D0072251

AURELIAN AND THE THIRD CENTURY

AURELIAN AND THE THIRD CENTURY

Alaric Watson

London and New York

First published 1999
by Routledge
11 New Fetter Lane, London EC4P 4EE

Simultaneously published in the USA and Canada
by Routledge
29 West 35th Street, New York, NY 10001

Typeset in Garamond by
Keystroke, Jacaranda Lodge, Wolverhampton
Printed and bound in Great Britain by
TJ International Ltd, Padstow, Cornwall

British Library Cataloguing in Publication Data
A catalogue record for this book is available from the British Library

Library of Congress Cataloging in Publication Data
Watson, Alaric
Aurelian and the third century / Alaric Watson.
p.   cm.
Includes bibliographical references and index.
1. Aurelian, Emperor of Rome, ca. 215–275. 2. Rome–History–
Aurelian, 270–275. 3. Emperors–Rome–Biography. I. Title.
DG308.W37   1999
937'.07'092–dc21
[B]   98-23382
CIP

ISBN 0–415–07248–4

TO MY FATHER

CONTENTS

CONTENTS

ILLUSTRATIONS

Plates

Maps

PREFACE

For too long the mid-third century has suffered from academic neglect. Though perhaps somewhat understandable, in view of the nature of the sources, this neglect is regrettable because of the importance of this period to our understanding of the history of the Roman empire as a whole. Recently, however, new information and new research has made possible a better informed and more balanced appraisal of this period and its overall importance in the development of Roman and indeed European history.

Few individuals more clearly epitomize this age or have a more justifiable claim to have influenced its course than Aurelian. But this book is not, and is not intended to be, a biography of Aurelian in the conventional sense of the term. Such an undertaking would be impossible. The evidence we possess does not permit us to draw a portrait of Aurelian the man, to investigate his personal life, or to get inside his thoughts. The literary sources present us with very little reliable information regarding Aurelian as an individual, and what is said about his character is somewhat suspect. We are told he was married, but all we know about his consort, Ulpia Severina, including even her name, is gleaned from the coins and inscriptions.

Nevertheless, a portrait of Aurelian's age, and the central role that he himself played in it, is not only possible, and indeed desirable, but long overdue. At the beginning of the twentieth century two substantial studies of Aurelian appeared, one in German (Groag 1903) and the other in French (Homo 1904). Since that time an ever-growing number of articles and monographs have appeared, each treating one or another aspect of his reign or of the period in general. No satisfactory full-length treatment of Aurelian has yet attempted to collate the information from these disparate secondary sources into an assessment of Aurelian's reign and its place in the history of the period. It is the fresh synthesis of this scholarship, together with a critical re-examination of the literary sources, which justifies the new appraisal of Aurelian's reign offered in the following chapters. In this way, it is hoped that we may arrive at a better understanding of this fascinating and crucially important period in Roman history.

To achieve this aim, I shall first consider the Roman world in the mid-third century in order to understand the context – political, military, economic, social and cultural – in which Aurelian operated. I shall then map out the sequence of events of Aurelian's reign so as to demonstrate the enormity of his military achievements. In the final part of the book I shall assess Aurelian's policies and his achievements beyond the field of battle.

While I accept responsibility for what follows, I am extremely grateful to all those who have helped me to realize this project or who have given me advice along the way. In particular, I wish to thank Averil Cameron for all the encouragement and input she has given me over the years, Richard Stoneman for his advice and his patience, and Roger Bland, Cathy King and Stephane Estiot for their assistance and for making available to me numismatic information and material. Finally, I would also like to thank my parents for their invaluable help and my wife for her patient encouragement.

Alaric Watson

ABBREVIATIONS

[Abbreviations not listed here are those of *Année Philologiques*]

Maraveille The catalogue of coins in Estiot 1983
Normanby The catalogue of coins from the Normanby hoard in Bland and Burnett 1988
RGDS Shapur's inscription known as *RES GESTAE DIVI SAPORIS*, as edited by A. Maricq, 1958 'Res Gestae Divi Saporis', *Syria* 35: 295–360
RIC Unless otherwise specified this refers to the coin catalogue for Aurelian in Webb 1927
Rohde The catalogue of coins in Rohde 1881
Sirmium The catalogue of coins in Kellner 1978

DATES

Alamanni and Juthungi invade Italy
Revolt of Postumus on the Rhine
261   Defeat of the Macriani in the Balkans
Odenathus seizes power in the east
262–7   Persian campaigns of Odenathus (now King of Kings)
Gothic invasions of Asia Minor
Postumus' campaigns on the Rhine
267–8   Gothic sea-borne invasion of the Aegean (sack of Athens)
Odenathus murdered
Zenobia assumes control in Syria
268   Revolt of Aureolus
Murder of Gallienus
Elevation of Claudius II
269   Alamanni (and Juthungi?) defeated at Lake Garda
Gothic invasion of the Balkans
270   Death of Claudius (July)
Reign of Quintillus (*c.* early September–late October)
Elevation of Aurelian at Sirmium (*c.* late September)
Palmyrene invasion of Arabia and Egypt
271   Aurelian's first consulship
Vandals invade Pannonia
Juthungi invade Italy
Revolt of Septiminus and Domitianus
Riots at Rome
Tetricus acclaimed emperor (in Aquitaine?)
Counter-offensive against the Goths
Withdrawal from Dacia
272   Recapture of Egypt
First Palmyrene campaign
Capture of Zenobia
Campaign against the Carpi
273   Revolts in Palmyra and Egypt, both suppressed
274   Aurelian's second consulship
Major reform of the coinage
Campaign against Tetricus
Reintegration of the west
Triumph at Rome
Dedication of the temple of Sol
275   Aurelian's third consulship
Campaigns in Raetia and the Balkans
Murder at Caenophrurium (*c.* early October)
Tacitus made emperor at Rome (*c.* late November)

276   Goths invade Asia Minor defeated by Tacitus, who is murdered
Reign of Florian (June–July)
Elevation of Probus

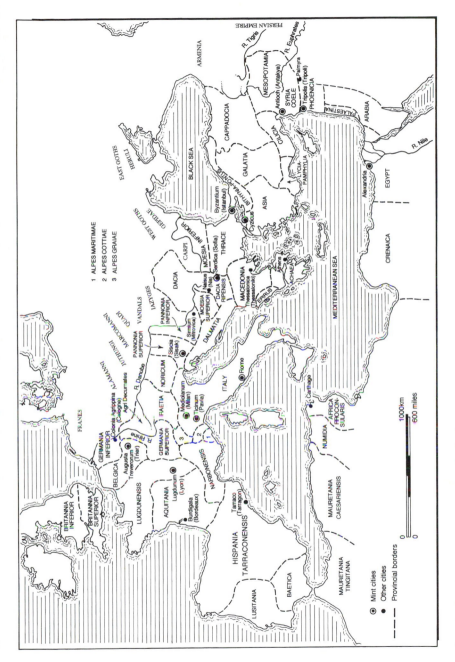

Map 1 The Roman empire in Aurelian's day

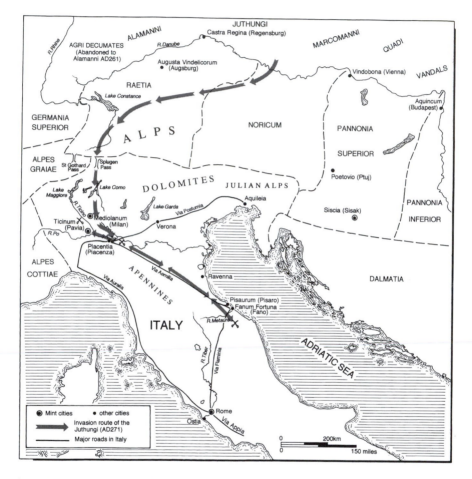

Map 2 Northern Italy and the upper Danube

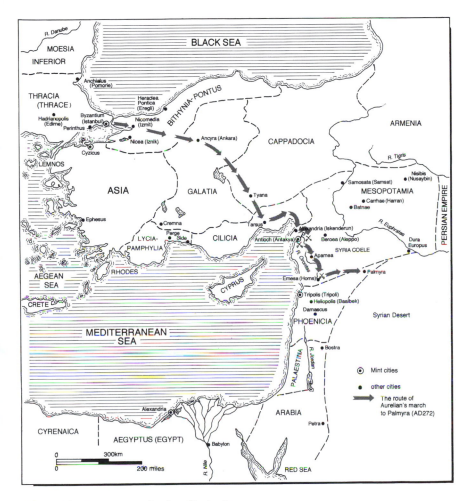

Map 3 The Roman east in Aurelian's time

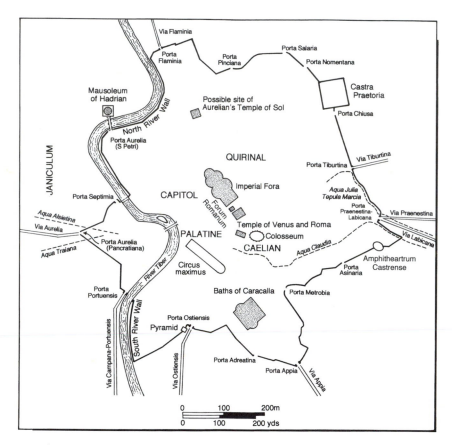

Map 4 Rome in the time of Aurelian

1

INTRODUCTION

The third-century 'crisis'

Lucius Domitius Aurelianus was born on 9 September in the year 214 or 215. He was a career soldier of humble Balkan origins. He came from a peasant family in the region just south of the Danube, possibly in the vicinity of Serdica, modern Sofia, or somewhat further to the north-west in modern Serbia.[1] Of his background and early life very little can be said with any degree of confidence. His native region was an especially rich source of recruitment, and like a good many of his compatriots Aurelian joined the army. As was customary, he probably did so at about the age of 20, that is around the year 235 – the year Severus Alexander, the last of the Severan dynasty, was assassinated. Nothing is known of his career before he emerged from the shadows onto the centre stage of history during the sinister events of the summer of 268. By that time he was already in his early fifties and a senior officer in the central imperial field army. His promotion to that rank clearly indicates that he must have impressed those who commanded him.

As with so many emperors in this period he was both elevated to the purple and then later assassinated by the army. He reigned for just five years, from 270 to 275, but what he accomplished in these few years is quite out of proportion with the brevity of his reign. Among his most important and lasting accomplishments were the reunification of an empire in the process of disintegrating into three distinct and mutually hostile dominions, the construction of defensive walls around the city of Rome against the ever-increasing barbarian menace and the first concerted efforts to halt and put into reverse the disastrous policy of monetary debasement that threatened to undermine the empire's economy.

Outwardly at least, the Severan age into which Aurelian was born was a time of great prosperity during which the empire reached its greatest geographical extent. The empire of Diocletian and Constantine

1

that followed the troubles of the mid-third century appears very alien to the empire of Aurelian's childhood. The apparent contrast is partly the product of periodization, an inescapable part of the historian's technique to simplify and make sense of the world he or she studies, but one that can easily lead astray. The mid-third century has been compared to a dark tunnel separating the comparatively well-illuminated worlds of the Severan age at one end and the age of Diocletian and Constantine at the other.[2] The lack of reliable information on the period has had two important effects. On the one hand it has, at least until recently, discouraged serious study. In this way the period has effectively been skipped over, thereby foreshortening the tunnel and throwing the periods at either end into even starker contrast. On the other hand, the portrayal of the third century as a Roman Dark Age has inevitably encouraged the attribution of observable changes in the empire to this period about which in fact very little is known. Both of these effects have tended to heighten the sense of catastrophe and to obscure continuity, allowing gradual developments and long-term trends to become easily overlooked.

The phenomenon of the 'tunnel' has thus helped to foster the characterization of the age in which Aurelian lived as one in which the Roman world was plunged into a crisis which precipitated the collapse of the classical world and out of which emerged the very different world of late antiquity. The label 'crisis' is, however, rather misleading. In trying to make sense of this pivotal period of Roman history it is vital to retain a sense of proportion. In the first place, it is difficult to defend the application of the term 'crisis' to a period of half a century or more.[3] Second, the term is usually applied generically, and somewhat indiscriminately, to a number of different developments in the military, political, social and economic spheres, the timings of which do not precisely coincide. A more discriminating approach is called for; one in which the interrelation of the different elements is mapped out and set within the context of the underlying developments in the empire.

POLITICAL INSTABILITY

The Augustan legacy

The most striking aspect of the so-called crisis was the political instability of the period. What Rostovtzeff labelled the 'Military Anarchy' traditionally began with the murder of Severus Alexander and lasted exactly fifty years, until the murder of Carinus in 285 left

Diocletian in control of the empire. During this half-century, in excess of sixty individuals laid claim to the imperial purple, and all but one or two of these claims were terminated by the sword. Almost invariably, these individuals were put up by the army, or rather by one of the several imperial armies stationed in different parts of the empire, often in opposition to the candidature of another else-where. While the rapid turnover of emperors is an indisputable fact, its causes and its significance are more open to debate. In order to approach this problem properly, it is necessary to understand the extent to which political instability was an inherent part of the anomalous system that Augustus bequeathed to the empire.

Due to the Roman aristocratic distaste for monarchy, the position of emperor was never properly institutionalized and the extra-ordinary power exercised by Augustus continued to remain highly personal and cloaked in deliberate ambiguity. There was, accord-ingly, no recognized constitutional mode of succession. In order to legitimate his authority, therefore, each new 'Augustus' represented himself as the ultimate successor of the first. For all the emphasis which Augustus placed on his role as *princeps* ('first citizen') and *Augustus* (something more than human, if somewhat short of divine), the symbolic representation of his authority never lost touch with its essentially military origins. Augustus understood, and fully exploited, the ideological nexus linking political authority to the divine sanction implicit in military victory that has come to be known as the 'theology of victory'.[4]

The subsequent invocation of the Augustan paradigm constantly reinforced the fact that Imperator Caesar Augustus had acquired his personal ascendancy through military victories in a succession of civil wars and had consolidated it by means of an impressive programme of foreign conquests. Already by the reign of Tiberius, the military salutation *imperator*, by which the armies of Rome traditionally greeted their victorious generals, had become an imperial monopoly and each new emperor dated the official inauguration of his reign (*dies imperii*) from the moment he was acclaimed *imperator* by the troops, rather than from when the senate ratified his powers.[5] To live up to the paradigm, emperors constantly represented themselves as victorious, valuing impressive-sounding victories over long-term strategic planning. More crucially, the Augustan legacy perpetuated the violence and civil war with which the empire had begun. For an emperor to die peacefully in his bed was always the exception rather than the rule, even in the first century. The civil war fought out between multiple contenders in 68–9 dramatically exposed the inherent political insecurity, simultaneously revealing what Tacitus termed a secret of imperial power, namely that emperors could be created elsewhere than in Rome.

In this respect, it is the second century rather than the third which must be regarded as anomalous. This anomaly owes a great deal to the comparative quiescence of Rome's neighbours and the ease with which the empire continued to dominate them. This could not last. Already by the reign of Marcus Aurelius (161–80) a dramatic and irreversible shift was under way in the relationship between the Roman empire and its neighbours. It soon became apparent that the empire was no longer the predator but the prey.

For most of the first two centuries of the empire it was exceptional for the emperor to assume personal control of the conduct of campaigns. As the external pressures on the frontiers grew and the barbarian incursions became more frequent, more penetrating and more devastating, emperors were increasingly expected not only to provide victories but to preside over them in person on the battlefield. Even before the end of the second century, the avowedly unmartial Marcus was obliged to spend nearly half his reign campaigning on the Danubian front in two arduous and costly wars (in 166–72 and 177–80). The military credentials and leadership qualities of the emperor thus became more critical and the relationship he maintained with the armies, on both a personal and a symbolic level, assumed an even greater significance. From this time, under the growing external military pressures, the soldiers openly took it upon themselves to determine who was capable of assuming this responsibility. In this new military ethos, the inexorable logic of the Augustan legacy ensured an ever greater propensity to civil war.

The underlying political instability resurfaced when Marcus' son and successor, Commodus, was assassinated on New Year's Eve, 192. Within a few months his immediate successor, Pertinax, was himself murdered. The praetorian guard, conscious that they could exact a higher price for their loyalty, effectively auctioned the position of emperor. The legions on the frontiers rejected the eventual winner of this shameless bidding, but without agreement as to his replacement. The Roman armies in Britain, on the Danube and in the east each chose to elevate its own general as emperor.

These events ominously demonstrated the escalating price the troops could demand for their loyalty and the growing factionalism and rivalry between the regional imperial armies. The ensuing power struggle was played out over a period of four years. The overall winner was Septimius Severus (193–211), the candidate of the Danubian army. The supremacy of the Danubian army was portentous, in view of the decisive role played by the troops and commanders from this region in the century that followed. On his deathbed, Septimius allegedly admonished his sons to 'Stand by each other, enrich the soldiers and scorn the rest.' Whether or not he ever uttered these words, they reflect an ugly truth that both he and his son and successor, Caracalla, understood.[6]

The 'infernal cycle'

In this new military environment, the emperor's presence was required wherever the military situation demanded, whether his enemies were internal or external. But he could not be everywhere at once. The sheer size of the empire, and the increasing disruption caused by the deteriorating military and political conditions, limited military communications and hampered the movement of troops and matériel. As the military pressures intensified, the 'tyranny of distance' increased the autonomy of the generals stationed on the frontiers.[7] Wherever the emperor did not personally assume the role of general there was always a chance that the general on the spot, if successful in repelling the invaders, might be encouraged by his troops to assume the role of emperor. The usurper would then march his army against his rival, leaving an inadequate garrison behind to guard the frontier. The barbarians would then take advantage of this weakness. If the local commander managed to defeat them, he often found himself acclaimed emperor in his turn. Thus there arose an 'infernal cycle' of civil wars and foreign invasions.[8]

In this context, it is both meaningless and misleading to attempt to divide those who claimed imperial power in the third century into 'legitimate emperors' and mere 'usurpers' based solely upon the historical accident of whether the claimant ever received the recognition of the senate at Rome. The assumptions underlying such a distinction are anachronistic and misguided. The senate's recognition never was more than one element in the complex process of imperial legitimation. From the late second century its significance diminished appreciably.

By the third century, the empire had simply become too unmanageable for a single person to be able to rule by himself for any length of time. The dilemma of the necessity for imperial omnipresence resulted in an extension of the well-established idea of shared rule. The elevation of sons to be co-emperors (either merely as

Caesars or often as full Augusti) became the norm. Although an important rationale of this co-rulership was to designate the line of succession, it also allowed the imperial college to be in more than one place at once. A number of vain attempts were made to search for a more systematic solution: notably the three-generation arrangement under Valerian in the middle of the century and the Tetrarchic system at its close. The problem remained unresolved in the fourth century and ultimately led to the permanent division of the empire that followed Theodosius.

MILITARY DEVELOPMENTS

Beginning around the time of Aurelian's birth, a marked shift in the relationship between the Roman empire and its neighbours irrevocably altered both the strategic balance of the empire and the context of imperial power. By mid-century, a number of archaeological clues bear witness to this rising tide of violence and prove it was no longer just the frontier provinces that felt its force: towns and cities shrank within hastily constructed circuit walls; coin hoards were buried but never recovered by their owners. Crucially for the empire, this intensification of the external pressures took place simultaneously on several fronts.

Developments beyond the Euphrates

The most important change took place in the east where, ironically, Rome's military successes were part of the problem. The expansionist wars of Septimius and Caracalla succeeded in humbling Rome's old arch-adversary, the Parthian empire, and in greatly extending Roman provincial rule in the region. But Septimius' annexation of Osrhoene and northern Mesopotamia overextended Roman lines of defence and communication, thereby stretching the military resources and logistical capacity of the empire. Moreover, it upset the regional balance of power, creating unsustainable strategic tensions between the Roman empire and its eastern neighbours which soon proved disastrous for Rome.[9]

The most immediate consequence of these campaigns was the crippling of the Parthian regime, fatally weakening the control which the Parthian rulers exercised over their regional viceroys. One such, Ardashir, the satrap of Persis (Fars), took advantage of this central weakness to strengthen his own power base in southern Iran.

Within a decade of Caracalla's campaign, Ardashir had completely overthrown the old Parthian regime, replacing it with his own Sassanid dynasty and thereby founding a new Persian empire.[10]

The appearance of this new and formidable force in the east soon placed an intolerable strain on the military resources of the Roman empire. Since the beginning of the Christian era, Rome had found the Parthian empire an easily containable neighbour and a relatively soft target for sporadic bouts of Roman military aggression. Though not necessarily more bellicose, the Persians were certainly more implacable, better organized and more inclined to take proactive measures to ensure their security and their interests. The defence of the eastern provinces of the empire became a costly exercise for Rome, altering the strategic balance of the empire and draining resources desperately needed elsewhere.[11]

Rome's military failures in the east fuelled the empire's internal political insecurity. The civil wars of 238 provided the opportunity for a spate of foreign raids, including a Persian invasion. The large-scale but ineffectual counter-offensive launched by Gordian III met with disaster at the hands of Ardashir's son and successor, Shapur I. In 244, Gordian was murdered and succeeded by his praetorian prefect, Philip. Usurpations and civil wars likewise followed in the wake of Shapur's great invasions of Roman territory in 252–3 and 260. Indeed it is no mere coincidence that the most testing years for the Roman empire in the third century, both in terms of external threat and internal political instability, were almost exactly co-extensive with the reign of Shapur I (241–72).

The Danubian frontier and the Gothic menace

Rome would undoubtedly have been better placed to deal with these troubles on the eastern frontier had they not coincided with an appreciable intensification of the external pressures along the length of the European frontier from the Black Sea to the Channel. The rich pickings of the Roman provincial farmlands and ill-defended towns of the frontier regions always presented attractive targets for opportunistic raids. The sporadic incursions of the second century gave way, during Aurelian's lifetime, to relentless pressure of a wholly different order, often exerted on several fronts at once. The most important factors behind this shift were the large-scale migrations of peoples from northern and eastern Europe and the greater co-operation, and in some instances even confederation, of peoples living beyond the frontier.

Starting at about the turn of the third century, a number of large populations of mostly Germanic peoples who had been migrating steadily south and west came up against and ultimately pressed on into the Roman empire. This massive and eventually irresistible *Völkerwanderung* placed an intolerable pressure on those peoples already living along the empire's northern border. The precise details of the reasons for the migrations, the routes they followed and the identity of the migrants are still not perfectly understood. But their impact on the Roman empire arguably provides the most fundamental distinguishing feature of the history of the later Roman empire.

By far the most significant of the new arrivals on the scene were the Goths. This large confederation of east German peoples arrived in the southern Ukraine no later than 230. During the next decade, a large section of them moved down the Black Sea coast and occupied much of the territory north of the lower Danube. This migration displaced the previous inhabitants of the area and in about 240 brought the Goths themselves into direct conflict with Rome. After another decade of intermittent raids, the Goths and their allies launched a full-scale invasion of the Balkan provinces, which resulted in the virtual annihilation of an entire Roman army together with the emperor commanding it. This signalled the beginning of a struggle that was to last for slightly over two decades and was only brought to a close by Aurelian himself. Meanwhile, the East Goths and their allies, who occupied the Crimea, took to the sea and inflicted devastating raids on the unprotected coastline of the Aegean and the Black Sea.[12]

Squeezed between the advancing Goths and the Roman province of Dacia were the Carpi, a free Dacian people who began to cause serious trouble around the time of Aurelian's birth. Philip defeated them in 247, but was unable to restore the Dacian *limes* completely, and this continued to weaken until Aurelian's reign. Further west, the arrival of the Vandals around the turn of the third century increased the pressure on the middle Danube. Throughout the third century, the Vandals themselves and their neighbours, the Sarmatian Iazyges and, still further west, the Suebian Quadi and Marcomanni, repeatedly broke through the Danube frontier. By 260 at the latest, a configuration of Suebian peoples calling themselves Juthungi began to make a devastating impact on the region.

The Rhine frontier and the west

The Rhine frontier suffered in much the same way. Although pressure on the upper Rhine began to mount early in the century, the full impact of the external pressures was generally felt rather later on the Rhine frontier than along the Danube. Nevertheless, when the intensification came, from the mid-250s, it was very marked. Britain, in contrast, appears to have escaped lightly at this time, remaining relatively prosperous and untroubled until roughly the time of Aurelian's death.

Partially under the impact of pressure from the interior, many of the hitherto independent tribes who had long been living along the Roman border came together to form much larger confederations. Though remaining politically loose, these new confederations proved militarily highly effective and their presence on the Rhine frontier played a key role in the military history of Aurelian's day. The Alamanni, a new and formidable confederation of tribes living in what is now north-western Bavaria, first appears in 213, when the emperor Caracalla fought against them on the upper Rhine. The situation deteriorated dramatically in the mid-250s, by the end of which decade the Alamanni were posing a real threat to Italy itself. To the north, at a rather later date, a number of tribes along the lower Rhine formed themselves into another new and equally destructive confederation: the Franks. The date of the earliest secure attestation of the Frankish confederation remains somewhat controversial, though it seems likely that it was already in existence by the late 250s.[13]

The Roman military response

Thus from the Arabian Desert to the North Sea the Roman empire faced an intensification of military hostility which gathered momentum in the 230s and reached its peak during the 250s and 260s. The empire's military resources were barely adequate to defend so vast a stretch of territory against such onslaught. The Roman military machine was designed primarily for delivering powerful offensive strikes at specific fixed targets. Even in the third century large-scale offensives remained the favoured military option wherever possible. But inevitably the empire's response to the mounting pressures became increasingly reactive and defensive, and containment was often the best that could be hoped for. The Roman military machine was forced to adapt to these new conditions. It did so by a series of *ad hoc* pragmatic responses to individual problems, which succeeded in averting catastrophe in the third century. But such responses should not be mistaken for a premeditated and consciously implemented programme of reform. The Roman empire never developed the kind of sophisticated strategic forward planning common to most modern states. It is very doubtful if it ever possessed what has been termed a 'Grand Strategy' as such.[14]

One area in which the empire responded to the changing situation was the gradual reform of the army itself. A significant aspect of this was the professionalization of the army command. The virtual monopoly which the social élite traditionally exercised over the command structure of the imperial army gave way during the course of Aurelian's military career to a corps of professional soldiers. Aurelian was himself one of this new breed of professionals, and by the time he reached the top ranks in the 260s the divorce between senatorial careers and the army command structure was effectively complete. Aurelius Victor alleges that this situation resulted from a formal imperial decree issued by the emperor Gallienus. For Victor, this was the disgraceful act of a disgraceful emperor. In recent years, more dispassionate research has promoted a more charitable view of Gallienus' reign. No other evidence attests the so-called 'edict of Gallienus', and it is preferable to regard the change as the culmination of a gradual trend rather than as the act of one individual.[15]

Another important aspect was the reduction in the size of the basic tactical unit. Detachments, or *vexillationes*, drawn from legionary and especially auxiliary units, had been used for some time. In the military context of the third century, which required rapid reinforcements of military units on the frontiers, these detachments, as opposed to whole legions, became the standard troop formation.

Two other fundamental military developments took place during Aurelian's military career, both of which were natural responses to the new warfare of rapid forced marches fought on multiple fronts. One was a steadily increasing reliance upon the use of cavalry. This development was actively fostered by Aurelian, who apparently excelled as a cavalry commander before he became emperor. The growing importance of the cavalry within the Roman army structure is reflected in the number of cavalry commanders, including Aurelian himself, who used this position as a platform from which to launch their bids for imperial power. The second development grew out of the first. In the 250s and 260s, the emperor Gallienus created a mobile central strategic reserve, with a heavy concentration of cavalry, comprising units drawn from a number of legionary bases together with new units formed by Gallienus, notably the Dalmatian cavalry. This strategic reserve, which he originally based at Milan and which prefigured developments in the next century, was a decisive element in the empire's ability to survive the onslaught of repeated barbarian incursions.[16]

THE MOUNTING COSTS OF WAR AND THE DETERIORATING ECONOMY

In a number of ways the costs of war escalated during the third century. Military expenditure far outweighed any other aspect of the Roman economy. The situation changed dramatically during Aurelian's lifetime. One very important factor was the shift in the nature and location of warfare. Whereas warfare had previously been conducted on or beyond the margins of the Roman world, in the third century the theatre of war shifted to being largely within the empire. The battlegrounds and the devastation left behind in the wake of passing armies, both enemy and Roman alike, were now situated in the empire's farmlands and provincial towns. Until the end of the second century, the costs of Rome's military offensives had substantially been met by the booty they returned. Now the booty captured by the Roman armies had only just been plundered from Roman provincials. The rising tide of civil war only made matters worse, since Roman armies were plundering Roman towns and settlements directly. Later in the century, brigandage and piracy, relatively contained for almost three centuries, were once again in the ascendant.

These conditions seriously affected trade and other commercial activities. Farming also suffered: farmsteads and crops were destroyed; livestock and stores carried off, if not by enemy marauders or local brigands, then by the Roman armies themselves. In many areas farmland, especially of the more marginal kind, was abandoned altogether. The situation was further aggravated by the continual recruitment of men from the land to replace those slaughtered in battle. Thus, the almost constant succession of bloody campaigns sapped the resources of the empire, both economic and human. The effects of the rising tide of civil wars were doubly deleterious: while frontier defences were depleted to furnish the rival armies, the dead and wounded on both sides helped to drain the empire's manpower, already depleted by a succession of plagues which swept across the empire from the late second century onwards.[17]

The rapid deployment warfare of the mid-third century also led to rising logistical costs. While the long, forced marches and problems of maintaining supplies inevitably created a logistical nightmare, the necessity of campaigning on several fronts at once contributed significantly to the empire's military expenditure. The cost of feeding and equipping the armies was further exacerbated by the increasing size of the armed forces and the rise in the price of transport costs. The Roman empire excelled all other pre-modern states in coping with the demands of logistics, but the constant rapid response needed to answer one emergency after another the length and breadth of the empire placed the expenditure on a wholly new footing. Another highly significant factor in the increasing military expenditure was the rise in army pay. Both Septimius and Caracalla substantially increased the basic army pay (*stipendium*). Even more crucial than the rise in basic pay, however, was the increase in the supplementary cash bonuses (*donativa*) distributed to the troops on occasions such as accessions, victories and anniversaries.

There were also indirect consequences of the escalating military and political difficulties of the times. In addition to the military donatives, emperors were obliged to distribute largesse to the urban populace on appropriate occasions. There were also Juvenal's 'bread and circuses': the food dole and the extravagant public shows and spectacles the emperors laid on in Rome and elsewhere in the empire. In these years of economic and political uncertainties, emperors could ill afford to cut back on such public relations exercises.

The measures by which the imperial government sought to finance its wars and recoup its costs were never popular and seldom economically sound in the longer term. The economic difficulties were aggravated by a lack of planning in the economy and the inefficient system of tax collection. The imperial government never systematically anticipated its economic needs. Inevitably, therefore, it employed short-term solutions. The burden of taxation fell unevenly. By exploiting legal exemptions and using bribes, many of the wealthiest individuals in the empire managed to evade the worst rigours of taxation, a disproportionate burden of which consequently fell on those who could less well afford it. Under the municipal system, responsibility for taxation rested on the curial class, membership of which became steadily more onerous as the system of tax collection became less efficient and ever more open to abuse.

The combination of an ailing tax system and rising military costs obliged the government increasingly to resort to other means to finance their expenditures. One such means was confiscation. The numerous civil wars gave ample opportunity for the proscription of the wealthy, whether or not the victim was truly guilty of supporting the losing side. Another was requisitioning. Both the imperial armies and the imperial retinue were supplied and billeted with little or no compensation. At the same time, the needs of the armies were met through a system of taxation in kind. Abuses of the system were many and caused much resentment. The increasing reliance upon taxation in kind must also be understood in relation to the decline in the value of the currency. In an inflationary economic climate, the government could more efficiently secure its needs, above all feeding and equipping the armies, by securing the goods in the form of direct taxation rather than by buying them.

The inflation was itself the direct result of another imperial measure designed to stretch the resources of the government: the irregular but persistent debasement of the currency. This policy had a profound impact upon the economy of the empire. Sporadic debasement was nothing new, but from about the time of Aurelian's birth it became more or less systematic. This rapid debasement had catastrophic consequences for the imperial government, the most serious of which was a crisis of confidence in the currency itself. This in turn accelerated the rate of inflation which eventually, in the late third and early fourth century, spiralled out of control. Since few sections of the Roman economy were fully monetized, the impact of this inflation may not have been too severe in the market-place. Its main victim was unquestionably the government itself. The effect of the continual debasement and inflation upon the structure of taxation and the administrative costs of the empire, including pay for the army and government officials, was considerable.[18]

Faced with relentless military pressures and inadequate manpower resources to meet them, successive emperors resorted to an expedient which drained the financial resources of the empire still further. During the third century, and still more thereafter, Rome tried to buy peace from its neighbours or buy their protection against more distant enemies. These subsidies, sometimes exacted over a number of years effectively as a form of Danegeld, represented the reversal of the policy of extortion by tribute which Rome had exercised over its neighbours during its ascendancy.

The overall impact of this deteriorating economic situation was cumulative. To contemporaries, the worst effects were felt towards the end of the century and into the next. In other words, the greatest misery coincided with the most determined efforts to put matters to rights, that is, roughly the period from Aurelian to Constantine inclusive. It is only with the benefit of hindsight that we can perceive the severity of the situation throughout the third century.

SOCIO-POLITICAL AND CULTURAL DEVELOPMENTS

The shifting sense of Romanity

From the late second century onwards the centre of power in the empire became increasingly itinerant, following the emperor as he spent ever more time in the frontier regions. 'Rome', as the conceptual capital of the empire, became divorced from the physical city on the seven hills; in Herodian's phrase, Rome was wherever the emperor happened to be.[19] With the emperor's presence demanded in the Balkans and the east, the strategic centre of the empire shifted gradually eastwards. His presence on campaign often necessitated the elevation of his provincial headquarters into *de facto* regional 'capitals': power bases in the frontier zones, often associated with regional branches of the imperial mint. This process culminated towards the end of the century in the establishment of a set of regional capitals under the Tetrarchy and ultimately in the foundation of Constantinople as a 'New Rome' on the Bosphorus.[20] The growing strategic and political significance of such new regional 'capitals' provided provincial strongholds from which rival emperors could more easily launch their bids for imperial power. Moreover, the augmentation of regional power bases at the expense of the centre allowed individuals to maintain political power on a particular frontier without controlling the rest of the empire. This political decentralization had a profound impact on the stability and even the integrity of the empire.

The decline of Rome as an administrative capital was both a symptom and an important cause of the decline of the senate that convened there. Although individual senators continued to be powerful within the entourage of the emperor wherever he might be, access to the emperor became increasingly restricted. The administrative and advisory roles of the senate could not easily continue when decisions of state were made at huge distances from the senate house. As an inevitable consequence of the emperor's protracted absences from the metropolis, the senate ceased to function as a central organ of government.[21]

At the same time, over the course of the second and third centuries opportunities for personal advancement through alternative channels in the imperial administration increasingly opened up for men of equestrian status. By reason of their virtual exclusion from military power, senators were soon effectively precluded from the pinnacle of political power. Aurelian was still a young child when the first non-senatorial emperor seized the purple. But throughout his military career imperial power lay almost exclusively in the hands of a succession of military commanders, very few of whom had any prior connection with the senate. Most, like Aurelian himself, were of humble provincial origin. For such men, faced with the dire political and military conditions of the mid-third century, the obsolescent senatorial ideals must have seemed an expendable luxury.

The decline of the senate reflects more fundamental changes taking place in the social framework of the empire at this time. The term 'Roman' was itself undergoing something of a metamorphosis, as the Roman empire ceased to be merely an empire ruled from Rome and developed towards a world community with which the provincial population could readily identify. Through the emergence of this 'new Romanity' the Roman empire was able to remain a meaningful political concept in both the east and the west well into the Middle Ages.[22]

One of the most crucial factors in this shifting perspective was the spread of Roman citizenship. Compared with most city-states in the ancient world, or indeed in almost any period, Rome was remarkably generous in allowing the rights of citizenship to the peoples she conquered. This process began with the incorporation of the Italian peoples under the republic and continued under the empire with the inclusion of large numbers of provincials from both west and east. In 213, only a year or so before Aurelian was born, the emperor Caracalla took this process to its logical conclusion by extending citizenship to all the free inhabitants of the empire. Literary sources hostile to Caracalla attribute to him the covert design of increasing the empire's tax base. Whether or not Caracalla had any such ulterior motive, the *constitutio Antoniniana*, as the decree is known, must be seen as the natural culmination of a long process.[23]

The ethnic make-up of the senate underwent a parallel transformation. By the end of the first century the senate began to admit the provincial élite of the western provinces. During the second century, and even more so in the third, the senate gradually incorporated increasing proportions of the provincial élites of North Africa and especially the Greek-speaking east. This realignment of the senate is significant because it reflected a much deeper realignment in the empire as a whole. Not only strategically, but also economically and culturally, the centre of gravity of the empire was decisively shifting eastwards.[24]

Cultural and religious developments

The mid-third century is often portrayed as an artistic Dark Age, heralding the death of classical culture. This is much too simplistic. Largely due to the changes in the economic climate discussed above, the era of extravagant municipal building programmes that characterized the Severan age did indeed grind to a halt and monumental architecture is therefore very much less abundant than in the preceding period. Conversely, some other arts were at their peak in this period: the mosaics of the mid-to-late third century are especially fine and the art of coin design and die-cutting reached unsurpassed heights in the 260s. Rhetoric and philosophy also flourished. One of the greatest cultural achievements of the third century was the emergence of Neoplatonism, a religious philosophy expounded by the Greek philosopher Plotinus in Rome in the mid-third century. Championed by his pupil, Porphyry, and counting the fourth-century emperor Julian among its followers, Neoplatonism came to exert a profound influence on the subsequent development of pagan thought in the fourth century.

Religion in the Roman world embraced a wide variety of beliefs and cultic practices and had a number of social, political and cultural dimensions. The cult of Dea Roma, the personified city of Rome, and the often associated imperial cult, the worship of Roman emperors both living and dead, originated in the Greek-speaking east. By the third century both had spread across the Roman world and acquired great social and political significance. The priests of the imperial cult enjoyed considerable prestige within their local communities. Both these cults acted as cohesive forces providing a concrete focus for the loyalty of the disparate communities of the empire towards Rome and the emperor.

The worship of local deities persisted and even spread alongside and often partially assimilated to the Roman pantheon. By Aurelian's time, a number of eastern religions had acquired considerable followings throughout the empire, including in Rome itself. Among these were the Egyptian cults of Isis and Serapis, the Anatolian cult of Cybele and Mithraism, a cult of Indo-Persian origin. This last was particularly widespread and appealed to a wide cross-section of society, not least the army rank and file. Mithras had strong solar affiliations and was sometimes referred to as Sol Invictus, the

Unconquered Sun. This name was also associated with a variety of other solar and quasi-solar cults popular in the east and the Balkans. One such came to be especially revered by Aurelian himself.

There was nothing mutually exclusive about any of these religions. They all coexisted within a polytheistic religious framework. A small number of religions in the empire, however, were exclusively mono-theistic. Of these, Judaism was the oldest and most respectable. Where it was suspected of involvement with militant Zionism, the Roman authorities were ruthless, but otherwise the practice of Judaism was largely tolerated.[25]

Christianity was a different matter. For Christians, their religious beliefs were incompatible with any other religious activities, including, for example, those of the imperial cult. Due to the inte-gration of religious beliefs and practices within the socio-political fabric of daily life in the empire, this had an impact far beyond what in today's terms might be seen as the religious sphere *per se*. For many pagans in the third century, Christianity posed a threat to the social, political and religious order of their world, wholly out of proportion to the numbers involved. From the pagan perspective, the comparative newness of Christianity, its strong emphasis on proselytism and its astonishing success, its exclusiveness and its secrecy all engendered suspicion. To the Roman authorities, the refusal to participate in religious expressions of loyalty to the emperor was a matter of grave concern. The growing troubles that confronted the Roman world in the mid-third century heightened this sense of insecurity. Serious confrontation between the state and its Christian subjects became almost inevitable.

The official persecutions in the middle of the third century, and again at the turn of the fourth, were marked by an appalling degree of violence. The emperor Decius was a deeply religious man who attributed the decline in Roman fortunes to the lack of proper religious observance towards the state gods. In 249 Decius instigated a call to all the citizens of the empire to offer prayers and sacrifices to the gods on his behalf. Those who refused suffered persecution. There was nothing in the original order aimed specifically against Christianity, but in the event the vast majority of those who fell victim to this persecution were Christians, whose stubborn resistance did not endear them to Decius and those who shared his view of the world. A few years after Decius' death, the emperor Valerian instigated a fresh call to sacrifice. This time the edict was directly targeted at the Christians. A new and more brutal wave of persecu-tion followed. But such coercion signally failed to achieve its aim and

Valerian's son and successor, Gallienus, put an immediate stop to the persecution.[26] The same futility awaited the great persecution at the turn of the next century. The scale of the martyrdoms and of the heroism they entailed earned the faith a new respect and even added to its appeal. Ironically, in the long term, the persecutions may thus have contributed to the spectacular success and ultimate triumph of Christianity.

A number of the more successful religions of eastern origin, including Mithraism and most especially Christianity, involved initiation ceremonies and held out the hope of individual salvation through some form of rebirth. How far and in what way the success of such religions can be linked to the more turbulent conditions of the times is a matter open to debate. Clearly, however, too simplistic a correlation must be avoided, especially where it is linked – either explicitly or by implication – to a characterization of traditional paganism as spiritually bankrupt and in the throws of irresistible decline.[27]

THE 'THIRD-CENTURY CRISIS' AND THE RHETORIC OF DECLINE

The Roman world in the third century was one in which old certainties were beginning to give way under the impact of new and unpredictable forces. It was above all a world dominated by military events and therefore, to a large extent, by the armies. The emperors, created by the armies, were almost exclusively men of humble origin promoted on merit rather than social standing. In this climate, the senatorial élite lost its pride of place. It no longer retained access to political power, still less controlled it. The destiny of the empire had passed into the hands of the great soldiers of the period, men like Aurelian himself.

By the fourth century, when the literary tradition upon which our knowledge of this period is founded was taking shape, the political, social and economic developments of the previous century were perceived in terms of a drastic and lamentable decline. The authors and the intended readership of these works belonged to the educated middle and upper classes, who identified with, if they did not actually belong to, the senatorial élite. For such writers, steeped in the traditions of Sallust and Tacitus, it was natural to attribute the ills of their own century to the erosion of senatorial power and dignity at the hands of a succession of uncaring and uncouth 'soldier emperors'. According to this highly conservative perspective, the third century was represented as a disastrous slide into arbitrary despotism. Such notions formed part of a wider rhetoric of decline which was soon adapted by both pagan and Christian apologists to suit the requirements of their opposing polemics.[28]

Until comparatively recently, scholars concerned with this period have broadly speaking shared the outlook of these authors so that the underlying rhetoric was seldom questioned. This factor, combined with the foreshortening effect of the 'tunnel' mentioned earlier, allowed the political, social, economic and cultural developments of the mid-third century to acquire the sweeping label 'crisis'. In the traditional view, the apparent stability of the second century was swept away along with the urbane government of the early empire. Out of the ruins arose the harsh world of late antiquity with its despotic government. Although this view has recently been called into question and the wholly misleading terminology of 'Principate' and 'Dominate' has now dropped out of vogue, these sentiments still largely colour the characterization of the 'early empire' and 'late empire' and of the 'crisis' which marks the caesura between the two.

Increasing awareness of the rhetoric overlaying the fragmented and tendentious literary accounts, coupled with a more systematic use of other sources, has encouraged a fresh approach. It is now apparent that the complex socio-political shifts of the period, including the waning political significance of the senate, can only properly be understood by taking a longer-term view. The mounting external pressures and the destabilizing effect this had upon the political system served not to produce but to accelerate such underlying developments.

The conventional thesis of a catastrophic 'third-century crisis' should be laid to rest. At the same time, it is vital not to minimize the gravity of the military and political situation. In the 250s and 260s barbarian invasions began to penetrate alarmingly deep into the empire's Mediterranean heartland, so that for the first time since Hannibal the city of Rome itself became vulnerable. The seemingly relentless Germanic menace along the entire length of the European frontier and the rise of first Persia and then Palmyra in the east led to a cycle of devastating military defeats, foreign invasions and internecine civil wars. By the time Aurelian seized power in 270 the cumulative effect of this rapidly deteriorating situation had precipitated a profound, if short-lived, political fragmentation of the empire which seriously threatened its long-term integrity. In this more restricted sense it remains meaningful to talk of a crisis. But the history of the third century is not the story of the collapse of an empire. Rather, it is a testament to the remarkable ability of the Roman empire to adapt and transform itself. This remains true even though ultimately, two centuries after Aurelian's death, the successive waves of barbarian incursions and the concomitant internal power struggles did prove fatal to the western part of the Roman empire. That they did not do so in the third century was in good measure due to Aurelian himself.

Part I

'RESTORER OF THE WORLD'

2

A DIVIDED EMPIRE

THE THREAT OF DISINTEGRATION

In 248, amid tremendous pomp and ceremony involving several days of magnificent and gory spectacles, the emperor Philip celebrated the millennium of the foundation of Rome. The celebrations were designed as a demonstration of Roman self-confidence, but the euphoric sense of optimism was short-lived. During the two decades that followed, under the impact of unprecedented external pressure exacerbated by numerous civil wars, the empire very nearly disintegrated. After a decade in which the defensive capacity of the empire was stretched almost to breaking-point, the events of the disastrous year 260 proved too much. The Roman empire effectively split into three. The emperor recognized at Rome, preoccupied with the defence of Italy and the Balkans and beset by numerous challenges to his authority from within, was incapable of giving the Euphrates and Rhine frontiers his personal attention. The defence and effective government of the east devolved upon the ruler of Palmyra, a semi-autonomous city in the Syrian Desert. At the same time, the defence and government of the western provinces was assumed by a local commander on the Rhine.

This tripartite political division of the empire was still in effect when Aurelian became emperor a decade later. Its forceful suppression and the reassertion of the political integrity of the empire were to occupy most of his regrettably short reign and must be reckoned Aurelian's greatest acheivement. This would not have been possible, nor would it have lasted as long as it did, had it not been for the underlying cohesion of the empire as a whole. Throughout the period of partition, the notion of the empire as an entity never lost its hold. Alongside the centrifugal forces outlined in the previous chapter there were countervailing forces which enabled the Roman empire to pull back from the brink of irretrievable fragmentation.

The impact of the Gothic menace

Even as Philip was celebrating his millennial festival at Rome, storm clouds were gathering over the Balkans. His departure for Rome, following the reasonably successful Danubian campaign of 247, left the region open to renewed Gothic raids. Early in 249, in response to the situation, the army of the Danube elevated their general Pacatianus to the purple. Philip apparently lost his nerve: rather than deal with the rebellion himself, he sent the well-respected general Decius to suppress the usurper. As Decius approached, the revolt collapsed and Pacatianus was lynched. Both armies immediately proclaimed Decius, himself a native of that region, as their new emperor. Reinforcing his own army with forces withdrawn from the Danube, Decius returned to Italy and eliminated Philip in a decisive battle near Verona.

While the armies of Rome were thus occupied in mutual destruction elsewhere, the Goths seized their opportunity. They crossed the Danube in force, plundering Moesia and Thrace and even attacking large cities like Philippopolis. At the same time, the Carpi raided Dacia with more or less complete impunity. Usurpations occurred at Rome and on the Danube, though both came to nothing. Decius returned to the Balkans, but after some initial success suffered a serious defeat at Beroea late in 250. In the spring of 251, while attempting to intercept the booty-laden invaders on their return journey, Decius and a considerable portion of his army were cut to pieces by the Goths at Abrittus. It was a staggering blow to Roman military prestige, and a terrible loss of manpower which the Roman empire could ill afford.[1]

The remnant Danubian army chose one of Decius' generals, Trebonianus Gallus, to succeed him. Powerless to intervene, Gallus allowed the Goths to return home with their ill-gotten gains. The elder of Decius' two sons, whom Decius had raised to rule as Augustus with him, had shared his father's fate. The younger, Hostillianus, who had remained at Rome with the junior rank of Caesar, still survived. Gallus immediately reached a compromise with him, whereby Gallus, his own son and Hostillianus formed a new imperial triumvirate. Hostillianus soon disappeared, murdered or perhaps succumbing to the plague.[2]

The military pressures in the region continued unabated. The Carpi raided across the Danube while the Borani and Goths raided the rich and vulnerable provinces of Asia Minor. In the spring of the following year, 253, a still more serious invading party of Goths and their allies crossed over the lower Danube.[3] This was intercepted by the governor of Moesia, Aemilianus, who was instantly proclaimed emperor by his troops according to the familiar pattern. Gallus, learning of Aemilianus' revolt and of his march westward, sent word to his general, Valerian, then in Raetia, to muster a large army and join him in Italy to crush the pretender. Before Valerian could even cross the Alps, Aemilianus confronted and soundly defeated Gallus in northern Italy. On hearing the news of the death of Gallus, Valerian's troops proclaimed him emperor in his own right. In the face of Valerian's advance, Aemilianus was assassinated by his own men. By early September 253 Valerian was left the dominant military commander and undisputed master of the empire.

The price was high. The situation in the Balkans remained critical. The virtual annihilation of a Roman army at Abrittus and the subsequent withdrawal of troops from the region by Aemilianus had left the Danube frontier desperately under-defended. When the Goths reached Thessalonica a ripple of terror spread throughout the Greek peninsula. On the upper Rhine, Valerian's withdrawal of substantial forces gave the Alamanni the chance to renew their attack. Meanwhile, in the east, the Persians had overrun most of Syria and a usurper had been acclaimed in Emesa.

The defence of the Danubian frontier was Valerian's first priority. His policy in the region included a scheme to fortify many of the major cities and strategic points, though the scheme was only partially implemented.[4] Valerian's attention was urgently needed in the east. His son and co-emperor Gallienus spent some time campaigning in the Balkans in the mid-250s, but his presence was also required on the Rhine. Gothic raids persisted on both sides of the Danube. In addition, the East Goths and Borani took to the sea. They plundered the northern coastal cities of Asia Minor from Trapezus to Nicea and on one occasion penetrated deep into Cappadocia.[5] The Gothic menace thus forms a backdrop against which the events in the east and the west must be viewed.

THE EAST: ROME, PERSIA AND THE RISE OF PALMYRA

The oasis and the eastern frontier

The eastern frontier of the Roman empire had no fortified line representing a clearly defined military or economic frontier, as did

Hadrian's Wall in northern Britain. Instead, the Syrian Desert acted as a natural frontier which served to channel both commercial and military activity along certain recognized and predictable routes.[6] One of the most important nodes on the caravan routes across the desert connecting Mesopotamia with the Mediterranean was the city of Palmyra. According to Jewish and Arab traditions, 'The City of Palms', or Tadmor to give it its Semitic name, was founded by Solomon (II Chronicles 8.4). The oasis in which it lay was poised, like the keystone of an arch, on the southernmost route across the desert that still had access to water. The growth of Palmyra's economic power in the first two-and-a-half centuries of our era was based not, like most other cities of the ancient world, on agriculture, but on commerce. The spice routes from the Gulf and the Silk Road coming overland from China via central Asia had for centuries passed directly through Palmyra. From here they went either north-west via Antioch to Asia Minor or south-west via Damascus to Tyre and Egypt.

Palmyrene merchants did very well out of this trade, but it was above all in providing protection to the caravans as they crossed the dangerous desert trade routes that the city earned its fabulous wealth.[7] With this wealth the aristocracy of Palmyra adorned their city, the tangible evidence of which can still be glimpsed in the impressive ruins set against the backdrop of the unrelenting desert beyond. The most striking of these is the magnificent temple of Bel, which together with its surrounding colonnade were on a scale, in both size and workmanship, to rival the greatest temples of the ancient world.

As a trading post poised between two great civilizations, Palmyra was naturally influenced by many different cultures and was home to many different peoples, who brought with them their own customs and their own religions. In certain ways, such as dress, both civilian and military, Palmyra looked more to Ctesiphon than to Rome. Its native culture was Semitic and the predominant language was a form of Aramaic. In contrast to the usual pattern in the Roman east, the Palmyrene vernacular was extensively used alongside Greek on civic inscriptions. Hadrian granted Palmyra the status of a free city as part of his rearrangement of the eastern frontier. It remained administratively semi-autonomous, even after Septimius incorporated the oasis within the Roman provincial structure, and around the time of Aurelian's birth was granted the status of *colonia*. This all reflects the exceptional status Palmyra retained long after its incorporation within the Roman empire.[8]

The strategic importance of the oasis had long been appreciated by

Rome. From the mid-second century, Palmyrene auxiliaries, notably archers, formed an integral part of the Roman defences of the eastern frontier region. In the third century the Palmyrene heavy cavalry was employed in the service of Rome as a useful counterpoint to the Persian cavalry, on which it was modelled. The marks left by Palmyrene units can still be seen up and down the eastern frontier and even further afield.[9] During the first half of the third century, as the caravan trade routes came more under threat from the Bedouin tribes of the desert and as the rise of Persia threatened Roman hegemony in the area, Rome looked increasingly to Palmyra for help.[10]

Palmyra had grown rich and powerful through the exploitation of the trade routes that ran across the desert. Maintaining full control over the desert traffic remained the city's paramount interest. The resurgence of the military power of Ctesiphon was thus viewed with some concern: Persian domination of eastern Syria and absolute control of these trade routes was an alarming prospect. In the long-running struggle between the two superpowers, therefore, Palmyra tended to side with Rome.

Shapur and the end of Valerian

After the failure of Gordian's Persian campaigns, Philip was obliged to sue for peace on terms very unfavourable to Rome. On the great rock monument at Naqsh-i-Rustam, Shapur represented his defeat of Gordian and humiliation of Philip as unmitigated triumphs. For his part, it is doubtful Philip saw himself as doing more than buying a breathing-space. Within two years he broke his word, refused any further tribute to Shapur and returned to the offensive. Once again, the Roman expedition was ineffective, since trouble on the Danube demanded the emperor's attention. During his absences, Philip left the east under the overall control of his brother Priscus, who now, in addition to being praetorian prefect, was given the grand title *rector orientis*, 'ruler of the east'. The administration of Priscus was deeply unpopular and helped to foment unrest in the region, which in 248–9 broke out into open revolt.[11]

Shapur was justly angered and distrustful after Philip's breach of promise. He took advantage of Rome's preoccupation with the Goths to intervene in Armenia in 251. The following year, Shapur unleashed the most devastating invasion the Roman orient had suffered since the last century of the republic. He utterly routed the Roman army of the Euphrates and captured or neutralized all the garrisons in northern Mesopotamia. The region was at his mercy. Striking deep into Syria, he sacked and plundered many wealthy cities in his path, including the great city of Antioch on the Orontes.[12] Renewing the offensive in 253, his progress was only halted by the hereditary priest-lord of Emesa, Uranius Antoninus. Uranius rallied the region's forces in the wake of this invasion and organized a spirited defence of the area. As a result, he was himself acclaimed emperor. His usurpation must be understood as a response to the military crisis of the moment and not seen as part of an assertion of Syrian autonomy.[13]

By 254, when Valerian finally arrived in the east, the crisis had somewhat subsided. Uranius Antoninus had apparently been eliminated and Shapur had partially withdrawn. However, the situation in the east remained unsettled. Over the next five years Valerian conducted intermittent campaigns against the Persians. He succeeded in regaining the important northern stronghold of Nisibis, which had long been, and long continued to be, a vital strategic point of contention between the two empires. But his responsibilities elsewhere prevented him from remaining permanently on the eastern frontier. Shapur was able to exploit his absences, for example capturing the valuable fortified outpost of Dura Europus on the Euphrates in 256 or 257.[14] Thus, the advantage swung back and forth between the two sides.

In 259, a serious Gothic invasion of Anatolia forced Valerian once more to abandon his efforts on the eastern frontier and march northwest to deal with the new threat. While in Asia Minor his army suffered severely from one of the periodic outbreaks of plague, which hampered his efforts to expel the Goths.[15] Again taking advantage of Valerian's absence, Shapur chose this moment to launch his third major offensive against Rome. He struck up through Mesopotamia, retaking Nisibis.

Valerian returned to the area as speedily as he could, massing his forces at Edessa for a final reckoning with his enemy. On a late summer's day in 260 he marched out of Edessa towards Carrhae. At a spot not far from where Crassus had suffered his catastrophic defeat a little over three centuries earlier, Valerian offered battle. The outcome was as disastrous for Valerian as it had been for Crassus. The Roman army was shattered. Worse still, Valerian himself was captured alive, an ignominy that had never previously befallen a Roman emperor. To reinforce the insult, Shapur is said to have used the captive emperor as a human mounting block and finally, when Valerian died in miserable servitude, he was flayed and his skin, dyed crimson, was hung in the temple at Ctesiphon. For the second time in under a decade a Roman emperor and his entire army had been eradicated by a foreign enemy. The defeat of Decius at Abrittus had been ruinous enough, but this time the consequences were far worse.[16]

In the short term, Shapur was able to unleash terrible destruction upon the region virtually unopposed. He overran Syria and then marched north into Cilicia and Cappadocia, apparently dividing his forces for a two-pronged attack. The trail of devastation might have been worse, but for the efforts of two of Valerian's generals who rallied the remaining Roman forces in the area and harassed the marauding Persian armies. Fulvius Macrianus led the forces stationed in Commagene in a kind of guerrilla action against the Persian army in eastern Cilicia, while Ballista (also known as Callistus) harassed the enemy column ravaging western Cilicia. In one such encounter Ballista even managed to capture Shapur's treasure chest and harem. Shapur decided to leave Cilicia and return eastward.[17] Before he reached the Euphrates, however, he found his way barred by yet a third and altogether more formidable adversary: Odenathus of Palmyra.

Odenathus 'Ruler of Tadmor'

The career of this illustrious individual is somewhat controversial, but the position of prominence he enjoyed in the region requires some attention.[18] Odenathus belonged to one of the leading families of Palmyra which had been granted full Roman citizenship by Septimius Severus at the turn of the century. There is, however, no reason to suppose that he was born into an ancestral ruling dynasty. His extraordinary position within the community, and later in the entire region, was of his own making.

Towards the middle of the third century, several inscriptions refer to one Septimius Odenathus son of Hairan son of Vaballathus son of Nesor as the 'Ruler of Tadmor (Palmyra)'. It has recently been shown that this individual is none other than *the* Odenathus and not, as was previously thought, his father or grandfather.[19] His title Ruler of Palmyra probably dates from around the 240s and indicates the personal ascendancy he had attained over his local community by that time. The same inscriptions also refer to him as a member of the Roman senate. This was an honour granted to him by a Roman emperor, most probably by Philip in recognition of his active involvement as commander of Palmyrene forces in the service of Rome during the Persian wars of the 240s. These two quite separate honours reflect his outstanding success as a military commander. His position of power is an indication of his personal role in bringing about the hegemony which Palmyra began to exert at this time over the Arab tribes of the desert marches of eastern Syria.[20] His pre-eminence at Palmyra is further demonstrated by an inscription dated to October 251 that acknowledges his son, Septimius Hairan, as his co-ruler with exactly the same honours.[21]

By the time Shapur launched his second great invasion of the Roman east in 252–3, Odenathus was thus already a powerful figure in the region. What part he played in these events is not certain, though the suggestion that he followed up the successes of Uranius Antoninus in chasing the Persians from Syria cannot be sustained.[22] It is alleged that Odenathus at some point tried to come to an arrangement with Shapur, who rejected his overture, contemptuously throwing his gifts into the Euphrates. The date of this alleged episode is not certain, but it fits in well with the events surrounding the Persian assault on Dura Europus in the mid-250s. Whether it should be taken to represent treachery towards Rome, or merely as an example of the Roman practice of buying off the enemy, is debat-able.[23] In any case, by the year 257/8 at the latest, Odenathus had apparently merited honorary consular trappings (*ornamenta consularia*) from Valerian for his sterling efforts in the service of Rome. This may well be connected to his response to Shapur's sack of Dura.[24]

By making himself the indispensable ally of Rome while steadfastly championing Palmyrene interests in the region, Odenathus thus skilfully exploited the situation in the east to his own personal advantage. In a bilingual inscription dated April 258, Odenathus is accorded the Aramaic title *mr* (in Greek, δεσπότης); the title, equivalent to the modern Arabic 'emir', was exclusively reserved for ruling princes.[25] Whether or not his ambitions at this time reached beyond eastern Syria, events were soon to grant him the opportunity of fashioning for himself a position of immense power.

His moment came in the aftermath of Shapur's great invasion of 260. With Valerian in Persian hands and the Roman army of the east in disarray, Odenathus realized the potential threat to Palmyrene interests presented by Shapur's overwhelming victory. The Persian forces were tired from their long campaign and from the harass-ment they had received in Cilicia at the hands of the Roman forces under Macrianus and Ballista. Odenathus' own army, consisting of Palmyrene auxiliaries reinforced by Roman soldiers, rallied from the frontier after the battle of Edessa, was comparatively fresh. Seizing his opportunity, he attacked Shapur's army as it marched back towards the Euphrates and drove it out of Roman territory.

As the news of Valerian's defeat and capture spread across the Roman world, a wave of spontaneous insurrections swept through the empire. Gallienus found himself in an extremely precarious position. The numerous revolts, combined with the ignominy of his father's fate, very nearly toppled him. Although he managed to hold on to power for a further eight years, he was never able to reassert his authority over the whole empire.

The first of these revolts took place in the east, where Valerian's capture had created a power vacuum. The heroic efforts of Macrianus earned him the respect of the troops, who promptly proclaimed his two sons, Macrianus and Quietus, as joint emperors. The eastern provinces and Egypt accepted this choice immediately.[26] In the spring of 261, the elder Macrianus determined to press his sons' claim over the whole empire. His decision to march west may partly have been prompted by the desire of those European troops that Valerian had brought east with him to return home. Leaving Quietus behind with Ballista as his praetorian prefect, Macrianus set out for the west accompanied by his elder son. Gallienus dispatched his best generals, Aureolus and Domitianus, to meet the threat. The armies met in the Balkans and the result was a resounding victory for the forces loyal to Gallienus.[27]

It is not clear whether Macrianus and Ballista came to an understanding with Odenathus before Macrianus set out for the west, or whether they simply calculated that he was of no consequence to their designs. Either way, when the news of the defeat in the Balkans reached the east it soon became clear that the Macrianic cause had made a grave miscalculation in underestimating Odenathus. At this critical moment, the Palmyrene prince came out decisively in favour of Gallienus. Once Macrianus and his main force had been destroyed in Illyricum, Odenathus rightly sensed the advantages in championing a distant and somewhat weakened Gallienus rather than in throwing in his lot with a local contender who lacked the forces to defend his dwindling cause.

Descending swiftly on Emesa, where Quietus had retreated for safety, Odenathus defeated Ballista and laid siege to the city. The Emesenes went over to Odenathus, murdered Quietus and threw his body over the walls. Thus the Macrianic revolt came to an end and the east, in name at least, returned its allegiance to Gallienus. It is clear, however, that the real power in the region remained with Odenathus.[28]

With the elimination of Quietus, Odenathus adroitly placed Gallienus in his debt while ensuring that his own army of Palmyrene and Roman units was the only sizeable force in the region.[29] Gallienus had no realistic option but to acknowledge his debt of gratitude to Odenathus and ratify the Palmyrene prince's position of power. He did so by creating him vice-regent of the east, with the title *corrector totius orientis*, much as Philip had with Priscus. Odenathus thus held supreme command of all the armed forces in the east and full authority over the provincial governors of the entire region from Asia Minor round to Egypt. As a result of this command Odenathus assumed the Roman military title *dux*.[30]

Under Gallienus' nominal authority, but in practice acting as a virtually autonomous ruler, Odenathus conducted the defence of the eastern provinces with vigour for a number of years. In 262 he managed to wrest northern Mesopotamia from Persian control, recapturing the vital stronghold of Nisibis, and launched a counter-invasion into the Persian empire. Upon his return, Odenathus assumed the title King of Kings, a title normally reserved for the monarchs of Persia (or Parthia). In a grand ceremony on the banks of the Orontes, not far from Antioch, he conferred this same title on his son Septimius Herodianus.[31] A few years later, in 266 or 267, he returned to the offensive and met with still greater success. This time he even reached the capital, Ctesiphon, though he was unable to take it.

As a result of these victories, Odenathus was acclaimed *imperator* by his troops. This technically exceeded his mandate since the emperor Gallienus, not his general, had the right to this salutation. Inasmuch as Gallienus permitted this infringement of his imperial authority, the incident clearly illustrates the emperor's impotence with regard to affairs in the east. It also explains the erroneous assertion in the *Historia Augusta* that Odenathus was made Gallienus' co-emperor. The acclamation demonstrates more eloquently than anything else the anomaly of Odenathus' position at this time: something between powerful subject, independent vassal king and rival emperor. In practice, however, he appears to have been shrewd enough not to flaunt the title, the significance of which remained entirely local until after his death.[32]

The policy Odenathus pursued was governed by his political acumen. His decision to support Gallienus, both against the Persians and against the usurper Quietus, was based on shrewd calculation regarding his own and Palmyra's best interests. By the year 267 he had reached a position of unprecedented power in the Roman east.

THE WEST: GALLIENUS AND THE REVOLT OF POSTUMUS

The western provinces under Valerian and Gallienus

In the joint reign of Valerian and Gallienus the situation on the Rhine frontier rapidly deteriorated. Taking advantage of the weakness caused by Valerian's march on Italy, the Alamanni breached the transrhenane defences and devastated much of the *agri decumates*, the area between the upper Rhine and the upper Danube roughly corresponding to modern Baden-Würtemberg. Gallienus was able to contain this invasion, but his energies were then diverted to the Danube frontier. While campaigning there in the mid-250s, Gallienus raised his elder son, Valerian II, to the junior imperial rank of Caesar. But the situation on the lower and middle Rhine soon demanded Gallienus' personal attention.

Leaving his son Valerian behind as a figure-head to represent the imperial house on the Danube front, Gallienus himself marched to the Rhine where a formidable barbarian army was plundering deep into northern Gaul.[33] Arriving in 257, he set about restoring the integrity of the Rhine frontier with great vigour. He set up his regional headquarters at Trier, giving himself easy access to a wide arc of the frontier. Using Cologne as a forward strategic base, he gained a number of significant victories and restored the defences on both banks of the river.

The experiment of co-rulership across three generations of the same family was short-lived: the young Valerian met an untimely end in 258. Undaunted, Gallienus decided to repeat it by elevating his younger son, Saloninus, to be Caesar in his brother's stead. Saloninus remained with his father on the Rhine, while the Danubian frontier, though still prey to constant barbarian raids, now lacked an imperial presence. Matters came to a head when news arrived of Shapur's great invasion of the east. An army commander called Ingenuus took advantage of the preoccupation of the two senior emperors to seize power for himself on the Danube. Gallienus responded with characteristic energy. By forced marches he managed to fall upon and destroy Ingenuus before the latter had fully established his position.[34]

Before Gallienus had had time to repair the disruption caused by the rebellion of Ingenuus, the news of the disaster which had overtaken his father Valerian in the east swept through the empire.

At this point, probably in response to the news, the Alamanni finally overran the whole of the *agri decumates*, the border of which had long formed a fortified communications corridor between the Rhine and Danube frontiers. The Juthungi, apparently with the Alamanni, then crossed the Danube in strength. As Gallienus hurried westward to meet their advance, they pressed on down into northern Italy as far as Ravenna. Rome itself was thrown into panic. Gallienus managed to defeat the invaders at Milan, but could not annihilate them. The Juthungi re-crossed the Alps, taking with them booty and captives from Italy.[35]

Meanwhile, on the middle Danube the disgruntled legions once again rose in revolt, choosing the general, Regalian, as their new emperor. Another usurper arose in Macedonia, and in the east the Macriani launched their bid for the empire.[36] In Gaul, meanwhile, the Franks renewed their devastating raids with fresh vigour. The effects of these incursions were felt alarmingly deep. One roving army even crossed the Pyrenees into Spain, where they sacked the major coastal city of Tarraco (Tarragona) and reached as far as Gibraltar.[37] But the most bitter news for Gallienus came from the Rhine frontier itself, where another revolt was to lead to a more personal tragedy.

The revolt of Postumus

In leaving the Rhine frontier precipitously, Gallienus had taken a calculated risk. Aware that the region was still vulnerable, he once again left behind him a young son to represent the ruling dynasty. Being no more than a boy, Saloninus was entrusted to the care of the administrator, Silvanus. The military defence of the Rhine frontier Gallienus left in the capable hands of his general, M. Cassianus Latinius Postumus.[38]

Postumus was a tough soldier of humble origin, probably from the region of the lower Rhine. He was a shrewd opportunist, whose sense of expediency always ruled his ambition. In the strained atmosphere following the news of Valerian's capture, which reached Gaul in the autumn of 260, he was challenged by Silvanus, on behalf of Saloninus, to hand over some booty recaptured from a Frankish raiding party. Astutely gauging the mood of his soldiers, Postumus insisted on distributing the booty among his victorious troops, a distribution in which he himself was not disinterested. When Silvanus persisted, the troops mutinied and proclaimed Postumus emperor. Silvanus and Saloninus tried to rally support from the troops stationed at Cologne. Saloninus, no doubt at Silvanus' suggestion, proclaimed himself full Augustus and issued coins advertising the fact. But the counter-coup was too late and the support for the house of Valerian too weak. As Postumus invested Cologne, the main regional mint at Trier began to coin in his name.[39]

Gallienus was in no position to intervene in Gaul. He was engaged in a desperate struggle for his own survival, trying to cope simultaneously with the Germanic invasion of Italy and the numerous other usurpers, from the Balkans to Syria. After a siege of several weeks the beleaguered townsfolk and garrison of Cologne turned against Saloninus and took matters into their own hands. Murdering the hapless youth and his guardian, they threw their remains over the ramparts and opened the gates to Postumus. With his power base in Germania Inferior and Belgica thus secure, Postumus was now in a strong position. The three northern provinces of Gaul, the two Germanies, together with the provinces of Britain and Spain, all went over to Postumus, as for a time did Raetia. In part this reflects the perceived weakness of Gallienus' position; it also reflects the real importance of the Rhine army as the defence mechanism for the entire region.[40]

The Frankish menace, the catalyst for Postumus' rebellion, did not subside. In the circumstances, Postumus decided to await the outcome of the impending civil wars which still loomed over Gallienus. The following year, 261, Gallienus regained control of the Balkans. Regalian was killed, perhaps in defending Panonnia against the Sarmatians, so too was Valens in Macedonia. Gallienus' generals, Aureolus and Domitianus, defeated Macrianus and, not long after, Odenathus eradicated Quietus in Syria. Only Postumus now remained.

The seizure of the *agri decumates* by the Alamanni effectively insulated Postumus' power base from attack by the legionary forces on the Danube.[41] Though eager to avenge his son, Gallienus needed to consolidate his hold on the central part of the empire before risking an adventure in Gaul. It is related that, under these circumstances, he challenged Postumus to single combat, which the latter declined.[42] Thus, an uneasy stalemate arose, each ruler having enough to contend with from barbarian pressure beyond their borders to wait for the other to make the first move.

In the mid-260s Gallienus finally judged the time was right. Taking the central reserve under the command of his brilliant but capricious cavalry commander Aureolus, Gallienus crossed the Alps and marched deep into Gaul. Here he won a substantial victory, but was unable to press home his advantage due to the deliberate hesitation of Aureolus. Though this insubordination smacked of treachery, Gallienus decided to err on the side of leniency; a decision that would later prove fatal. Gallienus renewed the offensive, but was seriously wounded during a siege and forced to withdraw. The entire campaign was then aborted and the military stand-off between the two rivals was resumed as before. Although neither ever formally recognized the other, nor did they make any further effort to remove each other.[43]

The position of Postumus

Postumus thus continued to rule and be recognized as the only rightful emperor throughout the western provinces from the Scottish Borders to the Straits of Gibraltar. His elevation to the purple must be understood in the context of the sudden intensification of barbarian pressure on the Rhine frontier in the late 250s. The military situation required an emperor on the spot. When Gallienus was no longer able to fill this role, his deputy was elevated in his place. In this, as in most other most respects, the revolt of Postumus followed the usual pattern of provincial usurpations in the mid-third century. The most important distinction was that Postumus continued to exercise his imperial power for a considerable number of years without ever receiving, or apparently ever actively seeking, the recognition of the senate at Rome. This matter requires closer scrutiny.

From the very outset, as was customary for usurpers at that time, Postumus immediately assumed the full titulature, regalia and prerogatives appropriate to a Roman emperor. These included issuing coins in his own name and designating the consuls. He thus secured for himself the consulship in the January immediately following his elevation. He also apparently assumed the suffect consulship directly upon his seizure of power, for his ordinary consulship the following January is recorded as his second.[44] Meanwhile in the east the brothers Macrianus and Quietus laid claim to exactly the same prerogatives, and for them also 261 was the year of their second consulship.[45] Since Gallienus himself assumed the consulship in Rome this same year, in order to reassert his own authority in the wake of his father's capture, there were in fact three rival sets of consuls in January 261. Which you accepted as the official consuls of the year depended on which part of the empire you were in, and, thus, which of the three rival imperial authorities you accepted.

The volatile circumstances that swept Postumus to power never fully abated. Unlike Macrianus, Postumus did not have a brother or son to guard his power base against further insurrections in the rear.[46] This certainly diminished the attraction of marching on Rome. Fully occupied with the defence of the Rhine, Postumus discovered that he could manage without the incremental legitimation of senatorial recognition. His tenure of power underlines how little that formal recognition mattered in the face of the harsh realities of the mid-third century. These events revealed another secret of imperial power as momentous as the Tacitean original of 68–9: an imperial contender could seize power and successfully maintain it without ever attaining the recognition of Rome and its senate at all. For the provincials and the soldiers such niceties were insignificant compared to the effective control of the barbarian menace. His success in defending the western provinces against further barbarian incursions, which he was at great pains to stress on his coinage, earned him considerable popularity among the civilian inhabitants of the region. His ability to give his undivided attention to this task must therefore be understood as the *raison d'être* of his prolonged tenure of power. His apparent willingness to accept the restriction of exercising his authority exclusively within the western provinces must be seen as a triumph of pragmatism over ambition and not as an attempt to set up a rival and totally separate empire in the west.

THE EMPIRE IN 267

Gallienus was a remarkable man. Anyone in that perilous period who could survive the ignominious capture of his father and the widespread unrest that inevitably followed deserves our respect. His talents have traditionally been rather overshadowed by the calamities that befell him and even more by the hostile press he received in the literary sources. It is true that he passed over the senate, especially in promoting men to the highest military offices, an offence for which the largely pro-senatorial sources could not forgive him. But in choosing instead to promote men of singular ability who had risen through the ranks, he proved he had an eye for spotting military talent not unlike that of Napoleon. Unlike Napoleon, however, his impetuosity did not inspire those around him with confidence in his leadership and, above all, he lacked the charisma to bind such men to him with undying loyalty.[47]

By the year 267 there were signs that Rome's fortunes might be about to pick up. The Danube frontier was comparatively quiet. The Persians were cowed by the spectacular military achievements of Odenathus, albeit only nominally under Gallienus' auspices. Gallienus himself even found time to be initiated into the Eleusinian Mysteries. His coins proclaimed that everywhere peace was restored.[48] It was, however, more a pious hope than a reflection of reality. The true state of affairs was altogether more sinister. In the next few years the Roman empire came close to disintegration. The wealthy east was under the increasingly hostile sway of Palmyra, the western provinces still recognized Postumus, and even after his death the bulk of this region refused allegiance to the emperor recognized at Rome. Meanwhile, the central portion of the empire was under the constant threat of Germanic invasions. Against this backdrop a deadly series of coups and attempted coups was played out, from which finally there emerged one sole victor whose ruthless courage enabled him to reunite the empire and pull it back from the brink of destruction. This man was Aurelian.

3

AURELIAN ASCENDANT

In the late summer of 267 news reached Gallienus in Italy of a massive
Gothic invasion of the Balkans and Asia Minor. Leaving Aureolus in
Milan to guard Italy against possible attack from either Postumus or
the Alamanni, Gallienus set out with his mobile strike force to meet
this new challenge. Aurelian, by this time in his early fifties, was
almost certainly among the senior officers accompanying Gallienus on
that march. For Gallienus, this campaign was to mark the beginning
of the end. For Aurelian, it was the end of the beginning.

THE ROAD TO THE PURPLE

The Gothic wars renewed

For two decades after the battle of Abrittus, in which the Goths
destroyed the emperor Decius and his army in 251, the Gothic
menace had a profoundly destabilizing influence upon the internal
politics of the Roman empire. After the invasion of 253, the Goths
and their allies concentrated their attacks upon Asia Minor. Several
separate raids, some of appalling destructiveness, ravaged the cities
of Asia Minor during the fifteen-year reign of Gallienus. Both the
coastal cities and those deep in the interior suffered. Among many
other casualties, the great temple of Artemis at Ephesus was burned
to the ground.[1]

Then in 267, the Heruli launched a sea-borne invasion which
sailed down the western shore of the Black Sea attacking coastal settlements. Although one raiding party was apparently defeated, another
succeeded in taking Byzantium. An abortive attack on the Bithynian
coast resulted in a naval encounter in which the invaders suffered
considerable losses. It may have been this setback which deflected the

course of their attack westward through the Dardanelles.[2] On reaching the Aegean, the German fleet headed out across the open sea making for the rich and poorly defended spoils of the Greek mainland. On the way, they sacked the islands of Lemnos and Skyros, making landfall in Attica, where they sacked Athens. There is a story that they were persuaded by one of their number to spare the great library, on the grounds that the Greeks were inclined to scholarship more than to warfare, thus it was wiser to leave them their books to study.[3] The Heruli then passed down through the Isthmus, with contemptuous disregard for the fortifications which had been started more than a decade earlier but left incomplete. Corinth, Sparta and Argos were all pillaged. Returning up through the Isthmus their advance was checked by an Athenian militia organized by the historian Dexippus, a fragment of whose account of these events survives.[4]

The invaders then turned up through Boeotia. Here, for the first time, they finally encountered a sizeable Roman army. It was commanded by Marcianus, one of Gallienus' top generals who was probably governor of Lower or Upper Moesia. The forces at his disposal were inadequate to stop the marauders completely, but he succeeded during the winter months in driving them northwards through Epirus and Macedonia towards Gallienus, who was advancing from northern Italy to meet them. Finally, in the spring of 268, in the valley of the Nessos (or Nestus) on the border between Macedonia and Thrace, Gallienus defeated them. Though the outcome of the battle was by no means conclusive, the emperor came to an arrangement with the Heruli whereby he offered them safe conduct out of the empire and granted *ornamenta consularia* to the Herulian chief, Naulobatus.[5]

At this point, news reached Gallienus that his gifted but wayward general Aureolus had revolted in northern Italy. Gallienus immediately perceived the gravity of the situation: if he lost control of northern Italy his position was hopeless. Leaving Marcianus in charge of the Danube frontier, he gathered together as large a force as he prudently could and set out for Italy to deal with the new threat. Once again Aurelian accompanied the emperor.[6]

The end of Gallienus

Instead of having himself proclaimed emperor, Aureolus immediately threw in his lot with Postumus, issuing coins from the mint at Milan in the name of the western emperor. This may have been the result of negotiations entered into between the two generals during the

abortive campaign a few years earlier, which would explain Aureolus'
apparent treachery at that earlier date. More likely it represents
the unilateral action of Aureolus, hoping to elicit the support of the
Rhine legions in his struggle against Gallienus. In any event he mis-
calculated: Postumus refused to become embroiled in Aureolus' risky
venture.[7]

Gallienus reached northern Italy with his army by early summer
and immediately engaged Aureolus' forces at a place subsequently
named Pons Aureolus (Pontirolo). The rebel forces were defeated
and Aureolus fell back into Milan. A lengthy siege ensued, which
was to outlast Gallienus himself.[8] Among the senior officers whom
Gallienus had brought with him from the Balkan war, there were
present in the loyalist army encamped around Milan that summer
several Illyrian generals who owed their promotion to Gallienus and
his father. Besides Aurelian, these included Aurelius Heraclianus, the
praetorian prefect, and M. Aurelius Claudius, an exact contemporary
of Aurelian whom Gallienus elevated to the supreme command of the
cavalry in place of Aureolus.[9] This Illyrian cabal had become increasingly dissatisfied with Gallienus. As the siege of Milan dragged on,
the three senior officers conspired to remove him. They already knew
they could count on the support of Marcianus. Others of a similar
background and opinion, such as Cecropius, the commander of the
Dalmatian horse, were brought in on the plot.

Early in September the trap was laid. One night, apparently while
Gallienus was eating a late supper, Cecropius brought him word
that Aureolus was preparing to make a sortie from Milan. Gallienus,
not suspecting a lie nor waiting for his usual armed bodyguard,
rushed off in his eagerness to stop his enemy. He was set upon
and killed. The conspirators then hastily organized the elevation of
Claudius.[10] Some credit Heraclianus with the ruse, one version says
it was Aurelian: there can be little doubt that all three were in on it
together. Much later, after Constantine had claimed Claudius as
an ancestor, versions were put about which attempted to exonerate
Claudius, either by professing his ignorance of the plot, by making
out he was absent at the time, or even by suggesting that the dying
emperor bestowed the purple on Claudius to mark him out as his
successor.[11]

Gallienus' fate was shared by his brother Licinius Valerianus, the
consul of 265. Some say he was with Gallienus at Milan, others that
he was at Rome, where the senate's hatred of Gallienus also resulted
in the murder of several of those closely associated with his regime.
Among the victims were his widow, Salonina, and their last and only

surviving son, Marinianus, who, though still a young boy, was in fact consul in that year. The coup was a success, its way smoothed by a large accession donative.[12]

The new emperor's right-hand man

Claudius immediately sought to stamp his authority on the situation. He not only curbed the excessive expressions of hatred that the senate was heaping upon the memory of Gallienus, but actually forced the senate to deify Gallienus. He also took steps to distance himself from the treachery which had brought him to the purple. For those directly implicated in the plot there were mixed fortunes. Of Cecropius, the actual assassin, no more is heard, but he was certainly relieved of his post and, if he did not commit suicide, was very probably executed: rulers are not generally well-disposed toward regicides, even, or perhaps especially, when they benefit directly from their actions. Heraclianus, too, disappears from view: he is said to have killed himself, perhaps fearing the same imperial vengeance as had befallen his agent, Cecropius.[13] Claudius' close confederate Aurelian, on the other hand, fared very well: he was immediately assigned Cecropius' old command over the Dalmatian horse, and in due course was promoted to the position of overall commander of the cavalry, vacated by Claudius himself. It may be that Aurelian's complicity in the plot to kill Gallienus was not as incriminating as that of the other two, or it may simply be that Claudius knew he could trust Aurelian. In either case, it suggests that Claudius had need of Aurelian, whose popular standing with the army helped to smooth the transition of power.[14]

There still remained the problem of Aureolus, immured inside Milan. It is possible that the beleaguered general, on coming to the realization that aid from Postumus would not be forthcoming, declared himself emperor in his own right. On hearing of the death of Gallienus, he decided to come to terms with the new emperor. If he hoped to gain by the removal of Gallienus, he was mistaken. According to one version, Claudius immediately had him put to death; according to another, his own troops dispatched him. There is a suggestion that Aurelian himself was implicated in the murder of Aureolus, but it is likely to be a later invention which, wishing to absolve Claudius of any possible blame, sought to pin the deed on another: and who better than his severe right-hand man, 'Hand-on-Sword'.[15]

The removal of the powerful and potentially dangerous Aureolus must have come as a relief to Claudius, who went to Rome to settle with the senate and enter into the consulship for the new year. But the relief was short-lived. The preoccupation of substantial numbers of Roman forces in the power struggles around Milan presented an opportunity for the barbarian tribes beyond the Danube to plunder Roman territory with relative impunity. It was an opportunity which the Alamanni were not slow to exploit. Together with their neighbours the Juthungi, they broke across the Danube, passed down through the Alps and began to pillage northern Italy. Claudius marched north to meet them. At Lake Garda, early in 269, he decisively defeated the enemy. The victory, in which Aurelian certainly played a part, earned the emperor the title Germanicus Maximus.[16]

Meanwhile, knowing the Roman defences in the Balkans were severely weakened by the events of the previous year, the Heruli decided to break their truce with Rome and repeat their venture. They had no difficulty in persuading both the East and West Goths to join the invasion, along with the Gepidae and the Peucini, a southern neighbour of the West Goths. Our sources speak of 320,000 men and 2,000 ships. Such figures are doubtless exaggerated, but the invasion represented an enemy force the likes of which were not seen again on Roman soil until the catastrophic Gothic invasion which destroyed the emperor Valens and his army at Hadrianople in 378.[17]

Having assembled their armada at the mouth of the Dniester, the Goths and their allies ravaged the Black Sea coast of Moesia and Thrace, attacking Tomi and striking inland as far as Marcianopolis. From there they sailed to the Bosphorus and, after being hit by a storm, they made unsuccessful attempts to sack Byzantium and Cyzicus on the way through the Sea of Marmara. Once through the Dardanelles, they sailed along the northern coast of the Aegean towards Chalcidice. They attacked Cassandrea and then laid siege to Thessalonica.[18] News of this Gothic invasion must have reached Claudius in northern Italy not long after the battle of Lake Garda, but his hands were still full dealing with the defeated enemy. He therefore dispatched his most trusted general, Aurelian, to proceed directly to the Balkans. Aurelian departed immediately at the head of a sizeable force, which included the Dalmatian cavalry.[19]

Claudius had another reason to delay his departure from Italy. On the Rhine, one of Postumus' generals, Ulpius Laelianus, had risen in revolt and the situation looked dire for Postumus. The centre of the revolt was at Mainz, but the coinage issued in Laelian's name was the work of the branch mint which Postumus had only lately set up in Cologne. Furthermore, certain of these coins suggest the support of at least part of the legion XXX Ulpia, the main base of which was at Xanten.[20] The implication is that disaffection towards Postumus was alarmingly widespread among the troops stationed along the middle Rhine. In rejecting Aureolus' overture the previous summer, Postumus may have suspected that some such trouble was near; on the other hand, his failure to seize the opportunity offered by the revolt at Milan may itself have contributed to the disaffection among his troops. Postumus advanced on Laelian, forcing him to fall back on Mainz. After a gruelling siege, Postumus' troops finally forced an entry into the city. Laelian was killed and the revolt effectively terminated, but when Postumus prevented his impatient and embittered troops from pillaging Mainz, they turned on their leader and killed him.[21]

Whether Claudius was tempted to intervene in the western provinces at this critical juncture is not certain. Faced with the choice between tackling Postumus or the barbarians, Claudius is said to have stated that war against a pretender was his own concern, whereas war against the barbarians was the state's, and that concerns of state must take precedence. This sententious rhetoric is almost certainly apocryphal, but the story suggests that Claudius did at least consider intervention in Gaul at this time. In the end, the situation in the Balkans was too serious for him not to go there in person. Leaving his younger brother Quintillus in command of the forces in Italy, Claudius set out for the Balkans with the main force of the central strategic reserve to join up with Aurelian and Marcianus. The recovery of the western provinces would have to wait.[22]

When the Goths learned of the approaching imperial army they abandoned their siege of Thessalonica and turned inward, laying waste north-eastern Macedonia as they went. Here, Aurelian caught up with them and, using the Dalmatian cavalry to great effect, succeeded in killing up to three thousand of them in a succession of skirmishes. By employing the cavalry continually to harass their flanks he managed to drive the enemy northward into Upper Moesia where Claudius had drawn up the main Roman force.[23] The battle was both bloody and indecisive, though it did halt the northward advance of the enemy. The Roman losses were sufficiently heavy to preclude chancing another pitched battle. Instead, Claudius managed to ambush the enemy. He succeeded in killing a large number, but the majority of the Goths escaped and remained under arms. The tactic succeeded in crippling their offensive capacity, but the invaders still represented a force to be reckoned with.[24]

The Gothic army began a slow and painful retreat south the way it had come. During the rest of the summer and into the autumn the invaders were once again harassed by Aurelian's Dalmatian cavalry. By this time running desperately short of provisions, the Goths and their animals began to suffer terribly from hunger. Perceiving their weakened state, Aurelian attacked them with the full force of his cavalry, killing many and driving the remainder westward into Thrace. In the mountains of the Great Balkan Range, at that time known as Haemus, the Goths found themselves trapped and surrounded. As winter set in, cold and disease added to the death toll caused by starvation. The harsh conditions were not easy for the surrounding Roman army either. Among certain units, discipline began to break down. The Romans may have written off the Goths too soon, for their fighting spirit was far from broken. Seizing the moment, they made a valiant effort to break out of their camp. Claudius apparently misjudged the situation. Ignoring advice, perhaps from Aurelian, he held back his cavalry and sent in his infantry alone. The Goths fought fiercely, inflicting serious damage on the Roman army, and a catastrophe was only averted by the timely intervention of Aurelian's corps of Dalmatian horse. The intervention was too late, however, to prevent the enemy from effecting their break-out.[25]

Throughout the spring the remaining Goths continued their roving march through Thrace, still shadowed closely by the Roman army. Short of supplies and weakened by hunger, many Goths fell victim to a devastating plague which swept through the Balkans during the spring and summer of 270. The pestilence spread to the Roman army too. Even the emperor became unwell and returned to his regional headquarters at Sirmium, leaving Aurelian in full command of clearing Thrace and Lower Moesia of the last of the marauding Goths. Aurelian succeeded in splintering them into smaller bands which were more easily dealt with. Those that did not die in battle or from the plague were gradually rounded up, together with whatever animals and booty remained with them. Some of the captives were recruited into the frontier units of the Roman army, others were settled as peasant farmers in the frontier regions, to be called upon as militia if the need should arise.[26] These mopping-up operations dragged on well into the summer. Meanwhile, Claudius himself accepted the title of Gothicus Maximus and celebrated his achievements on his coinage. The senate honoured him with a golden shield, like that which had been set up for Augustus. He did not have long to savour his success: he died that August at Sirmium, succumbing to the plague that had already sapped so much of Rome's military strength.[27]

Among the encomiastic accounts of the reign of Claudius there is a story which at first sight seems to contradict the well-attested version of the emperor's death given above. It is said that while the senate was debating how to combat the Gothic incursion, the Sibylline Books were consulted and found to demand the self-sacrifice of the leading senator to guarantee victory. Several members offered their lives, including Pomponius Bassus, at that time the senior consular, but Claudius declared that the oracular decree could mean none but the emperor himself. Having pledged his life to the state, he left for the wars and died heroically in fulfilment of his vow. It could be inferred that he died in battle, or as a direct result of wounds received in battle, but this is not stated directly. It is likely that this version of events is merely a highly rhetorical gloss inserted into the account of Claudius' deeds in order to represent his death, as a result of plague contracted while on campaign, as an heroic self-sacrifice.[28]

At the time of Claudius' death the Gothic wars remained unfinished business. In spite of Aurelian's tireless efforts, marauding bands of Goths still posed a menace to Thrace. One such was apparently strong enough to attempt an assault on the city of Nicopolis. At the same time, sea-borne raids continued throughout that summer. Though the forces involved were insufficient to pose much threat to the cities, the surrounding countryside suffered greatly. Anchialus on the Black Sea was attacked, as were many coastal areas and islands around the Aegean. Crete and Rhodes suffered particularly badly. The coast of Pamphylia was raided, though cities like Side managed to resist the assault. Even Cyprus may have been attacked. The impact of these raids was somewhat mitigated by the fact that the raiders were severely weakened by the effects of the plague.[29]

The struggle for power

When the news of his brother's death reached Quintillus in Italy, the troops that were with him immediately proclaimed him emperor. The senate at Rome must have been fully aware that the most powerful individual in the empire, and the one to whom the Balkan army would be most likely to turn as Claudius' natural successor, was unquestionably Aurelian. A significant lobby within the senate evidently found this prospect alarming as Aurelian had already earned a reputation as a strong-willed individual of stern temperament. More to the point, Quintillus' troops, though numerically and qualitatively inferior to those under Aurelian's command in Thrace, were much closer. Therefore, on receiving the news that Claudius was dead and his ineffectual younger brother elevated in his place, the senate did not hesitate to endorse Quintillus.[30] It was probably at this time that the senate voted to place Claudius among the gods and erect a golden statue of him in the precinct of the temple of Jupiter Optimus Maximus on the Capitol.[31] Otherwise, the reign of Quintillus has left very little trace. It lasted barely two months before it was overtaken by events in the Balkans.[32]

When the news of Claudius' death reached Aurelian in Thrace, where he was still occupied with the Goths, he knew what the army would expect of him. The outstanding part he had played in the Gothic wars, not least his quick and decisive action at Haemus, had already earned him the greatest respect among his fellow officers and the rank and file. Those officers who had supported Claudius over Gallienus now looked to Claudius' second in command as his natural successor. The precise timing of events is not certain. We do not even know whether they determined to act before or after news of Quintillus' coup in Italy reached the Balkans. Either way, they orchestrated the Danubian army to elevate Aurelian to the purple. Zonaras tells us that Claudius, on his deathbed, designated Aurelian as his successor and that the elevation of Aurelian was simultaneous with that of Quintillus. These assertions are best attributed to subsequent Aurelianic propaganda calculated to marginalize the reign of Quintillus. The date of Aurelian's elevation is uncertain, but it must have fallen roughly in the second half of September. He was just 56.[33]

When he heard of Aurelian's proclamation, Quintillus mustered his forces at Aquileia, a few kilometres north-west of the Gulf of Triest. As he prepared to meet his rival's advance there must have been many, including in all likelihood Quintillus himself, who doubted his ability to withstand Aurelian's challenge.[34] Of the two rival emperors, Aurelian's military reputation and the strength of his support among the soldiers gave him a distinct advantage. Furthermore, he had at his command the formidable and battle-hardened army which Claudius had assembled to fight the Goths in the Balkans. Against this, Quintillus' only advantage, the relatively insignificant incremental legitimation provided by the senate's recognition of his claim, was no compensation.

As Aurelian's army drew nearer, Quintillus must have sensed his cause was hopeless. There was no way he could confidently commit his officers and men to battle against the hero of the Gothic wars. By the time Aurelian reached Aquileia, both Quintillus and his cause were dead. One version says that he was murdered by his troops. It is just as likely that, anticipating the dishonour of defeat, he took his own life. His ephemeral reign was at an end, leaving Aurelian in undisputed control of the central portion of the empire.[35]

CONSOLIDATION: 270–1

Even with the removal of his immediate rival, Aurelian's position was far from stable. In the east, Palmyrene military expansion seriously threatened Roman interests, while the western provinces were still under the control of Postumus' successors. Nearer to hand, the Gothic problem remained unresolved, and was now compounded by the invasions of other Germanic peoples further up-river.

The sources for these events are very confused and no clear consensus has emerged among modern scholars as to how to interpret them. In particular, the identity, order, location and even the number of Germanic invasions during 270–1 remains controversial. What follows is, therefore, only what seems to me the most likely reconstruction.[36]

The early campaigns

At about the beginning of November, Aurelian entered Aquileia to receive the joyous acclamations of the troops that had so recently been sworn to defend Italy against him. The mint at Cyzicus had for some time issued coins in his name and that at Siscia had quickly followed suit. Now at last he also gained control of the Italian mints, at Milan and Rome. Among his first actions was to order these four imperial mints to prepare an issue of coinage to commemorate the deified emperor Claudius. In part this was intended as a genuine act of homage to his predecessor and former companion-at-arms. He also wished thereby to associate himself more closely with his illustrious and popular predecessor, and perhaps to reassure the senate of his intentions towards that body whom Claudius had treated well. Another reason was in order to marginalize still further the reign of Quintillus.[37] When news of Quintillus' death arrived in Rome the senate deftly changed its allegiance. While Aurelian celebrated his bloodless victory, a deputation of senior senators came north to greet their new sovereign lord and reassure him of their unswerving loyalty. Sometime in November Aurelian met them at Ravenna.[38] While he was there, word reached him of trouble brewing on the middle Danube.

Aurelian's march on Italy had left the Pannonian frontier vulnerable to attack. Seeing an opportunity, a large army of Asding Vandals were massing across the river in the vicinity of Aquincum (Budapest). Aurelian returned to Aquileia and, without delay, began to organize his army and the necessary supplies. He then marched back out of Italy the way he had come only a short time before, over the Julian Alps. By the time he arrived in Pannonia the year was drawing to a close. He set up his regional headquarters at Siscia, the mint city of the region. It was probably here, or at least while in Pannonia, that Aurelian assumed his first consulship, on New Year's Day 271. This was in accordance with a long-established imperial tradition which reserved the right of assuming the ordinary consulship for a new emperor in the first January of his reign. Foreign and civil wars permitting, this office would normally have been assumed at Rome. It was unusual for an emperor to assume the consulship without even setting foot in the old capital. The circumstances of Aurelian's first consulship are thus a further sign of the diminishing role of Rome in imperial pomp at this time.[39]

Meanwhile, the Vandals had crossed the river in force. They encountered little resistance as they looted the villages and countryside of the region. But the season was by now so far advanced that they were finding it difficult to live off the land through which they passed and were beginning to suffer from a shortage of food. Knowing that the enemy was not equipped for siege warfare, Aurelian sent word ahead to withdraw all the livestock and food supplies into the fortified cities.[40] Once he was satisfied that this war of attrition had sufficiently weakened the barbarians and that his own supply lines and troops were in proper order, Aurelian sought out the Vandals.

The campaign was long and made particularly arduous by the season. In the initial stages at least, Aurelian was unable to gain a conclusive victory. Finally, however, the Roman army succeeded in inflicting a defeat of sufficient magnitude to halt the barbarians. The Vandals, not wishing to test their mettle against Aurelian's army any further, sued for peace. An idea of the negotiations that followed and their results is preserved in fragments from the works of Dexippus and Petrus. The Vandals were bound over to keep the peace, in pledge of which they handed over hostages and furnished 2,000 horsemen for the Roman army. They also agreed to restrict their trade routes and allow the Romans to monitor their trade. In return, the Romans granted them safe conduct and enough food supplies to reach the Danube frontier. Some rogue bands of Vandals broke away from the main column and returned to pillaging, but were soon eliminated.[41]

Aurelian had little respite in which to savour his victory. Even before he could bring the campaign to a satisfactory conclusion, news reached him of a much more serious invasion that had broken across the Danube further upstream. Taking advantage of Aurelian's preoccupation in Pannonia, the Juthungi had cut a swath of destruction through Raetia as far as Lake Constance. They had then turned south over the Alps. Although their exact route is uncertain, it seems likely that they came over the Splügen Pass, since it was the area around Milan that bore the brunt of their attack. For the third time in only eleven years, a barbarian army was on Italian soil and the very heart of the empire was under threat.[42]

As soon as he heard of this invasion, Aurelian sent his main army on ahead to Italy, retaining only a few crack troops with him in Pannonia to oversee the Vandal withdrawal and the re-establishment of the frontier. Once he was satisfied he could safely withdraw, he hurried to Italy leaving only the frontier troops behind to secure the defence of Pannonia. He quickly caught up with his main army as it skirted the southern edge of the Dolomites along the Via Postumia.[43] Aurelian was anxious to engage the enemy as soon as possible and pressed on at great speed. As he drew nearer to Milan he discovered that the Juthungi had already moved south-east and sacked the city of Placentia (Piacenza). Whether Aurelian could have prevented this misfortune by diverting his approach further to the south and reaching Placentia before the barbarians is not clear. In any case, he sent word ahead to invite the barbarians to give themselves up and submit to his rule. They haughtily responded that they were a free people and if he wished to challenge them they would show him how free men could fight.[44]

The invaders withdrew with their spoils towards the south-east. Without being able to rest his army, Aurelian was immediately obliged to give chase. Had he taken a more southerly route earlier it is possible he would have been able to lie in wait for the enemy. As it was, his men were exhausted after their long series of forced marches from the Balkans. At dusk, in a wooded area just beyond Placentia, the advancing Roman army was ambushed and suffered significant losses. It was a humiliating set-back. As a direct result, the Germans were able to press on down the Via Aemilia in the direction of Rome.[45]

When the news of these disasters reached Rome an understandable panic gripped the city, for no significant force stood between the invaders and the metropolis. Rome had long since outgrown and built over its ancient city walls; the vast empire and its legions had long been an ample buffer to protect the city from external enemies. Now, with the approach of the Juthungi, the defenceless city seemed at the mercy of the forces of a foreign enemy. According to the *Historia Augusta*, the Sibylline Books were consulted and the religious observances they dictated were what eventually saved the city from the Germans.[46]

A more mundane view suggests that Aurelian managed to regroup his battered army and follow the trail of devastation that marked the enemy's route down the side of the Appenines towards the Adriatic. Aware that the Roman army was at their heels, the Juthungi did not pause to sack the defenceless coastal towns of Pisaurum (Pesaro) and Fanum Fortunae (Fano). Instead they began to turn inward along the Via Flaminia, which led over the Appenines towards central Italy and Rome itself. Here, on the banks of the Metaurus just inland from Fanum, Aurelian finally caught up with them. This time it was a pitched battle and Aurelian was victorious. The decisive moment came when a large section of the Juthungi found itself pinned against the river: as the barbarian line gave way, a great number were swept away in the river and drowned. The victory was commemorated on a pair of inscriptions from nearby Pisaurum, just to the north.[47]

The Juthungi sued for peace. They remained sufficiently confident to feel they could negotiate from a position of strength. Even though they had lost the battle, they still represented a formidable fighting force. A fragment from Dexippus' *Scythica* recounts the parley. Although the account is highly rhetorical and its reliability is not entirely above suspicion, it gives a flavour of the confrontation. After describing the display that Aurelian assembled to intimidate the enemy, Dexippus has the German envoys boast of the size and prowess of their fighting force and of how far they had managed to penetrate into the empire. Aurelian for his part was unimpressed. He was aware of the size of their army, but made it clear he was not about to let so considerable an enemy force roam unchecked through Roman territory on their way home laden with Italian spoils. The Juthungi were therefore denied the safe passage they sought and were sent away empty-handed.[48]

The Roman victory, though not conclusive, had been enough to ensure that the Juthungi could not continue their advance. In the circumstances, they had no option but to turn around and head back the way they had come up the Via Aemilia. Aurelian pursued them, waiting for the optimum moment to strike. He needed to be sure of a decisive victory, not only to avenge and expunge the memory of his earlier set-back but also to seize the booty the Juthungi were carrying. When the Juthungi reached the open plains near Ticinum (Pavia) Aurelian attacked. This time the victory was conclusive and the Juthungi were utterly routed. A few survivors formed into small bands, but these were easily run down and neutralized.[49] Thus, Aurelian was able to turn a campaign that had begun so badly into a complete triumph. In recognition of this he assumed the title Germanicus Maximus.[50] After a reign that had already lasted almost nine months, the emperor was at last in a position to head for Rome; but it was not to be the triumphant reception he could reasonably have expected.

Civil strife

While Aurelian was thus occupied in military activities in northern Italy, intrigue and civil strife once more reared their ugly heads. A revolt sprang up in Dalmatia, perhaps sparked off by the news of Aurelian's difficulties in Italy. The troops stationed there proclaimed Septiminus (or Septimius), who was perhaps their military governor, as emperor. The revolt was short-lived, and Septiminus was killed by his own soldiers.[51] A potentially more serious revolt at about the same time centred upon the figure of Domitianus, Gallienus' former general who had assisted Aureolus in destroying the Macriani a decade earlier. The location of the revolt is unknown. An apparently genuine coin issued in the name of Domitianus as emperor was found in France, implying that he revolted in south-eastern Gaul. A hoard deposited at Samoëns, south of Lake Geneva, suggests there may have been trouble in the area at this time.[52] If the revolt did take place in that region, it may have been sparked off by the Juthungian invasion to the east and it was probably suppressed by Julius Placidianus.[53] With the death of Domitianus, Aurelian was left as the last of Gallienus' great generals, the final victor in a power struggle played out over a dozen years.

Meanwhile, at Rome, where the German advance had caused general panic and unrest, a still more serious sedition erupted. The mint workers there had begun to defraud the government on a massive scale by issuing coinage which was markedly debased and underweight even by the poor standards of the day.[54] The effect of part of this fraudulent behaviour has recently been detected in much of the Divus Claudius coinage issued from this mint. The precise nature of this fraud is a matter of some debate, and the culpability of the moneyers may not have been as great as Aurelian later maintained. Certainly, however, the corruption went right to the top. The man responsible for the operation of the mint and the control of the supply of precious metals was the chief financial minister, or *rationalis*, Felicissimus.[55] It is clear that he was fully implicated, and it seems likely that his actions so far abused the responsibilities of his office that they amounted to treason. When he was challenged he incited the mint workers to open revolt, but apparently was almost immediately killed. He may even have been executed. In any case, his death, far from being the end of the affair, was the signal for some of the most appalling scenes of violence the city had witnessed since the last decades of the republic.[56]

Realizing the game was up, and fearing retribution, the mint workers took to the streets. The tensions of the preceding weeks had raised the stakes. Furthermore, Palmyrene aggression had recently led to troubles in Egypt (see Chapter 4), and it is more than likely that these had disrupted the grain supply for the city. Disaffection was widespread, and the situation quickly developed into a general uprising. A number of senators, perhaps those who had most strongly urged the elevation of Quintillus and thus had most to fear from Aurelian, seized the opportunity to conspire against the emperor. Perhaps emboldened by the news of the revolts in the provinces they began openly to incite the rabble. A full-scale and bloody riot ensued, ending in a pitched battle on the Caelian hill between the mob and the urban cohorts reinforced by regular troops from the imperial army. The carnage was certainly horrific, though the fatality figures given in the sources (a figure of 7,000 is mentioned) are dubious.[57]

Once order was restored, Aurelian dealt severely with the offenders. A large number, and not just the ringleaders, he immediately put to death. Several senators were among those rounded up and summarily executed, though the extent of their culpability is questioned by our pro-senatorial sources.[58] He then took the somewhat drastic measure of closing down the mint at Rome altogether. Some of the workers, those whom he had pardoned, he later took with him on campaign.[59] The immediate perpetrators of the upheavals were thus dealt with, but the dangerous combination of underlying factors which had led to the dangerous collapse of order at Rome had now to be addressed if a similar disaster were to be avoided in future.

The first such measure that Aurelian undertook turned out to be one of his most lasting legacies. To prevent, or at least mitigate, a repeat of the panic which had seized Rome as the Germans advanced, a panic which had been a spark to ignite the tinder of the other ills, Aurelian ordered the construction of the massive defensive walls around Rome that are still associated with his name to this day.[60] He also undertook to reform both the debased imperial monetary system and the arrangements for the urban food dole.[61] With regard to the latter, there remained the outstanding problem of Palmyrene interference in Egypt. Even if the supplies were by this time restored to normal, the threat that still hung over one of Rome's most vital lifelines was obviously intolerable. Aurelian therefore resolved to take on Palmyra. For the time being, however, he kept his intentions in this regard to himself. There was much preparation that would be needed for such a campaign and more pressing work awaited his attention in the Balkans. He did not delay any longer in Rome than was strictly necessary to ensure the restoration of his full authority in the city and to supervise the beginning of the construction of the walls. During the summer he set out from Rome, gathered his field army and headed for the Balkans.

The Gothic wars concluded

The efforts of Gallienus, Claudius and Aurelian to rid the Balkans of the Gothic menace had been only partially successful. Although Aurelian had managed to expel the Goths from Moesia during the previous summer, his elevation to the purple and the resulting contest with Quintillus had taken him away from the region before he could ensure a lasting solution. News of Aurelian's difficulties in Italy was the only invitation the Goths needed to renew their offensive against Moesia and Thrace. When Aurelian arrived in the area in the early autumn of 271, the Goths had already inflicted considerable damage. Aurelian defeated them and drove them back across the Danube, but was not content to leave it at that. Taking his army across the river he carried the war over into enemy territory. There he inflicted on them a crushing defeat, killing their king, Cannabas (or Cannabaudes), sacking their settlements and deporting the women who attempted to defend them. Years later, at his triumph in Rome, Aurelian is reported to have exhibited these captive women, dressed as Amazons, together with numerous other captives and Cannabas' royal chariot.[62] It was the most decisive victory a Roman army had won in that region throughout the entire troubled century. A sweet revenge for Abrittus, exactly two decades earlier, it earned Aurelian the title Gothicus Maximus.[63]

The resounding victory restored not only the Danube frontier, but the flagging morale of the region's defence forces. But that was not enough. The situation in Dacia was still tenuous, following the partial withdrawal of Roman forces from the province under Gallienus.[64] Aurelian could not spare the men and matériel that would be required to restore the transdanubian bulwark and the Dacian *limes*. He knew that, if he was to defeat the Palmyrenes, he needed to take with him to the east a sizeable army, one much larger than he had brought with him from Italy. He fully intended to levy more troops while in the Balkans, but raw recruits would be insufficiently reliable for the task in hand. But to deplete the already over-extended Danube army could be costly. For two decades the armies of Rome had been forced to defend the eastern Balkans from almost constant Gothic invasions. Aurelian himself had personally witnessed these bloody conflicts over the last four years. Nothing short of a drastic rethink of regional strategy would do.

Aurelian's solution was as radical as it was bold. He ordered the complete withdrawal of all the legionary forces stationed in Dacia and redrew the defensive line along the Danube, thereby greatly reducing the length of the frontier to be guarded. Furthermore, he evacuated from Dacia a sizeable proportion of its more important citizens and resettled them south of the river in a newly constituted province of Dacia Ripensis. As for the remaining population, Aurelian was in a position to impose terms on the Goths, and at the very least bound them over not to attack, possibly even engaged them to help defend, the territory north of the river, which thus retained some of its former function as a buffer.[65]

With the onset of winter, Aurelian began to make the necessary preparations for the confrontation with Palmyra: recruitment, training and logistical arrangements. The army he assembled was one of the most impressive of the century. In addition to the Dalmatian cavalry corps that had distinguished itself under his command in the Gothic wars, he had a troop of Mauritanian horse and he had legionary forces drawn from the full length of the Danube frontier, from Raetia and Noricum as well as the formidable regiments from Pannonia and Moesia. In addition to these, he had with him an elite corps of legionary vexillations, which probably represented the crack troops that had been with him since his first march on Italy, now augmented by units carefully selected for their outstanding ability from the legions and auxiliaries at his disposal.[66] With the approach of spring, his plans and preparations completed, Aurelian took this great army across the narrow neck of water that separates Europe from Asia, to Chalcedon. The game was afoot.

4

ZENOBIA AND THE EAST

In order to comprehend Aurelian's strategy in the east, we must first consider the situation from an eastern perspective. The rise of the fabulously wealthy city of Palmyra, the extraordinary career of its ruler Odenathus, and the dynamic enterprise of his shrewd and beautiful queen Zenobia, are tales that lend themselves easily to legend. We must discern the historical facts that lie behind these tales, for they are integral to the story of Aurelian's reign, just as his own career was to prove decisive in their conclusion.

THE MURDER OF ODENATHUS

The death of Odenathus of Palmyra is cloaked in sinister mystery. There is almost universal agreement that his sudden end was the work of an assassin; but who the assassin was and who may have put him up to it, how it came about, where and when, remain unresolved. Conflicting clues in the literary evidence tend to suggest either some political intrigue involving Rome, even implicating the emperor himself, or a family quarrel, possibly tinged with dynastic ambition.

In one version, a Roman official called Rufinus had Odenathus murdered on suspicion of plotting to rebel against Rome. When the victim's son, also called Odenathus, appealed to Gallienus, Rufinus not only defended his action but even persuaded the reluctant emperor to let him remove the son also.[1] Another version also reports a plot involving Gallienus, adding that Odenathus' widow Zenobia took up her husband's position and avenged his death.[2] Other clues lend fragile support to the allegation of antagonism between Rome and Palmyra around the time of Odenathus' death. Malalas records that Gallienus defeated the Persians and then fought against Odenathus for control of Arabia, defeating and killing him. He mentions no plot, but agrees that Zenobia's subsequent hostility to Rome was motivated by revenge. The *Historia Augusta* relates that when Gallienus heard of Odenathus' assassination he sent a large army to the east under his praetorian prefect Heraclianus, ostensibly to secure the Persian border. Zenobia, not trusting Gallienus' intentions, intercepted and repelled Heraclianus, destroying much of his army. Alas, neither of these accounts is very trustworthy. Malalas is very confused about the reign of Gallienus and, given Gallienus' preoccupation with the Goths, the story of Heraclianus should also be discounted.[3]

Another tradition paints a quite different picture. Zonaras tells how Odenathus' nephew, publicly humiliated by his uncle for failing to observe due protocol during a hunt, killed both the Palmyrene prince and his eldest son, and was then himself put to death. In Syncellus there is no mention of a murdered son and the murderer bears the same name as the victim. Though the relationship between the two is not spelled out, it looks like parricide. Zosimus says only that Odenathus fell victim to a conspiracy at a birthday party, apparently a family event.[4] The *HA* embroiders on this theme in typical fashion: in this version, Zenobia herself is the instigator of the plot, the murdered son, named as 'Herodes', is the son of Odenathus by a previous marriage; a wicked stepmother's jealousy thus provides the motive. The murderer, named as Maeonius, is a disgruntled cousin who, after murdering his kinsmen, is proclaimed emperor and is then himself immediately killed. Much of this is fiction.[5]

The sons of Odenathus present something of a problem. The epigraphic evidence does not support the notion that any son of Odenathus bore his name. On the other hand, 'Herodes' corresponds fairly closely to the name Herodianus, attested in epigraphic evidence, who vanishes without trace at this time and thus apparently perished with his father. The name Hairan, also attested in the epigraphic evidence as a son of Odenathus, likewise disappears at this time. It is possible that both names refer to the same person (Herodianos being a Greek version of Hairan), and conceivable that he was (or they were) of a former marriage. It is also likely that the offspring who survived were Zenobia's. The *HA* at first speaks of two surviving sons, named as Herennianus and Timolaus. 'Herennianus' may be a conflation of Hairan and Herodianus, 'Timolaus' may simply be a fabrication.[6] Later, the author specifically corrects himself, stating that Zenobia seized control in the name of one son only: Vaballathus. Julius Septimius Vaballathus Athenodorus is the only surviving son of whom we have any independent knowledge. He was unquestionably the son of Odenathus and Zenobia: named Wahb-Allat, 'the gift of al-Lat', after his paternal grandfather.[7]

The date of Odenathus' assassination has now been established on the basis of evidence from Egypt as falling between the end of August 267 and the end of August 268.[8] Only two accounts give any guidance as to location. Zosimus places the murder at Emesa, in Syria, while Syncellus says it took place in Cappadocia, as Odenathus was marching against the Goths who were threatening Heracleia Pontica in north-western Anatolia. The second account is usually preferred, partly because the *HA* seems to lend it some support. The timing now makes this less convincing, however, and it is clear that Syncellus has compressed into one brief narrative a number of separate Gothic raids on Asia Minor.[9]

No reconciliation of all these various accounts is possible, not least because the evidence is mostly hearsay and rumour. Perhaps it is not surprising that the death of this great man in suspicious circumstances should have given rise to so many conflicting 'conspiracy theories'. The western sources tend to present Odenathus as a loyal subject and stress that the relationship between Palmyra and Rome remained perfectly amicable up until his death. Only then was it blighted by the ambitions of his infamous widow. The suspicion that Gallienus might somehow have been implicated in the death of his eastern viceroy forces us at least to question this presentation. Whatever the truth, if the intention of those behind the assassination of Odenathus was to curb the power that he had built up for himself in the east, they reckoned without Zenobia.

THE ADVENT OF ZENOBIA

Consolidation

Septimia Zenobia (Bath-Zabbai in Aramaic) was as shrewd and capable as she was determined. She quickly perceived that her husband's death threatened everything he had worked for. If stability in the area was to be maintained, if Palmyra was to continue to enjoy the regional hegemony which Odenathus had so skilfully built up, above all if their son Vaballathus was to inherit any of his father's pre-eminence, she must seize the initiative.

Odenathus' extraordinary authority had been essentially personal in character, built up over a long period and based on a network of personal loyalties. To effect the transfer of such authority from one individual to another is always far more hazardous than is the case with an established monarchy. A similar problem had confronted Augustus just over two-and-a-half centuries earlier. Odenathus was certainly aware of this problem, which is why he had elevated his eldest son Herodianus to be his co-regent. The plan of succession had been destroyed, however, when Odenathus' assassin had also removed his heir apparent. Zenobia therefore wasted no time in securing for her son Vaballathus the titles and honours which his father had borne. Thus he immediately assumed the titles Lord of Palmyra and King of Kings as well as *corrector totius orientis*. To the first two of these titles he had a vaguely legitimate claim, as the son of Odenathus; to the last, denoting a very senior rank in Roman provincial military command, he had no official claim at all. The arrogation of this title was probably not meant initially as an affront to the Roman emperor, in whose gift the office rightly lay, but rather as part of a representation, for local consumption, of Vaballathus as the true heir of Odenathus' political authority.[10]

In this way, Zenobia secured both for her son and for Palmyra the continuity she desired. In this she had the backing of the nobility and the military establishment at Palmyra. The situation was none the less precarious. The network of alliances which Odenathus had built up in the region were not inherently stable and might not long outlast him. Furthermore, the boy was still young; his exact age is not known, but he was certainly a minor. For this reason, Zenobia, taking the titles queen and mother of the king, exercised the real power as regent herself.[11]

Her closest advisors were those who had been her husband's associates. Among these was Julius Aurelius Septimius Vorodes (Vorôd), apparently a man of Persian origin who had risen under Odenathus to become his top general during the wars against Shapur. Honoured by the Palmyrene city council for his military achievements, he became governor of the city of Palmyra around the time of Odenathus' death. To take her husband's place as supreme commander of the Palmyrene army Zenobia appointed Septimius Zabdas (Zabda), a man on whose military ability and unswerving loyalty she could justifiably rely.[12]

Military intervention: Arabia and Egypt

Whatever credence should be given to the accounts of antagonism between Gallienus and Zenobia at the time of her husband's death, there can be no doubt that the removal of Odenathus placed a serious and irreparable strain on the relations between Palmyra and Rome.

Although a *modus vivendi* appears to have been quickly re-established, there is no reason to suppose that Gallienus or Claudius ever ratified Vaballathus' assumption of the title *corrector totius orientis*. The boy's use of the title did not bode well for future relations, but as long as Zenobia did not intend to exercise its powers to the full, a tacit agreement could persist.

Zenobia was conscious both of the strength of the position she had inherited from her husband and of the weakness of Roman control in the east. Throughout 269, Claudius and his generals, including Aurelian, were engaged with the Germanic invasions of Italy and the Balkans. During this time, Zenobia consolidated her power base in the east. Inevitably, this created tensions. While certain Arab peoples accepted Palmyrene domination with equanimity, others, notably the Tanukh confederation in the Hauran, resisted strongly. As the friction worsened, the Roman authorities in the area found themselves rather awkwardly caught in the middle. Zenobia began to press her claim to exercise control over those parts of the empire which had lain within her husband's competence, and increasingly expected compliance from the Roman administration in the region. This included not just the Syrian desert and Arabia, but the whole region from Asia Minor to Egypt. She was fully conscious that she possessed the military might to back her claim, and also that, at least south of Cappadocia, she could count on considerable local support for her cause.[13]

At what precise point Zenobia determined to employ the military option to enforce the authority she claimed, or whether the confrontation escalated imperceptibly without there ever being a precise moment as such, is impossible to say. It was probably in the spring of 270, while Claudius and Aurelian were preoccupied with the Goths in the mountains of northern Thrace, that Zenobia sent her general Zabdas with a large army south-west into Roman Arabia. The Roman authorities there could scarcely ignore a deployment on this scale aimed, not at those beyond the frontier, but at Roman citizens. The *dux* of Arabia, a certain Trassus, marshalled the Roman legion stationed in that area, the III Cyrenaica, and confronted the Palmyrene army near the provincial capital, Bostra. Zabdas utterly defeated this force, killing Trassus. He then marched on Bostra and sacked it, destroying the temple of Zeus Ammon which had intimate links with the legionary garrison.[14]

The Palmyrene advance did not halt there. Zabdas marched down the Jordan valley, apparently meeting with little resistance. The exact route he took is not known. There is evidence to suggest that

Petra might have suffered attack at this time, though this may have been the result of an excursion not involving the main force.[15] Having thus easily secured Arabia and Judaea, it became clear that Zenobia's next objective was Egypt. It has been suggested that the entire campaign was motivated right from the start by the economic objective of securing new trade routes through Egypt, since the trade routes over the Euphrates had been cut during the conflict with Persia. However, this thesis ignores the considerable degree of continuity in the traffic across the Euphrates and underestimates Zenobia's political motivation in re-establishing her husband's former dominion.[16]

The arrival of Zabdas and the Palmyrene army at the eastern borders of Egypt coincided with, and indeed probably helped to provoke, serious unrest in Egypt. As in Arabia, the troubles had been fomented by friction between different local elements who either welcomed or resisted the idea of interference from Palmyra. The most experienced Roman military commander in the region was Tenagino Probus, who was prefect of Egypt by this date. Unfortunately for the Roman cause, at this precise time he was away commanding a naval expedition against 'pirates', who may be identifiable as the Goths whose attacks on Levantine ports have already been noted.[17] Taking advantage of his absence, a large number of Palmyrene sympathizers, led by Timagenes, an officer in the Roman forces stationed in Egypt, joined forces with Zabdas and overpowered the Roman garrison.[18]

The Palmyrene invasion of Egypt must have begun early in October, late enough for news of Claudius' death to have reached Zabdas in southern Judaea before he launched his attack. The timing suggests that the intervention in Egypt may have been more opportunistic than is usually supposed. Although Zosimus and the *HA* place the Palmyrene invasion of Egypt in the reign of Claudius, the accounts in Zonaras and Syncellus imply that the invasion took place shortly after Claudius' death. That Zabdas' expedition had begun in Arabia while Claudius still reigned, as Malalas rightly says, may be enough to explain the error in Zosimus.[19]

Advised of the situation, Probus hurried to Egypt and rallied the forces loyal to Rome. By early November he had regained control of Alexandria and was succeeding in driving the Palmyrenes out of the delta. But the Palmyrene forces managed to regroup and counter-attack. The main thrust of their advance was against Alexandria. It seems the Palmyrenes enjoyed considerable local support in the city, a prominent part of which may have come from the substantial Jewish community. Zabdas soon regained control of Alexandria.[20]

Probus retreated south to Babylon, the garrison city at the southernmost tip of the delta, in order to join forces with the Roman troops stationed there and secure the rest of Egypt. When Zabdas arrived, having marched south to challenge Probus, he found that the Roman general had taken up a strong position in the high ground to the east. Probus had chosen his ground well, but Timagenes, being familiar with the area, led a contingent of Palmyrenes around the Roman position and surprised Probus from the rear. The Palmyrenes were victorious and Probus committed suicide. The elimination of Probus and his army left Egypt firmly under Palmyrene control.[21]

PALMYRA AT ITS ZENITH

Syria and Asia Minor

Meanwhile, Zenobia also began to tighten her grip on northern Syria. Coin production at the imperial mint at Antioch, which had continued to issue in the name of Claudius up until the beginning of 270, faltered and then ceased altogether.[22] This coincided more or less exactly with the Palmyrene military advance into Roman Arabia. Unlike that episode, and the Egyptian campaign that followed it, the encroachment into northern Syria was more subtle, effected primarily through the influence of local agents sympathetic to the Palmyrene regime. Certainly in Antioch itself, the most important city in the region, evidence strongly suggests the presence of a significant faction prepared to support Zenobia's cause.

Among the influential citizens of Antioch alleged to have sought personal advantage by throwing in their lot with Zenobia was Paul of Samosata, the heretical bishop of Antioch. Though many local Christians were unhappy with both his behaviour and his theology, Paul had a substantial following in the city and in the surrounding countryside. His position remained none the less tenuous, especially so after he was excommunicated for heresy by a synod of his fellow bishops. He blatantly ignored their decision, but to remain in Antioch he needed all the support he could find. The requirements of his personal ambitions would have rendered an alliance with Zenobia an attractive proposition at just the time that she was seeking ways to exercise greater control over the area. It is said that they arrived at an understanding to their mutual advantage, whereby Zenobia gave her backing to the discredited bishop while he, in return, encouraged support for the Palmyrene cause at Antioch. The exact truth behind this allegation is now difficult to determine. It must be stressed, however, that it derives almost exclusively from later Christian writers who had every reason to blacken the name of Paul.[23]

Whatever Paul's relationship with Zenobia, we know there were many individuals at Antioch, including some of considerable standing in the community, who were ready to champion the Palmyrene cause. With their aid, Zenobia gradually came to exercise full control over the area. The mint at Antioch resumed production with an issue of antoniniani depicting Vaballathus on one side and Aurelian on the other, paralleling the tetradrachms being issued at that time in Alexandria.[24]

The Palmyrene domination over northern Syria was not complete before the arrival of Zabdas in the spring of 271, though it is entirely possible that military operations had already begun in this region under his second-in-command Septimius Zabbai. During the course of this year, Palmyrene control was extended across most of Asia Minor, including Galatia. The extent of active Palmyrene military involvement in this area is not known, but it may not have been all that great. We can be fairly sure that Zabdas and Zabbai were back in Palmyra by the summer, for in August of that year they dedicated a pair of statues, one to their former master Odenathus, the other to their present mistress Zenobia. The extreme north-western corner of Asia Minor, however, resisted Palmyrene rule. Zenobia's attempts to win over or subdue Chalcedon, the guardian of the Bosphorus, failed: the province of Bithynia, and with it the mint at Cyzicus, remained loyal to Aurelian.[25] This would provide Aurelian with a crucial bridgehead in Asia Minor when his offensive finally got under way.

Zenobia's power base

Palmyra was now at the height of its power. The position which Zenobia occupied cannot be explained in terms of a military conquest; nor should it be characterized simply as the triumph of one faction in the region over another. Numerous attempts have been made to find in Zenobia's religious and cultural affiliations a tidy explanation for her remarkable success. The reality was far more complex.

Although the Talmudic tradition is hostile to Palmyra, there was probably considerable support for Zenobia's cause among the Jews, as we saw at Alexandria. It seems she actively sought the support of the Jewish community, though we may safely discount stories of her flirtation with, or even conversion to, Judaism. It has even been suggested that the reputed involvement of Zenobia with Paul of

Samosata may have been influenced by her Judaic sympathies, for Paul's heresy had certain Judaizing tendencies. It is similarly claimed in various sources that Zenobia converted either to Christianity or to Manichaeism. While it is difficult to refute such claims, it seems more likely that Zenobia was careful to exercise religious toleration so as to cultivate the support of groups who had reason to feel marginalized under Roman rule.[26]

Zenobia's regime has also been interpreted primarily in the context of a more or less conscious power-struggle between the Semitic and Hellenistic cultures of the ancient Near East. Once again, her reputed alliance with Paul plays into the argument. It is possible that Paul appealed especially to the less heavily Hellenized Aramaic-speaking section of the population; but it is doubtful that this was his only constituency. We cannot even really be sure as to what extent this section of the population regarded the domination of Syria by Palmyra, as a predominantly Semitic power, as preferable to domination by Rome. In any case, how far a self-conscious cultural dichotomy along these lines really existed remains highly questionable.[27]

Conversely, great stress has also been laid on Zenobia's philhellenism. The fact that Zenobia went to great lengths to present herself and her regime in terms of continuity within the Graeco-Roman traditions is itself a powerful argument against too strong an identification between Zenobia and some form of anti-Roman or anti-Hellenic pan-Semitism. There is no doubt she deliberately cultivated the image of a Romanized Hellenistic monarchy, as demonstrated by the titulature she employed, both for herself and for her son, which was consciously modelled on Hellenistic and Roman traditions.[28] Furthermore, she openly identified herself with Cleopatra, even to the point of allowing herself to be styled thus. Apparently, she also took the trouble to restore several old traditions and monuments in Egypt, some of which at least had strong Ptolemaic connections.[29]

Zenobia deliberately fostered Greek culture and thereby won over many important cultural figures of the day. One of these, Callinicus of Petra, dedicated his ten-volume work on the history of Alexandria to Zenobia as 'Cleopatra'. Callinicus was almost certainly one of the many cultural figures of the eastern half of the empire who accepted Zenobia's patronage and moved to the court of Palmyra. Another such figure was Callinicus' compatriot Genethlius. A figure of far greater stature who was also drawn to the queen's court was the celebrated rhetorician and Neoplatonist philosopher Cassius Longinus. A Greek-speaking Syrian of roughly the same age as Aurelian,

Longinus had studied under Ammonius and Origen, after which he had taught for very many years at the Academy in Athens, where Porphyry had been among his pupils. In the late 260s, he accepted an invitation to the Palmyrene court, probably while Odenathus was still alive. In any case, he was certainly there in the period after Odenathus' death, when he acted as one of the dowager queen's principal advisers, possibly in the capacity of chief secretary for Greek affairs. The 'Nicomachus' whom the *HA* credits with a similar role is, however, a fiction. Another man of letters who took up the Palmyrene cause was the historian Nicostratus of Trebizond, whose history of his own times, covering the period from Philip to Gallienus, maintained a consistently eastern perspective and glorified the deeds of Odenathus, with whose triumphant victories over the Persians the work concluded.[30]

In as far as the cultural divide can be said to have existed, it is clear that Zenobia went out of her way to woo both sides, the Hellenistic as much as the Semitic. The secret of her success is that she managed to appeal to such a broad spectrum of different political, social and ethnic groups across the region. Her conscious self-alignment with the last of the Ptolemies may be partly understood as an anti-Roman gesture, indeed many contemporaries must have seen it in this light, for Augustan propaganda had firmly established Cleopatra as an implacable enemy of Rome. Nevertheless, it must also be understood within the wider context of the symbolic representation of Zenobia's political power, which drew, both consciously and unconsciously, on a rich tapestry of current modes of expression. In an era in which Roman imperial authority drew increasingly overtly upon Hellenistic royal symbolism, the use of such modes of representation cannot simply be dismissed as anti-Roman. Interestingly, as conflict with Rome became more and more inevitable in the last year or so of their reign, so the titulature applied to Zenobia and Vaballathus became increasingly closely aligned with the standard Roman imperial titulature of the day. It is insufficient to describe Zenobia merely as a usurper in the Roman mould, but nor was she a secessionist, in the full sense of one who rejected the very concept of the Roman empire. It should not be overlooked that it suited Aurelian's purpose well to encourage a representation of Zenobia as not only the enemy of Rome, but as alien to all that was Roman.[31]

THE ROAD TO WAR

Zenobia may have tried to convince herself and those over whom she exercised her dominion that she was acting in good faith with regard to Rome; that she was merely claiming what had been rightfully her husband's. Aurelian, at least, remained unconvinced. It is often suggested that Aurelian and Zenobia came to a formal mutual arrangement whereby Aurelian recognized Vaballathus as Odenathus' successor, with regard to his official status and Roman titulature, in return for which Zenobia promised to continue her late husband's policy of upholding the joint interests of Palmyra and Rome in the east. The notion is pressed to the point of accusing Aurelian of entering into this agreement in bad faith, using it to stall for time while he dealt with more pressing matters closer to home, but always intending to revoke the entente as soon as it suited him to do so.[32]

This hypothesis is based on the evidence of the coins, inscriptions and papyri from Egypt, Judaea, Arabia and Syria during the period December 270 to April 272. In fact, however, this same evidence can more persuasively be used to demonstrate that no such agreement ever existed. Rather, what happened was a series of incremental encroachments on Zenobia's part, starting with apparent appeasement and ending with overt challenge.

To consider this matter in detail we must start with the evidence from Egypt. From early December 270, the Alexandrian coins mention Aurelian and Vaballathus jointly. Although these coins grant Vaballathus the imperial title *Autokrator* (Imperator) along with the rank of consul and Roman general, they stop just short of claiming full imperial status for the young Palmyrene prince. Aurelian alone is accorded the most important imperial title Augustus, and on the earliest coins of this kind Aurelian alone is given a regnal year. From mid-December, the Egyptian papyri accord Vaballathus the same titles, this time advertising his status as a co-ruler, though still not emperor, by recording his regnal year (year I), together with the title of king. All these titles he assumed by right of heredity from his illustrious father, but in claiming regal status in Egypt, appearing on the coinage and allowing his name and titles to be used to date legal documents he had already gone far further than Odenathus.[33] It is most unlikely that Aurelian would have given his formal assent to this arrangement. He was merely powerless to prevent it. Over the ensuing weeks and months other encroachments of this kind demonstrate clearly that this amounts to no more than the unilateral arrogation of powers by Zenobia and her son.[34]

Sometime between the beginning of January and the middle of March 271, Zenobia instigated the next subtle move in this propaganda war. She chose to backdate the inception of Vaballathus' reign to the death of his father, thereby altering the reckoning of his regnal years. This meant that coins and papyri began to be dated by Aurelian year I and Vaballathus year IV, granting the young Palmyrene seniority of tenure. Aurelian's name still appeared first in the documents, however, so that the affront was deliberately muted.[35] Although Vaballathus still refrained from claiming imperial status outright, ways were found to hint at the parity of the two rulers. Coins were minted at Alexandria at this time which depict Aurelian and Vaballathus together on the obverse with the simple legend 'Aurelian and Athenodorus'. By leaving out Aurelian's imperial titles, the design makes no distinction in status between the two, except for the discrepancy in their regnal years prominently displayed on the reverse.[36] From late August 271, with the new Egyptian year, the reckoning of their regnal years automatically became Aurelian year II and Vaballathus year V.[37]

Meanwhile in Syria, the mint at Antioch began to produce coins which, as at Alexandria, honoured Aurelian with full imperial titles on one side and Vaballathus with the cryptic acronym VCRIMDR on the other. This, being the precise Latin equivalent of the contemporary Greek titulature used in Egypt, stood for 'V(ir) C(onsularis) [or 'Clarissimus']) R(ex) IM(perator) D(ux) R(omanorum)', titles derived as if by hereditary right from his father Odenathus. The mint mark on these coins appears on the side bearing Aurelian's portrait, which may indicate that this is the reverse. If Vaballathus does indeed appear on the obverse, this represents a further gesture of political defiance on the part of the Palmyrene regime.[38]

A number of inscriptions from this date are known for Vaballathus and Zenobia from Judaea, Arabia and Syria. These usually grant him the title of king or employ some variant of the contemporary titulature found in Egypt (including *Autokrator*), and refer to her as queen and mother of the king. Most of these, however, fail to acknowledge the Roman emperor at all.[39] On one inscription honouring Zenobia at Palmyra, dated August 271, she is accorded the title *eusebes*, the equivalent of the Latin title *pia*. Although this is not tantamount to claiming imperial status, it must be understood as a step in that direction, being a title often applied to Roman empresses in this era.[40] Another inscription from Palmyra of about this date honours a Roman emperor, whose name is now unfortunately missing, alongside Zenobia as *Sebaste* (Augusta) and 'mother of our unconquered lord imperator Vaballathus Athenodorus'. These titles are unequivocally imperial, although the inscription stops short of giving Vaballathus the title *Sebastos* (Augustus). The Roman emperor is still acknowledged and he is accorded pride of place, but this inscription none the less represents a further step on the road to a unilateral declaration of the right to imperial authority on the part of the Palmyrene royal family.[41] In Egypt, meanwhile, examples of similar encroachments can be found alongside the established titulature.[42] One grain receipt even goes so far as to place Aurelian and Vaballathus on equal footing, referring to them both as Augusti.[43]

It is scarcely credible that Zenobia seriously believed that Aurelian might ignore such encroachments upon the prerogatives of imperial authority as long as she stopped short of actually declaring Vaballathus a rival emperor. It is more likely that the intended audience of her caution was not Aurelian himself but the Roman administration in the east, which could more easily go along with her arrogation of power as long as their loyalty to the emperor was not overtly put to the test.

The final and decisive change came in about April 272. From this date, the mint at Alexandria abruptly ceased to recognize Aurelian and began to issue tetradrachms in the name of Vaballathus alone (year V), together with some in the name of Zenobia. The same decisive change is found at the Antiochene mint. In both cases, Vaballathus and his mother are accorded the unequivocal titles Augustus and Augusta respectively.[44] A milestone from Arabia, which must also date from this time, gives Vaballathus full imperial titles, complete with victory titles, and fails to acknowledge Aurelian in any way.[45] This outright defiance of Aurelian's authority was almost certainly a direct response to the launch of Aurelian's offensive.

5

THE PALMYRENE WARS

THE SHOW-DOWN WITH ZENOBIA

The war against Zenobia had two objectives. The first was to liberate those parts of the empire over which Zenobia had recently established a dominion and which were too sensitive to leave under the control of a potentially hostile power. The most important of these were the wealthy provinces of Asia Minor, with their significant tax contribution to the coffers of the imperial government, and Egypt, with its vital supply of grain.[1] The Mediterranean area of Syria, particularly the city of Antioch, was of secondary, but still considerable, importance. Aurelian's second objective was to eliminate Zenobia and to reduce the power of Palmyra so as to prevent a repeat of this dangerous situation. Because of the urgency of the first objective, Aurelian could not afford to wait until he had recaptured Syria, which he knew would be heavily defended, before reclaiming Egypt. Both for this reason and for the sake of opening up a second front, he made arrangements to send his fleet to liberate Egypt.

The recovery of Egypt

According to the *Historia Augusta*, Aurelian entrusted the command of the vitally important naval expedition to the future emperor, M. Aurelius Probus. Modern scholarship has naturally hesitated to accept the uncorroborated identification from such an untrustworthy source. Nevertheless, the idea should not be too hastily dismissed. There is nothing inherently unlikely in the idea that Aurelian should entrust his compatriot with such an important mission.[2]

Very little is known about the conduct of the campaign itself, except that it was all over in a matter of a few short weeks. Roman military operations must have been somewhat hampered by the lingering sympathy for the Palmyrene cause in Egypt, but the Palmyrene garrison there was probably not very strong. The chronology can be reconstructed from the Egyptian coinage and papyri with a fair degree of certainty. The fleet reached Egypt by the middle of May; by early June, Alexandria was safely back in Aurelian's control, with the rest of Egypt following no later than the third week in June.[3]

The march across Asia Minor

Meanwhile, Aurelian and his army had crossed Asia Minor. The initial stage of his progress was treated as a triumphant pageant by the inhabitants of Bithynia, who had successfully resisted Palmyrene domination. In Galatia, the loose Palmyrene hegemony evaporated before his advance, and he was welcomed without a struggle at Ancyra (Ankara), the provincial capital.[4] From here, he continued south-east towards the Cilician Gates, the pass through the Taurus Mountains that led from the Anatolian plateau down onto the Cilician coastal plain and thence into Syria. Before he could reach this pass, his route took him past the town of Tyana in Cappadocia, famous in antiquity for being the home of the first-century Neopythagorean philosopher Apollonius.

Tyana was the first point on Aurelian's march at which he encountered any appreciable show of resistance. Enraged by the decision of the townsfolk to close their gates to him, Aurelian swore he would not leave even a dog alive once he had captured the town. After a siege that lasted long enough to be a nuisance, but no more, the town capitulated. The *HA* tells us that Heraclammon, a citizen of Tyana, showed the emperor a weak point in the town's defences. For all his reputation for ruthlessness, Aurelian allowed sound political judgement to outweigh short-term military expediency. With an insight rare among third-century emperors, Aurelian realized that clemency would set a precedent far more potent in the coming struggle than he could hope to gain by terror. He ordered his army to spare the town and its inhabitants and was thus able to present himself as a liberator rather than a conqueror. His troops, spoiling for a fight, were disappointed and petulantly reminded him of his earlier angry outburst. The situation could have turned ugly: only a few years before, Postumus had been lynched by his troops for denying them the opportunity of sacking Mainz, an episode of which Aurelian was doubtless aware. Aurelian, however, was not to be intimidated: 'I did indeed decree that no dog should be allowed to live,' he declared, 'well then, kill all the dogs!' Pleased by the jest, the soldiers set about carrying out his orders. In this way, the situation was defused and the town was spared.[5]

There is another account of why Aurelian spared Tyana. In a lengthy digression, the *HA* recounts a fantastic tale in which the spirit of Apollonius appeared to Aurelian in his tent at night and, through a combination of wise counsel and ominous threats, persuaded the emperor to spare the town. Although the author of the *vita* goes to great lengths to argue the authenticity of this story, noting how he discovered it in the Ulpian Library, such protestations are always doubly suspicious coming from this author.[6] As the city's most famous son, Apollonius of Tyana was perhaps an obvious choice of saviour. The life and deeds of this mystic were legendary: he was credited with clairvoyance, healing the sick, raising the dead and finally ascending bodily into heaven. The parallels with the life of Christ were not lost on the pagans of late antiquity, who championed Apollonius as a kind of pagan saint to counterbalance the steady stream of Christian hagiographies. The story thus reflects the extra-ordinary prominence of Apollonius in the struggle between pagans and Christians in the later fourth century, when the traditions which lie behind the historiography of Aurelian's age were taking shape.[7]

The wisdom of Aurelian's leniency, whatever its origin, became immediately apparent as Aurelian marched down into Cilicia. At his approach, cities welcomed him without resistance. His route almost certainly took him directly south to Tarsus, the provincial capital, and then east by way of Issus, where Alexander the Great had won his famous victory over the Persians. From here, he reached the port of Alexandria ad Issum (Iskenderun) which marked the border with Syria. Thus Aurelian recovered control of Asia Minor with compara-tive ease.[8] Before him lay an altogether different prospect: the recovery of Syria, the heartland of Palmyrene power.

The struggle for western Syria: Antioch and Emesa

Zenobia and her generals, knowing that Antioch on the Orontes would have to be Aurelian's first objective on entering Syria, deter-mined to defend it in force. They drew up their army in the Orontes plain, on the western side of the Lake of Antioch, to the north of the city. Here they could intercept Aurelian's advance along the road from Alexandria at a point where the terrain was especially well suited to the battle tactics of the Palmyrene heavy-mailed cavalry, known as *cataphractarii* or more colloquially *clibinarii*.[9]

Before crossing into Syria, Aurelian received the unwelcome intelligence that Zabdas and the Palmyrene army lay between him and Antioch. To attempt a direct assault on the city from this direction would be to surrender tactical advantage to the enemy. Instead, Aurelian decided to outflank the enemy and attack from the east along the southern side of the Orontes valley. This manoeuvre had three advantages. First, the enemy, clearly anticipating a frontal assault from the north-west, might be confused by an attack from their rear. Second, he would cut off the enemy's line of retreat to the east and might even, if he reached the city, intersect the main route leading south. Finally, the eastern approach lay through terrain far less suited to the formidable Palmyrene cavalry. Aurelian therefore crossed over the mountains well to the north of the Palmyrene position and skirted round the eastern side of the lake.[10]

Zabdas got wind of Aurelian's manoeuvre. He realized he had to intercept the imperial army in the plain to the east of the lake before it could reach the hilly terrain further south, where his own cavalry would be at a comparative disadvantage. He swiftly dispatched the main body of his cavalry along the Orontes to reinforce the small contingent he had stationed on the eastern side of the lake to guard the road to Beroea (Aleppo).

When Aurelian found that his way was barred by the Palmyrene cavalry, he decided not to chance his infantry against this corps, whose fearsome reputation he had no reason to doubt. He elected instead to employ his cavalry in a risky but cunning manoeuvre. It was a hot morning in late May or early June. The Palmyrene cavalry had taken up a position on the Antioch–Beroea road just a few kilometres east of the Orontes. Drawing up his light-armed cavalry before the Palmyrene lines, Aurelian instructed them to give way before the first charge of the enemy and feign flight, inviting the Palmyrenes to give chase. This the Palmyrenes duly did, pursuing the Roman cavalry for several kilometres along the main road towards the town of Immae. Once the heavily armoured Palmyrenes had thoroughly exhausted themselves and their horses in the Syrian midday heat, the Roman cavalry turned on cue and countercharged. The slaughter was terrible. Those Palmyrenes who were not cut to pieces in the saddle were thrown from their mounts and trampled to death, as much by their own horses as under the hooves of the Roman cavalry. Few survivors made it back to Antioch.[11]

Aurelian's tactics at Immae relied on a remarkable level of discipline, co-ordination, and courage in the Roman cavalry. Their devastating success clearly demonstrates the emperor's skill as a tactician and his experience as a cavalry commander. At a stroke, Aurelian had crippled the enemy's most powerful weapon, the famous heavy-armed cavalry. The battle by no means marked the end of the affair; the Palmyrenes had other cavalry reserves and in fact overall their cavalry still outnumbered that available to Aurelian. Nevertheless, Immae would prove the decisive moment of the war.[12]

Zenobia had no option but to abandon Antioch. Too precipitous a retreat might have been dangerous, since the citizens might have turned on the Palmyrenes in order to curry favour with the victor. To buy some time, Zabdas employed a clever ruse. He found a man who roughly resembled Aurelian in age and build and, dressing him up in armour that could pass for imperial, paraded him through the streets of the city as if the Palmyrenes had captured the Roman emperor alive.[13] That night, Zenobia and Zabdas, together with their retinue, quietly left the city under cover of darkness. The army encamped outside already had orders to decamp and start south. Stationing a rearguard garrison on the heights above Daphne, a southern suburb of Antioch, Zabdas and Zenobia marched their army south to Emesa (Homs).[14] When the citizens of Antioch awoke to discover the Palmyrene retreat, a panic seized those who had most compromised themselves in supporting Zenobia's cause. Several, fearing Aurelian's wrath, fled into the surrounding countryside.

Meanwhile, Aurelian had spent the night encamped on the Orontes about twenty kilometres east of Antioch. His infantry had still not seen action, but with the enemy cavalry crippled he could now afford to deploy them. His intention was apparently to send his own cavalry round the city and attack the Palmyrene position from both sides.[15] At daybreak, learning of Zenobia's total withdrawal, he marched straight to the city, where he was warmly received. Again, Aurelian was not interested in retribution. He immediately promulgated a general pardon throughout the region in which he made it clear that he regarded the Antiochenes as having acted under duress rather than of their own free will. As at Tyana, his clemency paid dividends. Those who had fled into self-imposed exile returned to the city with gratitude.[16]

Both administrative and military considerations detained Aurelian at Antioch for a time. Years of increasingly antagonistic Palmyrene domination had left a legacy of administrative problems at Antioch, the metropolis of the east. Foremost among these was the imperial mint. It is possible also that the vexed question of the Christian schism at Antioch demanded his attention at this time.[17] On the military side, there remained the Palmyrene garrison at Daphne.

Though probably of no great size, its strategic position made it at once both impossible to ignore and difficult to dislodge. Aurelian decided upon a full-frontal attack up the steep sides of the hill, making use of the renowned *testudo* or 'tortoise formation' which the Romans had perfected during centuries of siege warfare. With their shields held close together over their heads, the soldiers were able to make the ascent without suffering unduly from the missiles being hurled down upon them by the enemy above. Once the Roman infantry gained the top of the hill, they made short work of breaking through the enemy defences and putting the Palmyrenes to flight. Some were driven over the precipice.[18]

There was also a second military reason for delay at this time. Aurelian had summoned reinforcements from a number of units stationed in the east. By the time he was ready to leave Antioch he had with him his original army, a small contingent from Tyana, fresh legionary reinforcements from the upper Euphrates valley and some Palestinian auxiliaries armed with clubs and maces.[19] With the road to the south now clear and the army fully assembled, Aurelian was at last ready to move out towards Emesa and Zenobia.

From Antioch, Aurelian marched south to Apamea and then on up the Orontes valley to Arethusa. Each town and village he passed through on his way gave him a hero's welcome. Continuing on south, Aurelian encountered the full force of the Palmyrene army, some 70,000 strong we are told, drawn up on the plain before Emesa. The terrain was of Palmyrene choosing and well suited to their heavy cavalry. Aurelian decided to try something similar to the risky but devastating tactical manoeuvre he had employed at Immae. The plan, however, began to go wrong from the start. Aurelian may have underestimated the strength of the Palmyrene cavalry still remaining; or perhaps the Roman cavalry was not as fresh as its opponents after the long hot march south. The Palmyrene cavalry got too close to the Roman lines. What had been planned as an orderly tactical withdrawal very nearly turned into a rout. Large numbers of Roman cavalry were killed as they caught the full force of the Palmyrene charge. When the Roman lines began to give way, the Palmyrene horsemen gave chase to the fugitives. In the euphoria of their initial success, the Palmyrene army pressed their advantage with undue haste. Their own line broke formation and the Roman infantry were able to wheel round and crash through the Palmyrene flank. In this counter-attack the Palestinian clubmen were apparently especially effective. The Palmyrene army suffered a shattering defeat. Its soldiers were either killed or driven from the field in total disarray, many being trampled to death in the ensuing stampede. Only a few, including the general Zabdas, made it back to Zenobia in Emesa.[20]

At Emesa, Zenobia hurriedly convened a council of war with her generals and advisers. The situation was deteriorating fast. Faced with a defeat on this scale, they could no longer count upon Emesene support. The council advised the queen that she had no option but to abandon Emesa and head straight for the relative safety of Palmyra. Once there, a new strategy might still be put together. Time was indeed running out for Zenobia. By this point she must already have known that Aurelian's naval force had recaptured Egypt. Even as her council was deliberating, Aurelian's army was preparing to close in on Emesa. Abandoning everything, including the treasure that she had with her in Emesa, Zenobia took flight across the desert for Palmyra. The Emesenes immediately threw open their gates and welcomed Aurelian.[21]

The push to Palmyra and the capture of Zenobia

Having thus accomplished the recovery of Egypt, Asia Minor and western Syria, Aurelian could now turn to the second of his objectives, to remove Zenobia and reduce the power of Palmyra. He immediately set out across the desert in pursuit of his enemy. It was now high summer, and the heat must have been almost unbearable for his soldiers. As they marched across the inhospitable terrain, they were harassed by guerrilla attacks from bands of nomadic Arabs who remained loyal to Zenobia, or at least preferred not to see the resurgence of Roman power in the region. However, if later Arab legend is anything to go by, Arab contingents, notably from the Tanukh confederation, served with Aurelian on his march against Palmyra.[22]

As soon as Aurelian arrived at the great oasis he invested the city, simultaneously entering into negotiations with those Bedouin in the area who chafed under Palmyrene hegemony to supply his army with the necessary food and fodder. Zenobia had clearly overestimated the loyalty or fear that she inspired among the surrounding nomadic tribes. Still she remained defiant. Trusting that the stores and granaries inside the city would enable her to outlast the siege, she rejected out of hand an offer of peace negotiations which Aurelian sent her.[23]

It soon became clear, however, that her only real hope lay in military intervention from Persia. Given that her late husband's reputation rested primarily on his spectacular humiliations of the Persian army, the idea of aid from that quarter might seem preposterous. The Persian king, Shapur, had doubtless witnessed Zenobia's growing confidence over the years with a degree of suspicion. Yet it made strategic sense to think of one's enemy's enemy as one's friend, and thus Shapur may have been willing to countenance a deal with Zenobia. Certainly the triumphant revival of Roman fortunes in the area cannot have been a prospect the Persians would have relished.[24] Nevertheless, Zenobia's bid for Persian support was an idea born of desperation. Shapur was nearly on his deathbed, and the transition of power was not running smoothly at Ctesiphon. The crown prince Hormizd Ardashir did not command the same authority among the Persian warlords as his father, and rival factions were at each other's throats. A small contingent of Persian mercenaries may have tried to assist the beleaguered Palmyrenes, but if so it is doubtful they acted with the blessing of the Persian government. In any case, their attempted intervention provided no more than a side show.[25]

Besides, there were Persian mercenaries, in particular archers, fighting on the Roman side. We are told that when a defiant Palmyrene was shouting insults at Aurelian from the walls of the city, a Persian archer asked the emperor whether he would like the insolent man silenced. Aurelian allowed him to try, and so the archer set a group of Roman soldiers with their shields before himself as a screen and fired his arrow. The bolt hit its mark and the offending Palmyrene fell over the wall to the ground.[26]

As the siege wore on and the plight of the Palmyrenes became more desperate, Zenobia and her generals realized that she would have to plead in person for Persian aid. Under cover of night she secretly stole out of the city and slipped through the Roman lines. Heading due east, she raced across the desert by camel. Aurelian soon learned of her flight and sent a cavalry detachment in hot pursuit. They caught up with her at the Euphrates and brought her back to Aurelian under military escort.[27] On hearing that their queen had fallen into Roman hands and that the sought-for aid would not be forthcoming the Palmyrenes were divided in their response. The hawks among them wished to fight it out, but the doves took matters into their own hands by shouting their offers of peace from the walls. Aurelian encouraged them to come out and surrender, offering the same magnanimity he had shown elsewhere. Tentatively, individuals began to leave the city and give themselves up, each bringing gifts and sacrifices to the emperor. He graciously received their offerings and pardoned each petitioner. Very soon the exodus became a torrent, and before long the city had renounced completely any pretence of resistance. Without further bloodshed, and in an atmosphere of general relief, Aurelian entered Palmyra.[28]

THE END OF PALMYRA

The aftermath of the siege

Towards the ordinary citizens of Palmyra Aurelian offered the same clemency he had shown the inhabitants of Asia Minor and western Syria. Unlike elsewhere, however, his clemency stopped short of a general amnesty. As Aurelian perceived it, the Palmyrenes had engaged in open revolt against Rome, and even the most lenient ruler could not pass over such actions lightly. Those suspected of being the principal instigators of the revolt were rounded up for trial. Besides Zenobia herself, these included several of her advisers, most notably the rhetorician Longinus. Moreover, not entirely trusting the sudden change of allegiance among the inhabitants of the oasis, Aurelian imposed a garrison on Palmyra, although he kept its size to a minimum. He also reduced some of the defences of the city and confiscated much of its military equipment.[29]

There was also a financial score to settle. The cost of the war had been considerable. Aurelian needed to distribute booty to his troops and to replenish the exhausted imperial coffers. The treasures captured at Emesa and the peace offerings made by the surrendering Palmyrenes were insufficient. Aurelian wished to exact considerable reparation from this city of fabulous wealth. A great deal of the city's visible treasures, including votive offerings and other precious objects from public and private collections, were carried off. Whether these were 'given' or whether he ordered their confiscation is not known.[30]

The eastern frontier had been thrown into serious disarray by these events. The situation could have been much worse: the Persians would surely have made more capital out of Rome's distress but for their own internal political problems. Aurelian had no wish to become embroiled in further unnecessary campaigning in the east, but he wanted to present his eastern victories as a triumph over Rome's traditional enemy in the region rather than merely as a civil war. He may even have directed minor military operations against some Persian troops who had encroached upon the frontier, but these were no more than punitive gestures: a shot across the bow. The Persians realized they had more to lose than gain by entering into open hostilities with Rome. Anxious to avoid a full-scale war they immediately sent an embassy to the victorious emperor to reassure him of their good intentions and to seek assurances of his. We are told that the Persian royal envoys presented Aurelian with a cloak of purple so rich in its dye that all others seemed ashen beside it.[31] In this way, Aurelian could justify his assumption of the title Persicus Maximus. Both the use of this title and the report in certain of the literary sources of a major victory over the Persians at this time reflect Aurelianic propaganda more than strict reality. It is unlikely that there were any serious hostilities between the two superpowers beyond the minor skirmishes already mentioned.[32]

Having come to an understanding with Persia, Aurelian was in a position to delegate to a subordinate the twin tasks of reintegrating the region into the empire and restructuring the Euphrates frontier defences. He entrusted these delicate and vital tasks to Marcellinus, one of his most reliable marshals.[33] The affairs of Palmyra and the eastern frontier were now arranged to his satisfaction. Aurelian therefore returned to Emesa taking with him the spoils from Palmyra and the prisoners awaiting trial.

At Emesa, Zenobia and her councillors and generals were put on trial. We are told that Zenobia pleaded she had been led astray by bad advice. Longinus was among several found guilty of conspiring against Rome and sentenced to death. It is said that he bore his sentence with a noble equanimity which helped to calm the indignation that his death evoked among literary and cultured people.[34] The identity of the other defendants is not known, nor their various fates, but most must have met with a similar end. Among those who probably perished at this trial was Zenobia's commander-in-chief, Zabdas, of whom no more is heard.

Zenobia herself was spared, not out of any regard for the dignity of her position, much less due to any scruples to do with her sex, but because of Aurelian's desire to display her in the triumph he planned to celebrate on his return to Rome. He also felt it expedient to parade the captive Zenobia in the cities of Syria. According to one account, Aurelian publicly humiliated Zenobia in certain key cities in the east, by parading her through the streets in chains seated on a dromedary. At Antioch, this public humiliation took place before the assembled populace in the hippodrome, after which she was chained up on a high structure resembling a pillory for three consecutive days.[35] Such actions were prompted not so much by cruelty as by political considerations: the manifestation and public mortification of the defeated queen was calculated to diminish any lingering sympathy for her cause in the urban centres of the east.

Aurelian now felt he had at last brought stability to the east. He assumed the title Restorer of the World (*restitutor orbis*) and set off for Europe with his prizes.[36] These included the treasures he had removed from Palmyra and the captives he had taken during the course of the war to grace his triumph, most especially the queen herself. The march back across Anatolia to Chalcedon passed without incident, although the Bosphorus crossing was hit by a storm in which one of the vessels, apparently transporting a number of Palmyrene captives, was lost. This mishap aside, Aurelian and his army arrived safely back in Byzantium.[37]

The war against the Carpi

At Byzantium, bad news awaited the emperor. The Carpi had begun to encroach on the area comprising the former Roman province of Dacia shortly after the formal withdrawal of Roman forces. They had now broken across the Danube and were causing havoc in Moesia and Thrace. Although it was already late in the year, Aurelian set about expelling the invaders without delay. Little is known about the campaign, besides the fact that it was successful. By the end of the winter the Carpi had been utterly defeated and driven back to the Danube. In a bold move, which set an important precedent, Aurelian settled a large group of these people on the Roman side of the frontier. As a result of this victory, Aurelian received the title Carpicus Maximus.[38] The general elation was soon shattered by an urgent and unwelcome message from Marcellinus.

After Aurelian's departure for Europe, the Palmyrenes began to show signs of unrest. Disillusioned by their recent change in fortune, they perhaps resented the manner in which their city had paid the price of defeat. The chief troublemakers rallied round the figure of Apsaeus, a Palmyrene noble who had escaped prosecution at the end of the war in spite of his association with Zenobia. As the discontent grew, Apsaeus approached Marcellinus, probing the strength of his loyalty to the emperor to see if they could not induce him to come over to the Palmyrene side. Marcellinus, was now attempting to stall them by appearing to give their offer serious consideration, while taking the opportunity to inform Aurelian of the situation.[39] On receipt of this sinister message Aurelian wasted no time in elaborate preparations but hastily marshalled his army and set out across Asia Minor once more. Speed was of the essence if the vigilance and loyalty of Marcellinus were to be turned to good account.[40]

The return to Palmyra

By a series of forced marches Aurelian reached Antioch by early spring. The Antiochenes had no warning of his approach and were gathered in the hippodrome for the horse races when the imperial army arrived. At Antioch, Aurelian learned that the situation at Palmyra was rapidly deteriorating. The Palmyrenes, under the leadership of Apsaeus, had slaughtered the garrison of 600 archers together with their captain, Sandario, and had proclaimed Septimius Antiochus as their king. An inscription found at Palmyra claims this Antiochus was the son of Zenobia.[41] The claim may exaggerate the closeness of their relationship for propaganda purposes. If true, it would seem likely that he was the son of Zenobia by someone other than Odenathus, in all probability after the latter's death. This would make Antiochus a boy of less than five years old at the time of this revolt, an age which fits well with Zosimus' description of him as 'insignificant'.[42]

For the second time in less than twelve months Aurelian marched against the city of Palmyra. The rebels' resistance did not last long. Surprised by the speed of Aurelian's advance, they were ill-prepared and ill-equipped to defend their city against a determined Roman assault. Furthermore, there is evidence that Aurelian had help from the dove faction within the city. One of the chief priests of Bel, Septimius Haddudan, a member of a distinguished Palmyrene family, was subsequently honoured in an inscription at the main entrance to the temple which records his (unspecified) help to the army of Aurelian.[43]

Considering the rebels had taken advantage of the emperor's leniency the previous year, when he had shown clemency in the interests of restoring stability to the region, the city could expect little mercy. The *HA* paints a vivid picture of his terrible wrath. But, as ever, this evidence is suspect. A more balanced view suggests that, once again, Aurelian showed remarkable restraint. To be sure, those directly involved were punished. The fate of Apsaeus is not recorded, but we can be certain he did not long outlast the suppression of his rebellion. But bloodthirsty reprisals were not exacted and even Antiochus was spared. Aurelian apparently considered him too inconsequential a figure to warrant destruction and probably too young to be held responsible for what had been perpetrated in his name. He was deported. Many more, besides, left the city of their own free will never to return.[44]

Palmyra itself apparently did not escape so lightly; Aurelian did not require the same degree of restraint from his soldiers as the previous year. Many of the city's magnificently adorned edifices were looted and much of the city's visible wealth was annexed to the imperial coffers, supplementing that already removed the previous year. Some of these treasures were destined to adorn the new temple that he intended to dedicate in Rome to the deity he believed had led him to victory over Palmyra, Sol Invictus. Doubtless, a number of buildings in the city also suffered physical damage, and certainly steps were taken, including the dismantling of the city's fortifications, to ensure that Palmyra never again would pose a threat to Rome. It is unlikely, however, that the great temple of Bel itself, the city's principal monument, was seriously damaged.[45]

Nevertheless, the undermining of the city's military and economic foundations was sufficiently thorough that Palmyra never recovered. The market, and therefore the trade, was relocated far to the north, at Batnae. The sheikhs who had operated from Palmyra to protect the caravans had never lost their contacts with the desert; they now simply returned to it. Of the prosperous and splendid city, the bustling hub of the caravan routes across the Syrian desert, little remained. The memory of Palmyra's former prosperity faded with its hour of glory, and from that time the City of Palms sank into quiet oblivion to become an unimportant provincial town on the outskirts of the Roman empire.[46]

The revolt in Alexandria

The revival of the Palmyrene cause in Syria had encouraged the pro-Palmyrene faction at Alexandria to reassert itself. The *HA* tells us that the leader of the revolt in Egypt was a rich merchant named Firmus, who used his wealth and his connections with the Blemmyes to the south to stir up trouble. If he ever existed at all, his ultimate aims are unclear, but it is most unlikely that he ever proclaimed himself emperor, or even intended to. In fact the 'revolt' probably never amounted to more than serious public unrest and violence on the streets of Alexandria. These riots were hugely destructive, however, causing widespread damage to a large part of the city, including the prosperous district of Bruchion where the Ptolemaic royal palace was sited.[47] Of Firmus himself, we have only the colourful but fantastic stories related in the *HA*. These are self-evidently padding: a pastiche of anecdotes cobbled together from stock literary descriptions and exaggerated beyond any semblance of plausibility. A character who swims with crocodiles, rides ostriches, drinks his wine by the bucketful and gets people to strike an anvil balanced on his chest while in the crab position is scarcely a credible historical figure.[48]

News of these disturbances reached Aurelian in Syria. As soon as he had finished in Palmyra, he swiftly descended upon Egypt and put down the fledgeling revolt with comparative ease.[49] The fact that Blemmyes are mentioned as being among the captives paraded in Aurelian's triumph does not indicate any punitive campaign to the south. If any credence is to be given to it, we must suppose that some Blemmyes, possibly merchant friends of Firmus from that region, were among those rounded up during the fighting. Firmus himself, we are told, was executed, by strangulation.[50]

Having thus restored order in Egypt, so vital to Rome's grain supply, Aurelian was finally able to turn his attention back to Europe. The eastern wars had occupied him for the best part of two years. It was at least the end of the year by the time he finally entered Rome to a tumultuous welcome from both the senate and the people.[51] He assumed the consulship for the year 274 and immediately began to implement his extensive reform of the coinage and to prepare the construction of his new temple of Sol. Preparations were also taken in hand for the most magnificent triumph that Rome had witnessed in living memory. The triumph itself, however, would have to wait, for there was still unfinished business in Aurelian's self-appointed task of restoring the Roman world. The provinces of Britain, Gaul and Germany still recognized an emperor based at Trier, as they had done ever since the revolt of Postumus in the autumn of 260.

The denouement

There is some disagreement in the literary sources as to the subsequent fate of Zenobia. One version, preserved in Zosimus, tells how Zenobia died in captivity *en route* to Rome, either from disease or from starvation brought about by hunger-strike. A similar story is also related by Zonaras, but in the same passage he also supplies another version, according to which she survived the journey to Rome safely. Since all the other literary sources agree on this point, it is clear that the Zosimus version must be rejected.[52] What happened to the unfortunate queen after her arrival in Rome is also contentious. Almost all agree that in due course she suffered the indignity of being paraded in Aurelian's triumph. She was indeed on this occasion almost literally the jewel in his crown: it is said she was made to walk before his triumphal car, bound in heavy golden chains and weighed down by jewels.[53] After the pageant was over, one might have expected a public execution. Indeed one source tells us that she was beheaded.[54] However, the majority agree that she received an imperial pardon and was permitted by Aurelian to retire with dignity into unobtrusive private life at or near Rome. The *HA* adds that the emperor granted her a villa at Tibur (Tivoli), just east of Rome, near the famous villa that Hadrian had built for himself. While this detail is typical of the spurious flourishes of this author, it need not be untrue.[55]

Several sources remark that her descendants were still known at Rome a century or so later.[56] Who these descendants were is not clear. One tradition maintains that Zenobia married into the Roman nobility, and it may be that they were descended from the progeny of this union. This is highly speculative, however, as the two sources that mention this union are late and, in any case, not among those which talk of the survival of her line.[57] Another possibility is that some of her earlier offspring shared her retirement; but if so, which?

The ultimate fate of Vaballathus is not known. There is nothing to suggest he did not share his mother's fate. Zosimus actually says that Zenobia's son, whom he does not name, shared her captivity and accompanied her on the journey westwards from Syria.[58] There is no mention of Vaballathus or any other child of Zenobia in the context of the triumph, but this may simply reflect his insignificance beside his more famous and more colourful mother. When speaking of 'Herennianus' and 'Timolaus', the *HA* at first suggests Aurelian had them executed but later emphatically states that they joined Zenobia in her retirement and were responsible for the line of descent still surviving in the fourth century. What may lie behind this and whether it allows us to draw inferences about Vaballathus is another matter.[59]

The ultimate fate of Antiochus is also uncertain, beyond that he was deported. It is very unlikely that Aurelian would have allowed him to remain in the east as a potential focus for discontent, but deportation doesn't suggest he was sent to Rome. Zonaras is the only source to mention that Zenobia had daughters. He claims that Aurelian himself took one as a bride and that the others were distributed as wives among the Roman nobility.[60] Although this detail is unreliable, not least because it is attached to the groundless story of Zenobia's premature death in transit, the silence elsewhere concerning Zenobia's daughters does not prove she had none.

EPITAPH FOR A FALLEN QUEEN

> Zenobia is perhaps the only female whose superior genius
> broke through the servile indolence imposed on her sex by
> the climate and manners of Asia.

With these words, Gibbon pronounced a fitting judgement upon the
Palmyrene queen: on the one hand justly commending her achievement; on the other hand doing so entirely within the terms of
the two prejudices which, from the earliest accounts to those of the
present day, have shaped the manner in which Zenobia has been
perceived. First and foremost, she was a woman; second, she was an
'oriental'.[61]

Much is made, in our literary sources, of her being a woman in a
world that rightfully belonged to men. In emphasizing her sex and
establishing the impropriety of Zenobia's claim to power on this
basis, the literary sources were able to reaffirm their own axiomatic
assumption that political power is a male preserve.[62] She is declared
to have been surpassingly beautiful, when the good looks, or
otherwise, of her male counterparts pass without mention.[63] She was
chaste, even to the point of being prudish.[64] She allowed her pride
to make her obstinate.[65] She possessed a womanly timidity and
inconstancy which together led her to betray her supporters in an
attempt to save herself and pleaded the frailty of her sex as an excuse
for her behaviour.[66]

The emphasis on her femininity somewhat detracted from the
glory of Aurelian's achievement in defeating her. This created a
presentational difficulty, most especially for the author of the *HA*,
who wished to portray Aurelian as a conquering hero. The difficulty,
which is occasionally made explicit in the sources, in part explains the
apparently converse tendency of stressing her virility.[67] In practice,
this served the same purpose, in that it reaffirmed the association
between masculinity and political power, while at the same time
allowing Aurelian to take the credit for restoring the rightful order
of things. Thus, in the end, we are shown the dangerous Amazon
queen tamed and domesticated, leading the life of an ordinary and
respectable Roman matron.

The *HA* in particular plays up this aspect, in order to further
another agenda. To underscore the inadequacy of Gallienus, one of the
principal themes in the last nine books of the work, the author
is at great pains to stress the effeminate nature of this emperor. To
enhance the effect of this characterization, the portrait of Zenobia in

the *HA* is suffused with expressions of her masculinity.[68] Thus, in her personal characteristics her voice was clear and masculine, her complexion swarthy as a man's.[69] In her behaviour, too, she is portrayed as essentially masculine in many respects: she dressed as an emperor, rather than as a lady, and was attended by eunuchs in preference to girls; she often rode on horseback, rarely in a lady's carriage (*pilentum*); she marched with the soldiers and drank with the officers, being well accustomed to the heat and dust of military campaigns; she is credited with being braver than her husband Odenathus, and is even given the credit for his victories over the Persians; she was wise and steadfast, a strict disciplinarian who could be generous when necessary, but was more careful with money than was customary for one of her sex.[70] She is also presented as a keen huntress. Her interest in this very masculine activity, combined with her extreme distaste for sexual intercourse, endured only for the sake of procreation, suggests a parallel with Atalanta or Artemis, or both.[71]

As a female ruler who set herself against the power of Rome, Zenobia is inevitably compared with Cleopatra. The analogy between Zenobia and the last of the Ptolemies, as we have seen, dates back to her own lifetime and was apparently even fostered by Zenobia herself. The *HA* offers us several spurious examples of the connections between them, including the assertion that she imitated Cleopatra in learning to speak Egyptian. The false story of Zenobia's suicide with dignity presented by Zosimus may also reflect a desire to equate the two tragic queens.[72] The analogy is influenced by the overriding consideration of her sex, rather than any genuine consideration of matters of policy, character or even circumstance. This is underlined in the further parallel the *HA* draws with Dido. Such analogies are both spoken and subliminal. Besides the manner of their deaths, both Dido and Cleopatra were best remembered for their captivating charms and their sexual liaisons with the most famous men of their day. It is reasonable to suppose that these ideas influenced the suggestion of Zenobia's great beauty and almost perverse chastity (the latter by reversal).[73]

Less pervasive, and certainly less overt, than the characterization of Zenobia in terms of her sex is that in terms of her cultural background. In our sources, with the *HA* once again to the fore, the concept of 'oriental' is associated with a whole set of negative propensities: 'orientals' are given to despotism, pomp, finery, luxury, effeminacy, weakness of character and faithlessness. Zenobia, either directly or through her family or her subjects, is constantly associated with or measured against these faults.[74]

With regard to both characterizations, Zenobia is represented as the 'other' in an historiographical tradition compiled and transmitted, for all intents and purposes exclusively, by western men. In view of the prejudices involved, a remark such as that Zenobia was 'the noblest of oriental women' is not as much of a compliment as it might seem.[75] The same may be said of the quote from Gibbon with which we started this chapter. That author's true attitude, characteristic of the tradition as a whole, is amply shown by his description of Zenobia's conduct at her trial:

> But, as female fortitude is commonly artificial, so it is seldom steady or consistent. The courage of Zenobia deserted her in the hour of trial; she trembled at the angry clamours of the soldiers, who called for her immediate execution, forgot the generous despair of Cleopatra, which she had proposed as her model, and ignominiously purchased life by the sacrifice of her fame and her friends. It was to their counsels, which governed the weakness of her sex, that she imputed the guilt of her obstinate resistance; it was on their heads that she directed the vengeance of the cruel Aurelian.[76]

To the effects of the above prejudices must be added that of excessive romanticism. Zenobia is, in the words of Harold Mattingly, 'one of the most romantic figures of history'.[77] She represents a blaze of colour against the rather bleak background of the mid-third century. She has, therefore, suffered rather more than most historical figures in being shrouded in legend; a rather more genuine point of comparison between her and Cleopatra. This process certainly began in her lifetime; it was taken to eloquent lengths by the *HA* and, largely under the influence of this source, has continued down to the present day. Legendary characters are always more susceptible to distortion for a variety of ends, and Zenobia has recently evoked a wide spectrum of interpretations.[78] Nevertheless, her ultimate triumph is that, through it all, something of the original historical figure has survived the rigours of historiographical reinterpretation down the centuries, to reach the attention of a more sympathetic age.

There can be no doubt that she lacked neither courage nor conviction. At the moment of her husband's assassination, the supremacy to which his diplomacy and military valour over two decades had brought his city and his family was in jeopardy. The power vacuum that loomed could well have been disastrous for both Palmyra and the region as a whole. By decisively seizing the initiative and carefully building on the political platform Odenathus had skilfully constructed, Zenobia managed to turn a struggle for survival into a glittering show of strength. We are not obliged to see in her actions either unbridled lust for power or altruistic self-sacrifice to a cause. A far more just epitaph than that supplied by Gibbon is to be found in the suggestion by David Graf 'that she took seriously the titles and responsibilities she assumed for her son and that her programme was far more ecumenical and imaginative than that of her husband Odenathus, not just more ambitious'.[79] She exercised her power with great sagacity and skill, taking whatever help she could get by playing opposing forces against each other, so that in a very short time she had become one of the most powerful individuals of her day and made Palmyra the most influential city in the region.

But the price was heavy. The course she embarked upon acquired a momentum of its own which, whether she fully intended it to or not, brought her to a point where the exercise of her policies conflicted with the vital interests of Rome. The control of the wealth of Asia Minor and above all the forceful appropriation of Egypt, with all its implications for Rome, were not circumstances a Roman emperor could afford to overlook. Conflict with Rome was sooner or later inevitable once the Rubicon of Sinai had been crossed. It was, perhaps, unfortunate for Zenobia that, in Aurelian, she found herself up against one of the few emperors of that century truly capable of rising to the challenge. An oracle she is supposed to have consulted on the outcome of the war warned the Palmyrenes that they were as doves quaking before their hawk-destroyer.[80] Less than six years after her husband's death, both her vision and her beautiful city lay in ruins, and she herself in chains.

6

WAR IN THE WEST

The reunification of the empire

By the early summer of 274, Aurelian was at last ready to take on his rival in the western provinces and thereby bring to a close the extraordinary train of events which had followed the revolt of Postumus fourteen years earlier. In order to place this campaign in its proper context it is necessary to review the events which led up to Aurelian's march into Gaul.

THE WEST BEFORE AURELIAN'S INTERVENTION (269–74)

The successors of Postumus

When Postumus was lynched by his own soldiers at Mainz in the spring of 269, his anomalous position might have been expected to vanish with him. As it turned out, Postumus' undeniable success and, above all, the length of his tenure of power had created a political momentum of their own. Furthermore, the military situation that had required an imperial presence in the region at the time of Postumus' elevation still obtained at his death. The soldiers, perhaps fearful of reprisals from the emperor Claudius for their sustained disloyalty to the emperor recognized at Rome, quickly proclaimed a successor in Postumus' place.

Their initial choice was not a happy one. M. Aurelius Marius possessed few of the qualities which had enabled his predecessor to maintain power in such troubled circumstances. The unfavourable comparison inevitably led to disaffection, and the support of the army quickly dissipated. After a very brief reign, lasting no more than a few weeks, the soldiers murdered Marius and acclaimed M. Piavonius Victorinus in his place. In him they found a far more worthy successor to Postumus. As a tribune in Postumus' praetorian guard, possibly even as its prefect, Victorinus had enjoyed Postumus' confidence. He had even shared the consulship with Postumus a couple of years before.[1]

With the death of Postumus, however, not all the western provinces felt constrained to continue their estrangement from Rome. In particular, the provinces of Spain switched allegiance and recognized Claudius.[2] More seriously for Victorinus, the Aedui in central Gaul declared their loyalty to Claudius. Early in the year 270, Victorinus marched south and laid siege to their principal city of Augusto-dunum (Autun).[3] In vain, the citizens of Autun looked to Claudius to come to their aid, but he was too preoccupied with the Gothic invasion to respond to their pleas. Claudius did no more than station a garrison to protect Italy against a surprise attack from the Rhine army in the new volatile situation in the west. Under strict orders not to intervene in the action to the north, this detachment sat tight and monitored events from a safe distance while the siege of Autun dragged on month after month. Eventually the citizens despaired of help and capitulated. Victorinus, mindful of Postumus' fate, gave his soldiers free rein in sacking the city. The devastation was terrible enough to leave deep scars, both physical and mental, which were still in evidence more than a generation later.[4]

In the spring of 271, only two years after he had seized power, Victorinus was murdered at Cologne. This time, allegedly, it was a private matter concerning his lascivious abuse of his officers' wives. He was succeeded by the governor of Aquitania, C. Pius Esuvius Tetricus. It is not entirely clear whether Tetricus, as one source has it, was still holding office in Bordeaux at the time of his elevation by the Rhine army. The distances involved and the volatility of the situation make it seem unlikely. One tradition suggests that the transition of power was smoothed by Victorinus' rich mother, who opened her coffers to bribe the army to accept Tetricus. The story may well be fictitious, as in all probability is the rich mother herself.[5]

The military stand-off

Apart from the abortive campaign that Gallienus launched against Postumus in the mid-260s, an uneasy military stand-off persisted for almost a decade-and-a-half, without either side attempting to challenge the other. This situation was partly the result of the fact that the Alamanni had effectively driven a wedge between the Rhine and Danube armies, exposing the flank of whichever ventured to march on the other. The emperors recognized at Rome opted instead for containment: thus the presence of Aureolus at Milan under Gallienus, and Julius Placidianus in the Rhone valley under Claudius.[6]

It has been argued that the presence of this forward garrison in Narbonensis proves that Claudius undertook a small but significant offensive in this region in order to recover control of the Alpine passes. If this were true it would represent a shift in policy away from mere containment. The argument is based on the assumption that Postumus controlled all of Narbonensis and also the Alpine passes.[7] There is, however, no evidence to support this assumption and it runs contrary to reason. Gallienus must have controlled the Alpine passes to have marched against Postumus. The reason Gallienus chose to station Aureolus at Milan rather than on the Rhone was not because he did not control the Alpine passes, but because the purpose of the exercise was to protect Italy, as much from the Alamanni and Juthungi as from the Roman army of the Rhine.

At the time of Tetricus' accession, in the late spring or summer of 271, Aurelian was already firmly established as ruler over the central part of the empire and had already amply proved his ability as supreme military commander. The events in Gaul were not uppermost in Aurelian's mind at this time. The Goths were still threatening the Balkans, and in the east the activities of Palmyra demanded Aurelian's attention. Tetricus must have taken comfort from the fact that Aurelian would be occupied elsewhere for the foreseeable future.

The fact that Aurelian felt secure enough to venture as far as eastern Syria on a campaign full of risks, leaving Tetricus on his flank in Gaul, speaks eloquently of Aurelian's assessment of the risk Tetricus posed. Aurelian controlled the Alpine passes and had a strong garrison on the lower Rhone. He evidently was confident that Tetricus had neither the inclination nor, in the final analysis, the capacity to make any serious attack against Italy.[8] Two years later, when Aurelian returned victorious from the east, Tetricus must have realized that it was only a matter of time before Aurelian would march against him. The fact that Aurelian did not celebrate a triumph immediately on his return from the east would have suggested that it would not be too long.

THE END OF TETRICUS

The gathering storm

At first, Tetricus' reign seemed relatively secure. The Rhine army, which had shown remarkable restraint during the tricky period between the death of Victorinus and the arrival of Tetricus in the frontier region, was apparently content to serve under him. The campaigns he undertook to repulse Frankish inroads seem to have been successful. Before long, however, he began to fall into financial difficulties. This is reflected in the drastic decline in the already highly debased coinage over which Tetricus presided.[9]

In the course of 273, Tetricus conferred many honours on his young son of the same name, raising him to share his rule as Caesar. He may have hoped the dynastic arrangement would help to strengthen his position, and he certainly issued coins stressing the nobility of his line. In the new year, he and Tetricus II took a joint consulship, which was widely commemorated on the coinage. Apparently in honour of this event, Tetricus arranged for his soldiers and subjects to make special vows which looked forward to the tenth anniversary of his accession. Although such vows were common at the start of a reign, and might be renewed at the fifth anniversary of the accession, their renewal at this date suggests that the loyalty they professed was perhaps not quite as secure as it might have been.[10]

During the first half of 274, as the prospect of Aurelian's military intervention in the region grew ever more inevitable, there are signs that the relationship between Tetricus and his army began to deteriorate. How far these tensions really existed and how much they were the invention of Aurelianic propaganda and hindsight, is difficult to determine. They were not a complete fabrication, as events early that summer demonstrate. One of Tetricus' provincial governors, Faustinus, made his own bid for the imperial purple. There is evidence to connect this rebellion with Trier, which would make Belgica the most likely province for Faustinus' governorship. If that location is correct, it was indeed serious for Tetricus. Trier was his capital city, the home of his mint and the base of his praetorian guard. But there is no apparent break in the sequence of Tetrican coinage from the Trier mint, so if the rebellion was at Trier, it cannot have lasted long. Polemius Silvius includes Faustinus in his list of those who claimed imperial status in opposition to Aurelian. This should not be taken to mean that the revolt of Faustinus occurred or even endured after the fall of Tetricus.[11]

The Faustinus incident, whatever its precise details and however dangerous it may have been in itself, left Tetricus deeply shaken and his authority in the region decidedly weakened. The outcome of the approaching conflict between Tetricus and Aurelian looked increasingly predictable. Provincial governors serving under Tetricus must have seen the writing on the wall, and the more politically astute doubtless began preparations to change sides.[12] For Tetricus, these were not the best of circumstances in which to face the advance of Aurelian's well-disciplined and victorious army.

The Châlons campaign

Administrative business and monetary reforms detained Aurelian at Rome during the spring of 274. By the early summer his preparations for the inevitable show-down with Tetricus were complete. Aurelian crossed the Alps, probably by way of the Little St Bernard Pass, into Narbonensis, where he joined forces with his advance guard already stationed at Grenoble. From here he marched up the valleys of the Rhone and Saone, retaking Lyon in his stride. Crossing the watershed at Langres he then marched down the valley of the Marne, intending to strike east towards the heartland of Tetricus' power on the Moselle.

Tetricus, meanwhile, had withdrawn a considerable force from the Rhine in order to halt his rival's advance at Châlons-sur-Marne. Here, in the Catalaunian Fields, the decisive battle was joined. The fighting was fierce, but Aurelian's superior generalship and the greater confidence and discipline of his army carried the day. During the battle, Tetricus himself was taken prisoner. As the news that their commander had fallen into enemy hands spread through the ranks of the Rhine army, the effect was devastating. In the panic and confusion their battle lines gave way completely. Aurelian's veterans seized the opportunity and surged forward. The resulting carnage was terrible. A generation later it was still remembered with horror and regret.[13]

One version suggests that Tetricus, weary of his predicament and bowing to the inevitable, had some time prior to the battle entered into secret negotiations with Aurelian. By way of overtures to these negotiations Tetricus is said to have sent Aurelian an invitation couched in terms of an apposite Vergilian quote: 'Rescue me, unconquered one, from these ills.' According to this version of events, Tetricus agreed to draw up his battle lines as if intending to make a fight of it and then, as soon as battle was joined, to surrender himself to Aurelian in exchange for the latter sparing his life.[14]

It has been rightly observed that this story must be largely a fabrication.[15] If the surrender of Tetricus had been pre-arranged, it is difficult to see why the heat of the battle was chosen as the moment, when a surrender just prior to the battle would have been just as devastating for the Tetrican cause and might have averted much of the carnage that followed. The decimation of the Rhine army was hardly to Aurelian's advantage. The subsequent defence of the Rhine frontier was his responsibility, and he would scarcely have jeopardized it lightly. As it turned out, the defence of the Rhine was severely weakened by the loss of manpower on the Catalaunian Fields that day, as the history of the next quarter-century was to prove.[16] It is not very credible that a commander of Aurelian's strategic ability would have been unaware of these consequences.

It seems reasonable to attribute the origin of the story of Tetricus' betrayal of his own army to a lost panegyric delivered to the victorious Aurelian or to one of his subsequent lieutenants in the region. Such a speech might well have wished to stress the weakness, the inconstancy and the unpopularity (or paranoia) of Tetricus.[17] Aurelius Victor and the *HA* adapted this account in order to serve one of their favourite themes. Only by presenting the slaughter at Châlons as part of a premeditated deal, a condition which the bloodthirsty Aurelian laid down for his clemency, could they reconcile the supposedly uncharacteristic leniency which Aurelian subsequently showed to Tetricus with their portrait of Aurelian as a man driven by cruelty.[18]

Tetricus was almost certainly sent on ahead to Rome to await his fate, while Aurelian remained in Gaul to oversee the reintegration and reorganization of the western provinces. The most urgent need was to secure the Rhine frontier. Aurelian had to replenish the depleted garrisons and see to the strengthening of the physical defences along the river. This was especially necessary along the upper Rhine, where the Alamanni posed a serious threat. He may even have conducted a brief campaign to repel an Alamannic raid. After mentioning an Alamannic invasion of Italy, Aurelius Victor says Aurelian expelled Germanic invaders from Gaul just prior to the defeat of Tetricus. It has been suggested that Victor might have misplaced this attack in time, so that it should relate to the period after the Châlons campaign. The evidence is inconclusive and it is preferable not to press Victor too far on these events.[19] Aurelian apparently also set about fortifying towns in the interior that were particularly vulnerable to attack from this quarter: a late tradition attributes the fortification of Dijon to Aurelian.[20] By the autumn, he felt able to hand over the supervision of these tasks to his subordinates and return to Rome to celebrate his long-delayed and much deserved triumph. Tetricus joined Zenobia as the star attraction among the captives displayed in this magnificent pageant.[21]

Although the humiliation of being led in a triumph should not be underestimated, Aurelian's subsequent treatment of Tetricus is revealing. As with Zenobia, his life was spared. Furthermore, his senatorial status and that of his son were re-confirmed. These gestures alone were magnanimous enough, and showed once again that Aurelian felt it more prudent to show clemency to his enemies, once humbled, than risk making martyrs of them. However, in the case of Tetricus he went further still. He created for Tetricus an administrative position over a region of Italy with the title *corrector Lucaniae*.[22] The report in one source that he was granted the greater distinction of *corrector totius Italiae* must be discounted, even though epigraphic evidence for this title does exist from earlier in the century and the earliest epigraphic attestations of *correctores* of the individual regions of Italy do not appear for another decade.[23] Nevertheless, to be granted the civil administration of even a district of Italy was, under the circumstances, a gracious gesture. The *Epitome* (35.7) relates that Aurelian mocked Tetricus with the jesting remark, 'It is more sublime to administer part of Italy than to rule beyond the Alps.' Even if the story is true, the 'elegant joke' detracted little from the generosity of the treatment that Tetricus received at the hands of his conqueror: a sentiment that Tetricus himself must have shared since he evidently accepted the post.

Reintegration of the west

Throughout the previous fourteen years the Rhine army had been the engine that had sustained the western emperors in power, although after the assassination of Postumus they did not remain true to any one individual for very long. Now that the Rhine army was defeated and its political power weakened, its role as king-maker was, for the time being, at an end. After Châlons, the allegiance of the western provinces simply and quietly returned to the emperor recognized at Rome. Militarily, the matter was all over. The political and social repercussions were not so straightforward.

The full and proper reintegration of the western provinces after fourteen years of political dissension was a delicate task which required careful handling. As far as the administration of the region was concerned, Aurelian appears once again to have exercised the utmost restraint. He did not, for example, condemn the memory of his defeated rival, as might have been expected. This can be seen from the fact that the inscriptions of Tetricus' reign, and indeed of his predecessors, were not systematically defaced. The numismatic evidence supports the inference that there was no official *damnatio memoriae*. That Aurelian did not de-monetize and recall the coinage of Tetricus and his predecessors is evident from its continued abundance in coin hoards.

By avoiding a condemnation of the regime as such, Aurelian was not obliged to distance himself from Tetricus' administration. Far from purging the western provinces of Tetricus' appointees in local government, there is every indication that Aurelian confirmed and even promoted those already in positions of authority in the region. In this way, he ensured the maximum of continuity and the minimum of disruption to the administration of the region as a result of the war. A good example of this policy is almost certainly to be seen in the career of the anonymous dedicatee of an inscription in Rome. Having held several minor posts in one particular (probably western) province, he was promoted to prefect of the public post throughout Gaul. He then served as procurator of the mint at Trier, was subsequently promoted to governor of Upper Germany and finally served on the staff of the praetorian and urban prefects at Rome, where he died and was given full recognition for his career. The most plausible explanation is that most of this career took place under Postumus and his successors, when the Trier mint was in full operation, and that his final post in Rome represents a continuation of his career after the reunification of the empire under Aurelian.[24]

Although Aurelian seems to have secured a peaceful transition of rule in this way, he evidently came to feel that the removal of the Gallic mint from Trier would be politically expedient. The proximity of Trier to the Rhine frontier and its army had proved a liability for Gallienus during the revolt of Postumus and could well do so again. Faustinus' rebellion may also have added to the sense that Trier was a vulnerable location. Moreover, as the effective capital of the western emperors, Trier had become too closely associated with the political dissension of the previous decade-and-a-half. Aurelian therefore decided to relocate the mint far to the south at Lyon.[25]

The numismatic evidence from this region in the period after reunification has brought to light a number of interesting anomalies. The coinage produced for Aurelian and his immediate successors at the Lyon mint does not conform precisely to the pattern found elsewhere in the empire at this date. Furthermore, the hoards discovered in this region from the period after the fall of Tetricus show a marked

preference for the highly debased coinage of Tetricus and his predecessors, including large numbers of debased forgeries, over the
new reformed coinage of Aurelian and his successors at Rome. These
observations have given rise to much speculation. Some scholars
regard them as evidence of continued political resistance to Rome. It
has been suggested that the mint at Lyon and, by implication, the
provinces of Gaul generally, were never under Aurelian's full political
control and that the pattern of hoarding is a symptom of the widespread rejection of the authority of Rome. Such political explanations
are far-fetched and unnecessary. It is preferable to understand these
peculiarities as responses to local economic conditions.[26]

The only other possible allusion to continued resistance to
Aurelian's authority in Gaul after the defeat of Tetricus is a somewhat
cryptic reference in Zonaras. He recounts that, when Aurelian set
out from Rome for the very last time in 275 after celebrating his
triumph, the emperor was obliged to intervene militarily to suppress
some 'unrest among the Gauls'.[27] To what this passage alludes is no
longer clear. It has been suggested it provides evidence of continued
armed resistance to Aurelian in Gaul, centred on the city of Lyon.
The supposition is based upon a casual reference in the *HA* which
mentions that the citizens of Lyon proclaimed Proculus emperor
in opposition to Probus because they had apparently suffered harsh
treatment under Aurelian.[28] The passage does not stand up to
scrutiny. The only other location mentioned in connection with
Proculus' revolt is Cologne.[29] The association between the rebel
Proculus and the Franks would suggest a location on the Rhine
frontier as altogether more credible than southern Lugdunensis.[30]
Furthermore, there is no indication that Probus' mint at Lyon fell
into his rival's hands. Returning to the *HA*'s allegation of Aurelian's
harsh treatment of Lyon with a more sceptical eye, the qualification
videbantur ('seemed') serves as a warning beacon. The context of the
passage declares its true worth: it is sandwiched between an account
of Proculus' vaunted lasciviousness and an elaborate joke on how
his proclamation came about as a result of a game. Such devices are
standard features of the *HA*'s inventiveness at its most waggish.

Far from Aurelian treating Lyon harshly, the facts appear to point
to a favourable disposition. The only certain indication we have of
Aurelian's relationship with Lyon is his decision to augment the
status of the city by relocating his Gallic mint there. This strongly
implies he felt secure in the political loyalties of the city. Furthermore, there is no discernible disruption to the operation of the Lyon
mint under Aurelian. Although this observation is, by itself, hardly

conclusive, it tends to argue against serious upheavals in the vicinity at this time. Whatever weight we choose to give these slight indications, it is certainly too much to read into the sources that Lyon remained stubbornly faithful to Tetricus or the 'Gallic cause'.[31]

This leaves us with the very vague statement in Zonaras that Aurelian suppressed some disturbance in the Gallic region in the last year of his reign. Aurelian may have been obliged to suppress an outbreak of the kind of brigandage that came to plague the Gallic provinces over the next decade or so. Such disturbances, which culminated in the revolt led by Amandus and Aelian in the mid-280s, feature prominently in the Gallic panegyrics of the period, where they are associated with the name of Bagaudae. To the extent that the Bagaudae had a quasi-political agenda, it had to do with land use and a reaction against the repression of the peasantry. Such civil disorders should not be taken as manifestations of political opposition to Aurelian's reunification of the empire nor as rejections of the sovereignty of Rome, still less as some kind of continuation of the cause of Tetricus.[32]

CODA: THE END OF AN ERA

With a single and decisive military victory Aurelian had at last succeeded in reuniting the whole of the Roman world, of which he was finally the undisputed master. The political aberration of parallel rulers holding sway in different parts of the empire, which had persisted for nearly a decade-and-a-half since the capture of Valerian, was at an end. The political turbulence of the mid-third century frequently resulted in divided loyalties, but these were usually resolved relatively quickly. Either the contender was eliminated or he supplanted the established emperor. The phenomenon of a sustained division of loyalties, lasting for years on end, was unprecedented.

In the aftermath of Valerian's disastrous defeat, as Gallienus struggled to reassert his authority in the central part of the empire, rivals inevitably filled the void elsewhere. The paramount need for an emperor on the spot prompted usurpations both in the east, where the Persian army was rampaging virtually unhindered, and in the west, where the Franks were constantly breaching the empire's defences. At the same time, the Danube frontier remained constantly vulnerable to attack. These exceptionally serious external military threats allowed the political divisions to persist, effectively creating a tripartite empire.

In the early stages, the parallel between the events in the east and those in the west was very close. With the elimination of Quietus at the hands of Odenathus, however, significant differences began to emerge. The west continued to recognize Postumus as emperor, whereas the east reverted to a nominal allegiance to Gallienus. The strength of the Palmyrene prince and the relative weakness of Roman power in the region enabled the eastern political divide to persist in practice, but it remained a special case. For all his acceptance of regal titles and an imperatorial acclamation, Odenathus never actually claimed imperial authority for himself.

Upon his sudden death, tensions that had been kept under control by the extraordinary position of power that Odenathus had built up for himself inevitably began to surface. In order to maintain Palmyrene domination in the region, Zenobia had to be more overt in her actions and in her claims. Under her rule, the political division took on another dimension. She resorted to military force to strengthen her control over the region and assumed ever greater pretensions in the titulature she allowed herself and Vaballathus. Those who harboured anti-Roman sentiments may have tried to exploit underlying ethnic tensions for their own ends, but for her part Zenobia was always careful to cultivate the Graeco-Roman constituency in the region. Until the end was in sight, her regime claimed control over the east without disavowing the sovereign authority of the Roman emperor. Only at the eleventh hour, when Aurelian was already poised to strike and there was nothing left to play for by subtlety, did Zenobia lay claim to full imperial status for her son and herself.

In the west, events had taken a rather different course. The military and political conditions which had enabled Postumus to seize power on the Rhine frontier still persisted so that he could not afford to risk an advance on Rome to challenge Gallienus. In choosing to remain on the Rhine frontier and confine his dominion to the western provinces, Postumus was able to reign for almost a decade. With the sole exception of his rival Gallienus, this was longer than any other emperor between Severus Alexander and Diocletian. Furthermore, the persistence of the need for an emperor on the Rhine and the political momentum of his actions allowed his position to continue after he himself was assassinated. A run of less effective and more ephemeral emperors successively took up his mantle. The last of these, Tetricus, was by no means ineffective or incompetent. The greater part of his troops stayed loyal to his cause to the end. It was merely his misfortune to find himself up against one of the greatest generals of the century, and one determined to reinstate the former unity of the empire.

We must reject the ascription of a deliberately secessionist programme to the events in the west during the decade-and-a-half which followed the revolt of Postumus. The 'Gallic separatist' explanation, together with its attendant terminology, 'Gallic empire' and 'Gallic emperor', are therefore wholly misleading. Like Postumus before him, the authority which Tetricus claimed, and which the armies of the Rhine and Britain and the general population of the western provinces recognized, was never anything other than that of a Roman emperor in the ordinary sense of the term.[33]

Even though the empire had come close to political fragmentation, there was always a strong underlying cohesion in the empire as a whole. The world which Aurelian reunited through his victory at Châlons was, thus, not an artificial construct held together by imperialist oppression. The great majority of Aurelian's subjects clearly shared his view that it was a world worth restoring.

7

THE END OF AURELIAN

Now that the Herculean feat of reuniting the empire was completed, Aurelian returned to Italy to celebrate his spectacular triumph in the late autumn of 274. A year later his outstanding career, crowned with military successes, was tragically brought to an abrupt and bloody end through ignominy, ignorance and treason. For at least a short period thereafter, the Roman world seemed to hold its breath while a successor was chosen. But it was only the following summer, with the elevation of Probus, that stability was once again restored. The history of Aurelian's final year is much less well documented than the foregoing period. What little evidence there is confirms what the nature of the times and our understanding of Aurelian's character would lead us to expect: that he had neither the leisure nor the inclination to rest for long on his hard-earned laurels.

THE CAMPAIGNS OF 275

The campaigns of Aurelian's final year remain obscure. We can be sure only that the barbarian menace showed little sign of abating and that Aurelian responded with characteristic energy. Piecing together the scant references from the literary sources, it is possible to discern three or four possible areas of military operation. The evidence for military campaigning in Gaul and/or Raetia is somewhat equivocal. A further Balkan campaign is more securely documented, though little is known about it. Finally, there is a suggestion that Aurelian was planning a full-scale offensive in the east against the old enemy, Persia.

Minor campaigns in the west

The evidence for Aurelian's military exploits in the first half of 275 essentially consists of two passing references. One appears in the

Historia Augusta and relates to a campaign in Raetia; the other (already referred to in the previous chapter) appears in Zonaras and speaks of unrest in Gaul. The *HA* says that after his triumph Aurelian 'set out for Gaul' and cleared the area around Augsburg of barbarian invaders before going on to Illyricum. The application of the term *Gallias* to include Augsburg seems rather loose. The author may merely have meant that Aurelian went via Gaul to Raetia. If so, the reason for this detour is not disclosed. It may be that the season dictated such a route. Or it may be that the invaders had turned westward, perhaps giving rise to the panic and unrest 'among the Gauls' referred to by Zonaras. The link remains tenuous at best, and how far we should even give credence to the *HA* with respect to a Raetian campaign remains an open question.[1]

Alamannic activity in the area of the Raetian *limes* early in 275 is certainly plausible. A year later they broke through the upper Rhine frontier in force, requiring a considerable effort on the part of Aurelian's successors to restore the frontier. It is highly unlikely, however, that the reference in Victor to Alamannic activity and a campaign in which Aurelian expelled barbarians from Gaul in the latter part of his reign has any relevance here.[2]

Aurelian in the Balkans

There is general agreement among the extant literary sources that Aurelian was in Thrace when he was killed, but very few offer us any kind of explanation of what brought him there. The sources are more or less unanimous in placing the fatal assault at a place called Caenophrurium (from the Greek, καινόν φρούριον, meaning 'new fort'), a minor staging post on the road between Byzantium and Perinthus (later renamed Heraclea) on the northern shore of the Sea of Marmara.[3] Syncellus and Zonaras explain his presence in the Balkans by reference to a campaign against the 'Scythians', that is apparently the Goths. An alternative explanation is offered by the *HA*: Aurelian was killed in Thrace on his way to the eastern frontier to conduct a major offensive against the Persians. No mention is made of any Balkan campaign.[4]

Certainly a Danubian campaign in the summer of 275 fits the chronology very well and the late Greek sources that preserve this information are generally well informed on Balkan events in this period. Some additional support comes from Malalas. Sandwiched between his account of Aurelian's creation of a new province of Dacia and his account of the assassination, Malalas states that the emperor started another war towards the end of his reign. He fails to specify where, but the implication is that the war was still in progress when Aurelian was killed, and thus that it was taking place in the Balkans.[5] The Herulian invasion of Asia Minor that followed not long after (see p. 107) might suggest that Aurelian had not satisfactorily completed his military operations in that region before he met his untimely death. There are good reasons, therefore, to accept that a Balkan campaign did take place at this time.

For the most part, however, modern scholarship has tended to give greater credence to the version given in the *HA*.[6] On its face, it is entirely plausible. A full-scale offensive against a Persian empire weakened by internal strife might well have been an attractive proposition for Aurelian in 275. Ever since the last century of the republic, Roman commanders had been drawn by the legacy of Alexander the Great to effect great conquests in the east, often to their own detriment or to that of Rome. Moreover, the location of Aurelian's death in the vicinity of Byzantium naturally suggests that he was *en route* for the Orient.

On closer scrutiny, the force of this geographical logic is not compelling. The literary sources imply, and some even explicitly state, that Aurelian was on the march when the assassins struck.[7] The exact location is described by most of these sources as being 'between Byzantium/Constantinople and Heraclea'. The order in which the cities are named hints at travel in a *westerly* direction. This is made explicit in a fragment of John of Antioch. Aurelian's presence in that area might therefore be explained by the military requirements of his Balkan campaign, and indeed he may have used Byzantium as an operational base. The *HA* reverses the names of the cities, thereby implying that the fatal march was heading east, towards the Euphrates frontier.[8] Zosimus appears to lend the *HA* some support here. He does not say in which direction the emperor was headed, but he does tell us that Aurelian was at Perinthus when the plot was formed, and that it was as he left this city that he was assassinated. Since the murder took place at Caenophrurium, an eastward journey is clearly implied.[9]

The very plausibility of a Persian expedition must put us on our guard: the plan is found nowhere outside the *HA*. Our suspicion is increased by the fact that the *HA* chooses this moment to announce that Aurelian had already gained a great victory over the Persians, at the time of the Palmyrene campaign. Doubtless, this latter assertion reflects Aurelianic propaganda, but its context suggests that the *HA* is at least improving upon, if not actually wilfully departing from, his source. The author's motive in linking Aurelian's murder to a Persian campaign is not that hard to guess. It was done in order to draw a closer parallel with another of his heroes, the emperor Julian, who was assassinated while campaigning against Persia.

Even if we accept a Gothic campaign as the most plausible explanation for Aurelian's presence in the Balkans, this does not preclude preparations for a Persian campaign. The two traditions are easily reconciled. Aurelian may have fought a successful campaign on the Danube in the summer of 275 and then may have been preparing for another campaign in the east at the time of his death in the autumn. It is, however, unwise to credit the *HA* with valid intelligence where this is uncorroborated. The evidence on Aurelian's campaigns in the late summer and early autumn of 275 thus remains inconclusive.

THE ASSASSINATION AND ITS AFTERMATH

Among Christian writers, Aurelian's death is linked to his intention to renew the persecution of Christians and is portrayed as an act of divine retribution. Sometimes, as with Lactantius, the link is explicit; usually it is more subtle.[10] Victor and the *HA* connect the assassination to Aurelian's cruelty: Victor linking it to the emperor's severity in dealing with corruption among provincial officials; the *HA* linking it to hatred aroused by the emperor's cruelty toward those in his immediate entourage.[11]

Neither the wrath of God nor the antecedents adduced in the accounts of Victor and the *HA* are historically very satisfying as explanations for the motives behind the murder. More interesting is the assertion in Malalas that Aurelian was killed by the army because he had commanded it badly.[12] This seems rather curious in light of Aurelian's spectacular and more or less unbroken string of military successes. Malalas may simply be mistaken. The assertion appears in no other source, though the inculpation of the army, or rather of certain of its officers, finds plenty of corroboration elsewhere. It may refer not to Aurelian's skill as a tactician on the field of battle or as a strategist in the management of campaigns, but rather to a strained relationship between the emperor and his men, resulting perhaps from his over-zealous enforcement of discipline. The imputation to Aurelian of severity as a military disciplinarian is found elsewhere, but such reports are probably somewhat exaggerated.[13] On the other hand, it may represent no more than an intelligent guess based on the complicity of the army. The evidence points to trickery rather than to any actual grievance.

Several sources preserve the story that a slave, or possibly freedman, on Aurelian's secretarial staff tricked the assassins into murdering the emperor. This man was called Eros according to the Greek tradition; the name 'Mnestheus' preserved in the *HA* is almost certainly due to the author's mistaken transcription of the Greek title, μενυτής, equivalent to the Latin *notarius*, in place of the man's name.[14] The secretary had somehow incurred the grave displeasure of the emperor and feared the consequences. Since he could imitate the hand of his imperial master, he forged a document or series of documents indicting various officers in the intimate circle of the emperor and condemning them to death.[15] Believing their lives to be in danger, the officers formed a conspiracy under the leadership of a general named Mucapor. When the army halted at Caenophrurium, the conspirators struck. Choosing a moment when Aurelian did not have his bodyguard with him, they set upon the emperor and stabbed him to death.[16]

The repercussions of Aurelian's death

The assassination of Aurelian left the Roman world in a profound state of shock. The elimination, at such a critical time, of one of the greatest generals the empire had known was a devastating blow. Even in a world well used to regicide, the news of Aurelian's sudden and senseless death was greeted with horror and disbelief. Nowhere was this state of shock more apparent than in the army.

Aurelian may have been renowned for his strict enforcement of discipline, but with this discipline he had gained spectacular results in the field of battle. It seems, *pace* Malalas, that this had earned him the admiration of his troops. Both the officers and the rank and file, therefore, sincerely mourned the loss of their great commander, the Unconquered Restorer of the World.[17] The implication of several senior officers in the bloody crime somewhat compromised these sentiments, not least when their motive of pre-emptive self-defence was immediately exposed as baseless. As the terrible truth about the secretary's mendacity was discovered, the conspirators were seized with remorse. Naturally enough, they turned their anger, sharpened by guilt, upon their informant. Eros was instantly put to death. The *HA* says he was bound to a stake and savaged by wild beasts, though this extra detail may be the author's interpolation.[18] Once the villain was dispatched, the army immediately prepared elaborate funerary rites in honour of their murdered emperor. Aurelian was buried with full pomp and ceremony in a magnificent tomb on the spot where he had fallen.[19]

The assassination had not been politically motivated. In their haste to rid themselves of their perceived peril, the conspirators had clearly not planned beyond the murder itself. There was no provision for a successor.[20] Now that the motivation for the treason had been exposed as false, there was even less for a potential candidate to grasp at. The army, so often ready to rally to the cause of a new contender after the murder of a reigning emperor, seems for once to have been utterly stunned. No one felt secure enough to push himself forward for fear of alienating the soldiers. In this strange mood, a kind of political paralysis ensued.

Meanwhile, the news that Aurelian had fallen victim to the basest of plots reached Rome. The urban populace, for whom Aurelian had been a great and worthy prince, deeply mourned his death. Even in the senate, where there was rather less cause to cherish Aurelian's memory, the prevailing mood was one of regret and unease rather than of relief, still less elation.[21] The days when the senate might have hoped to take a lead in selecting an imperial successor were long gone. Amid an air of resigned gloom, the senate awaited news of the inevitable proclamation of a successor by the field army in Thrace. Thus the political paralysis continued.

How long this state of affairs persisted and what happened to the government of the empire in the meantime is a matter of some dispute. Certain sources describe how the empire remained without an emperor for up to six months, or more. During this interregnum, it is said, the senate assumed control and eventually proclaimed a successor from among their own ranks: M. Claudius Tacitus. The pro-senatorial Latin epitomators portray Tacitus, in stark contrast to the usual rough soldier–emperor of the period, as a mild-mannered man. According to Victor and the *HA* he was one of the highest ranking senators at that time, and became the epitome of a senatorial emperor.[22] This testimony is highly suspect.

Leaving the improbable story of the interregnum to one side for the moment, everything else we know of the events immediately surrounding the accession of Tacitus suggests a different and more familiar pattern. It was a military coup. When news of Aurelian's death reached Italy, the army is said to have taken matters into its own hands and acclaimed Tacitus, who was at that moment in Campania. Though it is not stated explicitly, the context suggests that one of the corps stationed in Italy is meant, perhaps the praetorian guard.[23] Tacitus hurried to the city, where he accepted the acclamations of the praetorians with the customary promises of a sizeable donative. The senate promptly endorsed him as the new emperor.[24]

Tacitus is usually identified with the consul of that name who held office under Aurelian in 273. This is somewhat unlikely, given that Tacitus is said to have been 75 when he was acclaimed emperor. There is a suggestion, however, that Tacitus was actually a retired general and in reality nothing more than another in a long succession of military emperors of Illyrian origin. If this is true, it makes his selection by the army as Aurelian's successor more explicable and his late consulship somewhat less implausible.[25]

Whether or not he had been a consul under Aurelian, Tacitus made no effort to distance himself from his predecessor; quite the reverse. Among his first actions upon becoming emperor was to preside over the official deification of Aurelian.[26] By thus associating himself with his illustrious predecessor, the new emperor was attempting to improve his own personal standing. In particular, Tacitus hoped to win over the army, who remained loyal to the memory of Aurelian. Tacitus was thereby emphasizing continuity with the previous reign, much as Aurelian had done before him in presiding over the deification of Claudius.

The news of Aurelian's death soon reached beyond the frontiers. Germanic tribes began to renew their onslaught on the Rhine frontier.[27] Although the timing could be coincidental, it is likely that news of Aurelian's death helped to precipitate these attacks. Further east, a massive invasion of Heruli crossed the Black Sea from the Crimea to attack Asia Minor. Within a short space of time they overran much of Pontus, Galatia and Cappadocia, and penetrated as far south as Cilicia.[28]

Tacitus responded swiftly. Travelling to Thrace, he assumed personal command of Aurelian's imperial army. His first action upon arrival was to avenge his predecessor's death. He apparently chose to avoid a full-scale purge, confining himself instead to dealing only with those most directly involved in the assassination. These, Mucapor among them, were tortured to death as a terrible example.[29] Tacitus may thus have hoped to deter further would-be regicides from making any attempt on his own life. If so, he failed. After a brief campaign in which he managed to defeat the Heruli in Cilicia and drive them back towards the Bosphorus, Tacitus was himself murdered. It appears that at least some of those involved in the plot had also been accomplices to the murder of Aurelian. Once again, apparently, fear of imperial retribution was the motive for the deed.[30] The alternative version, that he died of disease, should almost certainly be discounted.[31]

Tacitus had been preparing to return to Europe, perhaps to deal with the Germanic invasions of Gaul, when he was struck down. He had assigned the conduct of the campaign in Bithynia to his praetorian prefect M. Annius Florianus, who may also have been his half-brother.[32] On Tacitus' death, Florian immediately assumed control of both the army and the state. He was duly acknowledged emperor by the senate and the western part of the empire from the Atlantic to Asia Minor, including Italy and North Africa. The legions of the east, however, elevated their own commander, M. Aurelius Probus.[33] Like Aurelian, and so many other emperors and would-be emperors of this period, Probus was a native of the Danubian provinces who had risen through the ranks to become a senior military commander. At the time of Aurelian's death, Probus was one of his most trusted and competent generals, a man very much in Aurelian's own mould, and as such an obvious successor. It is possible that Aurelian was specifically grooming him to be his eventual successor, though this idea is more likely to be a product of Probus' own subsequent propaganda.[34] Conscious of the numerical inferiority of the forces at his disposal, Probus did not seek to force the issue. Instead he bided his time, probably aware that Florian lacked the full confidence of his own troops. The strategy paid off. After an uneasy delay of several weeks, and an indecisive engagement between the two armies, Florian was lynched by his own men, leaving Probus master of the Roman world.[35]

Three imperial assassinations within such a short space of time might give any new emperor a sense of unease. To curb this trend, Probus chose deterrence over amnesty. He rounded up those responsible for the murder of Tacitus, together with all those in any degree connected with the assassination of Aurelian, casting his net far more widely than Tacitus had done. These he then put to death, allegedly by inviting them to a deadly banquet where they were set upon and slaughtered by Probus' soldiers.[36] The assertion in the *HA* that Probus showed more leniency than Tacitus had previously shown in this matter is certainly the invention of the author, for whom Probus was very much a hero.[37] With Probus' punishment of the last of those implicated in the murder of Aurelian we reach the end of this sordid affair. It only remains to investigate the reputed interregnum.

THE SO-CALLED INTERREGNUM

The story of the interregnum has achieved almost the status of folklore. Gibbon declared the episode to be 'one of the best attested, but most improbable, events in the history of mankind'.[38] In fact, only two sources describe this episode: Aurelius Victor and the *HA*. Although the details preserved in these accounts are precise, it does not follow that they are true. The more closely the chronology of the period has come under scrutiny in recent years the more the interregnum story has lost credibility. It is now almost universally accepted that the interval between the death of Aurelian and the accession of Tacitus cannot have lasted anything like the six months or more mentioned in these sources. Many scholars, however, seem reluctant to forgo the notion of some sort of interregnum.

The textual evidence and the chronology of 275–6

Victor relates that the army in Thrace, intimidated by their complicity in the murder of so stern and upright a ruler, sent an embassy to Rome to ask the senate to choose a successor. When the senate declined, referring the matter back to the army, the soldiers again petitioned the senate. Thus, with each rivalling the other in self-denial and modesty, rare enough virtues in such circumstances but virtually unknown among soldiers, six months elapsed in 'a kind of interregnum', longer and more glorious than that which had succeeded the death of Romulus. Finally, the senate exercised its ancient right to appoint the emperor by elevating Tacitus.[39]

The *HA* takes this story and, in characteristic fashion, embellishes it with fantastic inventions. The author even claims to report the very documents sent to and fro between the contrite army and the modest senate, together with the actual minutes of the senate, while it debated this weighty matter. This documentation is clearly spurious. The game is given away, here as elsewhere, by internal inconsistencies. It is stated that upon receiving the first embassy from the Balkans, the senate on its own initiative assumed responsibility for enrolling Aurelian among the state gods in a decree dated 3 February. In view of the uncertainty in the weeks following Aurelian's death, such an initiative is, in itself, highly unlikely. The senatorial decree which allegedly 'sanctioned' the elevation of Tacitus is dated to 25 September. The dates of these two would-be *senatus consulta*, if true, would give a gap of 7 months and 22 days; but elsewhere the *HA* repeatedly affirms the length of the interregnum as 6 months.[40]

In order to accommodate the literary evidence concerning the length of the interregnum, and to fit the facts as best as possible to these dates, it used to be assumed that Aurelian met his end early in 275 and that Tacitus acceded in late September. In fact, both dates are very much too early and must be rejected as fictitious.[41] It is now widely accepted that an interregnum of 6 months is out of the question.[42] In this debate, the Egyptian evidence has been decisive. It suggests that the hiatus between the death of Aurelian and the accession of Tacitus can have been no more than 10 or 11 weeks at the most, and very possibly as little as 5. Given the time it would have taken for the news of Aurelian's death to reach Italy, the interval required to be filled by any form of official interregnum has dwindled almost to vanishing point.[43] This totally undermines the credibility of the interregnum story as it is presented to us in Victor and the *HA*.

The origin of this fantastic story may be deduced from the *Epitome*, the only other literary source which refers to any form of interregnum. After dealing with the murder of Aurelian, it mentions that there followed 'a kind of interregnum'. The next sentence picks up with, 'After this Tacitus came to power'; a sentence lifted directly from Eutropius or his source.[44] But Eutropius makes no mention of any kind of interregnum. It is clear in his text that the words 'After this' refer to the murder of Aurelian, not to any supervening interregnum. It is quite likely that in this Eutropius has quite correctly understood the sense of his main source, the now lost Kaisergeschichte (KG). The KG must have contained a reference to 'a kind of interregnum', as the same characterization appears in Victor and the *HA*. In a revealing passage, the latter sums up Tacitus and Florian as in themselves sorts of inter-regent between Aurelian and Probus.[45] It is highly likely that this was the original significance of the phrase as used in the KG.

The KG was evidently also among those who ascribed to Tacitus a reign of about six months. This corresponds suspiciously with the length of the interregnum in Aurelius Victor.[46] The origin of the confusion becomes even more clear once it is observed that the sources furnish two distinct perspectives of the six-year span between the summer of 270 (the death of Claudius and thus the date of Aurelian's 'official' accession) and the accession of Probus in the summer of 276. The *Church History* of Eusebius, in whose lifetime these events occurred, records that Aurelian reigned for six years and was succeeded by Probus. Evidently, Eusebius considered Tacitus and Florian too insignificant to count, though he was undoubtedly aware of their existence. Indeed his *Chronicle*, at least in the version transmitted by Jerome, knew of them and assigns to Tacitus the usual six months. At the same time, it assigns to Aurelian a reign of five-and-a-half years.[47] Many later sources became confused by these two different perspectives. While they assign a reign of 6 years to Aurelian, they then still go on to give a reign of 6 or 7 months to Tacitus, evidently unaware that the 6 years already included the reign of that ephemeral emperor.[48] Just such double counting is also present in the case of Florian, whose reign of approximately 2 months was almost exactly coextensive with the first 2 months of Probus' reign.[49]

The germ of the interregnum story is therefore to be traced to an ambiguously worded reference in the KG to 'a kind of interregnum' following the death of Aurelian. The phrase was, it appears, mis-understood by Victor. The KG certainly described, and perhaps even exaggerated, the hiatus that followed immediately upon the death of Aurelian, doubtless mentioning that the news of the assassination was communicated to Rome (whether by formal embassy is doubtful) and also that the formal announcement of Tacitus' accession was communicated back to the army in Thrace. But the 'kind of interregnum' did not originally refer to these events. It was a figure of speech describing the interval between the death of Aurelian and the elevation of Probus. This description was transposed by Victor onto the (brief) hiatus between Aurelian and Tacitus, thereby allowing the interval to appropriate the 6 months elsewhere assigned to Tacitus and thus assume an unwarranted significance.[50] Thus, an entirely apocryphal episode came to be fashioned by the fertile imaginations of two fourth-century authors more interested in rhetoric than historical accuracy.

The myth of senatorial resurgence

For Victor, the story was a platform for sententious moralizing and conservative nostalgia. The Tacitean echoes with which the text is spangled set the tone. The episode is used as a vehicle for showing how much better the world would be if senators acted like senators and soldiers did not behave in their usual high-handed manner. In this make-believe, the opportunity is exploited to the full to stress the unruliness and illegitimacy of the soldiers' usual behaviour and to exaggerate the constitutional rights and political power of the senate. In particular, both the 'right' to choose the imperial succession, a right the senate never in practice possessed, and the right of senators to take up military commands are depicted as being restored to the senate.[51]

The elaboration on this theme found in the *HA* forms an integral part of a tendentious and entirely apocryphal account of the sudden renaissance in the political fortunes of the senate at this time. The author's portrayal of the resumption of senatorial government under the interregnum is in fact but the prologue to his representation of Tacitus as the last of the senatorial emperors in the true republican mould. The biography of Tacitus is a fantasy on the theme of the Principate as a form of restored republic.[52] It is studded with references to a more benign past. The emperor Tacitus himself is made out to be an urbane and bookish arch-conservative who championed the works of his namesake, the republican-minded historian, whose descendant he is said to have claimed to be.[53] This representation of the reign of Tacitus as an Indian summer of senatorial authority is as devoid of historical veracity as the story of the interregnum itself. The entire fiction must be understood in the context of the resurgence of senatorial self-importance at the close of the fourth century, when the *HA* was being compiled.[54]

Among scholars working in this field over the last 200 years, the story of the interregnum has found more apologists than sceptics. Even now that the evidence suggests an interval so short that an interregnum as such is unnecessary in anything but a *de facto* sense, the echo of this unbelievable story refuses to die away completely. Besides the texts discussed above, no evidence lends unequivocal support to the notion of an interregnum as such. Attempts have been made, however, to assign a number of known coin issues to the interval between Aurelian and Tacitus. The most famous example is a series of coins bearing the obverse legend GENIVS P.R. This issue, a number of which bear the letters SC, has been linked to the senate's assumption of executive control of government during the inter-regnum. This is nonsense. In the first place, as noted above, the senate's take-over is a myth. Second, the notion that the appearance of SC on the imperial coinage was indicative of senatorial *control* of the issue of bronze coinage at any period in the empire's history is open to very serious doubt. Certainly by this era the addition of these letters had nothing whatever to do with any genuine exercise of senatorial power.[55] Finally, in recent decades most scholars have preferred to assign this coinage to the reign of Gallienus, whose features bear an undeniable resemblance to those of the Genius on the obverse of many of the coins. While there are some who remain unconvinced, the Gallienic date must now be accepted as conclusive.[56]

Severina as dowager empress

The numismatic arguments in favour of the interregnum do not end there, however. In an attempt to rescue the story, some scholars have turned to the hypothesis that the government of the empire was vested, at least nominally, in the name of Aurelian's widow in the hiatus following his death. The theory, based on numismatic evidence, derives a certain strength from the fact that we know very little about Ulpia Severina. No literary source betrays the slightest knowledge of her. There are, indeed, only three allusions in the extant texts to indicate that Aurelian was even married at all. The *HA* makes a couple of elliptical references to Aurelian's wife and Zonaras presents us with the somewhat incredible story that Aurelian married one of Zenobia's daughters.[57]

Of her background, it can reasonably be conjectured that Severina came from Dacia or elsewhere in the Danubian region, where the *nomen* Ulpia was reasonably common due to the influence of Trajan (Ulpius Traianus). But her putative descent from that emperor is mere speculation, influenced by the mischievous nonsense of the *HA* concerning 'Ulpius Crinitus'. The *HA* has a great deal to say about this paragon of military virtue and senatorial sensibilities: it is said he claimed descent from the emperor Trajan, and was himself most like that emperor; his merits commended him to the emperor Valerian, who at one time considered promoting him to be his junior imperial colleague; he took an active interest in Aurelian's early career and eventually adopted Aurelian in a grand ceremony in the baths at Byzantium before the emperor Valerian; he remained close to Aurelian after the latter became emperor and a painting of himself and his young protégé was later hung in Aurelian's temple of Sol.[58] Few today credit the adoption, but the coincidence of the *nomen* has allowed another conjecture: might he have been the father of Ulpia Severina and thus Aurelian's father-in-law?[59] The charade must be ended. 'Ulpius Crinitus', along with all the anecdotes connected with his name, must be relegated to the long list of the *HA*'s fabrications.

As so often in this period, the scant information to be gleaned from the literary sources is in stark contrast to the specific details which can be ascertained from the contemporary epigraphic and numismatic evidence. It is only by virtue of this evidence that we can get any impression of Severina at all. Of the inscriptions mentioning Severina, the vast majority explicitly refer to her as the wife of Aurelian. All but two grant her the title of Augusta. It is probable that these two inscriptions, one of which gives her the title Pia, were erected before she was created Augusta. Of those that do accord her the title Augusta, none can be dated earlier than 274.[60]

From her coinage it is possible to be more precise about the date she was granted the title Augusta. Her coinage all post-dates the reform which took place in the early months of 274. The mint at Alexandria did not issue in her name until Aurelian's 6th regnal year (i.e. after the end of August 274). Recent studies of the post-reform coin sequences suggest that in fact it was probably not until well into the autumn of that year that Severina was accorded the title Augusta.[61] Certain bronze coins, evidently minted for a special occasion, portray Aurelian on the obverse and his consort on the reverse. The date of these coins is far from certain, but it is possible they were issued to coincide with Aurelian's triumph in the autumn of 274, which occasion may well mark the occasion of Severina's elevation to the rank of Augusta.[62] From this time, coins were issued for her at every mint operating for Aurelian, with the single exception of Tripolis. Her coins portray her, very much in the style of the day, with a somewhat austere expression, her hair braided and drawn up over the back of her head.[63]

Regrettably, however, we know almost nothing of her role as empress. Speculation as to her influence over Aurelian and the affairs of state is not merely pointless but dangerous. Those who have claimed to detect Severina's increasing political influence during the last year or so of her husband's reign have based this assertion merely on the increasing quantity of coinage in her name. This is not a safe inference.[64] The same relative abundance of the late coinage in her name has led to speculation of a rather different kind. It has been argued, with some degree of cogency, that certain late issues of coins minted in the name of Severina belong to the period following her husband's assassination and prove that the government of the empire was carried on in her name, whether or not with the co-operation of the senate.

One ingenious, but ultimately unconvincing, suggestion holds that the late coin types issued in the names of Aurelian and Severina bearing the reverse legend PROVIDENTIA DEORVM were minted posthumously and thus represent part of the interregnum coinage. The argument is largely based on the fact that the iconography apparently combines the Sol types from the latter part of Aurelian's reign with the Concordia types of Severina. The argumentation is thin and circular, deriving more from a desire to find some coinage that could possibly be dated to the interval after Aurelian's death than from any intrinsic feature of the coinage concerned.[65]

The most widely accepted version of the hypothesis centres on a series of coin types bearing the reverse legend CONCORDIAE MILITVM which depict the personification of Concord holding two legionary standards. The format allegedly reveals the efforts made in the name of the murdered emperor's widow to retain the loyalty of the soldiers in that potentially volatile period. The sequence of issues at most of the mint sites operating for Aurelian at the end of his reign appears to reveal an issue of these coins which apparently has no counterpart issued in the name of Aurelian himself. This apparent anomaly has allowed the attribution of these particular coins to the period following the emperor's death.[66] The hypothesis is especially convincing with regard to the output of the mint at Antioch, where a change in the mint marks used appears to confirm that these coins relate closely to the first coins issued in the name of Tacitus, and where the highly unusual obverse legend P(ia) F(elix) Augusta is found on a few rare coins bearing the reverse legend CONCORDIA AVG. The use of the singular AVG in place of the earlier AVGG is certainly striking.[67]

The assignment to Severina of an interregnum during which she ruled in her own right creates almost as many problems as it solves. In the first place, there is the universal silence of the literary sources, as remarkable as that of Sherlock Holmes' famous dog in the night.[68] In the second place, the attribution of identifiably post-Aurelianic issues at several of the mints remains controversial and no two accounts agree as to which mints operated the scheme. Most would agree that Rome, Ticinum and Antioch did produce such an issue; but there are serious doubts about such an issue at Lyon, Siscia, Serdica and Cyzicus. Tripolis, which never issued for Severina during Aurelian's reign, did not start to do so during the so-called interregnum. This state of affairs, which has been insufficiently explored by those who would see an interregnum issue, forces one to question whether we are dealing with an *ad hoc* response to the confusion that followed Aurelian's death rather than a period during which Severina ruled the empire in any meaningful sense. In trying to assess this problem, it should be borne in mind that the Balkan and eastern mints (Antioch, Cyzicus, Serdica, Siscia) would have heard of Aurelian's death a considerable time before they knew the identity of his successor, even assuming Tacitus was elevated almost immediately upon the news reaching central Italy. This does not, however, fit very well with the pattern we have, which suggests that the Italian mints (Rome and Ticinum), for which the gap would have been the least long, produced the bulk of these 'interregnum' coins.[69]

Although most numismatists currently working on this period are now prepared to see Severina's interregnum as beyond dispute, it still remains speculative, and serious doubts remain.[70] We must guard against over-hasty interpretations of the slight variations in mint marks that are unquestionably detectable: other explanations of these anomalous issues for Severina late in the reign may yet be forthcoming. The notion of post-Aurelianic coinage minted in the name of his widow certainly cannot be ruled out, but it should still be regarded with a degree of scepticism. Above all, it cannot be taken as in any way supporting the notion of an official senate-led interregnum of the kind portrayed in the *HA*.

Plate 1 Panorama of Palmyra
Source: Richard Stoneman

Plate 2: Legend

a   (obv) IMP AVRELIANVS AVG (rev) VABALATHVS VCRIMDR
(*RIC* 381)

b   (obv) IMP C L DOM AVRELIANVS AVG (rev) ADVENTVS AVG
(*RIC* 9)

c   (obv) SEVERINA AVG (rev) CONCORDIAE MILITVM (Concordia
with two standards) (*RIC* [Severina] 13)

d   (rev) RESTITVTOR EXERCITI (Mars hands emperor a globe) (*RIC*
366)

e   (obv) AVRELIANVS AVG (rev) RESTITVT ORBIS (Orbis Terrarum
crowns emperor with a wreath) (*RIC* 290)

f   (rev) VIRTVS MILITVM (Mars/Virtus hands emperor a globe) (*RIC*
147)

g   (rev) VIRTVS AVG (as above) (*RIC* 149)

h   (rev) VIRTVS AVG (Mars holding spear, shield and olive branch)

i   (obv) IMP C L DOM AVRELIANVS P F AVG (rev) VIRTVS AVG
(Mars with spear and trophy; at e a captive) (*RIC* 182)

j   (rev) PM TBPVII.COS.II PP (as above, wlthout captive) (*RIC* 16)

k   (rev) FIDES MILITVM (Jupiter hand emperor a globe) (*RIC* 344)

l   (rev) IOVI CONSERVATORI (as above) (*RIC* 227)

m   (obv) IMP AVRELIANVS AVG (radiate bust nude but for cloak,
with caduceus) (rev) VTVS MILITVM (as f above) (*RIC* 408)

Source: courtesy of the Trustees of the British Museum

Plate 3: Legend

a (obv) IMP AVRELIANVS AVG (radiate bust wearing trabea with eagle-topped sceptre)

b (rev) ROMAE AETER (Dea Roma seated with spear and shield offers a small victory to emperor which crowns him with a wreath) (*RIC* 142)

c (obv) SEVERINA AVG (rev) PROVIDEN DEOR (Fides or Concordia with two standards and Sol holding globe) (*RIC* [Severina] 9)

d (obv) IMP C AVRELIANVS AVG (rev) PROVIDEN DEOR (as above) (*RIC* 152)

e (rev) CONCORDIA AVG (emperor clasping hands with (Severina as) Concordia; above, a bust of Sol) (cf. *RIC* 80)

f (obv) IMP AVRELIANVS AVG (laureate bust with raised right hand) (*RIC* 81)

g (obv) IMP AVRELIANVS AVG (radiate bust with spear, gorgoneion on breastplate) (rev) ORIENS AVG (Sol with bow and branch trampling fallen enemy) (cf. *RIC* 64)

h (obv) IMP AVRELIANVS AVG (rev) SOLI INVICTO (Sol with globe, at feet two captives) (*RIC* 308)

i (rev) ORIENS AVG (as above) (*RIC* 279)

j (rev) VIRTVS AVG (Sol hands Hercules a globe; between them, a captive) (*RIC* 318)

k (rev) MARS INVICTVS (Sol with whip hands Mars a globe) (*RIC* 358)

l (obv) SOL DOM IMP ROM (frontal radiate bust of Sol; beneath, the four horses of his chariot) (*RIC* 322)

m (obv) SOL DOMINVS IMPERI ROMANI (bear-headed bust of Sol) (rev) AVRELIANVS AVG CONS (emperor sacrifices at altar) (*RIC* 319)

Source: courtesy of the Trustees of the British Museum

Plate 4 Aurelian's Wall
Source: Richard Stoneman

Part II

INTERNAL POLICIES

8

ECONOMIC REFORMS

THE ECONOMIC SITUATION IN THE 270s

The economic ills of the state had reached a critical point by the time Aurelian was elevated to the purple. The constant warfare, more often than not now fought on Roman soil, had brought about a marked increase in government expenditure while at the same time decreasing revenue. The military budget was the greatest part of this expenditure: soldiers had to be paid, and not infrequently donatives had to be found to supplement their income; they had to be fed and housed; in addition, in this age of rapid deployment, transport costs, of both men and supplies, became an ever larger consideration. To the effects of warfare were added those of an inefficient and burdensome system of taxation. This combination led to rising debts and to increasing amounts of farmland, particularly in the more marginal areas, being abandoned altogether as economically unworkable. The government's answer to its economic plight had been to resort to debasing the coinage, which in turn had helped to fuel inflation. The government tried to circumvent the worst effects of this by resorting increasingly to taxation in kind in order to supply the army more cost-effectively.

Debasement and its consequences

The Roman imperial government's debasement of its coinage effectively started with Nero, who both lowered the weight standard and adulterated the fineness, and was carried on at irregular intervals thereafter. In particular, the silver coinage suffered: with a few temporary exceptions to the trend, as under Domitian, the amount of base-metal alloy in the silver coinage was slowly augmented. It is

125

difficult to gauge the nature and consequences of this debasement down to the end of the second century. By the time of Septimius, however, the silver content of the standard Roman silver coin, the denarius, had sunk from its original 98 per cent under Augustus to approximately 50 per cent.

Up to this point, it might be said that the debasement amounted merely to tinkering with weights and measures. From the reign of Caracalla, however, something more like a massive and deliberate manipulation of the coinage came into play. Caracalla accelerated the policy of debasement in three ways: he markedly lowered the weight standard of the gold coin, the aureus, to fifty to the pound; he further adulterated the silver coinage; and in 215 he introduced a new silver coin, now known as the 'antoninianus' (from his regnal name Aurelius Antoninus) or 'radiate' (from the radiate bust of the emperor on the obverse), which he probably tariffed at the artificially high rate of two denarii. Although the new denomination was dropped for a time a few years later, it re-emerged in 238 and thereafter quickly established itself as the principal 'silver' coin in circulation for most of Aurelian's adult life. The debasement of this coin was not only rapid but thorough: under Gallienus the antoninianus effectively became a base-metal coin with the merest dash of silver, so that, by the time of Aurelian's accession, its silver content was little more than 1.5 per cent.[1]

The most significant effect of this rapid debasement was a loss of confidence in the monetary system, resulting in a high level of inflation which gathered momentum towards the close of the third century. By the very beginning of the fourth century, only a quarter of a century after Aurelian's death, when Diocletian issued his famous edict on maximum prices, the cost of basic commodities and transport had risen astronomically compared to the figures we know of for the second century. The cost of wheat, for example, was fixed at two hundred times its second-century level. The edict was designed to restrain inflation, so it is fair to assume wheat was trading at a still higher price at the time the edict was issued. The evidence is very patchy, but it seems to suggest that the worst of this inflation came quite late, so that during Aurelian's lifetime it was not as serious, and certainly not as apparent, as it became in the last quarter of the third century. In fact, the pace of inflation was so great by that time that the price edict did little to curb the inflationary cycle and prices continued to rise at an alarming rate in the early fourth century.[2]

Another direct result of the systematic debasement was the virtual collapse of the copper-based coinage. After the reign of Gallienus, the issue of the lower denominations of the imperial coinage, in bronze, copper and orichalc, virtually ceased. With this collapse came the end of the local civic coinage. At the time of Aurelian's birth a large number of provincial cities, especially in the Greek east, minted their own bronze or other base-metal coinage, but during the course of Aurelian's life this practice began to disappear. The attrition gathered pace from the middle of the third century – the greatest number of closures can be traced to the reign of Gallienus (253–68) – and thus precisely coincided with the fastest debasement of the imperial coinage. Under Aurelian, only four such civic mints were still functioning: Cremna, Perge, Side and Syllium, all in Asia Minor. The very last issue of civic coinage under the empire was produced at Perge within a few months of Aurelian's death.[3]

A more sinister consequence of the extreme and erratic debasement of the imperial coinage and the attendant collapse of the bronze coinage in this period was a rapidly increasing amount of fraudulent coining. One very important manifestation of this problem was the high level of fraud perpetrated by the mint workers themselves in the mint at Rome early in the reign of Aurelian, and perhaps for some time before this. This fraud, whatever its precise nature, was undoubtedly a factor in bringing about the most serious riot the city witnessed in imperial times.[4]

AURELIAN'S MONETARY REFORMS

The revolt of the mint workers and the full-scale riots to which it gave rise in the spring of 271 deeply affected Aurelian. He clearly resolved straight away to take measures to prevent such an occurrence happening again. He implemented a minor reform of the coinage to check the worst excesses of debasement and its potential for abuse. Subsequently, he overhauled the organization of the imperial mint system and, towards the end of his reign, introduced a significant and wide-ranging reform of the coinage. These measures, taken together, form one of the most comprehensive and complex overhauls of the Roman imperial monetary system ever undertaken by any emperor.[5]

To assist him in these difficult tasks Aurelian needed to appoint a man upon whom he could utterly depend to succeed Felicissimus as the new finance minister. He chose Gaius Valarius Sabinus. Sabinus is attested on an inscription from Placentia, probably dating from 271, with the title *agens vice rationalis*. This office, not otherwise known, strongly suggests that he was temporarily installed with the duties of the *rationalis* to replace Felicissimus in the immediate aftermath of the riots. At an uncertain but clearly later date he is accorded the title of *v.p. rationalis*. This must mean that his position was subsequently confirmed officially, presumably after the trouble at Rome had been suppressed. This second inscription was found at Ticinum, and it is reasonable to deduce from the location that he continued to hold this office at least up to the opening of the mint in that city in 274. If so, it follows that he was the minister responsible for the reform of the coinage in that year. It is thus fair to assume that Sabinus was in great measure responsible for implementing and perhaps even devising the key elements of Aurelian's financial and monetary policies.[6]

The first reform of 271

Having suppressed the moneyers' revolt, removed those who had conspired against him and re-established his authority in the city, Aurelian set about a minor reform of the coinage. These early measures amounted to little more than a holding operation, a slight reversal of the almost inexorable slide into ever more drastic coin debasement, while Aurelian concentrated on the military situation that confronted him in the Balkans and further east. A much more drastic solution to the crisis of the imperial coinage would have to wait until the impending conflict with Palmyra had been resolved.

The preliminary reform of 271 consisted primarily of a slight improvement to the weight standard of the billon (debased silver) coinage and a return to the silver levels that had pertained before the Divus Claudius issue. Certain stylistic changes can also be detected in the die-cutting, particularly an improvement in the lettering. This took place simultaneously across the mints operating in Aurelian's name, suggesting a tightening of central control over the operation of the mints.[7] As part of this restructuring, Aurelian moved the centre of his minting operation to Milan and set up two new mints in the Balkans. Both these measures set the tone for the restructuring of the mint system that was to follow.

The great reform of 274

Perhaps as early as the autumn of 273 Aurelian began the most comprehensive overhaul of the Roman monetary system since the reign of Augustus. The date has been the subject of much discussion. Formerly, it was linked to the introduction of coinage in the name of

Severina Augusta, which was known from Egyptian evidence to have occurred after the end of August 274. On the basis of changes in the coinage from Alexandria, some scholars pushed the reform back to approximately February of that year; more recently still it has been suggested it began the previous autumn.[8]

The only ancient source to mention the reform is Zosimus. He tells us that Aurelian recalled the old debased coinage and exchanged it for newly issued silver coinage.[9] It is clear from the coins themselves that this improved coinage was heavier and that its weight standard was more tightly controlled. Before the reform, the radiates were issued at between 86 and 98 to the pound; after it, the range was reduced to between 81 and 90.[10] The fineness was considerably improved: the percentage of silver was substantially augmented and once again the range was somewhat more tightly controlled. The modern scientific analysis of the billon alloy found in the coins demonstrates a rise in the silver content from a pre-reform average of 3.49 per cent to 4.1 per cent after the reform. This represents the silver content of the coins as they are found today; due to the surface leaching of the silver, the wear sustained by the coinage and the methods of cleaning necessary to obtain these results, it is fair to assume the silver content in antiquity would have been rather higher. For the post-reform coinage, this probably represents an intended average of about 5 per cent.[11] Finally, the coins themselves also show that, from the time of the reform, considerably more care was taken in the production of the coins, including more regular flans and more care taken to centre the reverse dies on striking.[12]

Except at the mint at Lyon, all the mints operating in the post-reform era mark the billon coins with a curious cipher. On the coinage from Rome, Siscia, Serdica, Cyzicus and Antioch, the mark is written XXI (at Siscia sometimes XX.I). On that produced at Ticinum, it is written XX only. At the mint at Tripolis, KA was used, which was also employed on some issues from Serdica. The meaning and implications of these signs have given rise to considerable debate among numismatists and ancient historians. All are agreed that the symbols relate to the number twenty (XX in Latin, K in Greek), but there agreement ends.

A recent and comprehensive review of this debate has classified the various interpretations into four groups.[13] The first three all take the symbols as value marks. The first assumes that the new radiate billon coins were intended to be worth precisely the same value as the pre-reform radiates. In this case, the marks are taken to signify that the new coins were worth either two pre-reform denarii or twenty asses, both of which, according to this argument, were possible ways of calculating the value of the radiate coin introduced by Caracalla. Neither version of this theory is very satisfactory.[14] The second interpretation assumes that, as the silver content of the radiates had declined so drastically since the introduction of the coin some 60 years earlier, it was necessary for Aurelian to devalue the radiate. This he did in one of 3 ways: either he made 20 of his new silver-alloy coins equivalent to one gold aureus; or he tariffed his new coins at 20 asses, deemed to be less than the value of the old radiate; or else he set their value at a twentieth of a first-century denarius. Such arguments founder on several counts, not the least of which is the absurdity of Aurelian choosing to tariff a coin of greater weight and silver content at a lower value.[15] The third version, also seeing the symbols as value marks, opts for the opposite interpretation, namely that Aurelian's measure was in essence inflationary. This takes the marks to indicate either that the new coin was worth 20 times the old radiate, or, somewhat more plausibly, that it was worth 20 sesterces, that is, 5 denarii.[16]

All of the above theories run up against serious difficulties, the most telling of which is the fact that Tacitus and Carus each produced coins alongside those marked in the Aurelianic fashion with the marks XI (or IA in Greek). This undoubtedly refers to the same thing, only indicating the figure 10 in place of 20. These coins cannot conceivably be tariffed at half the value of their contemporary counterparts marked XX or K. They are the same size and weight. The only difference between them, as careful scientific analysis has now proved, is that the X (or I) coins contain almost exactly twice the proportion of silver. Far from being worth half, they must in fact be worth twice the Aurelianic standard. This means that both the new marks introduced by Tacitus and Carus and by extension the marks introduced by Aurelian at the moment of his reform can only refer to the proportion of silver in the coins. It was a form of pledge or guarantee that the coins would contain 5 per cent silver (or 10 per cent in the case of the XI/IA coins). That is to say, 20 such coins would contain as much silver as one coin of pure silver.[17]

It is clear, then, that the marks on the coinage were placed there in order to reassure those to whom the coins were being paid, that is principally the soldiers, that the state guaranteed the standard of silver in them. It was essentially an attempt to restore confidence in the monetary system. The coinage minted at Lyon did not have this mark, either under Aurelian or under his successors. The weight is the same as elsewhere but the silver content is noticeably lower.[18] The absence of the mark under these circumstances helps to confirm its status as a guarantee of purity. Why the Gallic mint did not conform to the standard set elsewhere in the empire is still a controversial point in itself, to which we shall return below (p. xxx).

Gold, bronze and other issues

Gold coins were minted in the early part of Aurelian's reign at the ratio of sixty to the pound, following the standards of the day. After the reform, the average weight of the aureus was increased to 6.6g, equivalent to fifty to the pound. This represents a return to roughly the weight standard employed by Caracalla. Some of the coins are in fact marked IL (or I.L), clearly indicating that the coin weighed a fiftieth of a pound. By advertising the standard on the coin in this way, Aurelian no doubt hoped to reduce the risk of fraudulent minting or subsequent tampering.[19]

No bronze coinage was minted during the first three-and-a-half years of Aurelian's reign. This fact has sometimes been seen as proof of the antagonism between the emperor and the senate, centred on the right to issue such coinage. It has even been suggested that Aurelian formally removed this right from the senate.[20] No such political explanation is necessary. As already noted, the severe debasement of the billon coinage and the consequent inflation had left little room for base-metal coinage at the lower end of the monetary spectrum.

From the time of the reform, with its improved and more valuable 'silver' coin, the need for bronze coinage was revived. Three denominations of bronze coins were put out in the post-reform period, mostly at Rome. The largest was the least in demand, naturally in view of the debased billon coinage, and was consequently minted in extremely small numbers. The smallest, conversely, was minted in the greatest quantity, bearing laureate obverse busts of the emperor or a portrait of Severina wearing a stephane. A number of different reverse types are known. Between these two sizes there was a third denomination, bearing a radiate portrait of the emperor on the obverse and a bust of the empress on the reverse. The relative sizes and weights bear a certain correspondence to the system of bronze coinage which existed under Caracalla.[21]

After the reform, Aurelian also issued a small number of billon laureates, roughly corresponding to the old denarius which, like the bronze coinage, had found itself squeezed at the bottom end of the market and consequently had all but gone out of production. A number of these coins are marked with the cipher, VSV.[22] As with the markings on the radiate billon types, this mark has found a number of interpretations. The least likely is that it represents a value mark: given the dissolution of the theory of a value mark for the radiate coinage, this explanation is no longer tenable. A second explanation is that it stands for VSV(alis), that is, the usual coin, or denarius. A third explanation is that it stands for V(ota) S(oluta) V (i.e. Quinquennalia), that is, the vows taken at the celebration of Aurelian's fifth year as emperor. Between these last two explanations there is as yet no clear winner.[23]

REORGANIZATION OF THE MINT SYSTEM

The location of the mints which produced the money to pay the Roman armies acquired increased significance in the mid-third century. Throughout most of Aurelian's lifetime, and indeed for well over a century before his birth, the production of imperial coinage had largely been concentrated at Rome. Freshly minted coins with the ruling emperor's portrait, name and titles, essential not only for remunerating the troops but for disseminating the emperor's image and claim to authority, had to be transported huge distances to the far-flung frontiers. In the mid-third century, the growing barbarian pressure and the increasing threat of mutiny made it expedient for the emperor to have closer access to a mint operation to pay his troops in those frontier regions where the military conditions demanded his presence. The arterial road that formed the vital communications corridor running from northern Italy across the Balkans to the Bosphorus and Asia was an obvious line on which to site the forward outposts of the mint.

Aurelian's expansion of the mint network

The policy of minting money nearer to the scene of military operations came into its own under Valerian and Gallienus. Upon their accession in 253, these emperors inherited, in addition to the anomalous mint at Alexandria (see p. 214) and a number of local civic mints, three imperial mints located at Rome, Viminacium (modern Kostolac, on the middle Danube) and Antioch. During the course of their reigns they made use of a total of eight mint sites, of which a maximum of five, and for most of the time only four, were in operation at any one time. These new mints included Trier, Milan, Siscia (Sisak) and a mint somewhere in Asia Minor, possibly at Cyzicus or Ephesus. Trier fell to Postumus in 260, so that Claudius operated only from the mints at Rome, Milan, Siscia, Cyzicus and Antioch.[24]

Palmyrene expansion into the Levant in 270 took the mint at Antioch as well as that at Alexandria out of Roman control. Aurelian therefore began his reign with full control over only four imperial mints: Rome, Milan, Siscia and Cyzicus. At all four mints, the first types issued in his name maintained a striking continuity with those of his predecessors and, indeed, even with the final issues for Gallienus.[25] At each of these mints coins were also issued commemorating Divus Claudius. These issues either followed or were contemporary with the first issues for Aurelian at the respective mints. The Divus Claudius coinage of Rome was produced on a massive scale, a significant proportion of which was well below the appallingly low silver standard of the day. This fact very likely has a bearing on the subsequent revolt of the mint workers at Rome.[26]

Of the four mints Aurelian inherited, Rome was initially the largest concern, operating out of twelve *officinae*, or workshops. After the moneyers' revolt, Aurelian shut down the mint in the summer of 271, taking some of the workers with him on campaign to the Balkans. The mint never fully regained its earlier importance. When it reopened in the summer of 273 it was on a much reduced production level, putting out a couple of brief issues with various reverse types. From the late summer of 273, the number of workshops was steadily increased and the full range of denominations was minted.[27]

With the closure of the mint at Rome, that at Milan quickly established itself as the most important of Aurelian's mints. After the initial issues, the number of workshops was increased from three to four. Milan continued to operate on a large scale, including a fair proportion of gold issues, down to the end of 273. At the beginning of 274, with the introduction of the monetary reform, the mint was transferred to Ticinum (see p. 135 and Appendix B.3).[28]

Siscia and Cyzicus were the first mints to go over to Aurelian, after only a brief output in the name of Quintillus. At the outset of Aurelian's reign, Siscia was his principle mint. Following its initial issues, the mint increased its output, including issues of gold. Overall, it was Aurelian's second most important mint, responsible for about a quarter of his total coinage.[29] The fourth imperial mint operating for Aurelian at the outset of his reign was located at Cyzicus, on the southern shore of the Sea of Marmara.

After the initial issues, the number of workshops operating at Cyzicus was gradually increased from two, in the summer of 271, to five, by the summer of 273. There were apparently two issues here after the reform.[30]

During the course of his reign Aurelian managed to capture or regain the use of two imperial mints as well as the mint at Alexandria. The mint at Antioch at first issued coins in the joint names of Vaballathus and Aurelian, then for Vaballathus alone. From 273 there commenced a series of issues in the sole name of Aurelian and from late in 274 coins were also issued here for Severina.[31] The mint at Alexandria went through a parallel development in the early part of Aurelian's reign and only came under his full control in the late spring of 272. Early in his fifth regnal year, that is, approximately autumn 273, changes can be detected in the coinage which apparently reflect the great reform that Aurelian was set to introduce in the rest of the empire from this time. Some time after the end of August 274 the Alexandrian mint began to issue coins in the name of Severina.[32] After the battle of Châlons, Aurelian gained possession of Tetricus' mint at Trier. A second Gallic mint at Cologne, set up by Postumus towards the end of his reign, had most likely already been amalgamated with the operation at Trier under Tetricus. After a very brief issue for Aurelian, the mint at Trier was closed.[33]

Aurelian was also responsible for setting up five new mints during the course of his reign. On his arrival in the Balkans in the summer of 271, Aurelian set up a mint at Serdica (Sofia), on the main Milan to Byzantium road, using personnel withdrawn from Rome. Shortly thereafter, Serdica became the capital of his newly constituted province of Dacia south of the river. Though the types of the early issues are dominated by Jupiter, the association between this mint and Sol is especially pronounced and many of the most remarkable types of the reign were produced here. The volume of coinage in the name of Severina is small.[34]

The second mint set up by Aurelian was also in the Balkans, possibly initially as a camp mint to serve him during the campaign against the Goths in the autumn of 271, and subsequently as a stationary mint while he was preparing for his campaign against Palmyra over the following winter. In some of its earlier issues, probably lasting through the following summer, this mint occasionally placed a dolphin in the exergue, suggesting a maritime port. The most likely site is Byzantium, though other suggestions have been put forward.[35] The last issue from this mint was in the spring of 273, late enough to hail the emperor as Restitutor Orbis, but not late enough to embark on the predominantly solar programme of types found at every other mint from that summer. The output of this mint is now understood to be rather larger than was once supposed.[36]

In or about the late summer of 273, prior to the reform, Aurelian set up a supplementary eastern mint at Tripolis (Tripoli, in northern Lebanon), possibly in order to coin a donative issue to celebrate the victory over Palmyra and encourage his troops for their long and unanticipated excursion to Egypt. Only two reverse types are known to have been produced at this mint, the sequence of which may be determined from the mint marks. The overall output was small and no coins were minted here for Severina.[37]

The biggest of Aurelian's new mints was at Ticinum (Pavia), and was set up early in 274 as the successor to that at Milan. It was at Ticinum that Aurelian's finance minister, Sabinus, apparently set up his headquarters. The mint had a very large output and took over from its predecessor the role of Aurelian's principal billon mint. In fact, it has recently been calculated that the two mints of the Po valley account between them for two-fifths or more of all the billon coinage minted for Aurelian. This is perhaps not surprising given their strategic location.[38]

Finally, in the late summer of 274, after only a very brief issue at Trier, Aurelian relocated his Gallic mint to Lyon, confirmed by the mint mark L on Aurelian's later Gallic coins. As noted in Chapter 6, his choice of Lyon was presumably prompted by mistrust of the Rhine army, and was doubtless influenced by the fact that the city had formerly been the site of a very important imperial mint. The output of both the Gallic mints under Aurelian was negligible.[39]

Thus, from the time he established his authority in the summer of 271, Aurelian began to push still further the policy, developed under Valerian and Gallienus, of expanding and strategically relocating the mint system. Over the course of his reign he made use of eleven different mint sites, excluding Alexandria. Some of these represent relocations rather than brand new operations and never more than eight sites were in operation at any given time. Nevertheless, when he died there were eight imperial mints producing coinage in his name (not including Alexandria), and this represents an increase of 60 per cent over the number operating for Gallienus. Furthermore, Aurelian not only increased the number of locations at which his coinage was produced but also augmented the size of the operations at each location. One of the most important aspects of the increase in the minting operation over which Aurelian presided was thus an enormous increase in production levels.[40] It might be supposed that such increases in the number of locations and overall output would inevitably lead to a reduction in centralized control over the mint system as a whole. In reality, the reverse is the case.

Centralizing control of mint operations

From the outset it is clear that Aurelian meant to exercise a far tighter control over the operation of the mints than his predecessors had apparently done. This control embraced the weight standard, the silver content and the choice of types issued. The degree of standardization of weight and purity achieved by Aurelian was far greater than had been the case under his immediate predecessors. This new policy began to take effect as early as 271. As Aurelian's reign progressed, the standardization increased. In terms of fineness, as we have seen, only the mint at Lyon produced coins of a different standard after 274.

One of the most remarkable features of the coinage produced in Aurelian's reign is the degree of standardization in the choice of types. The earliest manifestation of this new policy is the simultaneous production of the Divus Claudius coinage at all four of the mints under his control. Soon after the Divus Claudius series had ceased, a number of mints issued coinage placing considerable emphasis on the support of the troops, notably types referring to Concordia. This theme re-emerged towards the end of Aurelian's reign. Although such types were fairly common in the mid-third century, the degree of uniformity is remarkable. In the series of coins depicting Jupiter handing the emperor a globe that were minted at several mints during the period late 271 to mid-273, the standardization of type is particularly striking. The policy of centrally imposed coin design is still more clearly illustrated by the numerous types advertising the emperor's title Restorer of the World, which began in 272 and continued to the end of the reign. This policy was taken to dramatic new lengths from the summer of 273. From that time, solar types, most especially those with the legend ORIENS AVG, began to be issued in great numbers from almost every mint. In fact the degree of similarity, one might say almost uniformity, between the output of the various mints, especially in the latter part of the reign, has posed severe problems for numismatists in sorting out the arrangement of the coinage and their allocation to different mints.[41]

FURTHER ECONOMIC MEASURES

In addition to his comprehensive reforms of the coinage and the mint system, Aurelian introduced a number of measures aimed at improving economic efficiency and stability. Measures to stimulate production of food and to aid the ailing agricultural infrastructure were combined with others designed to alleviate the effects of poverty and scarcity in Rome and elsewhere. Several of these measures were directly or indirectly related to the reforms he introduced to the urban corn dole at Rome.

Economic measures in Italy and the provinces

As we have already noted (above, p. 11), one of the most pressing economic concerns facing the Roman government in the late third century was the degree to which useful farmland was going out of cultivation. Among the areas most severely hit by this desertion of the land was northern Italy. As a means of halting this process and returning land to productive use, Aurelian encouraged cultivation (perhaps of vineyards) on deserted land by allowing its produce to be sold free of tax. The *HA* alleges that, in order to further this programme, Aurelian bought large tracts of land running all the way up the Via Aurelia. This is highly unlikely. The idea may have been suggested by the name of the road, which does not, as the author implies, reach the Maritime Alps. The Aurelianic programme of encouraging agriculture or viticulture on deserted land was apparently later continued and extended by Probus. Eventually, the burden on the fisc became too great, and in the next century the generous tax concessions which underpinned the project were curbed.[42] Another measure, at least in part connected with the abandonment of land, was the large-scale settlement of foreigners within the empire.[43]

Aurelian cancelled all outstanding debts owed by private individuals to the state and ordered the public burning of their records. This gesture, reminiscent of Hadrian, was designed to alleviate economic hardship. In reality, it may not have been quite as generous as it seems. The middle classes, on whom the main burden of taxation fell, were struggling, and the debts thus written off were unlikely to be met in any case. Moreover, cancelling such debts was, in the longer term, fiscally prudent in that it might help to stimulate the rejuvenation of the economy needed to fulfil the tax demands of the state. He is also said to have dealt harshly with state informers. These two measures may have been linked and both may have had some connection with the collection of import duties. If so, there is also, arguably, a connection here with the building of the city walls.[44] Aurelian is said to have declared an amnesty for all those accused of crimes against the state, and this measure may also be connected with import dues.[45] In addition, it is reported that he set aside the goods obtained from a tax in kind on certain goods such as papyrus and flax imported from Egypt for the people of Rome. How this measure worked in practice, if it ever did, is not certain. It may be that they were sold to raise revenue to subsidize Aurelian's reforms of the food dole.[46]

Reforms of the urban dole

The most important measures introduced by Aurelian in this field amounted to a complete overhaul of the system of urban food rations. Rome had long since ceased to be able to support its needs from Italian agriculture. Ever since Augustus' annexation of Egypt, the fertile flood plains of the Nile had annually contributed vast quantities of grain as a form of taxation in kind to supply the needs of Rome. North Africa also shipped substantial amounts of grain in a similar fashion. A proportion of this grain was distributed free to a sector of the urban populace. The rest was milled and sold to bakers who then baked their bread and sold it on at carefully controlled prices. The organization involved in this grain supply was immense and highly complex. Changes and additions were made to this dole from time to time, most notably by Septimius Severus and Severus Alexander, who made important changes to the organization of the city and certainly altered the way in which the grain was stored. Whether either of these emperors also began the distribution of baked bread in place of grain is far from certain; if so, it almost certainly was not on a regular basis and may not have been entirely free.[47]

Aurelian's reforms to the food supply of the metropolis were at least in part a reaction to the dangerous riots of 271, which almost certainly had economic as well as political and criminal motivations. The disruption of the grain supply from Egypt is a plausible inference from the events taking place in Egypt during the previous winter. The grain fleet would normally have sailed in the spring, as soon as the weather permitted.[48] By the time the riots broke out, therefore, the effects of the disruption, or of rumours which might portend disruption, would have been felt in Rome. Aurelian probably made up his mind, even this early in his reign, to increase the urban dole and very likely made his intentions known. How much, if any, of his planned reforms he was able to carry out at this early stage is uncertain, though probably most of it had to wait until his return from the east.

The most important aspect of the reforms relating to the food supply to the urban populace concerned the manufacture and distribution of bread. Aurelian reorganized the free distribution of bread to every recipient of the dole, now regularized on a daily basis. He made the right to receive this hereditary, and at the same time fixed the weight of these loaves at two pounds, evidently considerably higher than they had been previously.[49] He also, apparently at the state's expense, increased the weight of the loaves that the bakers were allowed to sell in the market by a full ounce per loaf, while maintaining the fixed price at its former level. Unlike the dole, this bread fed the entire population of the city, so that such a gesture must have been extremely costly, and was no doubt greatly appreciated.[50]

Such alterations to the manufacture and distribution of bread in the city would have required considerable administrative reorganization. This in itself underlines the extremely tight control that the state must have exercised over the milling and baking industries. The mills were located on the slopes of the Janiculum on the western side of the Tiber. They were powered by the aqueducts coming over the brow of the hill, the Aqua Traiana and the Aqua Alsietina. The mills and their associated water supplies were of profound strategic significance, the location of which helped to dictate the line of Aurelian's walls in this region.[51]

To what extent Aurelian's reforms of the urban dole may have necessitated the construction of more mills in this region is difficult to gauge. Recent excavations on the Gianiculo have revealed the remains of one such mill. It is an overshot mill, apparently employing the water supply of both aqueducts. After serving their function, the contents of both mill races flowed together into the Aqua Traiana and were carried on down the hill to power other mills below. The difference in the quality of water of these two aqueducts is quite marked, so that their confluence strongly suggests that the main purpose of this water supply by this date had become the driving of the mills. Whether this profound change was made under Aurelian or somewhat earlier is not yet clear. The relationship of the structure to the city walls at this point also remains to be determined.[52]

In addition to the bread supply for the city, Aurelian regularized, and possibly increased, the distributions of oil, which were originally introduced by Septimius Severus. Although they were reduced by Elagabalus and later restored by Severus Alexander, they had probably ceased to be regular by Aurelian's day. He also apparently regularized the inclusion of salt, heretofore sporadic, in the free dole to the populace.[53] Another, and altogether more ambitious, part of Aurelian's programme of reform of the urban dole was the free distribution of pork. Meat had sometimes been given out to the people, but never on a regular basis. The distribution may have been under the control of a tribune of the urban cohorts, whose new camp Aurelian had constructed in the vicinity of the forum suarium.[54]

Aurelian may also have considered including the distribution of free wine in the urban dole. Serious doubts must remain over this point, however, as it is mentioned only in the *HA*. If Aurelian ever entertained such a plan, he never carried it out. Rather, he arranged for wine belonging to the fisc to be sold at low cost to the people. The wine in question may well have been collected as a tax in kind on the importation of wine into the city. It was unloaded from barges on the Tiber at a point known as Ciconiae, and transported to the temple of Sol, where it was stored in the porticoes until such time as it could be distributed to merchants to be sold. This system of storing fiscal wine at the temple for sale at a subsidized price continued well into the next century.[55]

Some further measures, possibly connected with the reorganization of the urban dole, are referred to in the *HA*. Aurelian is said to have reorganized the shipping on the Tiber and the Nile, and to have reconstructed the embankment of the Tiber, apparently to improve the efficiency of the grain supply and the transport of other goods. But since these measures are only reported in a falsified letter the emperor purportedly wrote to his prefect of the grain supply, the usual caveat must apply.[56]

Finally, it is important to note that the city of Rome was not the only beneficiary of Aurelian's generosity. Many cities around the empire received sporadic help from the central government in times of need. For example, there is evidence to suggest that Aurelian intervened to help the city of Cremna in Pisidia after a particularly severe famine had struck the city.[57]

THE SIGNIFICANCE OF AURELIAN'S ECONOMIC REFORMS

The intention behind the measures that collectively made up Aurelian's economic reforms was essentially conservative. Aurelian saw himself as a *restitutor*. As usual in such cases, his immediate motives were mixed. A love of order, a determination to root out fraud, a desire to make tax gathering more efficient, the need to instil confidence in the medium with which he had to pay his troops, a determination to avoid the repetition of the economic circumstances that had helped to fuel the urban riots of 271, all these doubtless played a part. But Aurelian appears to have viewed these objectives from an essentially military perspective. His principal motivation was to keep his armies satisfactorily paid, fed, housed and ready to fight where and when he needed them. As far as the monetary reforms are concerned, it also seems very likely that he, or his financial advisers, had in mind as a model the monetary system that existed under Caracalla. In thus harking back to the era of his childhood, Aurelian was probably trying to restore, albeit in a somewhat artificial way, something of the comparative economic stability of the Severan period.

His monetary reforms were not, in the end, particularly effective. Although there is every indication that the new coinage was readily accepted in most parts of the empire, the greater value of the new radiates made them less useful for the average tradesman and merchant as a medium of exchange. In the western provinces in particular, the lack of bronze coinage and the relative expense of the new coin made the reformed coinage unwelcome. This is reflected in the make-up of the hoards in the west from the period following the reunification, which strongly favour the old debased Tetrican coinage over the new reformed coinage of Aurelian and his successors. It is likely that the reform coinage of Aurelian was rejected in favour of the old debased coinage of the region largely because the new coins were tariffed too high to form a convenient means of exchange. The pre-reform coinage thus continued to be used as the principal basis of daily trade. The fact that these coins were no longer in production led to a gradual decrease in their circulation through the natural attrition of wear and loss, including hoarding. This shortfall led to economic conditions in which large-scale forgery was a natural solution to fill the gap and produce a cheaper medium of exchange. Vast numbers of so-called 'barbarous radiates' and forgeries of lesser denominations were produced illegally. The forgers imitated the old debased coinage they had to hand, which for the most part was that of Tetricus and his predecessors. Attempts to explain these phenomena in political terms, as a Gallic resistance to reintegration into the Roman empire, are ill-conceived. The peculiarities of the reformed coinage produced for Aurelian and his immediate successors at the Lyon mint (the same weight standard, but lower silver content and no reform markings:

above p. 131) in my opinion lend support to the economic explanation by indicating an attempt to appeal to the local preference for coins of lower value. They certainly do not invite further speculation on political motivation.[58]

Some have argued that Roman emperors in general had little personal input into the choice of coin types. For Aurelian at least this is not so. It is obvious from the numismatic evidence that he took a very significant interest in all monetary matters, including the designs. While he clearly did not personally take decisions regarding each coin type minted in his reign, his involvement on a more general level is obvious. Furthermore, it is certain he appointed someone with the express mandate to keep a tight control over every aspect of coin production. That man was apparently Sabinus. Which initiatives we may assign to him and which were the emperor's own is naturally not possible to say. Sabinus was a subordinate who knew his master's mind. His importance with regard to Aurelian's monetary policies should not be underestimated.[59]

The immediate objectives of Aurelian's monetary reforms were realized. The mints and their workmanship were standardized, and doubtless the operatives were made more honest. The silver content of the radiates was raised and a degree of credibility restored to the currency. This may have gratified the soldiers but in the final analysis Aurelian's measures failed. Financial stability was not restored. Inflation galloped ahead with renewed vigour until it was running at a level virtually unknown before the modern world. The efforts of Diocletian, another arch-conservative, were very much along the same lines only even more Draconian, and achieved scarcely greater success.

The failure of Aurelian's monetary reforms cannot be laid too heavily at his door. It is doubtful that anyone in his unenviable situation could have done much better. A serious decline in agricultural and other productivity, such as the Roman empire experienced in the mid-third century, necessarily makes monetary stability almost impossible to restore. Aurelian also attempted to tackle some of the underlying ills of land desertion and poverty, but in the environment of continued military threat, there was little he could do to bring about the radical change that was required. In assessing Aurelian's performance on the economic front, it is important to place these reforms within their wider context, which included the programme of building and rebuilding and the reorganization of the administration that Aurelian undertook.

9

PUBLIC WORKS AND ADMINISTRATION

The military decisiveness and strategic thinking that characterized Aurelian's approach to economic reform can also be detected in his approach to public works and the reorganization of provincial administration. Foremost among these measures were the celebrated defensive walls that he built to protect Rome. Many of the other building projects attributable to his reign also reflect a desire to provide security or comfort. Strategic considerations show even more clearly in his reorganization of the Danubian frontier.

THE WALLS OF ROME

The city walls of Rome represent at once both the most emblematic and the most enduring monument of Aurelian's age. Nothing else so eloquently demonstrates that, by Aurelian's day, the Roman empire was now on the defensive. Although embellished, strengthened and restored many times down the ages, Aurelian's original structure remained the basis of the city's defences down to the nineteenth century and still today remains discernible along much of the walls' circuit.

The rationale

As already observed, the terrible riots that broke out in Rome in the spring of 271, more serious than any in the empire's history up to that time, were sparked off by panic at the imminent approach of the Germanic forces at that time ravaging northern Italy. It was the second time in just over a decade that the citizens of Rome had felt thus seriously threatened.[1] Their fear was not without justification, for the city was largely unprotected. For centuries prior to these events, the size of the empire and the strength of its armies had been sufficient protection for Rome. But that was effectively no longer the case. Elsewhere in the empire at this time, from northern Gaul to Asia Minor, the archaeological record reveals numerous instances of hastily constructed circuit walls around cities that had long since allowed their defences to fall into disuse and had extended well beyond their lines. In many cases, such as Athens and Side, these defences consisted of makeshift walls constructed out of any available masonry, including dismantled monuments and even statuary. Such a construction would hardly befit the eternal capital of the world.

Aurelian knew that he could not afford to leave behind in Italy an army of sufficient size to guarantee the defence of Rome against a potential recurrence of the Germanic threat. He needed to muster as large an army as he could for his projected campaigns in the Balkans and the east. Nor could he afford to leave Rome unguarded, for fear of renewed rioting at the first news of invasion from the north. His only option was to build defensive city walls behind which Rome could feel relatively safe from sudden attack.[2]

An undertaking of this magnitude required considerable planning and preparation. The line the walls were to follow had to be designated and prepared, plans had to be drawn up and approved and labour and materials had to be organized. Aurelian wasted no time. Before setting out for the Balkans to deal with the renewed Gothic threat, he personally oversaw the necessary arrangements for the project to get under way.[3] Although Aurelian may have consulted the senate on general matters, the plans for the walls were certainly drawn up by military architects expert in this type of construction.[4] Under normal circumstances, the most obvious labour force to carry out such work would also have been the army, but Aurelian could not spare the men. He therefore drafted in the city guilds to carry out the actual building work, perhaps under the supervision of a small number of military personnel. The use of the city guilds as conscript labour for building purposes was an innovation imposed on Aurelian by the circumstances, but in the next century it became increasingly common. In return for this undertaking, the guilds were granted the right to bear the name *Aureliani* in their official titles from this time.[5]

How much time was spent in the planning and preparation stages is not known, but the demolition work along the line of the new walls and the sinking of the foundations alone must have occupied a considerable time. Certainly the project as a whole occupied the rest of Aurelian's reign, and indeed remained still unfinished at his death in the autumn of 275. Malalas states that the walls were finished 'in a very short time', and implies that this happened within Aurelian's reign, but Zosimus says they were finally completed under Probus.[6] Probably the bulk of the project was achieved in Aurelian's reign but the whole not actually finished until the reign of Probus: a period of six years from conception to completion is hardly a long time for such an undertaking.

The extent and design of the walls

The ancient republican city walls, constructed in 378 BC following the sack of the city by the Gauls, had largely been subsumed and obscured by subsequent building; even by the reign of Augustus their exact line was uncertain. Repair to these walls was out of the question. It would also have been anachronistic, since the city had long since outgrown its earlier confines. By ancient standards, Rome in the mid-third century was very extensive: no European city exceeded it in size until London in the eighteenth century. To have surrounded the whole of the vast Roman conurbation with a circuit wall would have made neither economic nor strategic sense, and Aurelian did not attempt it. Even so, the circuit of the new walls was nearly 19 kilometres in length.

The line that Aurelian chose for his walls took in most of the fourteen Augustan regions of the city and enclosed all the major structures of economic and strategic significance. To the north and south it appears to have followed quite closely the old customs boundary of the city, which dated back at least to the reign of Vespasian and had been marked out by boundary stones in the late Antonine period.[7]

A salient to the south incorporated a section of the Via Appia within the walls so as to protect the Aqua Antoniniana and fortify the northern lip of the Almo valley, which would otherwise have dominated the city defences. This may represent a deviation from the customs boundary, though it is also possible that the old boundary came this far south. To the west, part of the fourteenth region on the right bank, an area roughly corresponding to modern Trastevere, was enclosed in a massive salient that stretched to the top of the Janiculum. Procopius rightly argues that this section was enclosed both because the Janiculum dominated the island and its bridges over the Tiber and because the region housed the city's flour mills, powered by the transtiberine aqueducts. Whether, in addition, the line of the walls was still following the customs boundary at this point is less certain.

Only in the east did the line of the new walls certainly abandon the customs boundary altogether, enclosing a considerable additional area bounded in the north-east by the praetorian camp and in the south-east by an important system of aqueducts. The Aquae Claudia-Anio Novus and Marcia-Tepula-Iulia provided a substantial part of the city's water supply and in themselves would have presented an enemy with a tactical vantage point had not the wall been set to pass along their outer side. Except for a short stretch either side of the Porta Praenestina–Labicana, the aqueducts themselves were not incorporated within the structure of walls as such, and thus economy of resources cannot be cited as the reason for the choice of line. Wherever deviations from the old customs boundary can be postulated, therefore, there existed sound strategic reasons for the line chosen.[8]

Strategy also demanded that the river bank itself should be strengthened to connect the fortifications on each side of the river. Two stretches of wall were therefore built on the topmost of three embankment tiers along the east bank of the Tiber: one in the south, of about eight hundred metres; the other approximately three times as long, linking the transtiberine walls with the Porta Flaminia in the north. The circuit thus incorporated all the urban bridges within the fortifications, with the possible exception of the Pons Aelius and perhaps the bridge of Nero, if the latter had not already been demolished by Aurelian's time. Though the evidence is wanting, it is highly probable that the fortifications reached across the Pons Aelius, incorporating the mausoleum of Hadrian (Castel Sant'Angelo), thereby making a bridgehead of this imposing structure. This was certainly the case in Procopius' time and, as the events he describes in his *Gothic Wars* make plain, it would have made little strategic sense for Aurelian to have left the mausoleum and the bridge outside the fortification system.[9]

In design, the main structure of the walls was simply built. It was constructed of a solid core of tufa aggregate held in a cement of lime and pozzolana sand faced, inside and out, with tiles or bricks broken into triangular pieces set in mortar. Unusually for this date, both the aggregate of the core and even that of the foundations consisted of new material and not rubble taken from demolished buildings. The tiles, on the other hand, as Vitruvius recommends, were reused and thus weathered: most were Hadrianic, though some were as late as Severan, and probably came from buildings demolished to make room for the passage of the walls. The faces were bonded to the core at irregular intervals with horizontal courses of large tiles reaching

146

into the core. The walls were constructed in short segments, and the absence of putlog holes implies the use of free-standing scaffolding. The quality of the workmanship varied considerably. In places, great care was taken to pack in the aggregate tightly behind the facing. For much of the circuit, however, the haste of the construction and the inexperience of the workmen are evident: in places the tiles were of insufficient depth to permit proper bonding to the core, allowing the facing to sheer off over time.

The foundations were 4 metres wide, and of varying depth, sometimes stepped to accommodate undulating terrain. The main solid structure of the wall was 3.65 metres thick and stood 6.1 metres high; this was crowned by a rampart walk made of fine cement, with a string course of tiles on the outer face of the wall. The whole was surmounted by wide-set and somewhat irregular battlements which raised the total height of the structure from the outside to just short of 8 metres. This simple structure is in keeping with other Roman fortifications of the day: in height it is about average; in thickness, somewhat above average. On certain sections the structure of the wall is of a quite different type, betraying Hellenistic influence. Here the wall is solid only to a height of about 3 metres, upon which base was constructed a barrel-vaulted gallery supporting the rampart walk at the standard height. The gallery was equipped with loopholes for archers. The tactical advantages for this type of construction in relation to their locations are not at all clear, and the difference may represent nothing more than the work of different personnel.[10]

For most of its length, the circuit was punctuated at regular intervals of about every 30 metres by a system of 381 towers. With very few exceptions, these towers were uniformly rectangular in shape, measuring 7.6 metres across, projecting 3.35 metres in front of the wall and flush with the back, and rising some 4.5 metres above the top of the wall. In most cases, the towers were solid to the height of the rampart walk, from which there was access to a triple barrel-vaulted chamber with a central stairway leading up to the crenellated roof. The chambers were usually equipped with two arched windows facing forward for the use of *ballistae*, with another such window on each side to allow the artillery to swivel at ninety degrees. On the galleried sections of the walls, the towers were only solid up to the height of the gallery floor, which passed through the rear of the towers, and were equipped with stairs that gave access to the upper-level artillery chambers and the rampart walk. Access to the ramparts from the ground was not possible by means of these towers, except where they were closely associated with posterns or minor entrances.

Access to the wall was exclusively via the gate towers, thereby enabling the defenders to control the unwanted interference of civilians.[11]

Aurelian's original walls were pierced by as many as twenty-nine entrances, including numerous posterns. These may be divided into four types. First there were the four great gates, each originally equipped with twin portals flanked by semicircular towers, which served the four main axial roads leading into the city: the Via Flaminia from the north, the Via Appia from the south and the two main roads either side of the river that led to the two ports of Rome, the Via Ostiensis on the east bank and the Via Portuensis on the west bank.[12]

The second category consisted of single gateways, again flanked by semicircular towers. Such gateways, serving the roads of secondary importance, were located at the intersection of the wall with the Viae Salaria, Nomentana, Tiburtina and Latina.[13] The Porta Praenestina–Labicana, built up against the outside of the monumental arches that Claudius I had erected to carry the Aqua Claudia and Aqua Anio Novus over the Viae Praenestina and Labicana, was a special case. It was effectively two gates of this second type juxtaposed, sharing a central tower which was constructed on top of an ancient tomb.[14] The gateway at the head of the Pons Aelius was probably also of this second type, though almost nothing is known about it.[15] The Porta Aurelia, spanning the Via Aurelia Vetus on the crest of the Janiculum, may also have been in this category, though its demolition in 1644 has left insufficient evidence.[16]

The third class of gate, serving only minor roads, consisted of a single-span archway in the curtain wall between two ordinary square wall towers spaced at the usual interval. Devoid of flanking towers, these gateways were originally scarcely more than posterns, though several of them received more serious treatment in subsequent phases. The best examples of this type of gate are Porta Asinaria and Porta Metrobia, both in the southern sector and both subsequently enhanced.[17] The gate now known as Porta Pinciana was an unusual example of this type: offset in order to accommodate the oblique angle of the road passing through it, the entrance was apparently guarded by a single, rather narrow, semicircular tower on the east side. Early in the fourth century, the western tower was added and the status of the gate upgraded.[18] Other gates of this class, if not simply posterns *per se*, were the so-called Porta Chiusa, just south of the praetorian camp, Porta Ardeatina (or Laurentina) and the transtiberine Porta Septimiana.[19]

148

Finally, there were a large number of anonymous postern gates and doorways in the wall, some of which probably served private needs. In addition to the small portal sometimes referred to as Porta Ostiensis West, four original posterns and two wickets are known in the main wall. Most, if not all, were blocked up at a very early date.[20] At least five posterns also pierced the stretch of river wall from the bridge of Agrippa up towards Porta Flaminia. These served the key ferry crossings and landing quays, including the quay known as Ciconiae, where the fiscal wine was unloaded for transport to the temple of Sol. Due to their commercial importance, these posterns remained open much longer than their landward counterparts, and by the Middle Ages their number had apparently even increased.[21]

The two most striking features of the Aurelianic walls are the simplicity of the overall design and the very high level of standardization imposed on almost every aspect of the construction. Apart from the galleried sections, mentioned above, and those sections where pre-existing structures were incorporated as part of the wall, the only notable exceptions are to be found in the treatment of the string courses and battlements at the top of the wall. Such standardization helped to save time and expense in the preparation and assembly of the materials. In addition, the simplicity of the design and remarkable uniformity were necessary to workmen who lacked the expertise of military engineers.[22]

Concessions were occasionally made for the lie of the land, however, so that the wall effectively became a revetment in places. Wherever possible, and strategically prudent, time and expense were spared by incorporating older structures within the wall. Of these, the most outstanding are: the retaining walls of the Horti Aciliorum and Horti Sallustiani in the north; the outer walls of the praetorian camp, which had to be raised; the side of a tenement block in the eastern wall, with its windows filled in; a short stretch of the Aqua Claudia-Anio Novus on either side of the Porta Praenestina–Labicana; the southern wall of the early third century *amphitheatrum castrense*, with its arcades walled up; and several tombs, most notably the pyramid of Gaius Cestius near Porta Ostiensis. As already noted, the mausoleum of Hadrian may also be counted in this list. In total, approximately one-tenth of the entire circuit was accounted for in this way. The appearance and configuration of the wall at these points obviously varied from the norm according to the idiosyncrasies of the original structures.[23]

Of those parts of the walls that were truly Aurelianic, the most distinctive deviation from the standard pattern was to be seen in the river walls. Here the walls were almost entirely devoid of towers, at any rate for long stretches, and, according to Procopius' experienced military judgement, presented a severe strategic weakness in the defensive line. This, it must be remembered, represents a sixth-century viewpoint; by that time the function of the city walls had changed considerably.[24]

The purpose and legacy of Aurelian's walls

The circumstances that inspired Aurelian to build the walls to a large degree dictated their nature. They had to be built in a hurry and with non-military labour and at a minimum cost. They had to be imposing enough to do the job required of them but the situation did not allow indulgence. The walls were therefore impressive rather than ostentatious; functional rather than beautiful. Only here and there, for example in the curtains of the major gateways, was there any attempt at aesthetic embellishment. It is clear from their structure and dimensions that the original walls were built to protect Rome from sudden attack by barbarian invaders long enough to allow relief forces to be sent to the city's defence. They were not designed to withstand concerted attack from an army equipped with sophisticated siege machinery. The large number of entrances clearly demonstrates the truth of this. The point is underlined by the fact that so many of the lesser posterns were closed and the remaining portals strengthened when the military circumstances altered to increase the likelihood of siege warfare. Certain strategic flaws in the design and construction of the walls, which once again point to the lack of experience in this kind of construction on the part of the workmen involved, indicate that the function of the walls was as much a psychological deterrent as a physical barrier. These flaws are most obvious at those places where pre-existing structures have been incorporated. A glaring example is the total lack of communication along certain stretches of the walls: at the pyramid, at the short sections of the Aqua Claudia around Porta Praenestina and at the tenement house just to the north of this. It is always possible wooden structures were added at these points which have now vanished without trace. The junction of the wall with the north-west corner of the praetorian camp and the unfortunate re-entrant east of Porta Ostiensis also created unnecessary weak points.[25]

The design of the walls was clearly made with artillery defence in mind. The provision of windows in the gate and wall-towers for the use of *ballistae* was a relatively innovative idea, and one perhaps born of the difficulties of meeting manpower shortages. Similar defensive systems are to be found in contemporary or very slightly later fortifications in Gaul and Spain. This design further reinforces the anticipated nature of the attack the walls were intended to withstand. The artillery system had a limited range in the area directly in front of the wall itself, thus providing effective deterrence rather than meaningful defence. Nor was it possible to defend much more than a single stretch of wall at any one time in this fashion. To defend the city from all sides, as would be required in a siege, by arming every artillery emplacement would have required a complement of well over 700 *ballistae* in working order together with the experienced personnel to man them. This was unthinkable in Aurelian's day, or at any other time in Roman imperial history. These machines did not have long service lives, and it is highly improbable that appreciable contingents of *ballistarii* were ever permanently stationed in Rome. Indeed, when faced with the serious prospect of siege warfare just over a century later, Honorius reverted instead to a primary reliance on archers, using artillery only as a reserve. Aurelian's walls thus represented 'a formidable barrier, not a fighting platform'.[26]

Both the line of the circuit and the nature of the walls themselves, including their numerous entrances, suggest that a secondary purpose may have been to reinforce the customs boundary itself and, in the east, to extend it. The construction of the walls may have been intended to put an end to smuggling as well as to provide security against foreign invaders. Evidence from the fifth century clearly indicates that customs were levied along the line of the new eastward extension by that time, and there seems no reason to doubt that this change was contemporaneous with the building of the walls and thus introduced by Aurelian. Part of the rationale for the eastward extension may thus have been the inclusion of the markets in region V, including the important *macellum Liviae*, within the customs area.[27]

In the centuries that followed Aurelian, the defensive walls with which he had surrounded Rome played an increasingly important military role. In the successive refurbishments and strengthenings that the walls received, their function was altered to meet the new military climate, turning Rome into a fortress. In the early fourth century, barely thirty years after the completion of the walls, Maxentius, faced with the prospect of defending Rome against a Roman army, doubled their height, began digging a ditch around the circuit, closed several lesser entrances and strengthened a number of the remaining gates. In the first decade of the fifth century, the walls and gates were reinforced again by Stilicho in the reign of Honorius. They proved an effective defence against two sieges by the Visigoths under Alaric, but failed to withstand the third attempt in August 410. The sack of Rome was an event that sent shock waves round the Roman world. Nevertheless, the walls continued to play a significant part in the history of Rome thereafter. Repaired twice in the mid-fifth and early sixth centuries, the walls and their associated defences played a crucial role in the sieges and counter-sieges of Justinian's Gothic wars, during which they were twice repaired and strengthened by Belisarius (536 and 547).

Throughout the medieval and Renaissance periods, the walls were maintained and added to, chiefly by the Papacy. The last occasion on which the walls proved a significant factor in the military history of the city was in the mid-nineteenth century, when the nationalist forces under Garibaldi managed for some time to withstand the French attack. Even today the visitor cannot help but be impressed by the imposing majesty of their remains.

OTHER BUILDING PROGRAMMES

Aurelian is credited with undertaking a number of other major construction projects in the capital. Besides the great temple of Sol which he erected in the Campus Agrippae, to which we shall return (in Chapter 11), he is said to have rebuilt the portico of the Antonine Baths on the Aventine, to have built a new camp within the city to house the urban cohorts and, more dubiously, to have erected a new portico in the grounds of the Horti Sallustiani.

In Aurelian's day, the Baths of Caracalla were among the most imposing civic buildings in Rome and an important focus for both the social and economic life of the city. We are told that Aurelian rebuilt the portico because it had burnt down. It is not entirely certain what part of the complex is meant, but it perhaps refers to the peribolus, which may have been added by Elagabalus and Severus Alexander. The outbreak of fire at public baths was a common enough occurrence in Roman times, but such fires rarely led to major structural damage. It is, therefore, a legitimate conjecture that part of this edifice may have been destroyed in the riots of 271. If so, Aurelian's decision to make good this damage would be all the more understandable. Either way, it is a reflection of the importance with which Aurelian regarded public opinion at Rome.[28]

Aurelian is also reported to have built a new camp for the four urban cohorts, who up until that time had been housed in the praetorian camp. We are told it was located in or near to the Campus Agrippae, in region VII, and thus near to Aurelian's new temple of Sol. This was a region of the city with an adequate water supply for such a camp, though as yet no identifiable trace of this, presumably large, structure has come to light. Very likely it was sited near to the forum suarium, since this was placed under the direct care of a tribune of the urban cohorts. It is generally supposed that the forum suarium was the central market for the swine trade in Rome, and as such there may have been a further administrative connection relating to Aurelian's distribution of pork rations.[29]

The *HA* informs us that, when in Rome, Aurelian preferred to reside in the Horti Sallustiani, rather than in the imperial complex on the Palatine. In itself this is not incredible, since it is known to have been an important imperial residence both before and after this time. It is difficult, however, to give any credence to the statement that Aurelian built a mile-long portico in which to exercise himself and his horses. Like so much of the unsubstantiated waffle with which that author has padded out his account of Aurelian's life, it should be treated with grave suspicion until such time as corroborative evidence can be found. The same must be said for Aurelian's reported intention to build new winter baths on the right bank.[30]

Building projects elsewhere in Italy during Aurelian's reign are more securely attested. We know at least that he ordered the construction of new bath complexes at Grumentum in the south and at Caesena (Cesena), just north of Rimini.[31] The *HA* also tells us of a plan to build a new forum, named after himself, at Ostia; a project which was apparently begun but later abandoned after the emperor's death. On the face of it this assertion seems more credible than the metropolitan projects alluded to above, and we should perhaps keep an open mind on the subject for the present.[32]

Outside Italy, Aurelian's highest priority lay in construction projects which facilitated the defence of the empire. The greater part of his reign, as we have seen, was given over to the defence of the empire and the elimination of its enemies. It is not therefore surprising to find this reflected in his provincial building projects. As at Rome, these included fortification or re-fortification of a number of vulnerable towns and strategic locations. The defensive walls at sites such as Dijon, Orleans and Richborough are among those which probably received attention at this time. There was, however, no systematic programme of urban fortification in this period. Another important aspect of Aurelian's building programme was the construction and maintenance of the provincial road network. To judge by the relative abundance of new milestones which have survived, especially in the arid and comparatively undeveloped North African provinces, a fairly systematic programme of repair to the road network was undertaken in Aurelian's reign. It is clear that this too was aimed at facilitating the defence of the empire.[33]

PROVINCIAL ADMINISTRATION

With regard to provincial administration, there were three areas to which Aurelian particularly addressed himself. The first was corruption in the provincial administration and the army stationed in the provinces. The second was the internal structure of the administrative hierarchy. The third, and most significant, was the restructuring of the Danubian frontier and the provincial map of the Balkans.

We are told that Aurelian cracked down very severely on extortion and embezzlement among provincial officials, presumably both military and civilian. Once again the accusation of cruelty is raised in this context, and indeed it is cited by one source as a factor contributing to his murder.[34] Extortion and embezzlement were perennial and widespread problems at this date. It stands to reason that curbing these activities would be unpopular with the class who regarded them as perquisites of their tenure of office. Nevertheless, for the general provincial population who had to furnish the bribes and extra taxation or commodities, such a stern approach might have been very welcome.

As for as the structure of the administration itself, it is quite likely that Aurelian was responsible for certain minor changes. Around this time, procurators of the rank of *ducenarius* began to be dignified with the title *vir perfectissimus*, where up to this point they had merely been entitled to be styled *vir egregius*. A date for this transition more precise than between 263 and 288 is difficult to argue, but evidence for this change occurring under Aurelian exists, and it is reasonable to postulate that the initiative was his.[35] In the regions of Italy, too, Aurelian may have been responsible for slight administrative changes. From this time, senatorial *correctores* are regularly attested for Italy, either as a whole or with jurisdiction over a particular region. The earliest of these is Tetricus, whom Aurelian appointed as *corrector* of Lucania in 275. On the other hand, the existence of regional *correctores* does not mean the office of *corrector Italiae* was abolished.[36]

The withdrawal from Dacia

The most significant change that Aurelian introduced within the provincial administration was the withdrawal from transdanubian Dacia and the creation of a new province (or provinces) south of the river. The details of this extremely important operation remain obscure and have given rise to considerable controversy.

The antecedents are clear enough. From the reign of Philip on, the province had known little respite from barbarian raids. Gallienus had been unable to spare the resources to expel the barbarians and indeed had even transferred part of the two Dacian legions, the V Macedonica and the XIII Gemina, back across the Danube to Poetovio (Ptuj) in Pannonia Superior. The rump garrison left behind in Dacia proved inadequate to protect the local population across the entire transdanubian territory. Under Claudius, the Roman forces in the region were powerless to rectify the situation, so that by the accession of Aurelian the defence of Dacia had become impracticable.[37]

Aurelian's resounding defeat of the Goths in 271, as already noted, afforded him the opportunity radically to overhaul the defensive strategy of the region. This is certainly the most likely date for his decision to withdraw all the Roman forces stationed in Dacia back south of the Danube. His victory would have enabled him to impose terms on the Goths that would allow such a withdrawal with relative peace of mind. The new Danube frontier could be held with far less military strength than would be needed to protect the whole of the transdanubian salient. This was timely, as he needed to collect as large a force as he could muster for his impending assault against Zenobia. Furthermore, the value of the Dacian salient as a buffer against barbarian attack had greatly diminished since, for the previous decade, a great many of the invasions that had caused such havoc had been sea-borne, giving the Roman forces stationed in the north a wide berth and attacking the undefended coastal regions.[38]

The withdrawal was undoubtedly put into effect immediately, though the entire operation must have taken a considerable amount of time. The logistics and military planning involved in such a strategic manoeuvre were complex, especially as it was vital to avoid giving the impression of weakness. The operation had to be seen to be an orderly withdrawal and not a hasty retreat. The old Dacian legions, V Macedonica and XIII Gemina, were eventually redeployed at strategic points along the new river frontier: the former at Ratiaria

(Arcar), guarding the route to Naissus (Nis) and Macedonia; the latter at Oescus, guarding the important crossing and the route that led through the Pass of Succi to Thrace and the Aegean coast.[39] Forward posts of these garrisons were still apparently guarding the main routes of this withdrawal, at least in the Olt valley north of Oescus, a year after the operation began. A coin hoard found in Oltenia suggests the presence of military personnel in the lower Olt valley as late as the early autumn of 272. Although the burial of the hoard does imply that the owner expected to remain in the area for at least a short while longer, it does not imply, as has been recently argued, that the withdrawal had not already started by this date.[40]

Although 271 is the most likely date, others ranging from 270 to 275 have been put forward by modern scholars at various times. The case for dating the withdrawal to the very end of Aurelian's reign is based primarily on the unsound premise that the event is mentioned late in the literary accounts of Aurelian's reign. This has more to do with style than chronology.[41] It has been supposed that a coin type with the reverse legend DACIA FELIX referred to this event. The type in question may now with certainty be dated to the very earliest issues at Milan, which started in the autumn of 270. This is quite certainly too early for Aurelian's withdrawal to have been the inspiration behind these coins. Their design is better understood as a reference to the homeland of certain troops for whom the coins were destined, who may even have been stationed in northern Italy.[42]

Aurelian's policy towards this region did not stop at a reorganization of military deployment. In addition to the military withdrawal, he undertook to evacuate from Dacia considerable numbers of civilians as well. It is unclear, on the basis of present evidence, precisely what this amounted to. It is highly improbable that he attempted a mass evacuation of the entire population of the old province of Dacia. Even though the population was no doubt depleted by the ravages of war, such an undertaking would have been wholly impracticable. Furthermore, the epigraphic evidence, which points to the survival of Daco-Roman civilization north of the Danube for more than two centuries after Aurelian, strongly argues against the wholesale removal of the population. This inference is further supported by the continuation of the Latin language in the region, of which modern Romanian is a direct descendant. Nevertheless, it is impossible to dismiss the reports that a large number of civilians, men and women, were evacuated south of the Danube. At the very least this would have consisted of the local dignitaries, administrators and officials, those in charge of the mines and many of the wealthier merchants and landowners: in short, anyone who had the means and who was inclined to follow the soldiers, or whose livelihood depended on them. These people, including their families and households, were relocated to an area carved out of a small portion of eastern Upper Moesia, the western end of Lower Moesia and part of Thrace.[43]

The area in which these people were settled was made into a new province called Dacia Ripensis, with its capital at Serdica (Sofia). It is possible that two new provinces were created simultaneously, one along the Danube, called Ripensis, and the other to the south, chiefly comprising the region of Dardania, called Dacia Mediterranea. If only a single province was initially created by Aurelian, it was subdivided into two provinces only a few years later under Probus or Carus.[44] Quite how this massive undertaking was carried out remains unknown. Neither the literary sources nor the archaeological evidence sheds much light on either the operation or its aftermath. To a certain extent the silence must be seen as a tribute to the efficiency with which the operation was undertaken.

The ravages of the preceding decades together with the constant recruitment of young men had severely depleted the population of the central Danube region, both north and south of the river. The consolidation of the population south of the Danube made perfect sense on economic and demographic grounds and may not have caused undue disruption. Not long afterwards, presumably during the winter of 272–3, we are told that Aurelian settled a large group of Carpi on Roman soil. This should mean south of the Danube, though it could perhaps be construed to mean that he allowed them to settle permanently in part of the old province of Dacia. If the latter, it suggests that even in the fourth century, transdanubian Dacia was conceived of as in some sense still Roman. Either way it is further proof of the relative under-population of the Danubian region at this time. The practice of settling Germanic and other tribes within the Roman empire accelerated during the next two centuries; again pointing to the amount of space available.[45]

AURELIAN THE MILITARY ADMINISTRATOR

Aurelian's campaign experience had shown him the value of defensive walls to protect cities from northern barbarians not equipped with siege engines. Valerian's walls around Thessalonica had enabled the city to hold out against the Goths until a relief army could reach it. Similarly, the fortifications with which Gallienus had enclosed Verona had allowed it to escape the ravages of the Alamanni in 269. The tactics which Aurelian had himself employed against the Vandals in the winter of 270–1 (above, p. 49) would not have been possible without such defensive structures. As with his relocation of the mints, it was first and foremost military requirements that determined his programme of repair to the roads and improved communications. His decision to abandon the transdanubian province of Dacia was governed by the need to establish a more manageable frontier. The abandonment of Dacia was a military mind's answer to an essentially military problem, and it was carried out in a military way. Doubtless the essentials of this policy also had been borne in on him during the course of his Balkan campaigns long before he became emperor. When he assumed the purple, he set about putting these realistic and essentially defensive dispositions into effect.

The attention that he lavished on building projects in the city of Rome, such as the walls and the baths, is not so much a comment on the strategic or political importance of the metropolis as on his conviction that Rome still mattered symbolically. As with his reform of the urban dole (see Chapter 8), his principal aim was to minimize the risk of the dangerous riots that erupted at the outset of his reign ever being repeated. His attempts to stamp out administrative corruption and embezzlement clearly mark his priorities. All these measures, just as with the economic measures discussed in the previous chapter, demonstrate a military attention to detail and a drive towards efficiency.

10

THE EMPEROR, THE SENATE AND THE ARMIES

From the perspective of the emperor, there were two groups within the empire who mattered above the rest and upon whose support and co-operation he depended: one was the military, both the army commanders and the rank and file; the other was the administrative élite, which certainly included senators but scarcely any longer the senate as such. Aurelian's relationship with these two vitally important groups is characterized in the literary sources by over-zealous enforcement of discipline and excessive cruelty.

ALLEGATIONS OF CRUELTY AND THE SENATORIAL RHETORIC

The emphasis on cruelty is particularly pronounced. He is accused of being cruel in his treatment of his enemies, in his treatment of senators, towards his officers and men and even towards members his own family. We are told he had his own nephew, or in another version his son-in-law, put to death. The *Historia Augusta* suggests it might have been a niece instead, or in addition. Which, if any, of these relatives is historical and whether there is any truth in the allegations, or which of them is the more accurate, is impossible to say.[1]

The Christian authors, of course, have a special grudge to bear: Aurelian was a persecutor, at least by intention (see Chapter 11). The influence of this tradition on the characterization of Aurelian in the literary sources generally should not be underestimated. The emperor Julian presents us with a portrait of Aurelian as a cruel man responsible for too many deaths, against which charge Sol alone among the gods is willing to defend him. Though Julian, it must be said, is certainly not one to have been swayed by Christian sympathies, he inherited a distorted caricature which he apparently accepted at face value.[2] The charge of cruelty against Aurelian is so commonplace that one is inclined to believe there is no smoke without fire. On the other hand, Malalas calls him magnanimous; and, with respect to Aurelian's treatment of his enemies at least, we have already observed ample proof that this characterization is nearer the mark.[3]

The theme of antagonism between the emperor and the senate is one of the most enduring throughout ancient historiography of the imperial period. This discourse is especially shrill in the literary sources dealing with the third century. It is nowhere more elaborate than in the pages of Aurelius Victor and the *HA* in their coverage of this period, in which the senate is portrayed as struggling against the erosion of its rights by a series of boorish and brutish emperors thrown up by the army. Gallienus, in whose reign senators effectively lost access to high military office, is denigrated, while Claudius, by virtue of his posthumous association with Constantine, is held up in contrast as the senate's benefactor. As we have seen (Chapter 7), the reign of Tacitus and the 'interregnum' that preceded it are presented as the renaissance of senatorial authority in which the emperor derived his power from the senate, the final effort to restore the senate to its rightful position of constitutional prominence, before this was swept aside by the autocratic regime that followed.[4]

This tendentious mythologizing naturally tended to blacken the reputation of Aurelian by comparison with the exemplary courtesy towards the senate ascribed to those whose reigns fall either side of his. It thereby exaggerated the caricature of a military autocrat as the implacable enemy of the senate. Only against the backdrop of this ongoing discourse can the portrayal of Aurelian, and in particular his relations with the senate, be properly understood. At the same time, it is important to bear in mind the contemporary epigraphic and numismatic evidence, from the study of which a far more complex and more balanced view is beginning to emerge. Modern prosopographical studies based on inscriptions have shed new light on Aurelian's relationship with the senatorial élite. Similarly, recent studies of coins and inscriptions have revealed far more about the emperor's relationship with the armies. Nevertheless, the traditional model casts a long shadow and the stigma still remains. To appreciate the legacy of the literary tradition, it is preferable first to consider Aurelian's relationship with the senate.

AURELIAN AND THE SENATE

Antagonism

The notion of a mutually antagonistic relationship between Aurelian and the senatorial élite centres particularly on the events of 271, when Aurelian proscribed and executed a number of senators in the aftermath of the urban riots. In order to judge these events properly it is vital to understand the political context in which they took place. When Aurelian was proclaimed emperor by the army at Sirmium in 270, the senate had already endorsed Quintillus, who was in Italy. Such an endorsement need not imply the wholehearted support of the majority of senators, but it is likely that at least some individual members of the senate actively preferred Quintillus to his rival. Supporting the losing side in those troubled times was often a costly mistake; and it requires no special reputation for cruelty on Aurelian's part to explain their fear of reprisals. Nevertheless, after the death of Quintillus and the spontaneous collapse of his cause, Aurelian met with a deputation from the senate at Revenna, and accepted the senate's protestations of loyalty without exacting reprisals of any kind. His magnanimity has largely been passed over without comment. In the event, his reward for showing clemency was further sedition.

In the spring of the following year, 271, Aurelian was obliged to suppress full-scale riots in Rome. While these riots unquestionably had significant political dimensions, what these might have been is not now easy to decipher from the cryptic notices we have in our sources. Certainly, senior members of Aurelian's administration, including the *rationalis* Felicissimus, were deeply involved. A number of senators were also implicated; presumably these included those who had most vociferously sided with Quintillus against Aurelian. Some of them may even have actively provoked the mob in order to further their own political agenda. It is clear that this agenda included the overthrow of Aurelian. The text of Zosimus implies, and there seems no reason for doubt, that these senators in some sense allied their cause with the two provincial rebellions that had broken out at this time: Septiminus in Dalmatia; and Domitianus, one of Gallienus' most powerful generals, probably in southern Gaul.[5] All this took place before Aurelian had had the opportunity to establish his authority, and against a backdrop of serious foreign invasions across the Danube, the last and most powerful of which threatened Rome itself. Small wonder, in these circumstances, that Aurelian's response to this sedition was vigorous and decisive.

Once the riots had been suppressed, those suspected of involvement, including a number of senators, were rounded up. Some were put to death. Others faced lesser punishments: at the very least the confiscation of their property. One of those executed at this time was apparently a member of that delegation which had greeted Aurelian at Ravenna in 270. The story, preserved in a couple of the late Greek sources, relates that at the audience in Ravenna the new emperor asked the assembled group of senators how he should rule wisely. One answered him that he should avail himself of both gold and iron: iron for those who proved recalcitrant and gold to reward those who co-operated. A short time later, this same senator was on the receiving end of his own advice, becoming the first to be given the iron.[6] We may presume, therefore, that the anonymous senator was found guilty of treason in the aftermath of the revolts at Rome in the spring of 271. How many senators shared in his fate, we have no way of knowing.

There is a presumption in some of our sources that the charges relating to senators were false. The real motive for such charges was the emperor's excessive cruelty; in addition, there was his desire to secure their wealth for the imperial coffers, emptied by the extreme demands of the previous few years. The latter allegation comes from a passage in Ammianus in which he compares the cruelty and greed of the emperor Valentinian, whom he strongly disliked, to Aurelian. This same comparison, again for the sake of denigrating Valentinian, is found in Jerome. These passages show that, certainly by the late fourth century, Aurelian's reputation for cruelty was undoubtedly a commonplace.[7] But its connection with the allegation of proscription for the sake of raising funds calls for caution. Allegations of this type were not new to Roman politics: Octavian and Antony and Septimius Severus are well-known examples. As with these earlier examples, however, there may be some truth in it. In 271 the imperial government was desperately short of cash, and Aurelian needed money to finance his projected eastern campaigns. The senatorial bias in the sources (notably those derived from the KG) easily lent itself to the conclusion that such proscriptions could only have been instigated by a cruel mind. We should not allow this to persuade us that Aurelian's actions were wholly unjustified or that replenishing the fisc was the sole motive for such proscriptions.

Modern scholars, taking their cue from the hostile literary accounts, have been all too given to exaggerating and complicating the rift between emperor and senate. This usually forms part of a wider presentation which seeks to portray Aurelian as a military despot inimical to the traditional values of the senate.[8] Various hypotheses have been advanced to support the inference of deep-seated antagonism. It has been argued that Aurelian removed the senate's right to issue bronze coinage and that this action in part led the senate to attempt his overthrow by inciting the urban riots in 271. This is highly unconvincing. As noted earlier, there is no reason to believe that the senate, at least by this date, possessed such a right for Aurelian to remove.[9] In the same vein, it has been suggested that the senate, in open defiance of Aurelian, issued coinage of its own, apparently with the full co-operation of the mint workers and Felicissimus. Some have identified the GENIVS PR coinage as being the product of this strange alliance: the SC marking on some of these coins being used to support the thesis of a senatorial issue. Again, the marking carries no such connotation at this date, and the attribution of this issue to the reign of Gallienus is no longer in doubt. Alternatively, it has been suggested that the coinage in question was the massive issue of DIVO CLAVDIO coinage, buying into the myth that Claudius was the senate's idol and Aurelian its enemy. The premise is ill-conceived and the issue of this coinage across the empire further undermines the thesis.[10] All this speculation must be laid to rest.

We are thus left with the bare facts that some senators were involved in the uprisings of 271, and that these men paid dearly for their treason. To extrapolate beyond this to a vision of mutual antagonism between Aurelian and the senate is both unwarranted and unhelpful. There is no evidence to suggest that a purge of the kind Aurelian apparently conducted in 271 was ever repeated during the rest of his reign. Nor is there any reason to believe in a smouldering hostility between the emperor and the senate for the duration of his reign. On the contrary, other evidence clearly demonstrates that Aurelian maintained a good working relationship with an important sector of the senatorial élite.

Co-operation

In contrast to the supposed antagonism between the rough soldier–emperor and the senate, portrayed in the literary sources, a quite different picture emerges from the prosopography of Aurelian's reign. It is clear from epigraphic and other evidence that Aurelian sought to promote and thereby associate himself closely with a number of individuals from the best-established families in the senatorial hierarchy. What is more, these connections clearly show strong continuity back to the reign of Claudius, universally acclaimed as a staunch supporter of the senate by the same writers who denounce Aurelian as the senate's implacable enemy.

Nowhere is this more strikingly illustrated than in his choice of consular colleague to share the honour of his first imperial consulship in January 271. Pomponius Bassus, one of the most senior and well-respected senators of the day, came from a distinguished senatorial family. He probably held his first consulship in 259 under Valerian and Gallienus. After holding various senior positions, including that of proconsul, he was appointed *corrector totius Italiae* by Claudius. Around the time of his second consulship he was appointed to the highly prestigious senatorial office of urban prefect. His tenure was not for a full year, and it is not clear whether it fell during the last few months of 270 or immediately following his second consulship in the latter half of 271. In the former, he may have owed his appointment to Claudius, Quintillus or Aurelian: if either of the first two, the continuity speaks for itself. If the latter date is accepted then he is certainly Aurelian's appointee, and the timing of the appointment, following the suppression of the revolts in the spring of 271, becomes highly significant.[11]

The same kind of continuity can be seen with the two ordinary consuls of the year 270, the last year over which Claudius presided. Flavius Antiochianus, for whom this was a second consulship and who was also urban prefect under Claudius in 269–70, held the prefecture again under Aurelian in 272; a very singular honour. Pomponia Ummidia, the wife of Antiochianus, was probably related to the well-placed Ummidii Quadrati and may well have been a relative of Pomponius Bassus. If so, this strengthens the idea of a group of leading senators who rose to prominence under Gallienus and Claudius and whose careers continued to prosper under Aurelian.[12]

The distinguished group of families (*gens*) of Virii also found favour under Aurelian. A certain Virius Orfitus was the consular colleague of Antiochianus in 270. Either the same man or, perhaps more likely, his father, was Antiochianus' successor as urban prefect in 273–4.[13] Another member of this same *gens*, Virius Lupus, was also an influential senator of his day. He was appointed governor of Arabia by Aurelian, possibly the first man to hold the post after Aurelian had reclaimed the eastern provinces from Zenobia in 272. He went on to become governor of Syria Coele, quite possibly still under Aurelian, in which capacity he clearly sided with Probus when the latter was proclaimed in 276. Under Probus he continued to prosper, becoming the emperor's consular colleague and urban prefect in 278.

He was also one of the earliest members of Aurelian's new college of priests, the *pontifices dei Solis*. The creation of this prestigious priestly college, the membership of which was almost entirely drawn from the senatorial aristocracy, further exemplifies the extent to which Aurelian did not snub the senate.[14]

T. Flavius Postumius Varus, a member of a well-connected family that had risen to prominence in the Antonine period, was Aurelian's choice of urban prefect for 271, and was thus presumably responsible for organizing the urban cohorts in defence of the regime during the riots of that year. If he was relieved from duty during the year, and replaced temporarily by Bassus, we cannot automatically assume disgrace.[15] Two other Postumii, probably related, found favour under Aurelian. Postumius Quietus was the ordinary consul for 272; his colleague was Junius Veldumianus, a member of a great and powerful senatorial family. Postumius Suagrus was appointed urban prefect as successor to Virius Orfitus in the last year of Aurelian's reign.[16]

The first-named consul for the year 273 was Tacitus. Some doubt has recently been cast on the identity of this individual. It is traditionally believed to be M. Claudius Tacitus, the future emperor. According to Zonaras, Claudius Tacitus would have been in his early seventies at the time: a somewhat improbable age for an individual to assume his first consulship. It has recently been suggested that Aurelian's consul might instead have been Aulus Caecina Tacitus, an important senator from a well-connected patrician family. If so, this provides a further example of the old-guard senatorial faction that prospered under Aurelian.[17]

The year 274, in which the emperor assumed his second consulship, was very important for Aurelian: it was the year in which he finally reunited the empire, celebrated both his quinquennalia and his triumph, introduced his great reform of the coinage, dedicated his temple to Sol and celebrated the first annual games in honour of the sun god. The man who was chosen to have the honour of sharing the consulship with the emperor in this highly significant year must have been a man of some consequence. It is therefore unfortunate that we know nothing at all about Aurelian's consular colleague in this year, one Capitolinus, whose place in this overall scheme is thus impossible to ascertain.

Nevertheless, the presence of all these other illustrious names among those who held high office under Aurelian should serve as a warning against the acceptance at face value of the portrait of Aurelian as the enemy of the senate. His appointment of individuals of senatorial rank to non-military administrative positions, including the appointment of the defeated Tetricus to a governorship in Italy, also serves to reinforce this warning. The picture that emerges from the prosopographical studies is of an emperor keen to work with the old senatorial order. There is no question of an emperor who either rejected the existing senatorial aristocracy or simply turned his back on the senate and regarded it with contempt. In fact, as we shall see, Aurelian promoted those who had done him the greatest service to high senatorial office, evidently considering this to be an honour befitting their loyalty to him. Far from revealing open hostility between emperor and senate, this suggests that he had considerable regard for the senate as an institution. This ties in with what we know, from other evidence, of Aurelian's naturally conservative character.

There is no need to attempt to whitewash Aurelian. That he had a number of individuals put to death during his reign there can be no doubt. In this period of almost constant sedition and assassination it would be remarkable had it been otherwise. Unsentimental and even severe he may have been, but the constantly repeated charges of excessive cruelty that we find in the literary sources must be treated with caution, especially where they relate to the senate. The imputation that Aurelian adopted an anti-senatorial stance, like the charge of excessive cruelty towards both senators and others, is largely based on a stereotypical caricature of the third-century *vir militaris*. With a more balanced assessment it appears that the reputation for cruelty of the alleged *paedagogus senatorum* has been grossly exaggerated.[18]

AURELIAN AND HIS ARMIES

Aurelian, like the majority of emperors in this period, was a career soldier. He understood the army's needs. In terms of inspiring loyalty in his officers and men, he fully appreciated the central importance not only of personal leadership and of winning victories but also of securing adequate payment, food, equipment and lodging for his troops. A supreme tactician, Aurelian understood the paramount importance of the kind of military discipline on the field of battle that had enabled Rome to conquer the Mediterranean world. Although highly conservative in outlook, he understood the need to adapt to new military circumstances, and many of his reforms look forward to the following century.

Trusted companions

Aurelian continued the policy of Gallienus of promoting to positions of military command men of an equestrian and military background rather than senators. At the same time, he rewarded those whom he trusted and who had proved their worth by appointing these new men to the highest senatorial offices alongside the established nobility.

Foremost among these was Julius Placidianus, the *praefectus vigilum* whom Claudius had stationed to guard the lower Rhone valley from attack from the north when Victorinus' Rhine army had marched on Autun. Some time in the early 270s he was promoted to praetorian prefect. He was also accorded senatorial rank, either by adlection to the senate at the time of his promotion to the praetorian prefecture or by virtue of his appointment to the consulship in 273, whether or not this occurred at the same moment. It may even be that he assumed the consulship, and perhaps the prefecture, *in absentia* while still stationed in southern Gaul. Such a rapid rise requires some explanation. The revolt of Domitianus in the spring of 271, which probably took place in southern Gaul, failed. We know that Placidianus was stationed in the right place at the right time. The most plausible inference from this data is that Placidianus' promotion was his reward for suppressing Domitianus' potentially extremely dangerous revolt.[19]

Another military man who apparently received high senatorial office in recognition of his loyalty to Aurelian was Marcellinus. After the initial victory over Palmyra in 272, the emperor entrusted him with the full command of the east, as prefect of Mesopotamia and *rector Orientis*. The identification of this Marcellinus with Aurelian's consular colleague of 275, though not conclusive, is very plausible. If the identification is accepted, then the honour of being adlected to the senate as the emperor's consular colleague was a fitting reward for the constancy that Marcellinus had shown during the spring of 273 when tempted by Apsaeus to turn against his master. It is far from improbable that this Marcellinus is also to be identified with the Aurelius Marcellinus who was *vp dux ducenarius* at Verona in the sole reign of Gallienus.[20]

M. Aurelius Sebastianus was the governor of Moesia Inferior during Aurelian's reign. The exact dates of his governorship are not known, but he seems to have been in office in 272 and very probably was entrusted with the defence of this critical part of the empire's frontier when Aurelian left the Balkans to march against Palmyra.[21] L. Flavius Aper had risen from *praepositus* with the Dacian legions stationed at Poetovio under Gallienus to become governor of Pannonia Inferior, possibly early in Aurelian's reign. He may well be the same man who later became father-in-law and praetorian prefect to the emperor Numerian.[22]

Four further *duces* close to the emperor are mentioned in the literary sources. M. Aurelius Probus, the future emperor, may have headed the forces which recaptured Egypt in 272. He may also have been promoted by Aurelian to the supreme command of the cavalry, an extremely powerful position previously occupied by both Aurelian himself and Claudius.[23] Jerome mentions a *dux* by the name of Pompeianus as one of Aurelian's principal generals in the campaign against Palmyra. We are told he was known by the *cognomen* Francus, and that his descendants, including the presbyter Evagrius, still lived at Antioch in the late fourth century. He may have been a native Antiochene, though this does not adequately explain his unusual last name. It is on balance preferable to accept that Pompeianus Francus was by origin a Frank who rose to high rank under Aurelian, served in the east and finally settled in Antioch, where his descendants continued to live for several generations.[24] Then there is Mucapor, cited by Victor and the *HA* as the ringleader of the plot which finally killed Aurelian. He was clearly a senior officer in the field army in Thrace at the end of Aurelian's reign and may have been of Thracian origin. No more is known, except that he was put to death by Tacitus.[25] Finally, the *HA* refers to a certain Firmus as *dux limitis Africani idemque proconsul*. A brave attempt has been made to rescue this individual from the fate of so many of the characters casually mentioned in that source by making him a governor of Crete and Cyrene.[26]

From papyri and inscriptions we know something of the governors of Egypt under Aurelian. The prefect of Egypt at the time of Aurelian's accession, Tenagino Probus, is not attested at all in the papyrological evidence, but his prefecture is alluded to in literary sources and confirmed by a single inscription.[27] When Probus committed suicide towards the close of the Palmyrene military operation in Egypt, perhaps in late November 270, someone must have taken his place. It now appears that the gap was filled by his deputy, Julius Marcellinus. This is possibly the same man who had been a military tribune stationed at Verona under his more illustrious namesake, Aurelius Marcellinus, in about 265; he may also have held a command in Alpes Cottiae in the intervening period.[28] The papyrological evidence has now been conclusively shown to prove that the acting-prefecture of Marcellinus preceded the prefecture of Statilius

Ammianus, the latter of which can now be very firmly dated to the late spring and summer of 272. It is therefore highly likely that Ammianus was installed as the new prefect by Aurelian's counter-invasion force in the late spring of that year. Whether Marcellinus remained as acting-prefect throughout the intervening seventeen or so months is not known; but it remains a plausible hypothesis.[29] From the beginning of 274, documents attest Claudius Firmus as the successor of Statilius Ammianus. He is given the unusual title of *corrector* of Egypt, instead of prefect, as well as the courtesy title, *vir clarissimus*. This implies that he was a senator, which is not without precedent. Nevertheless, Aurelian's appointment of a senator to this position of great responsibility is highly significant with regard to Aurelian's relationship with the senate and his co-operation with individual senators.[30]

Like Gallienus before him, Aurelian clearly had the ability to single out talented individuals for promotion. In marked contrast to Gallienus, however, he seems for the most part to have inspired great loyalty among his immediate subordinates, even when these generals, like Placidianus in southern Gaul in 271 or Marcellinus in eastern Syria in 273, were tempted by others to desert his cause. In view of this, it is perhaps slightly ironic that he should have shared Gallienus' fate, though the dedicated loyalty of the majority of his troops is probably the best explanation for the remarkable reluctance of any of his officers to push themselves forward in the aftermath of his assassination.

Military reforms and military discipline

Although very little can be said with any certainty, it appears that Aurelian presided over a number of subtle but significant military reforms. In his extensive and innovative use of light cavalry, most especially the units of Dalmatian and Mauritanian horse, he clearly continued the policies of Gallienus. At the same time, he also appears to have learnt the value of heavy-armed mailed cavalry, or *cataphractarii*, from his Palmyrene campaigns, and to have extended the use of such troops within the Roman army. In this, he appears to have anticipated developments in the early part of the next century.[31]

Aurelian anticipated future military developments in other significant ways. He recruited large numbers of foreign, mostly German, soldiers whom he apparently preserved as tactical units under their own commanders instead of integrating them into the existing Roman army structure. We know of a cavalry unit of

Vandals accepted as a form of tribute by Aurelian in 271 and it appears he also employed infantry units of Alamanni in this way. Like the promotion of German individuals to high military office within the empire, this looks forward to developments in the fourth and fifth centuries.[32] The emergence at around this time of a crack corps of hand-picked troops known as *protectores*, whose function was to serve the emperor as special guards, is an important development of the second-half of the third century. The names of two brothers, both styled *protectores Aureliani Augusti*, are preserved on a commemorative inscription from Bithynia.[33]

One of the secrets of Aurelian's success as a general was undoubtedly his emphasis on discipline, even if his reputation as a strict disciplinarian may be somewhat exaggerated in our sources. His employment of highly disciplined manoeuvres, like that which proved so spectacularly successful at Immae in 272, testify to the efficacy of his rigorous programme. He thereby rekindled army morale and earned himself the right to the title Restorer of the Army.[34] Aurelian may have hoped that strict discipline would also deter sedition. If so, it was a forlorn expectation, as his end all too clearly shows. Nor was the plot that killed Aurelian the only mutiny of his brief reign. Besides the dangerous, but ultimately abortive, revolts of Domitianus and Septiminus in 271, a fragment of Petrus Patricius records another incident in which Aurelian faced down a fledgeling rebellion by appearing in person before the mutinous troops.[35]

Symbolic expressions of the special relationship

In these troubled times, when the armies of the empire all too frequently acted as kingmakers, the special symbolic relationship between emperor and army which had always been a central feature of imperial ideology and iconography became still more prominent. This development is especially noticeable on the coinage, the principal function of which was to pay the troops. In various ways, the advertisement of this special relationship was designed to focus the loyalty of the armies on the emperor. These included titles borne by the emperor and his consort and the nomenclature of individual military units, various expressions of the armies' loyalty and of the success in battle which the emperor and his troops achieved, together with various forms of ceremony symbolic of these ideas.

In addition to financial reward, the armies' loyalty to the emperor had a religious dimension. The distribution of army pay was symbolically associated with the sanctity of the imperial image, just as it was literally connected to the exercise of imperial power.[36] Furthermore, the religious vows made by the soldiers on the emperor's accession were repeated annually, with special emphasis on multiples of five: the quinquennial and decennial years. These vows were sometimes advertised on the coinage, usually in association with imperial victory, presumably destined for special anniversary donatives. The existence of such references on the coinage of Aurelian is controversial.[37]

The military image that Aurelian wished to project can be assessed by looking at his coin portrait style. To a greater extent than for any previous emperor, the obverse portraiture of Aurelian is predominantly military in character: the vast preponderance of his coin portraits show him in armour. Many also show him wearing the *paludamentum*, the military commander's cloak. Certain coin portraits of Severina may also show the empress wearing this military garment, stressing her association with the armies.[38]

The association between the empress and the armies is made more explicit on inscriptions which refer to Severina as *mater castrorum*, 'the mother of the camps', a title occasionally applied to empresses from the mid-second century onwards. One of these also calls her the 'mother of the senate and the homeland'.[39] The predominantly military flavour of the coin types issued in Severina's name also shows how the symbolic ties between the emperor and his soldiers could be extended to his consort. By far the most common type for Severina bears the legend CONCORDIAE MILITVM, depicting the divine personification of Concord holding two military standards.[40] These coins stress the unanimity (*concordia*) of the troops in their support of Aurelian.

The emperor's own coinage placed an even greater emphasis on this idea. No other single concept is so persistently mentioned on the coinage throughout the entire length of Aurelian's reign. At one point early in the reign such types predominated.[41] They were, indeed, standard for this period, as were those which emphasized the fidelity (*fides*) of the troops, usually depicting the personification of good faith holding military standards. On the coinage of Aurelian's reign the special relationship between Aurelian and his men is underlined by a rare type depicting the emperor himself in place of Fides.[42]

Another important quality of the imperial armies which received much attention on the coinage of the early part of Aurelian's reign was their courage (*virtus*), without which the emperor could not be victorious.[43] The rise in the importance of the cavalry under Gallienus had been reflected on coins which singled out these units for special mention. In keeping with this idea, the coinage of Aurelian also praised the courage of the cavalry, which he himself had commanded just prior to his accession. The courage of the troops from Aurelian's native Illyricum also received special mention on his coinage, as did the personified spirit of the troops from this region and also that of the soldiers in general.[44] Certain coin types depict the emperor receiving a small victory from an armoured figure, who may represent the god Mars or the personification Virtus, but who in any case symbolically stands for the army as a whole. Some such were minted with the legends VIRTVS (or VIRT) MILITVM and VIRTVS AVG(usti) interchangeably, thereby graphically re-inforcing the symbolic relationship between emperor and soldiers.[45] The same parallel minting is found with types depicting the emperor riding on horseback, holding a spear with his right hand raised as if acknowledging the cheers of his men.[46]

A further aspect of this symbolic relationship was the practice of renaming military units in the emperor's honour. Traditionally, army units bore the name of the emperor who had raised them. The practice of renaming existing units after the reigning emperor, nominally at least on the basis of reorganization, was introduced by Commodus. The almost continual restructuring of the army in the third century allowed plenty of opportunity for this practice to continue. For Aurelian, two inscriptions bear witness to this practice, revealing a cohort and an entire legion with the surname *Aureliana*.[47] Aurelian's achievement in restoring the army to its former glory and self-respect and his close working relationship with his soldiers are further reflected on a coin type from Cyzicus late in the reign which hails him as *restitvtor exerciti*. The iconography shows Mars, as the personification of Rome's fighting force, handing the emperor a globe.[48]

Victory

The association between the emperor and victory was central to the way in which imperial power was perceived and legitimated in the Roman empire. More than anything else, an emperor was judged by his ability to secure victory in battle. This had always been true, but never more so than in the mid-third century. The emperors of this period thus bore a large number of titles which emphasized their role as supreme military commander and which trumpeted their successes in this role. None more deservedly than Aurelian. The references to victory on his coinage, though standard for the period, do not, for once, exaggerate. Specific victories are occasionally celebrated on inscriptions also.[49] The laurel crown, one of the most important imperial insignia from the time of Augustus, was also linked to the idea of victory. Its appearance on the coin portraiture of this period was limited by the infrequency of the denominations on which it was used. It was, however, standard on the principal gold piece, the aureus.

Following the general rule of the day, Aurelian's accession was an army coup, set in the military camp, and marked by ceremonial acclamations hailing the new emperor as *imperator*. These *acclamationes* were repeated annually, the tally sometimes being recorded on coins and inscriptions. At intervals throughout his reign, Aurelian also received further acclamations as *imperator* from his troops in recognition of particular victories and these too were enumerated on coins and inscriptions. As with other emperors of this period, the two systems of reckoning have given rise to some anomalies that cannot be adequately resolved and it has not been possible to relate the acclamations to specific victories in the field.[50] By the mid-third century such associations had begun to seem overworked. Apparently in compensation, Aurelian was hailed as *perpetuus imperator* on a large number of inscriptions, almost exclusively from North Africa. Many of these also include a number of other expansive titles which serve to underline the enormity of the emperor's achievement through his long series of victories.[51]

Invictus, meaning 'unconquered' or even 'invincible', was a title redolent with heroic and divine connotations. It was an epithet applied to a number of deities associated with victory, including Jupiter, Hercules, Mars and Sol. It was also an epithet strongly associated with Alexander the Great and adopted by some of his successors. It thus naturally came to be applied to Roman emperors, at first only unofficially in works of literature, but already by the reign of Trajan it is found on Greek inscriptions. In its Latin form it did not appear until the reign of Commodus, but by the mid-third century it formed part of the standard epigraphic imperial titulature. The word INVICTVS appeared on the reverse of imperial coinage from 193, usually in a context emphasizing its solar connotations. It is, however, only under Aurelian that the imperial title Invictus makes its first appearance on the obverse of the coinage. The innovation is only found at the mint of Serdica and reflects the adventurous spirit of that mint generally.[52]

In the title *magnus et invictus*, which is attested for Aurelian on a couple of inscriptions, the reference back to Alexander is still more overt. It must be understood in the context of the general *imitatio Alexandri* which, though always a significant element of imperial imagery, had become much more pronounced early in the third century.[53] The inscriptions of Aurelian also grant him the somewhat tautological title *invictissimus*, as well as another superlative with much the same sense, *victoriosissimus*.[54]

Even in anticipation of his reconquest of the east, he began to be referred to as *restitutor orientis*, presumably as a justification for his actions.[55] In the aftermath of the great victory in 272, he immediately assumed the grander title *restitutor orbis*, which by the summer of 273 had eclipsed the earlier title. Although both titles had been borne by Valerian and Gallienus, they more accurately reflect the reality in Aurelian's case. More than any other single title, *restitutor orbis* symbolizes Aurelian's achievement. From its first appearance in the late summer of 272, it rapidly became an important element in his titulature and was very widely used on coins, particularly in the period 272–4. More than any other emperor, Aurelian made this title his own. The sheer volume of coinage bearing this title for Aurelian was itself an innovation and it is also widely attested on inscriptions.[56] Inscriptions also accorded him the titles *restitutor patriae* and *conservator orbis*.[57] On the coinage, he is hailed as *restitutor gentis* and *restitutor saeculi*, in addition to the *restitutor exerciti* previously mentioned.[58] Following the defeat of Tetricus and the reintegration of the west, Aurelian was apparently acclaimed *restitutor Galliarum* and *restitutor libertatis* on inscriptions in that region.[59]

The emperor's victories were also linked to the provision of peace. From the time of Augustus, the title *pater patriae* had formed part of the symbolic representation of the victorious emperor as the bringer of peace. In keeping with the tradition of his age, Aurelian assumed the title on his accession.[60] Inscriptions from Gaul also accord him the title *pacator et restitutor orbis*. The date of these cannot be fixed either internally or from their location, since they were set up in Narbonensis. But the appearance of the title *pacator orbis* on the coinage of Aurelian after the Châlons campaign confirms the most obvious inference that the inscriptions and the title post-date the defeat of Tetricus in 274. Similarly, in 272, following the initial victory over Palmyra, Aurelian also assumed the novel title *pacator orientis*.[61] On certain North African inscriptions he is accorded the equally unprecedented title *pacatissimus imperator*.[62]

174

Among the titles which most directly related the emperor to victory were the *cognomina victoriarum*, the honorific titles awarded to the emperor in relation to victories over particular enemies. It is certain that Aurelian was accorded the titles Germanicus Maximus for his defeat of the Juthungi in 271 and Gothicus Maximus for the decisive Balkan victory later that same year. He assumed the title Parthicus (or Persicus) Maximus for his victories in the east in 272, on the excuse that the Persians had sent assistance to Palmyra, and Carpicus Maximus for his victory over the Carpi the following winter. These four titles are attested on a large number of inscriptions throughout the empire and are the only ones recorded on the papyri from Egypt. They also appear together on the important inscription set up at Rome in 274 by Virius Orfitus, his prefect of the city, to mark the emperor's triumph.[63] Most scholars therefore agree that these four, and these four alone, were the victory titles officially recognized by the senate at Rome. Whether or not one accepts the 'official' thesis, it is clear that other titles could be and were meaningfully applied to Aurelian.[64]

A number of other such titles are attested, though the attribution of some to Aurelian is questionable. The titles Arabicus Maximus and Palmyrenicus Maximus probably represent one and the same title (though they are certainly not to be elided with Parthicus/Persicus Maximus). In either version, the title clearly refers to Aurelian's defeat of Zenobia.[65] Dacicus Maximus, attested on only one or possibly two inscriptions, must refer to Aurelian's campaigns in the Balkans in 272; it is clearly not identical to Carpicus Maximus but its relationship with the latter remains unclear. It is unlikely to refer in any way to the withdrawal that Aurelian had recently ordered from transdanubian Dacia.[66] The title Britannicus Maximus, often attributed to Aurelian, is now doubtful. The same applies to the title Sarmaticus Maximus, which is also among the victory titles attributed to Aurelian in the *HA*. The remaining titles in the list supplied by that author, Armenicus [*sic*] and Adiabenicus, must simply be dismissed as fiction.[67]

Many of the titles reviewed above demonstrate the inflationary tendencies in imperial titulature of this period, either by the addition of the suffix *maximus* or by the use of a superlative form. This emphasizes the need for hyperbole to justify the claims of a particular individual in this period of almost constant rebellion. None of this is to detract from the fact that Aurelian deserved these accolades more than any other emperor between Septimius Severus and Diocletian.

Military ceremonial

The appearance of the emperor before his assembled troops afforded a valuable opportunity to strengthen the bond between them. Examples of such occasions included the formal address (*adlocutio*) and the audiences granted to foreign embassies following a Roman victory. By good fortune, a description of Aurelian's reception of one such an embassy has survived, preserved in a fragment from the contemporary Greek historian, Dexippus.[68]

After describing the battle in which Aurelian defeated the Juthungi, Dexippus goes on to give details of the parley that followed. Aurelian, sensing the self-assurance of the Juthungi, refused to grant their ambassadors an audience until the following day. As the next day dawned, the emperor,

> in order to intimidate the enemy, drew up his army in battle array. When the muster was to his satisfaction, he mounted a high rostrum wrapped in a purple robe, and arrayed the whole battle formation around him in a crescent. Beside him he placed his commanding officers on horseback. Behind the emperor were the standards of the select troops – golden eagles, imperial images, and banners with the names of the units highlighted in golden letters – all displayed on silver-plated poles. Once these things were all arranged in this manner, the Juthungi were brought in.

The embassy was suitably impressed, but none the less delivered the uncompromising terms under which the Juthungi were prepared to make peace. Aurelian, for his part, held his ground and gave the Juthungi no indication that he would give in to their demands. Despairing of reaching a settlement, the embassy returned to its people.

It must be conceded that the trustworthiness of this highly rhetorical description is not above suspicion. The figures are exaggerated and the speech and demeanour that Dexippus attributes to the representatives of the Juthungi owe far more to literary and rhetorical topoi than to factual information. Nevertheless, the elaborate reception which Dexippus here describes gives us a reliable sense of what this kind of imperial pomp must have been like in the mid-third century. The original audience whom Dexippus was addressing was contemporary with this event. The precise details of what was said at the parley may well have been distorted, but the overall flavour of the pageant must retain a ring of truth.[69] Such ceremonies were designed to impress those present with the splendour of the emperor's majesty: not merely the enemy but also, and perhaps more importantly, the emperor's own men.

THE TRIUMPH

Public spectacle played a vitally important role in justifying an emperor's claim to rule the empire, especially where it could be linked directly to military victory. It also formed an important aspect of his relationship with his subjects, most particularly, but not exclusively, the armies. The emperor's arrival in a given city or town was a ceremonial occasion. The ceremony of *adventus* was often commemorated on the coinage of this period. Several coins of Aurelian's reign depict his ceremonial entry into a city on horseback carrying a long sceptre and raising his hand in salutation.[70]

Of all the imperial ceremonies which served to cement the bond between the emperor on the one hand and his troops and his subjects generally on the other, none was more splendid or more central to the symbolism of imperial authority than the triumph. A profoundly traditional Roman religious festival, the triumph was the clearest expression of the link between divine favour and military victory. In the traditional triumph of republican times the triumphant general came as close as Roman tradition would allow to assuming the status of a divine ruler: so close that a slave was required to travel behind the triumphant whispering in his ear the reminder that he was mortal. Under the empire, triumphs had preserved a special place in Roman ceremonial, not only because they remained an imperial monopoly but also because of their comparative rarity. Few emperors in the third century could have claimed a triumph with as much justification as Aurelian. It was held to mark his victories over the Vandals, the Juthungi, the Goths, the Carpi and (nominally, at least) the Persians. It was also held to celebrate the restoration of the unity of the empire and the emperor's decisive victories over Zenobia and Tetricus.[71]

The event was staged in the autumn of 274, after Aurelian's return from Gaul. It was timed, probably consciously, to coincide with the celebration of Aurelian's quinquennalia. Aurelian had also chosen the year 274 to assume his second ordinary consulship, as was customary for a quinquennalian year.[72] The triumph was, without doubt, a magnificent spectacle. Regrettably, there is no reference to the event on the extant coins and inscriptions and the literary sources for the most part make only passing references to it. Eutropius is somewhat more informative than most. He tells us that Aurelian returned to Rome where he held a noble triumph in celebration of his recapture of both east and west, in which Zenobia and Tetricus were paraded before the emperor's triumphal chariot.[73] The only surviving account to go into the details of the event is that in the *HA*. It is in typical style:

> [*Aurel.* 33] Aurelian's triumph . . . was a most splendid affair. There were three royal chariots: one was Odenathus', elaborately worked in gold and silver and spangled with gems; another, equally elaborate, had been presented to Aurelian by the king of Persia; the third Zenobia had made for herself, hoping to survey the city of Rome in it. Indeed her hope was not in vain, for it was in that chariot that she entered the city, but as a defeated woman and a captive. There was another chariot, drawn by four stags, said to have belonged to the king of the Goths. It was in this, as many have passed on the memory, that Aurelian rode to the Capitol, there to sacrifice the stags which he had vowed to Jupiter Optimus Maximus when he had captured them at the same time as the chariot. This was preceded by twenty elephants and two hundred tamed wild beasts of various kinds from Lybia and Palestine. These Aurelian presented to private citizens immediately afterwards so as not to burden the privy purse. Four tigers were also led in procession, and giraffes, elks and other such beasts each in order. Then followed eight hundred pairs of gladiators in addition to the captives of the various barbarian peoples: Blemmyes, Axomites, Arabs from Arabia Felix, Indians, Bactrians, Iberians, Saracens and Persians, each bearing gifts; Goths, Alans, Roxolani, Sarmatians, Franks, Suebi, Vandals and Germans, all with their hands bound. Foremost among these passed the chief citizens of Palmyra who had survived and also some Egyptians, on account of their rebellion.
>
> [34.1] Ten women were also led in the procession. They had been captured while fighting in men's attire among the Goths after many of their number had been destroyed. These women carried a notice which indicated that they were of the Amazon race. Indeed notices were borne before each of the captive peoples giving their names.
>
> [34.2–3] Among the captives was Tetricus, dressed in a

scarlet cloak, a yellow tunic and Gallic trousers, and with him his son, whom he had proclaimed as emperor in Gaul. There too Zenobia was paraded, adorned with jewels and in golden chains held aloft by others . . .

[*Tyr. trig.* 30.24–6] She was . . . led in triumph in such splendour that nothing more magnificent was ever seen by the Roman people. First of all, she was covered with huge gems, such that she laboured under the weight of her jewellery; indeed it is reported that, though a very strong woman, she very often came to a halt, saying she was unable to bear the weight of the gems. Besides this her feet were fettered with gold and her hands were in golden manacles; not even her neck lacked a golden chain, which was supported by a Persian guardsman.

[*Aurel.* 34.3–5] . . . Golden crowns from every city were paraded, recorded on prominent notices. Then came the Roman populace itself, followed by the banners of the guilds and of the military camps, the heavy-mailed cavalry, the royal treasures, the whole army and the senate (though rather more sadly, as they saw senators being led in triumph). Each added on more to the length of the procession. It was already almost the ninth hour by the time it finally reached the Capitol, and late into the night when it got back to the palace.

[34.6] During the following days spectacles were given for the people: theatrical plays, chariot racing in the circus, wild beast hunts, gladiatorial shows and staged sea battles.

All this makes excellent reading, but how much of it was based on anything more than the author's fertile imagination is another matter.[74] Among his embellishments should probably be placed the impressive-sounding list of conquered peoples. It has been suggested that this may originally have been composed of two lists, one of envoys and the other of captives; but it certainly cannot be relied on as historically accurate. Another of the *HA*'s fictions is almost certainly the stag-drawn chariot of the Gothic king. Zonaras tells us, more plausibly, that Aurelian rode in a chariot drawn by elephants; the version in the *HA* may have been inspired by a mistranslation from a Greek source.[75]

The details aside, we can legitimately infer it was a truly spectacular event, even by Roman standards. The days of spectacles that the author tells us followed the event itself were a standard feature of such occasions. Altogether it must easily have measured up to the other two grand spectacles that the city had witnessed in living memory: the millennial celebrations under Philip and the decennalia of Gallienus. And more than on either of these last two occasions, the soldiers and the people of Rome, indeed of the whole empire, had much for which to give thanks to the gods.

AUTOCRATIC IMAGERY AND MILITARY DESPOTISM

Many modern scholars have postulated a shift towards a more overtly autocratic style of rulership and imperial imagery under Aurelian. This must be seen in its proper context. Generally speaking, the extent to which autocratic and regal imagery had surrounded imperial power from its inception has not been appreciated. Augustus had been careful to avoid presenting too overtly monarchical a self-image, but the theology of victory by which his position of power was expressed and legitimated was inevitably influenced by the image of the archetypal divinely inspired victor, Alexander. Thus, under the growing influence of the Greek-speaking part of the empire, Hellenistic royal titulature and insignia became increasingly acceptable under his successors. What we find in the age of Aurelian is a great deal of emphasis on tradition and a tendency to exaggerate and embellish time-honoured formulas rather than a break with the past.

The problem is exemplified in the use of the title *dominus* (*noster*), '(our) lord'. It is most commonly associated with the period which began towards the end of the third century, until recently known as the 'Dominate', when autocratic rule allegedly became the accepted norm. In practice, the title had always been applied to emperors in common parlance and literary works; during the course of the second century it became an established part of the imperial titulature on inscriptions. Its first appearance on the imperial coinage under Aurelian must therefore be understood as part of a gradual trend rather than a radical step towards autocratic representation.[76] Inscriptions to Severina likewise accorded her the title *domina*. Aurelian is styled 'ruler of the earth, of the sea and of the whole world' on an inscription from Moesia Inferior.[77]

The emblem most closely associated with royalty and autocratic rule in the ancient world was the diadem. In origin it was a cloth fillet worn round the head, adopted by Alexander the Great as a token of his victories over the Persians. It acquired such strong monarchical connotations during the Hellenistic era that it was deliberately avoided by Roman emperors, at least in public, down to the mid-third century. From the early fourth century, Constantine and his successors adopted an elaborately bejewelled version of this royal headband. There is evidence to suggest that Constantine's act was anticipated in the third century, as part of an increasingly overt *imitatio Alexandri*. A statue of Severus Alexander, now in Naples, shows the emperor nude but for the victor's fillet around his head. Although the athletic context provides a plausible 'excuse' for him to be sporting such a headband, the allusion to the royal diadem of Severus Alexander's Macedonian hero cannot have escaped his contemporaries.[78]

A less oblique reference is to be found on a medallion of Gallienus, portraying him with flowing locks, head tilted back, his gaze upturned in the classic pose of Alexander the Great and wearing a fillet tied at the nape. Although part of the fillet is hidden by his hair the allusion to Alexander is unmistakable. The identification of this headgear as a diadem is confirmed by a local coin type from Iconium. The medallion thus anticipates by some sixty years the *vicennalia* portraits of Constantine I, and apparently vindicates the statement in the *HA* that Gallienus was the first Roman emperor to wear the diadem.[79]

The same claim, however, is made elsewhere in the extant literature on behalf of Aurelian, linked to his alleged adoption of other regal and bejewelled garments. In one source, his diadem is said to have been decorated with a star, suggesting an image of the emperor as cosmocrator – universal ruler – which may point to the origins of the decorated diadem of later centuries. No coin portraits of Aurelian wearing the diadem have yet come to light, and without them it is unwise to trust the literary notices too far. Nevertheless, the evidence as it stands helps to confirm that Constantine's decision to adopt the diadem had antecedents in the third century, and ties in well with other evidence suggesting that Aurelian took on a more overtly autocratic style of representation.[80] In common with all third-century empresses, Severina is depicted as wearing the stephane. This crescent head-dress, not unlike a plain modern tiara, was in origin a divine emblem, which had become the standard head-dress of Hellenistic queens. As such, it is another aspect of the imperial adoption of Hellenistic royal imagery found on the coinage and inscriptions of Aurelian's time.[81]

The titles and imagery applied to Aurelian do not suggest a radical departure from Roman traditions and ideals. On the contrary, the main emphasis is on reiterating and amplifying images already imbued with the sanctity of tradition. Nor should Aurelian's adoption of certain elements of monarchical titles and insignia be seen as a slap in the face for the senate. The senate was by this time a somewhat anachronistic institution, and its influence was sharply declining. It is not that Aurelian had contempt for the senate: he was far too traditional. He may have been somewhat blunt, but his priorities remained the serious military and economic problems facing the empire which the senate as an institution could do little to help solve.

In these circumstances, the emperor's relationship with the armies was crucial. In the drive to improve the efficiency of the Roman military machine in this period, senators had inevitably lost out to professional soldiers, both as commanders and consequently as emperors. Aurelian was an army man; he understood the army, and the army apparently believed in him. The symbolic ties which bound emperor and army together had evolved over centuries, but in Aurelian's case they contained a more literal truth than for many of his predecessors.

11

THE EMPEROR AND THE DIVINE

In the Roman world, just as military success was understood to be proof of divine favour, so the emperor's relationship with the divine was seen as the key to his success. The representation of that relationship, to be found on the coins, inscriptions and monuments of the period, was thus central to the legitimation of an emperor's power. Under Aurelian, these ideas reached new heights and in particular found expression in the association of the emperor with a new solar religion. This must be understood in the context of the conservatism of both Aurelian and his age, and against the backdrop of continued emphasis on the traditional Roman pantheon and the imperial ruler cult. Such was the importance placed on these ideas that those who obstinately refused to participate in such activities were seen as jeopardizing the safety of the empire as well as committing treason and sacrilege.

DIVINE PATRONAGE AND DIVINE POWER

Aurelian and Severina are represented on their coins and inscriptions as having a very special relationship with the gods. They are sometimes depicted with specific divine attributes. While some of this may appear quite startling to modern eyes, brought up in a long tradition of Judeo-Christian ideology, it should be noted that such associations were customary. Indeed, in this respect the coinage of Aurelian's reign falls far short of the divine identifications applied to Gallienus only a few years before.

The emperor's piety towards the gods was the cause of his good luck, which in turn enabled him to reign victorious and undefeated. This special relationship is reflected in the standard imperial titles *pius felix invictus*. Aurelian's only innovation was to include the title Invictus in his obverse titulature.[1] The emperor's piety, reflected in his title Pontifex Maximus, is stressed on certain coins depicting the emperor and the personification Pietas sacrificing at an altar. Severina is accorded the unusual superlative title *piissima*.[2]

Victoria, Mars, Hercules

The deities with whom Aurelian was directly or indirectly associated were often closely linked with the notion of imperial victory and often portrayed as the emperor's companions-at-arms.[3] Given the pervasiveness of the theme of victory on his inscriptions, references to the goddess Victoria on Aurelian's coinage are surprisingly few. She is sometimes depicted on certain coins with the legend RESTITVTOR ORBIS crowning the emperor with a wreath. On an inscription, Severina is herself referred to as an incarnation of the goddess of victory.[4]

Another deity very closely associated with the idea of imperial victory on the coinage of this period is Mars. The association itself dates back to Augustus.[5] Mars is mentioned specifically on a number of Aurelian's coins, usually with the epithet *pacifer*, but on a few coins with the epithet *invictus*. These coins imply that Aurelian could count on the assistance of the god of war to bring about victory and peace, and they also draw a parallel between the warrior–ruler and his divine partner. This identification with Mars is taken still further on coin types which portray the god encircled by the emperor's titulature.[6] Similarly, on other types with the same or analogous iconography, Mars represents the emperor's, or else embodies the armies', courage (*virtus*). Obverse coin portraits of Aurelian in a three-quarter back view, nude but for a strap over his shoulder, holding a spear and shield, are likewise almost certainly meant to represent the emperor as Mars; even those that do not depict the emperor in heroic nudity may retain an echo of this divine association.[7]

Similarly Aurelian associated himself with Hercules. The mortal hero who became a god after ridding the world of terrible monsters was an obvious choice of model for the emperors of the third century. Such symbolism had been thoroughly exploited by both Gallienus and Postumus. As with Mars, Hercules is represented as the embodiment of Aurelian's valour. On a pair of inscriptions set up at Pesaro in 271, Hercules is represented as Aurelian's co-regent who helped him to defeat the Germanic invaders.[8]

Other divine allies

Venus was another deity intimately connected with Rome's destiny, as the mother of Aeneas the founder of the gens *Iulia* from which all the emperors symbolically traced their descent via Augustus and Julius Caesar. A coin type issued for Aurelian at Cyzicus early in the reign depicts Venus Victrix, helmeted and carrying her spear and shield. Towards the end of Aurelian's reign, Severina was associated with both Venus Victrix and Venus Felix, whose cult at Rome was centred on the temple of Venus et Roma in the Forum. The temple, built by Hadrian, was in some sense a counterpart to the provincial temples of the imperial cult dedicated to Roma et Augustus.[9]

Aurelian is also associated directly with the eternity of Rome. Coins with the legend AETERNITAS AVG depict the she-wolf suckling the twins Romulus and Remus, while others depict Roma Aeterna holding a small Victory who crowns the emperor with a wreath.[10] We are told that Aurelian erected a golden statue of the Genius of the Roman people on the rostra in the forum at Rome. Such a prominent position, at the religious and civic heart of Rome, presupposes an act of deliberate policy if not also of religious sincerity.[11]

Minerva, Neptune and Mercury were also associated with Aurelian on his coinage.[12] A coin type depicting Mercury celebrates the divinely inspired foresight with which Aurelian ruled the world. A statue of Mercury was erected in the forum beside the sacred way in the last year of Aurelian's reign; again the location implies the emperor's approval. More significant is a small number of obverse busts which represent Aurelian as Mercury, nude but for a cloak and carrying the caduceus over one shoulder. The iconography of this portrait type, which is so far only known on billon radiates, was taken from certain unusual types minted for Gallienus. These coins were most likely intended to represent Aurelian as the divine guarantor of *felicitas saeculi*, emphasizing his ability to provide the conditions necessary for commerce to thrive. Aurelian's safe return from campaign was presided over by the goddess of fortune, whose cult was also associated with renewal and plenty.[13]

Apollo is described as Aurelian's protector, which may be an allusion to Apollo's function as a healer. On the other hand, Apollo was also regarded in the third century very much as a solar deity (see below, at n. 64). Aurelian is also represented on his coinage as being under the tutelage of Aesculapius, a deity more specifically associated with health.[14]

Aurelian and Jupiter

Jupiter, whose cult on the Capitol was the central focus of the Roman state religion, features very largely in the imperial symbolism of the first three centuries of the empire. The idea of imperial power deriving from some form of Jovian investiture goes back to the beginning of the empire and was given particular currency under Trajan and Hadrian. For a time in the early part of Aurelian's reign, it is clear that he regarded himself as being in a very special relationship with Jupiter. For two years, from the summer of 271 to that of 273, Jupiter was represented as Aurelian's principal divine sponsor. This special relationship was depicted in a number of ways referring to several cultic forms. Among the earliest Jovian coin types for Aurelian were some referring to Jupiter Stator. Among the very latest were some radiates minted at Rome referring to Jupiter Victor. An inscription from the Balkans set up in 273 apparently gives thanks to Jupiter Optimus Maximus for Aurelian's victories over Palmyra and the Carpi, and another from North Africa asks the god to protect Aurelian.[15]

The theme of Jupiter as the emperor's protector is combined with that of divine right on a very great number of billon radiates bearing the legend IOVI CONSERVATORI or CONSER that were issued from all the imperial mints operating for Aurelian between the two dates mentioned above. The iconography of these coins displays a scene of divine investiture, where the deity hands his protégé a globe, the symbol of dominion over the world. The repetition of the theme in such quantities, across such a number of mints and for such a sustained period of time is exceptional, and must be taken to indicate the emperor's personal intervention.[16]

These coins were largely minted in the first instance to pay the armies, and it seems reasonable to suppose that this assertion of divine right was aimed primarily at the soldiers. Aurelian's divine right as Jupiter's chosen superseded the volatile whims of the armies. In an age of endless coups and civil wars, the attraction of such a claim is obvious. The point is underlined by certain other types minted for Aurelian alongside the IOVI CONSER types at Cyzicus from late 271 to the middle of 272, which combine the iconography of Jovian investiture with legends that stress the support and loyalty of the troops.[17] These types, even more emphatically than the main series of Jovian coins, suggest that the soldiers owed allegiance to Aurelian precisely because he was the god's chosen one on earth. The message is echoed in a fragment which describes how Aurelian confronted an assembly of mutinous troops. Standing before them and lifting his imperial cloak with his right hand, he declared that god alone could bestow the purple; it was for god to determine the length of time his chosen should continue to rule, he told them, and not even fifty seditions like that just attempted could deflect this divine pre-ordination.[18] The representation of Aurelian as Jupiter's vice-regent may be implied in the numerous bust types of his reign which apparently depict part of the aegis on his shoulder. The aegis, symbolic of Jupiter's power, was strongly associated with military victory. The iconography suggests that the emperor is to be seen as the instrument of Jupiter's divine will.[19]

The cult of Juno Regina, whose temple was on the Aventine, was also closely associated with the idea of victory. Like other empresses of this period, Severina is associated with this important cult on her coinage. By extension, the relationship reflects upon Aurelian. The parallel between the relationship of Severina to the consort of Jupiter and that of Aurelian with Jupiter himself was probably quite intentional.[20]

The divine emperor

The imperial cult, which accorded the reigning emperor divine honours and worshipped past emperors, individually and collectively, was both politically and socially hugely important in the first three centuries of the Roman empire. The association of the reigning emperor with his deified predecessors was significant as an expression of political and religious continuity, which formed part of the process of legitimation. Aurelian's decision to issue coinage in honour of the deified Claudius must be seen in this light.[21]

Aurelian's assimilation to the divine is suggested on Greek inscriptions referring to him as 'greatest and most godlike', and on a Latin inscription he is given the epithet 'most sacred'.[22] A number of inscriptions attest the posthumous deification of Aurelian, using the standard Latin term *divus*, applied to deified emperors and distinguishable from *deus*. The *HA* says that after Aurelian's death Tacitus set up a silver statue of his deified predecessor in Aurelian's new temple of Sol.[23] Exceptionally, the Latin term *deus* is applied to Aurelian on a group of Latin inscriptions found in Italy, Spain and North Africa. These suggest that he was worshipped as a god in the west during his own lifetime. No such subtle distinction exists in Greek, and Aurelian and Severina are both accorded full divine status on Greek inscriptions in their lifetime.[24]

The numismatic evidence confirms that the term *deus* was applied to Aurelian in his lifetime. The formula DEO ET DOMINO appears for Aurelian on the obverse of certain rare coins. They were minted at Serdica, the most innovative of Aurelian's mints, towards the end of his reign. The unusual nature of the style of address is underlined by the use of the dative case, which is extremely rare, though not unheard of, on coin obverses of this date. One type even refers to Aurelian as DEO ET DOMINO NATO, stressing his divinely ordained destiny.[25] Almost two centuries before Aurelian, the emperor Domitian desired to be addressed as 'our lord and god' (*dominus et deus noster*).[26] Although these Aurelianic coins represent the first occasion on which either title had been applied to an emperor on an imperial coin, there was no longer anything radical in the sentiment they expressed. The formula was repeated later for Aurelian's successors.

AURELIAN AND SOL

In the second half of his reign Aurelian came to feel a special affinity with Sol, the Unconquered Sun, to whose divine protection he attributed the remarkable series of victories, especially in the east, which had enabled him to restore the empire. The exact nature and identity of Aurelian's solar religion is controversial, but it was undoubtedly influenced by the prevailing tendency towards syncretism, the coalescence of diverse religious elements within a single cultic framework. In order to understand this development in its proper context, it is necessary to take full account of the centrality of solar imagery in the symbolic representation of political power in the ancient world.

Solar imagery and imperial authority

The association between solar imagery and political power in the ancient world was entrenched by Alexander the Great. The central role of such imagery in the symbolic scheme of Augustus' self-presentation, and its association with his triumph over the east, as represented by Cleopatra, is well documented.[27] As imperial ideology came increasingly under the influence of ideas and images associated with Hellenistic rulership, the emphasis on solar imagery inevitably increased. One important aspect of this development was the adoption of the radiate crown, in origin a divine attribute particularly associated with the Greek sun god Helios. In keeping with Hellenistic tradition, Septimius and Julia Domna were represented as Sol and Luna, imagery that became standard with the introduction of Caracalla's new silver-alloy coins on which the emperor was portrayed radiate while the busts of empresses were depicted over a crescent moon. Such imagery was a strong feature of the coinage of Valerian and, especially, Gallienus, including coins associating the emperor with the rising sun (ORIENS AVGVSTI).[28]

It is against this backdrop that we must understand the use of solar imagery on the coinage of Aurelian's reign. The coinage of the first two years of his reign gave no hint as to the extraordinary representation that was to follow. On one early type, Aurelian is associated with the eternity of the sun god and coins issued to celebrate his first consulship in January 271 link his authority to the image of a radiate lion, a beast associated with solar cults in the east of the empire.[29] In 272, as Aurelian's great military expedition against Zenobia was under way, coins were issued from two mints in the Balkans with the reverse legend ORIENS AVG. Such types, depicting Sol with one or other of his two most distinctive attributes, the globe and the charioteer's whip, were not in themselves exceptional.[30] For the time being, Jupiter continued to be the principal divine sponsor of Aurelian's reign.

The change came in the summer of 273, apparently marking Aurelian's final suppression of Palmyra. Right across the whole empire, at every mint that operated in his name, there was a marked shift in emphasis. Sol had supplanted Jupiter as the emperor's divine sponsor. The initiative must have been Aurelian's own, and its implementation can to some extent be traced as it moved from east to west. The solar types begin to appear at Antioch and the Balkan mints in the early summer of 273, and at the Italian mints a little later.[31] From this point until his death just over two years later, coins referring to this special relationship were minted constantly at all the mints operating for Aurelian. SOLI INVICTO types are common, but the reverse legend that predominates is ORIENS AVG. The iconography of these solar types varied subtly from one issue to another, but in general they show Sol standing, radiate, naked but for his cloak, holding a globe or occasionally other attributes such as the whip, with his right hand raised in benediction. Usually one or two captives are at his feet.[32]

A couple of inscriptions call on Sol Invictus to protect the emperor.[33] The theme of Sol as Aurelian's tutelary deity is echoed on a number of coins which explicitly refer to SOLI CONSERVATORI.

One such type, minted at Cyzicus, depicts Sol handing the emperor a globe. This scene of Solar investiture, which echoes the earlier scenes of Jovian investiture, is also found on coins with other legends, including some which proclaim Aurelian to be the Restorer of the World and others which show Sol as the inspiration for the emperor's valour.[34] On yet others, the emperor's *virtus* is personified, as elsewhere, by Hercules and Mars: on these types it is they who receive the globe from Sol.[35]

On coins minted for Aurelian and Severina to mark the reunification of the empire in 274, bearing the legend PROVIDENTIA DEORVM, or simply PROVIDEN DEOR, Sol is depicted carrying his globe greeting a female deity (Concordia or Fides) who holds a military standard in each hand. The scene as a whole represents the divine pre-ordination by which Sol guaranteed Aurelian's authority and required the allegiance of his soldiers.[36] Sol is also represented as the bringer of peace in the wake of Aurelian's reunification of the Roman world.[37]

Perhaps surprisingly, no coins of this reign refer to Sol as *comes Augusti*, the emperor's companion, either explicitly (as later for Probus) or even iconographically by depicting the bust of Sol jugate behind that of the emperor (as appeared for Victorinus). The bust of Sol does appear, however, in the field above the emperor as he clasps hands with a female figure (either intended to be Concordia or Severina) on bronze types with the legend CONCORDIA AVG. These were probably issued to coincide with the triumph late in 274, and symbolize the way in which Sol presided over the public acceptance of Aurelian's rule.[38] In his obverse portraiture Aurelian's special relationship with the sun is also brought out. The solar connotations of the radiate crown continued in spite of its denominational meaning, as did the lunar significance of Severina's crescent portraits. On one obverse type, Aurelian's cuirass is decorated with busts of Sol and Luna. Aurelian is also, though very rarely, represented with his right hand raised in the gesture characteristic of Sol.[39]

Finally, we come to the most remarkable, and also the most controversial, coins of the reign. A few rare and highly distinctive coins, probably issued from the mint at Serdica, single out Sol as the heavenly ruler of the Roman empire. Traditionally classed as bronze, metal analysis has recently revealed a silver content which suggests that they may have been intended as a new coin worth double the new radiate. The obverse of these coins bears the legend SOL DOMINVS IMPERI ROMANI, or an abbreviation thereof, and displays a bust of Sol; beneath the bust on some versions the four horses of his solar chariot are depicted in miniature. On the reverse, Aurelian is shown sacrificing at an altar, either in a toga or in military dress, with the legend AVRELIANVS AVG CONS. The reverse legend has been variously interpreted, the most common assumption being that the final letters stand for CONS(ul). But this is not the usual abbreviation for consul; nor is the reverse iconography, especially where Aurelian appears in military dress, relevant to his role as consul. It is preferable, in view of the iconography, to restore CONS(ecravit) or perhaps CONS(ecrator), referring to the consecration of Aurelian's new temple of Sol at Rome and to the sacrifices Aurelian made at that time. This suggests that Aurelian conducted the ceremony in person.[40]

Much has been written on the significance of these unique coins. Their very uniqueness, however, makes their significance more difficult to assess. These rare coins, produced in billon in minute quantities and probably at a provincial mint, scarcely support the thesis of a far-reaching and revolutionary religious reform, still less the existence of an imperial decree on the supremacy of Sol. The fact that the emperor has ceded his place to the deity on the obverse of the coin is not in itself unprecedented in this period, as is shown by the GENIVS PR coinage issued for Gallienus only a few years earlier. While these coins, and in particular their extraordinary obverse legend, confirm the exalted position that the god held in the emperor's religious scheme, they do not actually tell us as much about Aurelian's religious policies as is usually supposed.[41]

The temple, the priesthood and the games

The coins honouring Sol Dominus Imperi Romani were minted at the climax of Aurelian's programme of religious reform. Exactly what that programme signifies and of what it consisted is still controversial. We know that it involved the construction of a new temple at Rome, with a new priesthood and the institution of elaborate games.

Preparations for the building of the temple probably began early in 274, upon Aurelian's return from the east.[42] The consecration ceremony appears to have taken place on 25 December 274, that is, on the feast of the winter solstice, thereafter known as *dies Invicti Natalis*. This day was a significant one in the Roman religious calendar, and does not correlate with the sacred day of any known Syrian cult.[43] The exact whereabouts of the temple is a matter of some dispute, as no remains have been positively identified. We are told it was erected in the seventh region, in or near the Campus Agrippae, more or less adjacent to the new camp that Aurelian built to house the urban cohorts. The most likely location is not the large remains discovered under the Piazza S. Silvestro but a rather smaller complex to the north lying just east of the Corso. This location would tie in well with the probable location of the Ciconiae, the landing quay for the fiscal wine that we are told was stored in the portico of Aurelian's temple.[44]

It was, by all accounts, a splendid edifice, adorned with gold and precious jewels.[45] It is likely that the materials for this lavish temple were gathered from a number of places, including the treasures taken from Palmyra. The building incorporated eight splendid porphyry columns which Aurelian may have transposed from another temple elsewhere, very possibly at Palmyra. Such borrowings were not uncommon in the Roman world at this time, as the Arch of Constantine demonstrates, and the antiquity and possibly the religious significance of the stones would quite probably have added to their appeal. In just the same way, we are told, these same porphyry columns were transported to Constantinople in the sixth century on the orders of Justinian, to adorn his new church of Holy Wisdom (St Sophia).[46]

Aurelian inaugurated special games in honour of Sol, the *agon Solis*, to be held every four years. They were first held in the year 274, very probably on 22 October, and may have marked the beginning of the celebrations that followed Aurelian's triumph.[47] The model Aurelian had before him was a specifically Roman one: the *agon Capitolinus* inaugurated by Domitian.

Aurelian also founded a new priestly college to look after the religious and administrative needs of all aspects of the new cult, including the temple and the games. He may also have set aside large funds for the administration and maintenance of the cult and its buildings.[48] The new priesthood consisted of pontiffs, *pontifices dei Solis*. The nomenclature is instructive, indicating very clearly that Aurelian viewed the cult as essentially Roman and traditional in character. The new college was clearly intended to parallel the existing college of pontiffs, whose functions were particularly associated with Vesta and Jupiter Optimus Maximus. It did not supplant or even overtly challenge the older college: both priesthoods happily co-existed at Rome and indeed the same individuals were often proud members of both. Furthermore, members of the older priesthood were designated *pontifices maiores*, a title which clearly demonstrates that the established state religion was not instantly relegated to second place. By the mid-fourth century, the designation *pontifices Vestae* had come to replace the earlier *pontifices maiores*, implying a shift in their relative ranking; but we should be wary of transposing this situation back into the third century.[49] Aurelian himself took no special title relating to the newly established cult. Henceforth, his title of Pontifex Maximus referred simultaneously to his position as head of both pontifical colleges, old and new. This also emphasizes how much he regarded his new cult of Sol as being within the framework of traditional Roman religion.

Homo purported to detect three separate phases by which Aurelian established his new cult of Sol: first, Aurelian installed Sol as the supreme deity of the state by decree; second, he saw to the construction of a new temple and the inauguration of special games; and third, he created the new pontifical college.[50] This three-phase scheme has been followed by most scholars since, but there is no real evidence to support it. Homo's first phase is, in reality, a phantom based on an over-interpretation of the coinage; and common sense dictates that the new priesthood must have been conceived and put in place at the same time as the temple and the games, even though the earliest attested epigraphic evidence for the new college comes from early in the reign of Probus.[51]

The identity of Aurelian's Sol

The identity of Aurelian's sun god remains highly controversial. The Romans had their own sun god, Sol Indiges, whose main temple was on the Quirinal, associated with a feast day on 9 August, and who also had a shrine shared with Luna in the Circus Maximus, associated with a feast day on 11 December. This cult was already closely associated with those of both Helios and Apollo by Augustus' day.[52]

There were many other solar cults under the empire, notably those of eastern origin including cults from Egypt, Mesopotamia and especially Syria, which came increasingly to influence solar worship at Rome and elsewhere in the empire. This was a two-way process of assimilation, so that the development of the oriental solar religions was influenced by Greek and Roman ideology and imagery. This syncretic tendency was already far advanced when, under Septimius and Caracalla, there was a marked increase in the influence of Hellenized Syrian solar cults, in particular that of the Emesene god, Elahgabal, whose hereditary high priest was Caracalla's maternal grandfather.

It is usually assumed that the solar cult Aurelian introduced to Rome was in essence an eastern, more specifically Syrian, solar cult. Some have suggested that the emperor adapted the cult of Elahgabal to suit Roman tastes, reconstituting the Syrian cult in order to avoid the opprobrium associated with the spectacularly unsuccessful attempt by Caracalla's unstable cousin Elagabalus, then high priest at Emesa, to impose the cult upon Roman religion two generations earlier.[53] The disgrace and *damnatio memoriae* suffered by the adolescent emperor Elagabalus and the nature of the cult he championed, renders this an unlikely choice of model for Aurelian's new religion. There are in fact grave problems with this identification, which is based on the use of the epithet Invictus and on highly suspicious information provided by the *Historia Augusta*.

The epithet Invictus ('Aνίκητος) was never exclusively the property of the Emesene god and indeed was applied to a wide variety of deities, by no means all solar, as well as to rulers in the ancient world. Except where Elahgabal is specifically named or where some other link to Emesa can be established, it is therefore very dangerous to assume that references on inscriptions to Sol Invictus or Deus Invictus must refer to the Emesene god; still more so, references on coins.[54] Like most Baal cults in the Near East, which had solar associations but were often identified with Jupiter, the cult of Elahgabal ('god of the mountain') was not in origin solar. Again not unusually, the Emesene god was worshipped in the form of an aniconic black stone, almost certainly a meteorite, and tended by priests invariably referred to as *sacerdotes*.[55]

The relevant passage in the *HA*, which must be regarded as pure fabrication, has caused considerable mischief. The author reports that during the decisive battle against the Palmyrenes at Emesa in 272, Aurelian was aided by a shining 'divine form' which rallied the spirits of his soldiers. After the victory he entered Emesa and, proceeding to the temple of Elahgabal, instantly recognized his divine helper. He promptly established new temples at Emesa, dedicating great riches to them, and vowed to build a temple of the sun god at Rome, which promise he later kept. The story is clearly bogus, inspired by the obvious coincidence of Sol Invictus and Emesa and by the memory of Elagabalus. The coins clearly indicate that Aurelian's special relationship with Sol began in the summer of 273, not a year earlier. Whether or not the biographer intended the story as a pagan counterpart to the vision of Constantine at the Milvian Bridge forty years later, it certainly cannot be used as evidence of the identity of Aurelian's Sol.[56] It remains very unlikely, therefore, that the new religion was simply a remodelled version of the Emesene cult previously sponsored by Elagabalus.

Among the other quasi-solar deities strongly associated with the epithet Invictus, the most important was Mithras. Many of the same objections as we saw in the case of Elahgabal apply equally to Mithras, whose iconography almost invariably shows the god in a very specific pose, referred to as *tauroktenos*, in which he wears Persian dress and kneels on the back of a bull plunging a sword into its neck. The priests of Mithras were called *patres patrum*; once again in marked contrast to the *pontifices* of Aurelian's Sol. Furthermore, both Mithraism and its priesthood continued at Rome and elsewhere in the empire after Aurelian had established his new religion. We even know of individuals who were able to boast of having been both *pater patrum* and *pontifex dei Solis*. If the two cults were the same, this would be meaningless.[57]

Far more credible are the links to the gods of Palmyra. The connection between Aurelian's solar imagery and his subjugation of Palmyra is abundantly clear. *Oriens Augusti* was at once the emperor and the god, whose daily triumph over darkness matched Aurelian's triumph over his enemies in the orient. Sol's assistance is specifically acknowledged on certain coins proclaiming the emperor as Restitutor Orientis and Restitutor Orbis. The captives frequently depicted on the ORIENS AVG and other solar types are invariably shown in oriental dress.[58]

Zosimus tells us that Aurelian 'set up cult statues of Helios and Belos' in his new temple at Rome. This either indicates that the two statues were seen as different incarnations of the same deity or that the temple was dedicated to a pair of gods.[59] This may indicate that a cult statue of Bel, presumably from the great temple at Palmyra itself, was brought to Rome and set up in the new temple. This hints at the possibility of the ancient ritual of *evocatio*, by which the presiding deity of an enemy was ritually summoned out of their city with the promise of a new cult home at Rome. The problem here is that Bel was not a solar deity. At Palmyra he was associated with two other deities: Yarhibol, a god with strong solar associations (though his name, 'lord of the months', suggests a lunar origin), and Aglibol, the Palmyrene moon god. This latter pair are represented as the acolytes of Bel and form part of a divine triad with Bel at its centre.[60] The HA says that Aurelian intended to set up in his temple of Sol a statue of Jupiter, evidently in foreign guise, seated on an ivory throne. The context of this passage is highly suspect, but it might just conceal some half-understood allusion to the Palmyrene god Bel, who was usually depicted fully armoured and, like other Syrian Baal cults, was closely associated with Jupiter.[61]

Besides the indigenous Yarhibol, there were two other sun gods worshipped at Palmyra. One was the Arabic sun god, Shamash; the other, more enigmatic and less clearly solar in origin, was Malakbel (whose name probably means 'messenger of Bel'). Malakbel was worshipped jointly with Aglibol, the moon god, as heavenly brothers in a temple known as the Holy Garden. The worship of the sun and moon was widespread in northern Syria. Malakbel and Aglibol were also worshipped at the temple to the Unknown God, probably the Phoenician Baal Shamin, where they were represented as the acolytes in the city's second sacred triad. The worship of Malakbel was widespread in the empire and from the early second century he had a shrine on the right bank of the Tiber, apparently in the vicinity of the wine warehouses just outside the future Porta Portuensis. He was commonly identified with Sol and sometimes bears the epithet Invictus. At Rome he is also known as Deus Sol Sanctissimus. It may be relevant that Aurelian too bears the epithet Sanctissimus on an inscription from Capena.[62] The Holy Garden at Palmyra, the site of which has not yet been located, may have been the temple that Aurelian plundered for the treasures and cult statues he removed to Rome. The reference in Zosimus to Helios and Belos might therefore conceal a transformed version of the twin cult of Malakbel and Aglibol, subsumed and transformed into a new and essentially Roman cult of Sol and Luna. In this respect, it is interesting to note that one source refers to Aurelian's temple as a temple of Sol and Luna.[63]

It must be stressed, however, that this is only speculation. What is certain is that the new cult was very strongly solar. The iconography which pervades Aurelian's later coinage is entirely drawn from Graeco-Roman religious imagery associated with the iconography of Hellenistic ruler cult. Like Helios, Aurelian's Sol also retained a close connection with Apollo.[64] To what extent the cult of Sol championed by Aurelian was a syncretic amalgam of one or more of these oriental religions, or what precisely was its relationship to the Palmyrene cults of Bel or Malakbel, must remain unresolved.[65]

The nature of the new religion: polytheism, henotheism or monotheism?

The story that he was brought up to honour the sun god by a mother who was herself a priestess of Sol, believable as it may sound, is to be regarded as nothing more than fiction born of hindsight.[66] Solar cults were, however, prevalent in the Balkans, especially in the army, during the third century. There is, indeed, some indication that eastern solar imagery may have influenced imperial ritual at this time: the soldiers that elevated Aurelian to the purple may have done so in a literal fashion by raising him on a shield symbolizing the sun-disk. This identification of the new emperor with the rising sun, an identification which dominated Aurelian's coinage, was in later centuries to become a central part of imperial inauguration ritual.[67]

The devotion which Aurelian showed towards Sol in the last years of his reign appears to have been both sincere and personal.[68] But this does not mean he attempted to supplant the old Roman pantheon by the imposition of a solar monotheism or even a solar henotheism (the belief in a single god to which other gods are subordinate). For an emperor in the third century, the perception of a special relationship between himself and a particular deity was fairly commonplace. That Aurelian took this to far greater lengths than had been done before does not mean the measures were intended to overturn Roman religion. On the contrary, it is clear that everything he did was very much in keeping with the traditions of ancient Roman religious practices. There is indeed every reason to suppose that Aurelian was, in religion as in much else besides, deeply conservative.

It is often alleged that Aurelian relegated all other gods to being mere manifestations of the power of his new syncretic solar deity. But there is every indication that a vast variety of cults, including those of the traditional Roman pantheon, continued to thrive at this time. Other deities, such as Mars and Hercules, continued to appear on the coinage alongside Sol, precluding the notion that they might represent different facets of a single solar deity. Dedicatory inscriptions prove the continuation of other cults, and the priests of Sol were often, indeed usually, priests of other cults as well, without any sense of incongruity or sacrilege. On the contrary, it clearly indicates that polytheism was alive and well.

For many modern scholars, the trend towards religious monotheism is closely allied to a drastic shift towards greater autocracy in Aurelian's reign and to his desire to unify the Roman world under one ruler.[69] Such assumptions lack foundation. Neither the idea of henotheism, still less monotheism, nor its alleged link to greater autocracy has ever been properly demonstrated. There is no evidence that Aurelian wished to have himself represented as 'Sol-on-earth' in any way which implied a new imperial solar monotheism. In spite of the existence of coins and inscriptions which allude to his godhead, the emphasis is much more one of ruling by divine right than of declaring his own divinity.[70] The gradual trend towards a more overtly autocratic representation of imperial power in the Roman empire, noted earlier, has very little to do with Aurelian's religious policies.[71]

Scholars who wish to see in the religious policies of Aurelian's reign the official inauguration of an inexorable trend towards solar monotheism have undoubtedly been led astray by a Judeo-Christian cultural outlook which fails to understand the very nature of polytheism.[72] Some have even gone so far as to see Aurelian's cult of Sol as a reaction to the threat to paganism posed by the rise of Christianity. This is a fourth-century view, impossible to hold much before the reign of Julian, whose personal beliefs it indeed closely echoes. Solar henotheism, far from being a necessary third-century precursor of the drift towards the acceptance of monotheism and Christianity in the next century, must rather be understood as a fourth-century reaction to Christianity and its spectacular advances. The standard view of Aurelian is therefore anachronistic and wholly unacceptable. Furthermore, it has encouraged the perception of Aurelian's decision to renew the persecution of the Christians as a conflict of monotheistic beliefs. This is quite clearly nonsense. The conflict between Christianity and paganism in the third century was most emphatically a conflict between uncompromising monotheism and inclusive polytheism.[73]

AURELIAN AND CHRISTIANITY

Christianity was undoubtedly one of the fastest-spreading religions in the third century. Its success can be put down to the extraordinary level of commitment shown by believers, to the highly developed organization of the Church, to the impact and good example of Christian charity and to many other reasons besides. The rapid rise of Christianity during the middle decades of the third century was observed with disquiet by conservative pagans like Aurelian. The problems that had brought the conflict between the state and the followers of Christ to a head during the 250s had not gone away by the time Aurelian himself was acclaimed emperor.

To the old problems, new ones had been added. In the decade or so following the end of the Valerianic persecution, Christianity had continued to grow in strength and socio-political importance.

Christian bishops were by this time becoming figures of considerable stature in their local communities. Some, like Paul of Samosata, the bishop of Antioch, apparently allowed this sense of importance to go to their heads. Paul was elected bishop of Antioch shortly after the Persians retreated from their great invasion in 260. Both his doctrine and his attitude soon aroused disquiet and, in about 264, a synod was held to consider his suitability. Nothing was resolved. Paul's overbearing behaviour, which had more in common with a magistrate or tyrant than a bishop, together with the heretical views he blatantly expounded in Church, which denied the full divinity of Christ, convinced many to try again. Shortly after the death of Gallienus, probably in the autumn of 268, an even more substantial synod was convened, including deputations from as far afield as Egypt and Italy. Paul was found guilty of heresy, impeached and excommunicated.[74]

This was by no means the end of the affair. Paul had a powerful following in and around Antioch. He arranged a personal body-guard for himself and, in defiance of the Church ruling, refused to relinquish the bishop's house, presumably continuing to preach there. With the rise of Palmyra under Zenobia, Paul's behaviour was of more than purely local political significance, though he was probably too crafty a player to display his allegiance quite as overtly as his detractors have maintained.[75] In a highly significant move, his enemies within the Church, having failed to dislodge him with a purely ecclesiastical ruling, turned to Aurelian to intervene in the dispute. This Aurelian did. On receiving the petition, Aurelian found in favour of the 'bishops of the doctrine of Italy and Rome'. Paul was forced to surrender the buildings belonging to the Church of Antioch which he had appropriated and was banished from the city.[76]

Essentially, the dispute concerned the ownership and use of property. Appeals to the emperor were the usual recourse of last resort for settling such disputes between citizens in the empire. But in this particular appeal we have a new and highly portentous development. This episode marks the very first instance of a Roman emperor's direct involvement in Church affairs. As the subsequent history of the empire and the Church would show, it was the first of many. In fact it anticipated by almost precisely forty years the appeal to Constantine in the Donatist affair, which, like the Aurelianic episode, concerned property rights. The formula discovered by Aurelian for settling the dispute at Antioch was virtually identical to that employed by Constantine on the later occasion.

The appeal to Aurelian is yet another indication of the growing prominence and self-awareness both of Christianity as a whole and of the bishops in particular. Throughout the last four decades of the third century, the relationship between the Roman government and the Christian community, especially its increasingly powerful bishops, remained uneasy. The possibility of a renewal of the persecutions was never far away. This threat came very close to being realized at the end of Aurelian's reign, according to Christian accounts written shortly thereafter. The uncompromising attitude of the Christians precluded the worship of both the emperor himself and his divine protectors, including his patron Sol Invictus. Like other conservatives of his era, Aurelian seems to have regarded the refusal of the Christians to honour the gods of Rome and to recognize his own quasi-divinity not only as a threat to society but as a challenge to his personal authority. Whatever his reasons, Aurelian apparently determined to renew the persecutions in the last few months of his life. It is said he had even drawn up the orders for them to begin when he was struck down by his assassins. The orders were never issued.[77]

Of special interest in this context are several accounts of martyrdoms which allegedly took place under Aurelian in Italy, Gaul and Asia Minor. At first glance, the existence of these accounts would appear to suggest that Aurelian's orders for a persecution had actually been issued by the time of his death. It has been shown, however, that these martyrologies are not reliable. Furthermore, the dates of the martyrdoms do not fit the known chronology for the end of Aurelian's life. If such martyrdoms ever occurred at all at this time, they more plausibly represent sporadic isolated incidents involving purely individual cases. They certainly do not amount to proof that a general persecution was actually renewed.[78]

It appears that in the confusion which followed Aurelian's death, all such plans were forgotten. The respite was short-lived, however. A quarter-of-a-century after Aurelian's death, under the auspices of the Tetrarchs, Diocletian and Galerius, the horror of renewed persecution finally broke upon the Christian world with unprecedented intensity. It was not until the rise of Constantine in the second decade of the fourth century that Christianity was finally set free from the atrocities of persecution, only to plunge almost immediately into interminable internal schisms.

The majority of those responsible for instituting the persecutions in the third and early fourth centuries suffered premature and sometimes gruesome deaths. Although most emperors in this period met with similar fates, the Christian writers who lived through these terrible times not unnaturally saw in these deaths the hand of divine retribution. For these authors, the assassination of Aurelian just as he was on the point of renewing the persecution was thus seen as an example of God's providence.

THE RELIGIOUS POLICIES OF AURELIAN

Aurelian was a traditionalist who honoured the Roman pantheon, most especially those deities, such as Mars and Jupiter, strongly associated with military victory and the destiny of Rome. In the latter part of his reign, he developed a personal devotion to Sol who came to eclipse the other deities on his coins. The persistent production of the solar coin types and the timing of their introduction, together with the symbolism of their iconography, suggest that Aurelian personally attributed his success against Palmyra to a close alliance between himself, Imperator Invictus Augustus, and his divine protector, Deus Sol Invictus. The exact identity of Aurelian's tutelary deity is not resolved, but it appears it was at least in part a creation of his own, influenced by oriental solar cults but at the same time firmly rooted in the tradition of Roman imperial solar iconography.

The relationship between Sol and Aurelian as it is represented on his coinage is arguably the most remarkable of all the expressions of divine tutelage ever to appear on the imperial coinage. But it must be understood in its rightful context, both alongside other expressions of divine tutelage on the coinage of the period, notably for Gallienus and for Postumus, and alongside the other religious aspects of Aurelian's reign.

Aurelian raised the status of his new solar religion to a level comparable with the existing state religion at Rome and placed it within the formal structures of that state religion. He built a magnificent temple to Sol at Rome worthy of this new status, which he adorned with the rich spoils of Palmyra and in which he placed cult statues of Sol and Bel side by side. He consecrated this temple according to proper Roman ritual and instituted four-yearly games and a new college of priests who, by their very title of *pontifices dei Solis*, emphasized the official Roman nature of the cult. By these measures, Aurelian ostentatiously acknowledged his debt of gratitude to his divine patron.

He did not, however, impose the cult of Sol above the existing Roman state religion, as the emperor Elagabalus had attempted to do with the Emesene god. The traditional college of pontiffs remained senior to the new college he created for Sol, and as Pontifex Maximus he remained the head of both. Nor did he attempt to overturn the established religious order by imposing his new cult of Sol as a kind of exclusive monotheism, along the lines of Christianity. On the contrary, it is clear that the new religion drew its strength from the place it was accorded within traditional Roman polytheism. In fact, Aurelian was apparently greatly disturbed by the Christians' obstinate refusal to participate in traditional state religion or to honour the gods of Rome. His decision to renew the persecution is better explained in terms of his religious conservatism than in terms of a religious radicalism resulting in a clash of monotheistic beliefs.

The success of Aurelian's achievement can to some extent be measured by the important status his cult continued to enjoy for well over a century after his death. Tapping, as it did, into ancient and deep-rooted ideas about the nature and representation of rulership, the solar theology which Aurelian did so much to foster continued to influence imperial ideology even after the emperors had found Christ and turned their backs on paganism. Indeed, partly as a result of this influence, it came to have a profound effect upon the representations of Christ himself as well on the subsequent royal ideology of both Byzantium and Christendom.[79]

CONCLUSION

The world which Aurelian knew was one dominated by warfare which stretched the resources of the empire to the limit. Repeated Germanic and Persian invasions penetrated deep into the empire along the entire length of the European and eastern frontiers. The empire, once the aggressor, found itself increasingly on the defensive. The military situation created impossible demands on the emperor's presence and exacerbated the underlying political instability. The political price of failure was high. If the emperor could not be on hand to deal with the barbarian menace in a particular region, the general on the spot who successfully repelled the invasions would often be invited to assume the imperial purple. Inevitably, this resulted in a multiplicity of mutually hostile emperors and precipitated a series of civil wars.

The cycle of foreign and civil wars not only drained the empire's resources but also caused unsustainable disruption to the economic infrastructure of agriculture and commerce. The situation was further exacerbated by administrative corruption and by the government's short-term expedient of debasing the coinage, which lead to a collapse of confidence in the monetary system, to widespread fraud and ultimately to galloping inflation.

The spate of military coups that followed the ignominious defeat and capture of Valerian by the Persians in 260 set the scene for a new development which threatened the very integrity of the empire itself. While Gallienus managed to cling on to and re-establish his authority over Italy and the Balkans, the army of the Rhine and the western provinces remained loyal to their chosen emperor, Postumus. The east, meanwhile, came increasingly under the effective rule of Odenathus, whose allegiance to Gallienus was merely nominal. For more than seven years, the responsibility for the defence of the empire was divided between these three individuals. Within a short space of time (perhaps as little as twelve months, from the spring of 268 to that of 269) all three were assassinated. Far from bringing it to an end, their deaths merely served to entrench the effective tripartite division of the empire. In the west, a series of emperors were proclaimed by the army of the Rhine. The east was ruled from Palmyra by Zenobia with increasingly hostile autonomy.

It is in these critical circumstances that Aurelian first comes to our attention as a leading member of the cabal of Illyrian officers who conspired to eliminate Gallienus and replace him with one of their own. The brief reign of Claudius was fully occupied in repelling Germanic invaders from northern Italy and the Balkans. He had neither the time nor the resources to deal with the tripartite division within the empire. When he succumbed to the plague two years later, the road was open for Aurelian to take up the reins of state himself.

Aurelian may be fairly said to have epitomized the new breed of military commanders, the majority of whom came, like himself, from Illyrian peasant stock. In physical appearance, his coin portraits depict the close-cropped hair and short beard typical of his kind. They reveal a powerful and uncompromising countenance: the personification of 'grim-visaged war'. As with so many of his fellow soldiers and compatriots, his general outlook was highly conservative and he remained steadfastly loyal to the traditions and integrity of the Roman empire. It was through the courage, determination and leadership of such men that the empire was salvaged from the threat of disintegration and left arguably more brutal but unquestionably better adapted to the hostile environment in which it found itself. None deserves more credit for this achievement than Aurelian himself.

With characteristic energy and determination, Aurelian systematically set about tackling the ills that beset the empire. In rapid succession he eliminated his immediate rivals, repulsed a number of dangerous Germanic invasions that broke across the Danube and put down the most serious riots the city of Rome had experienced in imperial times. By the early summer of 271 his position was sufficiently secure for him to turn his attention to broader issues. From this point until his death, somewhat over four years later, Aurelian devoted himself, both on and off the battlefield, to restoring the empire to something of its former glory.

Aurelian was first and foremost a soldier, nowhere more at home than on campaign. He was an exceptionally capable military commander who won the complete support and admiration of his troops. It was this special relationship which had allowed him to seize power in a military coup and which enabled him once emperor to win such a spectacular series of victories. His inspirational leadership, his grasp of both strategy and tactics and the impressive discipline he instilled in his troops are all evident from the results of his campaigns. Nowhere were these qualities more clearly manifested than in his extraordinary victory over the Palmyrenes at Immae.

His greatest achievement, and the one which was to occupy most of his brief reign, was the reunification of the Roman empire. By taking on and crushing first Zenobia and then Tetricus he eliminated the rival powers that had effectively divided the Roman world into three parts ever since the capture of Valerian. It must have been a daunting task, but one which was accomplished through his unflinching determination, evident from at least the summer of 271. In this decisive action he averted the permanent disintegration of the empire and ensured its survival as a political entity for a further 200 years. The significance of this achievement for the subsequent development of Europe and the Mediterranean is incalculable.

His military successes also extended to Rome's external enemies. In a tireless series of campaigns he managed to restore a degree of security to the shattered frontiers of the empire. From the perspective of his subjects in such troubled times, this protection was the most crucial benefit the emperor could provide. In driving back and decisively defeating the Goths, Aurelian effectively brought to an end their twenty-year-long rampage through the Balkan lands and the Aegean. He also took the momentous decision to withdraw all Roman forces still stationed north of the Danube and to evacuate a substantial number of civilians from the Dacian salient, resettling them south of the river. The main purpose of this move was to rationalize the strategic defence of the area, while giving more room to ease the barbarian pressure. In this way he hoped to make the new frontier along the river more readily defensible. After defeating the Carpi, he settled substantial numbers of them within the Roman empire, thereby setting an important precedent that would dramatically effect the course of Roman and indeed European history in the centuries that followed.

One of his most significant decisions was to build defensive walls around the city of Rome to provide its inhabitants with some security against the potential renewal of Germanic attack. The walls still bear his name to this day and in large measure still stand, with later accretions, where he erected them. They are at once both the most enduring monument of his age and the most eloquent statement of the changed military conditions with which the empire was now faced.

His military background and bearing should not be taken to mean that he was *ipso facto* particularly hostile to the senate or the senatorial élite. That this element of society had lost much of the political influence and significance it had once wielded is a simple truth. In as far as Aurelian chose not to defer to the outmoded ideals for which it stood, he was not unusual for his time. It is undoubtedly true that he had his enemies among the senatorial aristocracy and, equally, that he had no compunction about eliminating them. The senatorial blood on his hands, excusable under the circumstances, was no worse than in the case of many highly regarded emperors who had acted in a similar way in just such circumstances before him: Octavian, Hadrian or Septimius, for example. His reputation for cruelty, much trumpeted in the literary sources, has received undue credence. As Malalas reminds us, he was capable of great magnanimity. Nowhere is this more dramatically illustrated than in his final treatment of his defeated rivals, Zenobia and Tetricus, both of whom he allowed to live on in honourable retirement after their part in his magnificent triumph.

Aurelian also set about trying to find proper solutions to the many economic woes which faced the empire at his accession. He implemented much-needed reforms of the utterly debased and discredited imperial coinage. At the same time, he overhauled the mint system. Not only did he extend the number of mint sites and increase their output, he simultaneously imposed far greater central control over the whole operation. In so far as these measures were not particularly effective in producing the stability he desired, the blame does not lie heavily on Aurelian himself. The effects of the systematic abuse of the monetary system over the previous half-century and more, together with the momentum of the inflationary pressures on the empire's economy, could not be checked merely by introducing these much-needed reforms. The conditions which had brought about these difficulties persisted still, and inflation in fact spiralled further out of control in the decades that followed.

Aurelian also attempted to tackle some of the other economic problems of his day. He took steps to curb the corruption of provincial officials and discharged the considerable arrears of public debt. He implemented measures to encourage the productive use of deserted farmland. He also reformed the system of food supply for the capital, making more goods available at subsidized prices and increasing the urban food dole.

His successes, especially in the field of war, he himself credited to the support of his divine patron, the sun god Sol Invictus. To this deity he dedicated a magnificent new temple at Rome. The cult he established at Rome was specifically Roman in character, and was tended by a new explicitly Roman priestly college of pontiffs. Although, under the influence of Neoplatonist philosophy and Christian doctrine, this cult of Sol took on an increasingly mono-theistic aspect in the fourth century, there can be no doubt that in Aurelian's day it was conceived in terms of an exalted place within the structure of traditional Roman polytheism. This is not to deny that Aurelian was aware of its potential as a cohesive force within the empire. Like the imperial cult, it doubtless played a key role as a focus for unity across a wide spectrum of his subjects.

One group of his subjects in particular ostentatiously refused to participate in these two cults, or indeed in any other religious activities besides its own. Aurelian's decision to renew the persecution of the Christians must be understood in the context of the disloyalty and social disruption implied in such stubborn refusal, rather than as a clash between two monotheistic faiths. On the other hand, Aurelian was the first emperor to whom the Church turned to help settle its own internal difficulties. Aurelian's intervention in the dispute over Paul of Samosata represents the dawn of a new era in the relationship between church and state.

Two abiding themes, closely linked, governed almost every action and policy of Aurelian's brief reign: his deep-rooted conservatism and his fierce loyalty to Rome. Both were common among men of his kind, as can be seen, for example, in Diocletian. In his style of representation, in his monetary reform, in his desire for unity and prosperity in the empire, he appears above all to have looked back to the era into which he had been born. From the perspective of the 270s, the Severan age must have seemed tinged with gold. In his religious reforms and in his adoption of more overtly autocratic insignia and titles, Aurelian appears to look forward to the later empire and Byzantium more than back to Augustus. But this is largely an illusion: a trick of the light, or rather the lack of it. For in the dark 'tunnel' that is the mid-third century, the contrast between the early empire and the late empire has been exaggerated at the expense of the strands of continuity and gradual development. The traditional view underplays the degree to which Augustus' rule was both autocratic and legitimized by divine sanction. Insufficient account is therefore taken of the extent to which the emperors of the third century saw themselves as continuing within a tradition which went back to the founder of the empire.

Just as Augustus had claimed a special affinity with Apollo and

Sol, whom he repeatedly associated with his victory over Antony and Cleopatra, so Aurelian claimed an affinity with Sol Invictus, whom he credited with the victory over the new Cleopatra, Zenobia. Similarly, Constantine would later represent first Apollo then Sol Christus as his divine patron. Very real distinctions exist between the ways in which these emperors at different times chose to represent their authority in relation to their divine sponsors, but to dwell on these distinctions is to overlook the far more significant elements of continuity. The age of Aurelian must be taken not as a catastrophic break, but as a vital link in the development from Augustus through Constantine and beyond.

Aurelian was supremely a man of the moment. He was a man of action; a soldier in a soldier's world. His approach to the problems he faced betray his military mind: his use of force to reunite the empire, as opposed to stabilizing the *modus vivendi* by negotiation; his tighter control over the mint operations; his decision to evacuate Dacia; his decision to surround Rome with fortified walls. Unquestionably a man of stern resolve, he had a strong concern for order and discipline. He may have lacked finesse in his dealings with the senate, but the accusations of extreme cruelty levelled against him in the literary sources are certainly over-exaggerated.

If the literary tradition has at times been a little hard on him, his achievements speak for themselves. In so short a time and against such odds, to turn the tide of the empire's fortunes so dramatically around is an achievement almost without parallel in the annals of imperial Rome. With no hint of irony, the *Epitome* (35.2) likened his achievements to those of Alexander the Great and Julius Caesar. As the splendid pageant of his triumph passed through the streets of Rome in the autumn of 274, those who witnessed it could be forgiven for believing that here at last was an emperor who was truly the Restorer of their World. A year later he was dead. He died as he had lived, by the sword. Who can say what he might not have achieved but for the perfidy of a disgruntled secretary and the gullibility of his fellow officers. His brief but glorious reign lasted no more than five years and two months. In that short span he inspired renewed hope and vigour which gave the empire a new lease of life. For this, he earned the respect and affection of his subjects. The *Historia Augusta* asserts that Aurelian was loved by the people. Even if this was an idea added by that author, there may be considerable truth in it. He had certainly given them cause enough.

APPENDIX A
Excursion on sources

No study of the mid-third century can evade the constraints imposed by the unsatisfactory nature of the literary sources, which are generally tendentious and often heavily coloured by hindsight. Some are fragmentary, most are sketchy, and none is particularly reliable.[1] There is by contrast a wealth of information to be gleaned from the contemporary coins, inscriptions and papyri and from archaeology. These provide us with a direct and concrete link to the period in which Aurelian lived. The growing awareness of and interest in sources other than literary, and the increasing technical and conceptual sophistication of the research applied to such sources in recent decades, have begun to allow a critical reappraisal of the literary testimony which has unlocked the door to a far better understanding of the period as a whole.

THE LITERARY SOURCES

Of all the texts that have come down to us pertaining to this period, none is more vexing than the notorious *Historia Augusta*. The scholarship entirely devoted to sorting out the labyrinthine contortions of this one work is now voluminous.[2] No study of this period in general or of Aurelian's reign in particular is possible without first coming to terms with this wayward fantasy. Purporting to be the work of six authors writing under Diocletian and Constantine at the turn of the fourth century, it is in fact the creation of a single individual writing almost a century later.[3] The anonymous author was a rogue who deliberately set out to mislead. He clearly valued jokes above veracity and never hesitated to insert extraneous material to give his text more colour. We may never know exactly why this hoax was perpetrated in the form that it was. Indeed, the more we find out about the author's convoluted and impishly inventive mind, the more complex the picture seems to become.

The author's outlook on politics, society and religion was highly conservative and heavily influenced by the milieu in which he worked. While the work is not exactly an anti-Christian polemic, indeed it has no observable coherent programmatic purpose of any sort, it does display a marked pagan bias.[4] The author's view of the world is centred very much on Rome and coloured by the traditional values of the Roman senate. His intended primary audience was certainly the pagan senatorial aristocracy of the late fourth century, on the fringes of which world he may himself have moved. The *HA* should therefore be seen in the context of the resurgence of senatorial self-importance that characterized late fourth-century Rome.[5]

The *vita Divi Aureliani*, containing fifty chapters and occupying over fifty pages of text in the Loeb edition (thirty-eight in Teubner), is longer than any other life in the entire work, with the sole exception of the elaborate encomiastic fiction that serves for a biography of Severus Alexander. It is twice as long as the next longest biography in the final section of the work (that nominally written by 'Vopiscus'). Unfortunately for us, this bulk is largely composed of blatant fabrications. Some of the fabrications are of great length and complexity: the prologue (1–2); the account of Aurelian's adoption by one 'Ulpius Crinitus' (10.3–15.2); the elaborate digression on the Sibylline Books (18.7–20.8); the account of the interregnum (40–41); and the sermon on good and bad emperors, studded with bogus anecdotes (42.3–44.5). In effect, virtually everything relating to Aurelian's early life and career is pure fiction. In addition, there are a large number of bogus documents and fictional characters.[6] Although potentially of immense value in the study of the *HA* itself, such fictions have only served to confuse our understanding of Aurelian's reign. The quantity of padding and fictional material suggests that the author felt Aurelian *deserved* to be dealt with at such length and indulged in so much fabrication to stretch out the meagre details with which his sources furnished him.

The excesses of the *HA* are made doubly deleterious by the deficiency of reliable information from other sources. This situation has not been assisted by the attrition of time. Of works written in Latin, the relevant books of Ammianus Marcellinus are sadly missing, and the references in the extant portion of his work tantalizingly few.[7] Both Ammianus and the author of the *HA* probably made use of the *Annales* of Nichomachus Flavianus, now also lost. Another lost work was the imperial history ('Kaisergeschichte', or KG) of Constantinian date postulated by Enmann.[8]

The KG offers the most satisfying explanation for the similarities between the *HA* and the various extant Latin epitomators of the fourth century, the *Caesares* of Aurelius Victor, the *Breviarium* of Eutropius and the anonymous *Epitome de Caesaribus*. The conciseness of the texts is compounded by the ignorance and bias of their authors. Though not formally structured as a series of imperial biographies like the *HA*, these works were written on an essentially biographical formula which, as in the *HA*, not only divides the history of the period up into the individual reigns but also subdivides the account of each reign thematically. Typically, an account of the origins and character of each emperor is followed by a main narrative of military events, which in turn is followed by an account of internal policies and other important events, often without regard to relative chronology. Modern scholars have occasionally been misled into dating a particular event according to its position in the narrative.[9]

The prejudices of Aurelius Victor are particularly intrusive: his bias against the military and his traditionalist, pro-senatorial viewpoint at times wholly distort the narrative to suit his rhetorical purpose.[10] A further problem, peculiar to Victor, is provided by the lacuna in the text of the *Caesares* towards the end of the account of Claudius' reign (in the middle of what is now 34.7). The lacuna is almost certainly extensive, covering Victor's concluding remarks on Claudius, his account of Quintillus and the early part of the narrative on Aurelian, including his accession, the early Germanic Wars and his Palmyrene campaigns. The existence and/or import of this lacuna has often been overlooked.[11]

Among the other Latin authors whose works provide some further information on this period, particularly noteworthy are the Christian writers. Jerome compiled a Latin version of the lost *Chronicle* of Eusebius. *On the Lives of the Persecutors* by Lactantius, though almost contemporary, is too polemical to be reliable. The same bias infuses Orosius' *History against the Pagans*. Such texts, reacting to the pagan polemics of their day, blame the ills of their times on the persistence of paganism. Further information is also to be gleaned from the *Breviarium* of Festus and from the *Romana* and *Getica* of Jordanes. Additional information is to be found in the speeches of the western orators at the turn of the fourth century preserved in the *Panegyrici Latini*. Further hints can also be found in the works of other minor Latin authors such as the Chronographer of 354, Polemius Silvius, Cassiodorus and Gregory of Tours.

Among the most important Greek authors, the loss of all but fragments of the works of the contemporary historian Dexippus is particularly frustrating. He wrote a history of the Gothic wars (*Scythica*), covering the period 238–71, and a general *Chronicle* down to 270. Doubt has recently been cast on the historical worth of these works. Dexippus was a contemporary but, with the exception of the campaign to repel the Goths from Attica, was not an eyewitness to the events he describes. His style is highly rhetorical and an uncritical acceptance of the fragments at face value is to be avoided. Nevertheless, it is going too far to dismiss the information they contain as wholly unreliable.[12]

The sophist, Eunapius, wrote a continuation of the *Chronicle* of Dexippus, starting with the reign of Aurelian, but this too exists only in fragments, none of which is directly relevant. Both Dexippus and Eunapius were apparently used by the historian, Zosimus, writing at the close of the fifth century, whose unsatisfactory *New History* forms a regrettably important source for the events with which we are concerned.[13] Though his narrative is chronological his sense of chronology is not reliable. Like his model, Eunapius, Zosimus was staunchly pagan and his work must be understood as part of the late pagan polemical tradition which sought to blame Christianity for the ills that beset the empire.

The *Church History* of Eusebius of Caesarea, a near contemporary of the events with which we are concerned, provides some limited help, particularly on Christian affairs. Of the later Greek chroniclers and minor historians, some additional information is provided by Syncellus and by the twelfth-century Zonaras. The *Chronographia* of John Malalas is also useful, especially concerning events in the east; but it is generally speaking not a reliable source. Further information is to be found in the fragmentary remains of the works of John of Antioch, Peter the Patrician and the anonymous Continuator of Dio.[14] Still more cryptic clues are provided by the thirteenth book of the Sibylline Oracle, a contemporary work written (after the event) in the form of prophetic verse. Unfortunately, it ends shortly before Aurelian's accession.[15] In relation to affairs in the east, especially concerning Zenobia, some further information is also preserved in Jewish and Arabic texts.[16]

Besides the literary texts, further useful information is to be found in the law codes and digests. Regrettably, however, the surviving material from this period is unimpressive. A mere handful of Aurelian's own legal pronouncements are preserved and, additionally, there are some subsequent imperial pronouncements which have a bearing on the legislation of his reign.

COINS, INSCRIPTIONS, PAPYRI AND OTHER ARCHAEOLOGICAL EVIDENCE

In recent decades the situation has been transformed by tremendous advances in the study of what may broadly be termed archaeological evidence, in particular coins, inscriptions and papyri. As the value of sources other than literary has become more widely appreciated, the volume and sophistication of work carried out in these fields have greatly increased.

These advances have been most spectacular in the field of numismatics. Since coins were being produced at a far higher rate in the mid-third century than in previous periods, and the number of coin hoards buried but not recovered by their owners increased with the political, military and economic insecurities of the time, there is an abundance of coinage from this period that can be studied. The coin evidence for Aurelian's reign has proved notoriously recalcitrant, but even here progress has been remarkable. A number of important numismatic articles and monographs devoted to the coinage of his reign have recently appeared. In particular, our present understanding has been significantly advanced by the excellent work on the numerous coin hoards of this period, studying both their composition and location.[17] Inferences can often be drawn from such studies relating to monetary policy and to the workings of individual mints, their output and their location. Though somewhat more controversial, the study of coin hoards has even been used to plot the most likely route of barbarian invasions.[18] The metrology of coins and the scientific analysis of their metal content are now very precise and have contributed immensely to our understanding of monetary policy and the sequencing and attribution of coins. Studies devoted to coin types have revealed much about the imperial titulature and iconography in use at this date, and reflect further on both policies and events.[19]

Important advances have also been made in the field of epigraphy. Although the numbers of extant inscriptions from this period are considerably smaller than for the Severan period, the information they contain is none the less illuminating. Epigraphic studies have proved especially useful in relation to questions of chronology and imperial titulature. Certain types of inscription have also provided evidence relating to building and repair work, for example milestones in relation to the provincial road network. The careful assemblage, collation and analysis of the inscriptions of Aurelian's reign, either as a whole or in relation to some specific aspect, has greatly added to our understanding of the period.[20] Epigraphy has also provided the raw material for the study of individual careers; and prosopography has in turn added greatly to our knowledge of political, social and administrative developments in this period.[21]

Papyrology has also contributed to our knowledge of this period, not least in the area of chronology. The Egyptian evidence, whether coins, inscriptions or papyri, is especially important for chronology because, although restricted to one geographical area, it provides unusual precision. Egypt had never been admitted within the ordinary provincial structure of the empire, but remained a separate imperial domain with its own closed monetary system. The mint at Alexandria was thus an anomaly, operating on a different basis from the other imperial mints and in a different currency, based on the Ptolemaic tetradrachm. The coinage from this mint continued to bear Greek legends and carry the emperor's regnal year, based on the Graeco-Egyptian calendar which ran from approximately 29 August to 28 August.[22] The papyri regularly provide even greater precision, mentioning not only the regnal year but the month and often the day as well. As with inscriptions, the papyri help to sort out the elements of imperial titulature. They also provide vital information on economic and social matters.[23]

Other forms of archaeological evidence have also provided helpful information. Excavation and analysis of archaeological remains, both on land and under the sea, have yielded a great deal of information on trade and other socio-economic developments. The study of structural remains has likewise contributed substantially to our understanding of this period. Some of the most significant work in relation to Aurelian's time has been carried out on the fortifications erected in this troubled period, often in some haste. The studies that have been made of the walls of Rome itself have revealed much valuable information on their design, construction and purpose.

APPENDIX B

Problems of chronology

1 GOTHIC INVASIONS UNDER GALLIENUS AND CLAUDIUS

The sources present us with two sets of data: (a) [Sync. 717; SHA *Gal.*; Zos. 1.39] A sea-borne raid swept down the western shore of the Black Sea, attacking the coastal cities, including Byzantium, crossed the Aegean and sacked a number of cities in Achaea, including Athens, before turning north to Macedonia where Gallienus defeated them; (b) [Zos. 1.42–46; SHA *Claud.*; Zon. 12.26] A sea-borne invasion on a quite unprecedented scale ravaged the western shore of the Black Sea, passed into the Aegean, besieged Thessalonica and was finally defeated by Claudius.

The traditional view accepted there were two major invasions: one late in Gallienus' reign, the other under Claudius. In 1939, Alföldi argued for one single invasion, pointing to the high level of coincidence between the two versions. He suggested that Gallienus was responsible for its defeat and that the credit was only later transposed to Claudius as part of the general denigration of Gallienus in the literary sources.[1] This theory has been broadly accepted by most scholars since, though some would date the invasion to the reign of Claudius.[2] It has the beauty of simplicity, but the truth is not always simple.

If there were two distinct invasions, elements of each have become confused in our sources. This might be partly because, at least initially, the two invasions followed similar routes. The *HA* describes how two of Gallienus' generals, whom he names as 'Cleodamus and Athenaeus, the Byzantines', defeated the barbarians 'circa Pontum'; he also mentions a naval victory over the Goths in this region during which the Roman admiral Venerianus was killed.[3] Conversely, Zonaras records that 'Cleodamus Athenaeus', i.e. Cleodamus the Athenian, defended Athens by defeating the barbarians at sea.[4] This appears to be a garbled version conflating the two notices in the *HA* (for nothing in the text of *Gal.* 13.6 indicates that the battle fought by Cleodamus and Athenaeus was at sea). Alföldi preferred Zonaras, but for once the *HA* seems more trustworthy.

Zonaras went on to recount an incident during the sack of Athens in which the invaders burned the books; the story appears again in Petrus, and in both cases the incident is placed in the reign of Claudius. Syncellus, the *HA* and Zosimus, on the other hand, all place the sack of Athens in the reign of Gallienus. That the invasion of Greece took place under Gallienus is further supported by Victor and Eutropius.[5] It must be accepted that only one invasion of Achaea took place, but that does not mean there was only one invasion overall. Alföldi also pointed to the references to a siege of Thessalonica. Only the *HA* refers to a siege of Thessalonica under Gallienus; all other sources date this event to Claudius' reign.[6]

Finally, the *HA* and Zosimus place Gallienus' victory over the Goths in the Balkans; Syncellus adds that the battle occurred on the banks of the Nessos (Latin Nestus).[7] The only source to name the site of Claudius' victory is Zosimus, who says it was at Naisus (modern Nis).[8] Naissus was the birthplace of Constantine, who later 'adopted' Claudius as his ancestor. The association between Claudius and Naissus may have been one of the reasons why Constantine singled out Claudius in particular. If Zosimus is correct in placing the battle there, the coincidence may help to explain the confusion between the two campaigns in the literary sources.

The evidence is simply too confused to say with any certainty whether there were two (or more) invasions, or only one. On balance, I believe the weight of evidence points to there being two (as set out in Chapter 3 above). Either way, it is clear from the account in Ammianus, which pays scant attention to chronology, that even the Claudian campaign was not decisive, and that the matter was only finally concluded by Aurelian.[9]

2 AURELIAN'S EARLY CAMPAIGNS, 270–1

Controversy also surrounds the number of Aurelian's campaigns in the first few months of his reign and the precise identity of the peoples against whom they were fought. Once again the problem turns on how to reconcile contradictory evidence and once again Alföldi has proposed a solution which elides two supposed invasions into one.

The starting point is two fragments from the *Scythica* of Dexippus. Fragment 6 describes Aurelian's parley with the Juthungi after he had defeated them beside a river. Fragment 7 describes Aurelian's negotiations with the Vandals, after which Aurelian hastened to Italy when he learnt the Juthungi had invaded 'again'.[10] The problems arise in reconciling these fragments with the information provided by the other literary sources and with the chronology of the first twelve months of Aurelian's reign.

A fragment of Petrus also refers to Aurelian's negotiations with the Vandals, which approximates to Dexippus' fr. 7.[11] Zosimus (1.48–49.1) tells how Aurelian went from Rome, via Aquileia, to Pannonia, where he fought the 'Scythians', who sued for peace. Aurelian then heard that the 'Alamanni and their neighbours' were about to invade Italy. Fearing for Rome's safety, he marched to Italy, killing a great many barbarians in battle beside the Danube. The *HA* (*Aurel.* 18.2) says that Aurelian fought fiercely against the 'Suebi' and the 'Sarmatae', and won a great victory. The author then (*Aurel.* 18.3, 18.6, 21.1–4) describes in some detail the invasion of Italy by the 'Marcomanni', who defeated the Romans at Placentia (Piacenza) but were finally vanquished by Aurelian. A fragment of the Continuator of Dio refers to negotiations after the barbarians had sacked Placentia, and the *Epitome* recounts the barest outline of a campaign in Italy in which Aurelian won three battles at Placentia, beside the Metaurus River near Fanum (Fano) and on the plains of Ticinum (Pavia).[12] Both Zosimus and the Epitomator pass on directly to describing the revolts of Domitianus and Septiminus and the major rioting at Rome, which is implicitly linked to the barbarian invasion of Italy. The causal link is made explicit in the *HA*.[13]

The traditional view supposes that there must have been two Juthungian invasions of Italy in rapid succession early in Aurelian's reign, one either side of a campaign against the Vandals. The first, perhaps launched under Quintillus, was defeated by Aurelian on the Danube (Dexippus fr. 6); the second, more serious, invasion is that indicated by the 'again' of Dexippus fr. 7.4, and described by the other sources mentioned above. After this, Aurelian proceeded direct to Rome to suppress the riots.[14] There are difficulties with this view. First, it requires two major invasions of Italy by the same Germanic people within a few months of each other; second, Dexippus is the only possible evidence for the first invasion; third, realistically speaking, there is insufficient time for a Juthungian campaign before Aurelian set out for Pannonia.

Alföldi reversed the order of the Dexippan fragments, suggesting

Aurelian fought only one Juthungian campaign, which took place after the Pannonian campaign. The 'again' of fr. 7.4 therefore referred back to some earlier invasion. Alföldi postulated that the Juthungi took part in the invasion of Italy under Claudius alongside the Alamanni.[15] This simplification has been widely accepted among modern scholars; but it too is not without its difficulties. Many of these were exposed in a recent article by Saunders.[16] They may be summarized as follows:

1 The received order of the Dexippan fragments should only be altered on compelling evidence. It is unlikely that these passages were not in their correct chronological order in Dexippus' original text. Nevertheless, it is not at all unthinkable that they were reversed by the excerptor or early in the history of the text's transmission.[17]

2 Zosimus, upon whom Alföldi heavily relied, is not a reliable source. His account of Aurelian's reign begins with Aurelian setting out from Rome. Although Alföldi and many other scholars have assumed that Aurelian visited Rome at the beginning of his reign, there is no credible evidence to suggest that he did so; in fact the assumption is based on an anachronistic view of the importance of Rome in this regard, backed up solely by Zosimus.[18] Furthermore, Zosimus is clearly confused over the identity of the various Germanic peoples north of the Danube at this time (see below).

3 Both the content and the tenor of the speeches in Dexippus F. 6 present serious difficulties. The Juthungi boast about how they have overrun most of Italy, and Aurelian describes them as laden with Italian spoils. Furthermore, the Juthungi wish to negotiate their safe passage home and at the same time argue as if from a position of strength, a position which Aurelian does not deny. Also, Aurelian reminds them of the lessons the empire had recently taught the Goths and the 'Galmioni' (probably a textual corruption of Alamanni) but omits to mention his victories over the Juthungi themselves in Italy. All this is very out of place if we accept Alföldi's notion that the Juthungi have already retreated as far as the Danube, in other words, are virtually home, and have been twice defeated by Aurelian already (the second time, at Pavia, decisively according to the *HA* and the *Epitome*).[19]

4 It is simply not credible that Aurelian chased them some 600 kilometres over the Alps to the Danube and then had to come all

the way back before marching to Rome at a time when he must have known Rome was in turmoil.[20] Nor is it credible to suppose that the unrest caused by the Barbarian victory at Piacenza and their advance as far as Fano would have persisted all the while Aurelian marched not just to Pavia, but all the way to the Danube and back (which would require the best part of three months in total).

This last objection was noted by Cubelli, who attempted to rescue the thesis by suggesting that Dexippus mistakenly set the final victory on the banks of the Danube when in fact it was the Po: that is to say, the episode described in fr. 6 refers to the battle at Pavia.[21] This is ingenious, but still fails to explain the factors mentioned at (3) above. It also leaves Aurelian faced with a large hostile force in northern Italy which he would still have had to neutralize, in some final battle of which we know nothing, before he could turn his attention to Rome.

These problems all virtually disappear if Dexippus fr. 6 actually took place after the battle of Fano, which was the first set-back for the Juthungi and which still left them in a position of considerable strength. The boast to have overrun 'all but a little of Italy' is far better suited to the context of their point of greatest penetration. In this context it assumes the import of a veiled threat: if they are not given what they ask for, they will go on and conquer the rest. Furthermore, it makes better sense of an otherwise unexplained riddle in the *Epitome*. The author's style is extremely compressed, and not given to adding superfluous details. The fact that he bothers to mention the name of the river beside which the battle of Fano was fought strongly suggests that the river figured prominently in the account of the battle he was using. The only part of fr. 6 to locate the scene on the Danube is the introduction, which represents the Byzantine excerptor's précis of the battle that preceded the negotiations in the main body of the excerpt. Dexippus may not have known the name of the Metaurus. The only river actually mentioned in the body of the text is the Ister (i.e. the Danube). It would therefore have been very natural for the excerptor, who was interested in the rhetoric and not the historical setting of Dexippus' text, to have assumed that the battle too was set on the Danube.[22]

If we are to accept that the Dexippan fragments are now in the wrong order, we must explain the use of the term 'again' at the end of fr. 7.4. To do this we must first establish the identity of the various invaders in this period. Dexippus, the only contemporary source, speaks of none but the Juthungi in relation to the invasion of Italy under Aurelian. Indeed (in fr. 6.4), the envoys make much of the fact that their vast army is made up purely of Juthungi, unmixed with other (and by implication, lesser) peoples. This would be meaningless if Dexippus had just described an invasion comprising joint forces of Juthungi and Alamanni. The involvement of the Alamanni in this invasion depends entirely upon Zosimus, who calls the invaders 'the Alamanni and their neighbours'. Such a description could include the Juthungi, who were indeed neighbours of the Alamanni, and many scholars have seen fit to accept this.[23] But Zosimus' grasp of ethnology is at best shaky. He apparently refers to the Vandals as 'Scythians', a somewhat generic term more usually reserved for Goths in this period.[24] Earlier (1.37.1–2, 1.38.1), Zosimus describes the invaders of Italy in 260 as 'Scythians', here specifically identifying them as a branch of the Goths. According to Victor (*Caes.* 33.3) these invaders were 'Alamanni', an identification apparently confirmed by Zonaras (12.24), who adds that they were defeated by Gallienus near Milan.

A recently published inscription found near Augsburg sheds new light on this matter.[25] The inscription comes from an altar to Victory, set up to celebrate the defeat of the Juthungi in Raetia on their return from plundering Italy, laden with booty and transporting 'thousands' of captives taken in the raid. The inscription is dated 11 September in the consular year of the emperor Postumus and Honorationus. In publishing the inscription, Bakker dated it to 260, suggesting Postumus took up an *eponymous* consulship in that year. This suggestion is at odds both with imperial practice and with the chronology of the period: the consulship Postumus assumed in the latter part of 260 was a suffect consulship. Bakker's suggestion was based on a false premise, for iterations of consular years are frequently omitted at this date (as the editors of *AE* rightly remark). Both the battle (24–5 April) and the inscription are best dated to 261.[26]

The Augsburg inscription therefore shows that the Juthungi, whether alone or more likely as allies of the Alamanni, were involved in the great invasion of Italy in 260–1. Given that the Juthungi were involved in a major invasion of Italy during the decade before Aurelian's accession, it is conceivable that Juthungian forces were also with the Alamanni at Lake Garda in 269. Indeed, this would make the best sense of the Juthungian boast in fr. 6.4 that this time (unlike at Lake Garda) they had no weak allies. Zosimus nowhere describes the invasion of 269, and it is possible that in his 'Alamanni and their neighbours' he has mixed up aspects of the two invasions, in both of which Aurelian figured prominently.

Neither the Continuator nor the Epitomator name the invaders of 271. The *HA* refers to them as 'Marcomanni', a Suebian people living in Bohemia. The identification is suspect. The author probably borrowed the name to evoke the great struggle under Marcus Aurelius. The Juthungi also comprised Suebian peoples, notably the Semnones who had been among the allies of the Marcomanni at the time of Marcus Aurelius. The *HA*'s use of 'Marcomanni' in this context is therefore best taken as a misnomer for the Juthungi.[27] What significance should be attached to the 'Suebi' and 'Sarmatae' mentioned by the *HA* (*Aurel.* 18.2) is controversial. The passage actually implies it is referring to events that occurred under Claudius. If so, this victory over the 'Suebi' (i.e. Juthungi and Alamanni) may be that at Lake Garda, which otherwise the *HA* fails to mention.[28]

The author also omits any mention of the Vandals at this point, though they figure alongside the Sarmatians, the Suebi and the 'Germani' in the list of conquered peoples paraded in Aurelian's triumph (*Aurel.* 33.4). The Marcomanni, interestingly, do not appear in this list as such, though the invaders of Italy may be hidden in the generic 'Germani'. The attribution to Aurelian of the title Sarmaticus Maximus, implying a Sarmatian victory, is no longer safe. It may be that the Sarmatian Iazyges assisted the Vandals or that 'Sarmatae' here means Vandals. At the very least, the author is clearly confused.[29]

It is still possible that the traditional view is correct, as Saunders concludes. Further inscriptions, such as that found at Augsburg, may yet throw some further light on this vexed question. In the meantime, no explanation can be definitive. In my view, however, the version given in Chapter 3, and the explanation offered above, is the most satisfying on the evidence as it stands at present.

3 THE POWER STRUGGLES OF 270–2

The chronology of the events that took place in the months following Claudius' death is clouded by a lack of firm data and by numerous seeming contradictions. Nevertheless, a plausible reconstruction is now feasible on the basis of the activity of the various imperial mints and the evidence from Egypt.[30]

Claudius must have died in about mid-August. The mint at Alexandria only received news of his death after it had begun to issue coins for Claudius' year III (29 August 270 to 28 August 271). At Oxyrhyncus, a good five days' journey to the south, a papyrus still recognized Claudius around the end of September 270.[31] The Alexandrian mint briefly issued coins in the name of Quintillus, all dated year I. His official *dies imperii*, being the day on which he was proclaimed emperor in Italy, must therefore have fallen just after the beginning of the Egyptian year, that is, on or shortly after 29 August 270.[32]

The literary sources allow Quintillus only a brief reign, ranging from seventy-seven days to as little as seventeen.[33] The Roman imperial mints that had been under Claudius' direct control at the time of his death (Rome, Milan, Siscia and Cyzicus) all began to issue coinage in the name of Quintillus. Their output in his name is such that a reign of only a few days' duration can be ruled out; something around two months is more likely.[34] The emission for Quintillus at Cyzicus is small, suggesting a very short duration.[35] This ties in well with what we can infer about Aurelian's proclamation at Sirmium, news of which caused the abrupt cessation of coin production at Cyzicus in the name of Quintillus. Allowing for the various travel times involved, this would place the elevation of Aurelian at Sirmium in late September.

Returning to the Egyptian evidence, the papyrological record to date suggests that the reign of Quintillus was never recognized in the Nile valley south of Memphis. Instead, in this region, for a period of a month or two, starting no later than 12 October and extending down to mid-November, or even mid-December, papyri were dated by the Roman consuls. This unusual formula suggests some confusion, or hesitation, in the minds of Egyptian officials in that area concerning the identity of the reigning emperor. When papyri resume the more usual form of regnal dating, Aurelian and Vaballathus are named jointly.[36]

Clearly, news of Claudius' death reached Memphis by early October, but the recognition of Quintillus attested by the Alexandrian mint was never communicated up-river before being overtaken by some other event. The most likely explanation for the severe disruption to the official channels of communication from Alexandria implied by these events is the civil unrest and uncertainty occasioned by the Palmyrene invasion.[37] This places the initial Palmyrene assault at the very beginning of October.

During the ensuing troubles the mint at Alexandria may have partially or even totally shut down for a brief time. For a short time the mint did issue coins in the name of Aurelian as sole ruler (year I), though not apparently working at full production. This issue probably coincides with the interlude during which Tenagino Probus regained control of the city.[38] It appears this was in approximately early November. The disruption caused by the invasion prevented the restoration of official communications to the south before the Palmyrenes struck again. As a result, the sole reign of Aurelian was not recognized south of the delta, where dating continued to be by the consuls. During the latter half of November and into December the Palmyrenes regained control of the delta. Thereafter, both the Alexandrian coinage and the papyri from further south honour Aurelian and Vaballathus jointly, at first according them the same regnal years but soon prioritizing Vaballathus by dating his regnal years from the date of his father's death.[39]

Until the early 1970s it was generally thought that Vaballathus' year IV was the Egyptian year 269/70, which conventionally placed the death of Odenathus in 266/7. However, papyrological research has conclusively shown that Vaballathus' year IV was in fact 270/1. Although this dating is now universally accepted, the necessary inference that his father's murder must have fallen in the Egyptian year 267/8 (i.e. between late August 267 and late August 268) has yet to be properly acknowledged.[40]

An analogous situation occurred in Syria. Towards the end of Claudius' reign the mint at Antioch closed down and did not reopen for several months until well into the reign of Aurelian. In view of the other available data, it is reasonable to attribute this hiatus to the growing disruption in the region caused by Palmyrene aggression. The interruption was followed, in the winter of 270/1, by an issue in the joint names of Vaballathus and Aurelian. At a later point, which can now be shown to have been the spring of 272, coins were issued in the names of Vaballathus and Zenobia alone, in defiance of Aurelian, but production was short-lived, ceasing abruptly with Aurelian's recapture of the city.[41]

The date of this last event, and the chronology of Aurelian's Palmyrene campaign, depends once again on the Egyptian evidence. The system of dating by Aurelian year II and Vaballathus year V continued to be used at Oxyrhyncus until at least the middle of April 272. By 24 June, Aurelian was already recognized as sole ruler on a papyrus from Oxyrhyncus.[42] This document, however, uses a new computation for Aurelian's regnal years: the current year, 271/2, is given as Aurelian's year III. Evidently Aurelian had decided early in his reign, as part of his efforts to marginalize the reign of Quintillus, to backdate his *dies imperii* to the date of Claudius' death (that is, to the Egyptian year 269/70). This fact had never been understood in Egypt as long as it remained under Palmyrene domination.[43]

The new reckoning of Aurelian's regnal years must therefore have been recognized in Alexandria no later than 19 June at the very latest. Aurelian's expeditionary force must have regained control of Alexandria at some point considerably anterior to this. The mint at Alexandria had time to prepare a small issue of coinage in the name of Aurelian alone using the old reckoning (i.e. year II) before the error was understood and corrected and a fresh issue put out dated year III.[44] Aurelian therefore cannot have been recognized as the sole rightful ruler at Alexandria any later than the end of May, providing a *terminus ante quem* for the recapture of Alexandria. It may be assumed, on the basis of the papyrological evidence, that the Alexandrian mint was still issuing the joint coinage up to the beginning of April at least. This was followed by the issue in the names of Vaballathus and Zenobia, which cannot have ceased appreciably earlier than mid-May. It appears, therefore, that the battle for Alexandria took place during May 272. The rest of Egypt apparently offered little resistance, and the entire campaign was all over in a matter of weeks.

By working backwards, it is therefore possible to conjecture as to a timetable for the beginning of Aurelian's great campaign. The expeditionary fleet must have set sail from Byzantium no later than the very beginning of April. The Alexandrian mint received the instructions from Zenobia in Syria to abandon the joint coinage in favour of coinage recognizing Vaballathus as Augustus in approximately mid-April. Allowing time for these instructions to arrive from Syria, Zenobia must have taken her momentous decision some time in the second half of March. Aurelian's preparations to cross the Bosphorus would have made his intentions unequivocal some time before this. It seems reasonable to conjecture that it was this intelligence which prompted Zenobia to change her policy.

4 THE CHRONOLOGY OF 275–6

The chronology of the end of Aurelian's reign and the events that occurred in the months that followed his death have provided historians with particular difficulties. The bibliography on the subject is now extensive.[45] The starting point for any such enquiry is the date of Aurelian's death. Coins from Alexandria dated year VII for Aurelian suggest he was still recognized as the reigning emperor in

Egypt at the end of August 275. The papyrological evidence pushes the *terminus post quem* even later. A document dated 19 October, found at Oxyrhynchus, strongly suggests that Aurelian was still reigning well into September 275.[46]

The earliest known Egyptian evidence dated by reference to Tacitus does not appear until 9 May 276, but other evidence helps to narrow this gap. It is known that Tacitus took up the consulship as emperor on 1 January 276. Since he received a second grant of tribunician power, which would usually fall due on 10 December, it is probable that he was emperor by the beginning of December 275.[47] The literary sources mostly give Tacitus a reign of about six months, though some give him nearer seven.[48] He was still recognized in Oxyrhynchus at least up to 25 June 276. Coinage from the mint at Alexandria suggests that Probus was acknowledged as emperor in that city well before the end of the Egyptian year; possibly as much as two months before. Allowing time for the news of Tacitus' death to reach Probus and for that of Probus' proclamation then to reach Egypt, Tacitus probably met his end sometime in (mid-to-late?) June.[49] This appears to confirm a date in late November or very early December 275 as being the most likely date of Tacitus' accession.

The news of Aurelian's assassination must have taken about four weeks to reach Rome from Thrace. It seems reasonable to assume there was then some delay, of days or perhaps even a few weeks, while the news travelled further to reach Tacitus in Campania. If he was not acclaimed in Campania itself, but by the praetorians in Rome, he must have had time to hurry north to the metropolis. Even assuming the assassination took place as early as mid-September, the interval between the arrival of this news in Rome and the proclamation of Tacitus can scarcely have exceeded seven weeks. In fact, however, there is no sound evidence to preclude Aurelian having lived on well into October and some slight evidence to suggest that a later date for his death is more plausible.[50] If Aurelian was killed in late October, the interval of uncertainty at Rome cannot have been much more than a matter of days. This latter suggestion is far from improbable, given the notice to this precise effect in one source and the silence of most of the others.[51]

NOTES

1 INTRODUCTION: THE THIRD-CENTURY 'CRISIS'

1 Birthday see *Chron. 354* (*Chron. Min.* I 148); Philocalus *CIL* I²: 272, cf. 356. Year see Malal. 12.30 (301 Bonn); *Synopsis Sathas*: 39. Place see Eutrop. 9.13.1; Epit. 35.1; SHA *Aurel.* 3.1f., cf. 24.3. The suggestion of Sirmium (Mitrovica) may be derived from the fact that he was acclaimed emperor there. The parentage in *Epit.* 35.1, though plausible, is probably fiction. See Syme 1971: 208–10, 222–3; Syme 1983: 65, 123, 159; Paschoud 1996: 71–2.

2 A.H.M. Jones, *The Later Roman Empire, AD 284–602*, vol. 1, Oxford 1964: 23; cf. R. MacMullen, *Corruption and the Decline of Rome*, New Haven 1988: 111.

3 Traditionally the 'crisis' covers the period 235–85, but it has often been extended to embrace the third century as a whole and sometimes even beyond. R. Rémondon, *La Crise de l'Empire Romain de Marc Aurèle à Anastase*, Paris 1964, postulated a crisis lasting 330 years.

4 The phrase was coined by J. Gagé, 'La théologie de la victoire impériale', *Rev. Hist.* 171 1933: 1–43; see further Zanker 1988.

5 On the imperial monopoly, see Tacitus *Ann.* 3.74; the dating of the *dies imperii* began with Claudius I: see Campbell 1984: 93ff.; cf. A. von Premerstein *Vom Werden und Wesen des Prinzipats* [*Abt. B.A.W.* N.F. 15], Munich 1937: 245–60. Octavian's names, Imperator and Caesar, have thus given to modern European languages their terms for 'emperor' (empereur, imperatore, Kaiser, Tsar, etc.).

6 Dio 77.15.2. In fact, both Septimius and Caracalla augmented army pay (see p. 12). The regionalism evident in the events of the 190s indicates that it is scarcely meaningful to speak of 'the Roman army' in the singular by this date.

7 The phrase is borrowed from Geoffrey Blainey, *The Tyranny of Distance: How Distance Shaped Australia's History*, Sidney 1966. On the dilemma of the necessity for imperial omnipresence see F. Millar, 'Emperors, Frontiers and Foreign Relations 31 BC–AD 378', *Britannia* 8, 1982: 1–23, 11–15.

8   The phrase 'le cycle infernal' was coined by J.-J. Hatt, *Histoire de la Gaule romaine (120 av. J.-C. – 451 ap. J.-C.). Colonisation ou Colonialisme?* (2nd edn), Paris 1966: 227.

9   Isaac 1990: 15–16; Potter 1990: 8.

10 Most likely in 226. See R.N. Frye, 'Parthia and Sasanid Persia', in Millar 1981: 249–67, esp. 257f.; and, more generally, A. Christensen, *L'Iran sous les Sassanides* (2nd edn), Copenhagen 1944: esp. 84–98.

11 Isaac 1990: 19–53.

12 On the Gothic migration see G. Kossack, 'The Germans', in Millar 1981: 294–320, esp. 317–19; and, more generally, E.A. Thompson, *The Visigoths in the Time of Ulfila*, Oxford 1966. Among the more influential allies of the Goths were the Gepidae (in eastern Romania) and the Heruli (near the Crimea).

13 Millar 1981: 319–20 (G. Kossack, op. cit.). Barnes 1994 argues that the earliest secure reference to the Franks is in the reign of Probus, but as he himself admits (pp. 17–18) this ignores the evidence of Zon. 12.24 and of Jerome *Chron.* 223 (Helm).

14 The analysis of Luttwak 1976: 127–94, esp. 145–54, must be heavily qualified: see Isaac 1990: 372–418; cf. also J.C. Mann, 'Power, Force and the Frontiers of the Empire', *JRS* 69, 1979: 175–83; Millar 1981: 240f.

15 Victor *Caes.* 33.34 (still believed by some, e.g., Cizek 1994: 68–70). On the development, see H.-G. Pflaum, 'Zur Reform des Kaisers Gallienus', *Historia* 25, 1976: 109–17; Millar 1981: 60–1; Potter 1990: 56–7.

16 Alföldi 1967: 1–15; L. de Blois, *The Policy of the Emperor Gallienus*, Leiden 1976: 26–36; cf. M.R. Alföldi, 'Zu den Militärreformen des Kaisers Gallienus', *Limes Studien* 3, Basel 1957: 13–18.

17 The plague was first brought back from the east by the army of Lucius Verus in the 160s. On manpower see A.E.R. Boak, *Manpower Shortage and the Fall of the Roman Empire in the West*, Ann Arbor 1955. While Boak probably exaggerates the position, it was none the less a serious factor.

18 On debasement and inflation see Chapter 8.

19 Herod., 1.6.5; cf. *Dig.* 3.2.2.4, 48.22.18 (*pr.*), 50.1.3. Note also, Millar 1977: 39, 'the emperor functioned as a sort of moving capital of the empire in himself'.

20 Millar 1977: 40–53. Even before founding Constantinople, Constantine referred to Serdica as 'my Rome': Petrus Patr. *FHG* IV 199 (= Dio, ed. Boissevain, III 748, fr. 190). On the strategic shift eastwards, see Millar 1981: 239–41, 245.

21 Millar 1977: 277, 619; Hopkins 1983: 176–84.

22 On the development of 'une nouvelle Romanité' see G. Dagron, *L'Empire romain d'Orient au IVe siècle et les traditions politiques de l'Hellénisme. Le Témoinage de Thémistios*, Paris 1968: 83–119; cf. E. Kantorowicz, *The King's Two Bodies: A Study in Mediaeval Political Theology*, Princeton 1957: esp. 82f., 246f.

23 A.N. Sherwin-White, *The Roman Citizenship* (2nd edn), Oxford 1973 (note esp. 221f. on the concept of 'Roman' in relation to the spread of citizenship).
24 Hopkins 1983: 184–200; cf. Millar 1977: 375–447 on the increasing confidence of the Greek east.
25 Wardman 1982: 123–7. For a much more antagonistic view of the relationship between the empire and Judaism see Isaac 1990.
26 Alföldi 1939: 202–7; Friend 1965: 422–9; Wardman 1982: 127–34; Potter 1990: 42–3, 49, 68–9, 261–7. Gallienus' edict of toleration: Euseb. *HE* 7.13.
27 E.R. Dodds, *Pagan and Christian in the Age of Anxiety: Some Aspects of Religious Experience from M. Aurelius to Constantine*, Cambridge 1965, must be regarded as taking an over-simplified approach.
28 See Appendix A and also Chapter 7.

2 A DIVIDED EMPIRE

1 Potter 1990: 44–6, 278–82.
2 Herennius, the elder son, may have been killed in an earlier battle (Beroea?), according to Jordanes *Get.* 103; on the sons of Decius see Potter 1990: 282–3. On the Goths retaining their booty see Zos. 1.24.2.
3 Zos. 1.27 (AD 252), 1.28 (AD 253). See Potter 1990: 310–12 (cf. 47) for the distinction between these two Gothic attacks.
4 Thessalonica was fortified, but plans to fortify both Athens and the Isthmus of Corinth lapsed.
5 The chronology of Zos. 1.31–6, our fullest source, is regrettably unclear.
6 On the Roman frontier in the east see now Isaac 1990, esp. 14–18, 372–418; see also Freeman and Kenedy 1986.
7 Matthews 1984, esp. 164–70; Isaac 1990: 144–6; Stoneman 1992: 31–49; and see J. Teixidor, *Un port romain du désert: Palmyre et son commerce d'Auguste à Caracalla*, Paris, 1984.
8 Isaac 1990: 147: 'Palmyra could never have been – and never was – an ordinary provincial town, whatever its formal status.' On the status of Palmyra in the 250 years from Antony to Caracalla see Graf 1989: 144; Isaac 1990: 141–7, 225; cf. Stoneman 1992: 20; see also J. Starcky and M. Gawlikowski, *Palmyre*, Paris 1985.
9 For example, the Palmyrene cohort stationed at Dura: see J.G. Février, *Essai sur l'histoire politique et économique de Palmyre*, Paris 1931: 74; de Blois 1975: 18. On military and strategic importance of Palmyra see Isaac 1990: 144, 228; Stoneman 1992: 27–8, 52.
10 The Bedouin threat see Graf 1989: 144 .
11 Zos. 1.20.2; Victor *Caes.* 29.2; *Orac. Sibyl.* XIII 61–3. On Philip's eastern policy, the role of Priscus and the revolt of Jotapianus at Emesa see Potter 1990: 37, 39–40, 212–16, 220–5, 229, 245–7, 248–9.

12 Shapur's second great invasion represented a total defeat for Rome in the east: *RGDS* 13–17; Zos. 1.27.2; Zon. 12.21; *Orac. Sibyl.* XIII 110–33. Potter 1990: 46–7, 290–308. On Antioch specifically see G. Downey, *A History of Antioch in Syria from Seleucus to the Arab Conquest*, Princeton 1961: 587–95; Alföldi 1967: 125.

13 *Orac. Sibyl.* XIII 150–4; Malal. 12.26 (296 Bonn). Potter 1990: 48–9, 323–7 (and the modern works there cited); Peachin 1990: 296; cf. Bowersock 1983: 128.

14 Dura was a strategic point on the Euphrates frontier, it fell to Shapur on his homeward route in 252 (*RGDS* 17), was regained by Valerian and sacked by Shapur in the mid-250s (probably 256) see Potter 1990: 50, 292 (esp. n. 252), 296; de Blois 1975: 9–10.

15 Zos. 1.36.1.

16 *RGDS* 24; Eutrop. 9.7; *Epit.* 32.5; Zon. 12.23; *Orac. Sibyl.* XIII 158–61; cf. Zos. 1.36.2; Petr. Patr. (*FHG* IV 187) fr. 9; and on the subsequent fate of Valerian, Petr. Patr. (*FHG* IV 188) fr. 13; Lactant. *de mort. persec.* 5.1–7 (esp. 5.6). See Potter 1990: 50–1, 329–37, cf. 292–3; and for date see König 1981: 20–31.

17 *RGDS* 26–34; cf. the somewhat confused accounts in Malal. 12.27 (297 Bonn); Sync. 716 (Bonn); Zon. 12.23; *Orac. Sibyl.* XIII 162–4. See also E. Kettenhofen, *Die römisch-persischen Kriege des 3. Jahrhunderts n. Chr. nach der Inschrift Sahpuhrs I. an der Kaaba-ye Zartost*, Wiesbaden 1982: 106–22; Potter 1990: 337–41.

18 For the controversies surrounding Odenathus, see Potter 1990: 381–94; de Blois 1975.

19 M. Gawlikowski, 'Les Princes de Palmyre', *Syria* 62, 1985: 251–61 (esp. p. 260); cf. Potter 1990: 381–4.

20 Against 'dynasty' see Isaac 1990: 226; Potter 1990: 388–90; cf. SHA *Tyr. trig.* 15.2, rightly stressing the novelty of Odenathus' assumption of the regal title. On hegemony over Arab tribes see Bowersock 1983: 132–7; Graf 1989: 150–5; Potter 1990: 389. This hegemony is reflected in the title 'king of the Saracens' in Malalas, 12.26 (297 Bonn) and 'ruler of the Saracens' in Procop. *Pers.* 2.5.

21 *Inv.* III 16 (*CIS* II 3944); see Potter 1990: 384.

22 So de Blois 1975: 17f., taking the actions of 'Enathus' reported in Malalas 12.26 (297 Bonn) to refer only to the events of 252–3; in fact it is clearly a conflation of the events of the period 252–66. That Malalas' account is confused is proved by his descriptions of the death of 'Valerian' (confused with Gallienus) and of the reign of 'Gallienus' (confused with Valerian, among others).

23 Petr. Patr. (*FHG* IV 187) fr. 10; cf. the echo of a similar story in Malalas 12.26 (297 Bonn).

24 On the title ὁ λαμπρότατος ὑπατικός (consularis) and the *ornamenta consularia* see Potter 1990: 389–90. For a more elaborate, but less convincing, account of Odenathus' exploits in the late 250s see de Blois 1975: 12–20.

25 *Inv.* III 17 (*CIS* II 3945; *IGR* III 1031); cf. Potter 1990: 388–9.

26 Peachin 1990: 40–1.

27 Potter 1990: 53, 344 (giving credence to Zon. 12.24 concerning pressure from European troops). It is probable that Aurelian himself, then in his mid-forties, took part in this campaign on the loyalist side. On Ballista as praetorian prefect see Howe 1942: 81f.

28 SHA *Gal.* 3.1; Zon. 12.24; *Orac. Sibyl.* XIII 164–9; cf. Potter 1990: 53–4, 343–6 (noting possible arrangement between Macrianus and Odenathus). Whether Odenathus acted at the express invitation of Gallienus is unclear and is largely irrelevant.

29 Some clues as to the forces available to Odenathus are provided in the sources, though they tend to underestimate the extent to which these forces constituted a regular army; see Festus *Brev.* 23; Jerome *Chron.* 221 (Helm); Oros. 7.22.12; Jord. *Rom.* 290.

30 Sync. 716; Zon. 12.23–4; cf. also the wide-ranging powers in Eutrop. 9.11.1; SHA *Gal.* 1.1, 3.3, 10.1; *Tyr. trig.* 14.1 (see below, n. 32, on *imperator*). It must be stressed that neither *dux* nor *imperator* are recorded on inscriptions of Odenathus. The reservations on the title *corrector* expressed by J. Cantineau, 'Un *restitutor Orientis* dans les inscriptions de Palmyre', *Journal Asiatique* 222, 1933: 217–33, 217–23, and Millar 1971: 10, are unwarranted; see now Potter 1990: 54, 390–2.

31 The inscription (see D. Schlumberger, 'L'inscription d'Hérodien: remarques sur l'histoire des princes de Palmyre', *Bull. d'ét. orient.* 1942–3: 36–50; cf. *Inv.* III 3; *IGR* III 1032: relating to the elevation of Herodianus) is now dated to the period of Odenathus' Persian campaigns. The nomenclature of Odenathus' sons has proved problematic: Septimius Hairan may have died sometime between 251 and 262 so that by the latter date Herodianus was Odenathus' eldest surviving son (though it is also possible that they were the same person), see Potter 1990: 385–8 (together with the works he cites). On the co-rulership of 'Herodes' (Herodianus) at this time, see also SHA *Tyr. trig.* 15.5; cf. *Gal.* 13.1. The title King of Kings is also given on a posthumous inscription in Aramaic (*mlk mlk'*): *Inv.* III 19 (*CIS* II 3946). See also SHA *Tyr. trig.* 15.1, and Potter 1990: 385, 390–3.

32 The acclamation of Odenathus as *imperator* is in fact conjectural, based on its use by Vaballathus (see above n. 30 and also Chapter 4). Co-rulership see SHA *Gal.* 12.1.

33 Almost certainly the first appearance of the Franks see Zon. 12.24; cf. Chapter 1, n. 13.

34 The date is controversial. Victor *Caes.* 33.2 states it was in the wake of the news of Valerian's disaster, which led Alföldi 1939: 184, to postulate 260. J. Fitz, *Ingenuus et Régalien*, Brussels 1966, among others, preferred a date as early as 258, while still retaining the relationship between this revolt and that of Regalian (see p. 34). The year 260 is to be preferred, though the revolt must have occurred on the news of Shapur's invasion rather than of Valerian's disaster.

35 Zon. 12.24; cf. Zos. 1.37.1–38.1; *AE* 1993: 1231; see also Appendix B.2. On the strategic importance of the Alamannic migration see Drinkwater 1987: 226–8 and in this book, Chapter 6.

36 Valens, the usurper in Macedonia, is attested in Amm. 21.16.10 and *Epit.* 32.4, as well as the largely spurious accounts in SHA *Gal.* 2.2–4, *Tyr. trig.* 19 and *Tyr. trig.* 21.1–3.

37 Victor *Caes.* 33.3; cf. H.D. Gallwey, 'A hoard of third-century antoniniani from southern Spain', *NC* 1962: 335–406.

38 Possibly governor of one of the Germanies: see König 1981: 53; cf. *PLRE* I 720, n. 2.

39 König 1981: 41–51.

40 Drinkwater 1987: 116–18 (cf. 27–8). On Raetia also going over to Postumus see *AE* 1993: 1231.

41 Furthermore, the allegiance of the *legio III Italica* stationed at Regensburg is not entirely clear in the light of *AE* 1993: 1231; Gallienus would not have wished to denude northern Italy of forces as long as Raetia remained loyal to Postumus.

42 Cont. Dion. (*FHG* IV 194–5) fr. 6.

43 SHA *Gal.* 4.4–6; cf. *Tyr. trig.* 3.5, 11.3. The date is controversial, but the consensus is for 265; cf. Alföldi 1939: 186 (dating to 263). The assertion in Drinkwater 1987: 89, that Postumus controlled the Alpine passes, is incorrect; on this and the stand-off, see Chapter 6.

44 Elmer 1941: 28; cf. König 1981: 65, suggesting he received *ornamenta consularia*; followed by Drinkwater 1987: 67. The assumption of a suffect consulship in the last part of 260 is much more satisfactory in view of the parallel with the Macriani (see following note).

45 *P. Oxy.* 34. 2710.8–9 (the iteration for Quietus is restored). The insignificance of this pair of youths (as opposed to their father) before their revolt precludes the idea that they might have been granted the *ornamenta consularia*.

46 Postumus Junior (SHA *Tyr. trig.* 4) is fictitious.

47 Among the top generals that Gallienus promoted, Ingenuus, Regalian and Postumus had already openly revolted against him; Aureolus, Heraclianus, Claudius and Aurelian would do so in the sequel.

48 Mysteries see Alföldi 1939: 189; on the VBIQVE PAX coinage and its date (on returning from Athens) see Göbl 1953: 11, 16.

3 AURELIAN ASCENDANT

1 Sync. 716–17; cf. SHA *Gal.* 4.7–8, 6.2, 11.1, 12.6; Jord. *Get.* 20.107–8. These sources have clearly elided the events of several raids into one catalogue. See Alföldi 1939: 141–50, 721–3; Demougeot 1969: 422–5; cf. Potter 1990: 44–7, 55–8.

2 SHA *Gal.* 13.6 (campaign near Pontus); *Gal.* 13.7 (naval victory); Sync. 717 (general route and sack of Byzantium). The East Goths may have

been involved in this invasion, and parhaps split off into Asia Minor, where they were halted by Odenathus (see Chapter 4, n. 9).

3 Sync. 717; cf. Zos. 1.39.1 (sack of Athens). Book burning see Petr. Patr. 169 (= '*Cont. Dion.*' fr. 9.1 *FHG* IV 196); Zon. 12.26 (both erroneously placing the incident under Claudius: see Appendix B.1). On the archaeological evidence for the sack of Athens see H.H. Thompson, 'Athenian Twilight: AD 267–400', *JRS* 49, 1959: 61–72, 62–5.

4 Sync. 717; SHA *Gal.* 13.8; Dexippus *FGH* 100, fr. 28.

5 Sync. 717; SHA *Gal.* 13.8–9, cf. 5.6–6.1 (a generalized introduction to the Gothic troubles in Gallienus' reign: see Appendix B.1); Zos. 1.39.1 (confused chronology); Victor *Caes.* 33.3; Eutrop. 9.8.2.

6 Date of Aureolus' revolt, see now Bastien 1984. Victor *Caes.* 33.17 (Aureolus held a command in Raetia, only moving to Milan after his revolt); but cf. Zosimus 1.40.1 (specifically locating his command at Milan). Marcianus' command see Zos. 1.40.1; SHA *Gal.* 13.10; *Claud.* 6.1; cf. *RE* 14, 1511.

7 Alföldi 1967: 1–15; König 1981: 125–31; Drinkwater 1987: 31–3; Bastien 1984.

8 Zon. 12.25; Victor *Caes.* 33.18; *Epit.* 33.2.

9 Heraclianus: *RE* 13, 361; Howe 1942: 82. Claudius as *hipparchos*, Zon. 12.26. See Syme 1971: 210f.

10 Zon. 12.25; SHA *Gal.* 14; Zos. 1.40.2–3; cf. Victor *Caes.* 33.19–22 (less reliable) and John of Ant. fr. 152.3 (*FHG* IV, 599), confusing Heraclianus with Cecropius); see also short notices in *Epit.* 33.2; Eutrop. 9.11.1; Jerome *Chron.* 221 (Helm); Oros. 7.22.13; Jord. *Rom.* 287; Sync. 717. Malalas 12.27 (298 Bonn) is wrong.

11 Victor *Caes.* 33.21 (stressing Aurelian's popularity with the army, but apparently confusing him with Heraclianus: see *PLRE* I, Heraclianus (6)). Claudius exonerated see SHA *Gal.* 14.2; *Claud.* 1.3. Both this and the deathbed scene (Victor *Caes.* 33.28; *Epit.* 34.2) as the product of either Claudian or, more likely, Constantinian propaganda see Syme 1971: 205–6; Syme 1983: 69, 152.

12 Gallienus' family see SHA *Gal.* 14.9–11; Zon. 12.26; Eutrop. 9.11.1; John of Ant. fr. 152.3 (*FHG* IV 599); Victor *Caes.* 33.31–4. Marinianus as consul see A. Alföldi, 'The Numberings of the Victories of Gallienus and the Loyalty of his Legions', *NC* 1929: 218–79, at 266f. Accession donative see H. Huvelin and J. Lafaurie, 'Trésor d'un navire romain trouvé en Méditerranée: Nouvelles découvertes', *RN* 1980: 75–105; cf. SHA *Gal.* 15.

13 Zon. 12.25; John of Ant. fr. 152.3 (*FHG* IV, 599; but cf. n. 10 above).

14 Aurelian's cavalry command see SHA *Aurel.* 18.1; on which see Homo 1904: 38–9; Fisher 1929: 130; but see now Paschoud 1996: 113–14.

15 Zos. 1.41; Zon. 12.26; SHA *Claud.* 5.1–3. Aurelian as perpetrator see SHA *Aurel.* 16.2; cf. Magie 1932: 222–3, n. 5; Paschoud 1996: 109–10 (for the epithet, cf. SHA *Aurel.* 6.2). On Aureolus as emperor see Alföldi

1967: 2ff., 9f.; *RIC* V.2, 589; but see now Bastien 1984: 133–4, 140; Drinkwater 1987: 146, n. 82.

16 *Epit.* 34.2–3; arguably also SHA *Aurel.* 18.2 (and perhaps even Zos. 1.49.1: on this and the conjectural involvement of the Juthungi see Appendix B.2). See H. Huvelin 'La victoire du lac de Garde de Claude II', *NAC* 9, 1982: 263–9. For the title Germanicus see for example *CIL* XII 2228 (but cf. Peachin 1990: 86).

17 Prelude see SHA *Gal.* 13.10; *Claud.* 6.1; Zos. 1.42.1. Size and ethnic make-up see SHA *Claud.* 6 ('Greuthungi' equivalent to 'Austrogothi' or East Goths; 'Tervingi' to 'Visigothi' or West Goths); cf. 7–9.2; Zos. I.42.1 (6,000 ships); Amm. 31.5.15. See Appendix B.1.

18 Zos. 1.42–43.1; SHA *Claud.* 9.3–4, 9.7–8; cf. Amm. 31.5.16.

19 Timing inferred from SHA *Claud.* 6.2.

20 The revolt see Victor *Caes.* 33.8; Eutrop. 9.9.1; *Epit.* 32.4. See König 1981: 133–6; H.H. Gilljam, *Antoniniani und Aurei des Ulpius Cornelius Laelianus, Gegenkaiser des Postumus*, Cologne 1982: esp. 16–18; Schulte 1983: 44–8; Besly and Bland 1983: 57 (cf. 53–8); Drinkwater 1987: 139, 146, 175–7; Bland and Burnett 1988: 147.

21 Eutrop. 9.9.1; Victor *Caes.* 33.8; John of Ant. fr. 152 (*FHG* IV 598); cf. SHA *Tyr. trig.* 3.7, 5.1. See König 1981: 136.

22 Zon. 12.26; cf. SHA *Claud.* 6.2–3 (an apology for Claudius being 'occupied elsewhere' at the time of the Gothic invasion). Quintillus in northern Italy see SHA *Aurel.* 37.5; cf. below n. 34 (and see Paschoud 1996: 179).

23 Zos. 1.43.1–2; cf. SHA *Claud.* 9.9. The siege of Thessalonica must have been relieved by the vanguard of the imperial army under Aurelian (*pace* Zosimus). On Aurelian and the Dalmatian horse see below, nn. 25, 26 (cf. above n. 14). Claudius probably linked up with Marcianus at this time.

24 Zos. 1.43.2; cf. 1.45.1 (see Appendix B.1); SHA *Claud.* 9.9. Victor *Caes.* 34.5 (no loss of life on the Roman side) is a post-Constantinian invention.

25 Zos. 1.45; SHA *Claud.* 11.3–8 (cf. 11.9 on the outstanding role of the Dalmatian horse in the campaign as a whole). The date of 270 in SHA *Claud.* 11.3, though not totally reliable, remains plausible.

26 Zos. 1.46; cf. SHA *Claud.* 9.4–6; *Aurel.* 16.4 (cf. 17.3–4); see Paschoud 1996: 110–113 and see also above, n. 14.

27 Thus coins: VICTORIAE GOTHIC, *RIC* V.1, 251, 252. The title Gothicus is attested on inscriptions: e.g. *CIL* XVII 159; cf. *CIL* XII 5511 (but see *CIL* XVII 149 and Peachin 1990: 377, n. 11); but there remains some doubt whether he was granted the title in his lifetime: cf. the posthumous DIVO CLAVDIO GOTHICO (*RIC* V.1, 263, 264; on which see below, at n. 37); see Peachin 1990: 86–7. The golden shield (and a golden statue) see Eutrop. 9.11.2; Oros. 7.23.1; Jerome *Chron.* 222 (Helm); Jord. *Rom.* 288; cf. below, n. 31. Death see Zos. 1.46.2; SHA *Claud.* 12.2; Eutropius, Orosius, Jerome, loc. cit.; Malalas 12.28 (299 Bonn). For the date see Appendix B.3.

28 Victor *Caes.* 34.3–5; *Epit.* 34.3–4; cf. Amm. 31.5.17.
29 Zos. 1.46.1; SHA *Claud.* 12.1, 12.4; see also Dexipp. *FGH* 100, fr. 29 (Side); Amm. 31.5.16 (Pamphylia; Nicopolis; Anchialus); cf. (Anchialus) Jordanes *Get.* 108–9, though reconciling this account with the others is not easy.
30 A military coup (subsequently endorsed by the senate) see Eutrop. 9.12; Oros. 7.23.2; Zon. 12.26; Jerome *Chron.* (222 Helm); Jordanes *Rom.* 289. The stress on the senate is only in contrast to the overwhelming support which Aurelian enjoyed in the army. See also Zos. 1.47; SHA *Claud.* 12.3; John of Ant. fr. 154 (*FHG* IV 599). Zonaras almost implies a palace coup, perhaps by the praetorians (cf. the lukewarm support for Quintillus subsequently shown by the troops in northern Italy).
31 Above, n. 27; also *Epit.* 34.4 (strongly suggesting posthumous honour); cf. SHA *Claud.* 12.3. Deification confirmed by coinage (see below at n. 37), but the statue, and indeed the golden shield, are most likely post-Constantinian propaganda.
32 On the length of his reign see Appendix B.3.
33 Deathbed scene see Zon. 12.26; see P. Damerau, *Kaiser Claudius II. Gothicus*, Leipzig 1934: 90; Alföldi 1939: 193.
34 Throughout the empire, many of those in positions of authority must have hedged their bets, which may account for the consular dating in Egypt: see Appendix B.3. Quintillus at Aquileia see Jerome *Chron.* (222.6 Helm); Chron. 354 (*Chron. Min.* I, 148).
35 Murder: Eutrop. 9.12; *Epit.* 34.5; Jerome *Chron.* (222.6 Helm); Chron. 354 (*Chron. Min.* I, 148); SHA *Claud.* 12.5 (cf. 12.6, purporting to pass on the neutral verdict of Dexippus). Suicide see Zos. 1.47; Zon. 12.26; SHA *Aurel.* 37.6. For the date see Appendix B.3.
36 See Appendix B.2.
37 On the date and purpose of the Divus Claudius issue see Bland and Burnett 1988: 144–6. On the supposed connection to senatorial opposition see Chapter 10 (at n. 10). On another measure to marginalize Quintillus' reign, by redating Aurelian's *dies imperii*, see Appendix B.3 (and also for chronology).
38 Aurelian at Ravenna see *Cont. Dion.* fr. 10.1 (*FHG* IV 197). On the timing (and the fact that Aurelian did not go to Rome at this time) see Appendix B.2.
39 On Siscia as Aurelian's temporary headquarters at this time and his assumption of the consulship see Manns 1939: 19; Estiot 1983: 14, n. 26; cf. Estiot 1995a: 15. Aurelian's route via Aquileia to Pannonia see Zos. 1.48.1 (cf. Appendix B.2).
40 Zos. 1.48.1. Groag 1903: 1369; Homo 1904: 70ff.; cf. Cubelli 1992: 32 (in my opinion wrongly suggesting Noricum and north Italy); see also Appendix B.2.
41 Dexippus *FGH* 100, fr. 7 (*FHG* III 685–6, fr. 24); Petr. Patr. fr. 12 (*FHG* IV 188). Note also Zos. 1.48.2 (saying the battle was on the

Danube and was inconclusive; both points are questionable, though he may well be referring to an earlier battle. The passage is not without its problems: see Saunders 1992: 317, and Appendix B.2); cf. SHA *Aurel.* 18.2. See also Mattingly 1939: 299; Mócsy 1974: 211.

42 See Map 2. The route is suggested by a number of hoards: see Cubelli 1992: 33 (and his map, p. 35; but cf. my reservations on the route and timing of the invasion and the identity of the invaders in Appendix B.2), and by the fact that the region of Milan lay in their direct path (SHA *Aurel.* 18.3). The German army must have crossed the high Alps as soon as they became passable (i.e. probably towards the very end of March). The date of 11 January given in SHA *Aurel.* 19 is worthless (as is the rest of this passage from 18.5–20.8: see below at n. 46).

43 See Map 2. Dexippus *FGH* 100, fr. 7.4; the route within Italy is suggested by subsequent events, see nn. 44–5 below.

44 *Cont. Dion.* fr. 10.3 (*FHG* IV 197); the sack of Placentia may be part of what lies behind the 'disaster' mentioned in SHA *Aurel.* 18.3 (cf. the following note).

45 SHA *Aurel.* 18.3–4, 21.1–3; the scale of the defeat is almost certainly an exaggeration of the author. *Epit.* 35.2, erroneously classes this battle among Aurelian's victories (accepted as such by Alföldy 1966, but is now universally rejected: see Saunders 1992: 323–4 and n. 62; cf. n. 46 below); cf. Groag 1903: 1371.

46 SHA *Aurel.* 18.5–21.4. For Alföldy 1966 this passage was an anachronistic commentary wholly influenced by pagan reaction to the burning of the Sibylline Books on the orders of Stilicho during the invasion of Italy by Radagaesus in 405/6. This thesis has now been discredited: see Lippold 1972, who preferred (p. 163) to see the passage as pro-senatorial rather than pro-pagan. See also Saunders 1992: 314.

47 *Epit.* 35.2; Dexippus *FGH* 100, fr. 6.1 (the battle is said here to have been on the Danube but cf. Appendix B.2). The inscriptions see *CIL* IX 6308–9 (Pisaurum).

48 Dexippus *FGH* 100, fr. 6 (*FHG* III 682–5, fr. 24). The size of the Juthungian army given in Dexippus is certainly an exaggeration: see Saunders 1992: 324, n. 64 (cf. Appendix A, n. 13). See also Chapter 10, n. 68 and Appendix B.2.

49 *Epit.* 35.2; SHA *Aurel.* 18.6.

50 Attested on numerous inscriptions and papyri: see Sotgiu 1961: 17ff., 1975: 1042; Kettenhoffen 1986: 142–3; Peachin 1990: 91–2. It is reasonable to suppose that the title also covered the campaign against the Vandals (cf. Appendix B.2).

51 *Epit.* 35.3; Zos. 1.49.2; cf. *RE* 2A, 1560, Septiminus (2). He may have been lynched on the news of Aurelian's victory at Ticinum.

52 Zos. 1.49.2 stresses the charge rather than the act of treason (as also with 'Septimius' and a certain Urbanus), however, there is the coinage: *RIC* V.2, 590; cf. *RN* 1901: 319ff.; *RN* 1930: 7ff. On the hoard, see

S. Estiot and M. Amandry, 'Aurélien: trois monnaies d'or inédites de l'atelier de Milan (270 AD)', *BSFN* 45, 1990: 727–32, 728 n. 3.

53 On Placidianus, see Chapter 10 (at n. 19).

54 Link to German advance see Cubelli 1992: 37. On the scale of the fraud and of the workers' involvement see Mattingly 1939: 300; Palmer 1980: 219; Cubelli 1992: 49. Date, see Appendix B.2; cf. (all probably on the early side): Cubelli 1992: 30 (spring 271), 39 (March); Gatti 1961: 94f. (end 270/ beginning 271).

55 On the DIVO CLAVDIO coinage in question see Bland and Burnett 1988: 144–6; cf. catalogue, pp. 186–7, nos. 1110–45. On the nature of fraud/crime see Cubelli 1992: 43–6, cf. 10–18 (a useful review of earlier hypotheses); cf. Crawford 1975: 576 (the mint workers more as scapegoats than genuinely culpable). This Felicissimus (*RE* 6, 2162–3) is plausibly to be identified with the 'Aurelius Felicissimus v. e. proc[urator]' of *CIL* IX 4894 (*RE* 2.2, 2491): see *PLRE* I, Felicissimus (1). On the standing and power of Felicissimus as *rationalis/procurator a rationibus* see Cubelli 1992: 40–3; cf. 44–5.

56 Polemius Silvius 49 (*Chron. Min.* I, 151–2) places him alongside Tetricus and Zenobia and Vaballathus as imperial pretenders in opposition to Aurelian; but Eutrop. 9.14 implies he was killed before the revolt got under way. That he was a victim not a protagonist of these events should be rejected, see Fisher 1929: 144.

57 Trouble at Rome early in reign see SHA *Aurel.* 18.4, 21.5; Zos. 1.49.2. Mint workers' revolt see *Epit.* 35.4; SHA *Aurel.* 38.2 (cf. 38.3–4); Victor *Caes.* 35.6; Eutrop. 9.14.1. The *Epitome* is the only source directly to link the two, though it is highly suggestive that the *HA* uses the verb *compescere* to describe Aurelian's retaliation in each case, but nowhere else throughout the entire work (C. Lessing, *Scriptores Historiae Augustae Lexicon*, p. 82 sv.). On the episode as a whole and its scale see Mattingly 1939: 300; Groag 1903: 1372–7; Homo 1904: 162–4; Palmer 1980: 219; Cubelli 1992: 49–50 (accepting the numbers given). M. Peachin, 'Johannes Malalas and the Moneyers' Revolt', in C. Deroux (ed.), *Studies in Latin Literature and Roman History III*, Brussels 1983: 325–35, used a reference to unrest among the mint operators at Antioch in Malalas 12.30 (301 Bonn) to relocate the revolt to Antioch; now refuted by Bland and Burnett 1988: 146; cf. Cubelli 1992: 19–25.

58 SHA *Aurel.* 21.5–8, 38.2, 39.8; Eutrop. 9.14.1; Zos. 1.49.2; Ammianus 30.8.8; see Chapter 10.

59 Estiot 1983: 33; cf. 25.

60 Zos. 1.49.2; Victor *Caes.* 35.7; *Epit.* 36.6; Eutrop. 9.15.1; SHA *Aurel.* 39.2; see Chapter 9.

61 See Chapter 8.

62 SHA *Aurel.* 22.1–2, cf. 33.3–4, 34.1; cf. Oros. 7.23.4; Eutrop. 9.13.1; Jordanes *Rom.* 290.

63 The decisiveness of the victory (with respect to earlier victories) is made clear by Ammianus 31.5.17. Groag 1903: 1378, ingeniously postulated

that the 'Cannabas' of SHA *Aurel.* 22.2 is to be identified with 'Kniva' or 'Cniva', the victor at Abrittus; Barnes 1978: 70, suggested rather this man's son of the same name. Gothicus Maximus, *ILS* 8925 (271–2). cf. VICTORIA GOTHICA (*RIC* 339).

64 See Chapter 9 (at n. 37).

65 Although the Carpi overran part of Dacia a year later, the Goths appear to have hesitated for a time: Cizek 1994: 145–7; cf. Mócsy 1974: 211. See more fully, Chapter 9.

66 Zos. 1.52.3–4. As the headquarters for these operations he apparently used the city of Byzantium: *CJ* 5.72.2 (cf. Chapter 8, n. 35).

4 ZENOBIA AND THE EAST

1 Petr. Patr. fr. 166, 168 (Biossevain III, 744 = *Cont. Dion. FHG* IV 195, fr. 7). The story is rhetorical and not very credible.

2 John of Ant. fr. 152.2 (*FHG* IV 599).

3 Malalas 12.27 (298 Bonn); cf. 12.28 (299 Bonn); SHA *Gal.* 13.4–5. Revision of the dates for the death of Odenathus (see Appendix B.3) and the revolt of Aureolus (Chapter 3, n. 6) now virtually preclude Heraclianus' expedition, though Gallienus possibly threatened it. (On the alleged campaign see G.M. Bersanetti, 'Eracliano, prefetto del pretorio di Gallieno', *Epigraphica* 4, 1942: 169–76, 171–3.)

4 Zon. 12.24 (neither nephew nor son are named); Sync. 716–17; Zos. 1.39.2.

5 SHA *Gal.* 13.1; *Tyr. trig.* 15.5, 17. 'Maeonius' might be a corruption of the Aramaic Ma'nai (see Graf 1989: 145), but both the name and his elevation are probably fictitious. Zenobia as the evil stepmother, see SHA *Tyr. trig.* 17.2 (the story is introduced with *dicitur*, 'it is said'); cf. 16.3. This aspect of Zenobia's character is one of the very few negative traits in the *HA*'s portrait of her: see Wallinger 1990: 141.

6 On Odenathus' sons see Chapter 2, n. 32 and also Alföldi 1939: 175–7; Stoneman 1992: 114–15 (suggesting 'Timolaus' may be a corruption of Wahballath); cf. n. 8 below.

7 SHA *Tyr. trig.* 17.2, 27, 28, 30.2; *Gal.* 13.2; but cf. *Aurel.* 38.1. This last is the only mention of Vaballathus in the literature, other than in the bare list of usurpers at the time of Aurelian in Polemius Silvius 49 (*Chron. Min.* I 521). 'Athenodoros' ('the gift of Athena') is the nearest Greek equivalent.

8 See Appendix B.3.

9 Zos. 1.39.2; Sync. 716–17; cf. SHA *Gal.* 12.6–13.1. Odenathus may have repulsed the Goths in Cappadocia (in 267?) and then been killed (at Emesa?) in 267/8.

10 Vaballathus as King of Kings see *CIS* II 3971.

11 Zenobia as regent see SHA *Gal.* 13.2. Queen see *IGR* III 1028–30.

12 On Zenobia's advisors see Zos. 1.39.2. Vorodes may have been Odenathus' envoy to Persia in the 250s, if he can be identified with the

Vorôd mentioned in *RGDS* line 67. A key player in the defeat of the Persians, he probably figured prominently in the ceremony on the banks of the Orontes in 262, for he personally dedicated the inscription honouring Herodianus as co-regent (Chapter 2, n. 32). See *CIS* II 3937–42 (cf. *IGR* III 1036, 1040–5; the date of the last is problematic). In general, see D. Schlumberger, 'Vorôd l'agoranome', *Syria* 48, 1972: 339–41; Graf 1989: 155; Potter 1990: 377 n. 30, 383; cf. Alföldi 1939: 176–7; Stoneman 1992: 117, 122. Zabdas see *RE* 2A 1575–6.

13 Zenobia and the Arabs see Graf 1989: 150–5; Bowersock 1983: 131–7 (cf. Odenathus' title king of Saracens, Chapter 2, n. 20, in this volume. Local support see Graf: 1989: 145–59.

14 Potter 1990: 247, cf. 58–9; Isaac 1990: 222–3; Graf 1989: 143–4. Defeat of Trassus see Malalas 12.28 (299 Bonn); cf. Zos. 1.44.1 (size of army). On the temple see *IGLS* 1907; cf. J.-P. Rey-Coquais, 'Syrie romaine de Pompée à Dioclétien', *JRS* 68, 1978: 44–73, 56–60; Hanslik 1972: 3.

15 Graf 1989: 143–4; cf. Isaac 1990: 222–3. Some of the epigraphic evidence cited by these authors probably belongs to a slightly later period (perhaps 271–2).

16 See Graf 1989: 146, and the bibliography cited there.

17 Zos. 1.44.2; Sync. 721; Zon. 12.27; SHA *Claud.* 11.2 ('Probatus'). On the connection with the Gothic raids against, e.g., Cyprus (see Chapter 3, n. 29), see Alföldi 1939: 180.

18 Zos. 1.44.1 (combined army of Palmyrenes and Palmyrene sympathizers amounted to 700,000 men). The loose wording of SHA *Claud.* 11.1 has been used to identify Timagenes as a Palmyrene by origin, but this is doubtful; see Graf 1989: 144.

19 Zos. 1.44.1; SHA *Claud.* 11.1–2; Malalas 12.28 (299 Bonn). For timing see Appendix B.3.

20 J. Schwartz, 'Les Palmyréniens et l'Egypte', *Bull. Soc. d'Arch. d'Alexandrie* 40, 1953: 63–81, 77; see also Hanslik 1972: 3–4; Graf 1989: 146.

21 Zos. 1.44.2–45.1; cf. SHA *Claud.* 11.1–2; Zon. 12.27; Sync. 721; cf. *Prob.* 9.5. The battle for control of the delta took place during November, and Palmyra had gained control of the whole of Egypt by early December: see Appendix B.3.

22 Alföldi 1939: 178–9; Callu 1969: 220–1.

23 Millar 1971: esp. 12–13 (somewhat underplaying the influence of Palmyra in the region under Odenathus); cf. Baldini 1975; J.H. Declerck, 'Deux nouveaux fragments attribués à Paul de Samosate', *Byzantion* 54, 1984: 116–40; Potter 1990: 48; Stoneman 1992: 148–51. The Palmyrene connection is stressed by later Christian authors, who saw Paul's denial of the full divinity of Christ as very similar to the heresies against which they were writing: in particular Athanasius *Hist. Ar.* 71; cf. John Chrysostum (*Hom. 8 in Joannem*).

24 Support at Antioch see Zos. 1.51.3. On coinage see below, n. 38 and also Appendix B.3.

25 Zos. 1.50.1. On Zabdas and Zabbai see Stoneman 1992: 122; their inscriptions: (a) to Odenathus see *CIS* II 3946 (*Inv.* III 19; cf. Potter 1990: 390–1); (b) to Zenobia see *Inv.* III 20 (*IGR* III 1030).

26 Graf 1989: 147–9; Stoneman 1992: 151–3.

27 For the dichotomy see, e.g., F. Altheim and R. Stiehl, 'Odainat und Palmyra', in *Die Araber in der Alten Welt* 4, Berlin 1965: 251–73, 270; I. Shahid, *Rome and the Arabs. A Prolegomenon to the study of Byzantium and the Arabs*, Washington 1984: 152; but cf. Graf: 1989; see also Homo 1904: 88–9.

28 Bowersock 1986.

29 G.W. Bowersock, 'The Miracle of Memnon', *Bull. Am. Soc. Papyr.* 21, 1984: 21–32; Graf 1989: 146–7; cf. SHA *Tyr. trig.* 30.19–21; *Aurel.* 27.3; *Prob.* 9.5. On the Cleopatra connections see further, Chapter 5, nn. 41, 72.

30 On Callinicus see Bowersock 1983: 175–6; Graf 1989: 146. On Genethlius see Bowersock 1983: 135. On 'Nicomachus' (SHA *Aurel.* 27.6) see Syme 1968: 111 (not to be confused with the late fourth century Nicomachus Flavianus, of whose works the SHA made extensive use). On Nicostratus see Potter 1990: 70–2. On the early career of Longinus see Porph. *V. Plot.* 20; Eunapius *V. Soph.* 4.1.2–3; and at Palmyra see Zos. 1.56.2–3; SHA *Aurel.* 30.3; see also Suidas (Longinus sv); *PLRE* Longinus (2). Generally, see also Stoneman 1992: 129–32.

31 On Zenobia as an imperial usurper see Bowersock 1986: 21; Graf 1989: 159.

32 For example Groag 1903: 1365f. (Vaballathus' titles were granted by the senate at Rome on Aurelian's instructions, this even applied to Zenobia's title of Augusta!); Homo 1904: 66–9. For Mattingly 1936: 101–13 (cf. Mattingly 1939: 301), Zenobia reached a concordat with Claudius which Aurelian refused to renew (cf. Graf 1989: 145, suggesting the concordat was first reached with Gallienus). In my opinion, there is no evidence for any concordat after the death of Odenathus, merely *de facto* positioning for power.

33 Coins (with the titulature *Hupatos Autokrator Strategos Rhomaion*, usually abbreviated, e.g., VAVTCPω) see Milne 1933: 103, nos. 4303–7. The same titles, along with *ho lamprotatos Basileus*, are recorded in full in the contemporary papyri: first such, *P. Oxy.* XL 2921.6–11; last such, *P. Oxy.* XL 2908.ii.20–5.

34 C. Gallizzi, 'La titolatura di Vaballato come riflesso della politica di Palmira', *NAC* 4, 1975: 249–65.

35 First papyrus thus see *SB* XIV 11589.20–3 (mid-March 271); coins see Milne 1933: 103, nos. 4308–26; Rathbone 1986: 123–4.

36 Milne 1933: 104, nos. 4327–9 (paired obv.; rev. LA | LΔ in a wreath).

37 Coins see Milne 1933: 104, nos. 4330–48; papyri see, e.g., *P. Oxy.* X 1264.20–6.

38 *RIC* V.1 (p. 260) 381; Manns 1939: 22; Peachin 1990: 403, no. 152 (cf. his n. 31), see Plate 3,a. On the Alexandrian titulature, cf. n. 33 above. For interpretation see Mattingly 1936: 112–13; Mattingly 1939: 301; Alföldi 1939: 179. It must be pointed out, however, that these coins are unquestionably intended as antoniniani (radiates), and it is Aurelian who wears the determinative radiate crown, whereas Vaballathus is depicted laureate. While these coins are unfortunately still too rare for die studies to be of any assistance, it is conceivable that future die studies may be able to reveal which side was technically the obverse.

39 Several milestones of this kind for Vaballathus are now known from Arabia and Judaea: see T. Bauzou, 'Deux milliares inédits de Vaballath en Jordaine du nord', in Freeman and Kenedy 1986: 1–8; Isaac 1990: 223 (esp. n. 22); Graf 1989: 143–4. It is far from certain that these delineate the route of Zabdas' march in 270, as is claimed by these authors. For Syria see, e.g., *IGR* III 1028.

40 *IGR* III 1030 set up by Zabdas and Zabbai (above, n. 25); the title is found in the epigraphic evidence for Gallienus' consort, Salonina.

41 *CIG* 4503b (*OGIS* 647; cf. *IGR* III 1027). The missing emperor is traditionally restored as Claudius, but the titulature for Zenobia and Vaballathus fits far better into the sequence in early 272 (when Aurelian would have borne the title consul restored in the inscription); the absence of victory titles for Aurelian is not conclusive for dating purposes on Greek inscriptions.

42 *BGU* III 946 gives Vaballathus the imperial title 'our lord' in March 272; although Oxyrhyncus *P. Oxy* X 1264.20–6 (March 272) and *P. Oxy* XL 2904.15–23 (17 April 272) preserve the conventional formula, the latter being the last example to do so.

43 *O. Mich.* 1006 (dated May/June 271, though it is possibly backdated).

44 Last joint dating, see above n. 42. Milne 1933: 104, nos. 4349–52, and for Zenobia, 4353. Antioch see *RIC* V.2 (p. 585) nos. 1–8; for Zenobia see *RIC* V.2 (p. 584) nos. 1–2; cf. Manns 1939: 23. The authenticity of the Zenobian coinage has been called into question see, e.g., Mattingly 1936: 113.

45 *AE* 1904: 60: *Im* [sic] *Caesari L Julio Aurelio Septimo* [sic] *Vaballatho Athenodoro Persico Maximo Arabico Maximo Adiabenico Maximo Pio Felici Invicto Au* [sic]. On the chronology of this period see Appendix B.3.

5 THE PALMYRENE WARS

1 Zos. 1.50.1.

2 SHA *Prob.* 9.5 (confused with Tenagino Probus); accepted by Homo 1904: 89; cf. more cautiously *PLRE* Probus 3.

3 See Appendix B.3.

4   Zos. 1.50.1–2; SHA *Aurel*. 22.3. For Aurelian's route on this campaign see Map 3.
5   SHA *Aurel*. 22.5–23.3 (stressing the rarity of such effective restraint upon soldiers); *Cont. Dion*. fr. 10.4 (*FHG* IV 197). The significance of Tyana is reflected in Zos. 1.50.2. On Heraclammon see SHA *Aurel*. 22.6, 24.1, cf. 23.4–5.
6   SHA *Aurel*. 24.2–6; see Brandt 1995: 111–12; cf. Paschoud 1996: 140–1. Reference to the library is particularly suspicious, since he invokes its authority at other untrustworthy points of this biography.
7   The episode derived from the *Annals* of Nicomachus Flavianus, who had himself translated Philostratus' biography of Apollonius, see Syme 1968: 111. On Apollonius in fourth-century anti-Christian polemics, see Brandt 1995: 115–16; N. Horsfall, 'Apuleius, Apollonius of Tyana, Bibliomancy: Some Neglected Dating Criteria', *Historia Augusta Colloquia NS III, Marceratense*, Bari 1995: 169–77, 170–4; Paschoud 1996: 141. See also Appendix A.
8   Zos. 1.50.1.
9   Malal. 12.30 (Bonn 300.8–11); Zos. 1.50.2; Downey 1950: 68, and n. 18. (For what follows, I largely adopt Downey's reconstruction.)
10 Downey 1950: 62–4; see also Groag 1903: 1383–4.
11 Zos. 1.50.3–51.1; Downey 1950: 64–6.
12 That Immae was pivotal is reflected in the fact that the epitomators tend to cite it rather than the later battle of Emesa see Eutrop. 9.13.2; Fest. *Brev*. 24; Sync. 721.10–12; Jordanes *Rom*. 291; Jerome *Chron*. (222 Helm). For a reconciliation of these texts with Zosimus see Downey 1950: 67–8. On the continued numerical superiority of the Palmyrene cavalry see Zos. 1.53.1.
13 Zos. 1.51.1 (cf. Pisistratus' re-entry into Athens in Herodotus 1.60).
14 Zos. 1.51.2, 52.1; cf. Downey 1950: 57–8.
15 Zos. 1.51.2. Zos. 1.50.3 states that, before the engagement the previous day, Aurelian had sent his infantry across the river (apparently in order to protect them from the Palmyrene cavalry). For an ingenious, if not entirely satisfactory, attempt to reconcile the difficulties presented by this passage, see Downey 1950: 65 and 66, n. 17.
16 Zos. 1.51.2–52.1; SHA *Aurel*. 25.1.
17 Zos. 1.52.1. (On Christian schism see Chapter 11, nn. 76–8.)
18 Zos. 1.52.1–2; cf. SHA *Aurel*. 25.1 (wrongly placing this 'brief confrontation' before Aurelian's entry into Antioch). See Downey 1950: 67f. on confusion in some sources between this minor and comparatively easy victory and either Immae or Emesa.
19 Zos. 1.52.4.
20 Zos. 1.53; SHA *Aurel*. 25.2–3, suggesting the Roman cavalry was tired. For the size of Zenobia's army see Zos. 1.52.3. (On divine intervention, SHA *Aurel*. 25.3–4.)
21 Zos. 1.54.1–2; SHA *Aurel*. 25.3–4.
22 SHA *Aurel*. 26.1. Graf 1989: 150–5.

23 Zos. 1.54.2. Offer of parley see Cont. Dion. fr. 10.5 (*FHG* IV 197); SHA *Aurel.* 26.6–27.6 (the letters themselves are naturally fiction), 28.2.

24 On the possibility of Shapur's support, or at least tacit approval, early on in her ascendancy, see Graf 1989: 155ff.

25 SHA *Aurel.* 28.2; cf. Aurelian's assumption of the title Persicus Maximus.

26 Zos. 1.54.2–3. We are also told that Aurelian himself was wounded by an arrow during the siege, see SHA *Aurel.* 26.1.

27 Zos 1.55; SHA *Aurel.* 28.3 (dromedary).

28 Zos. 1.56.1–2.

29 Zos. 1.56.2; SHA *Aurel.* 31.2 (600 archers).

30 Zos. 1.56.2; SHA *Aurel.* 28.5. These reparations may have included treasures from the temple of Bel, possibly offered by the priests to mollify Aurelian.

31 SHA *Aurel.* 28.5–29: the existence of this parley, though un-corroborated, can safely be inferred.

32 SHA *Aurel.* 35.4, 41.9, cf. 28.4; Victor *Caes.* 35.1–2. There is no other reference to this victory over the Persians; the absence of any such reference in Festus (24), though not conclusive, is highly suggestive.

33 Zos. 1.60.1.

34 Zos. 1.56.2; SHA *Aurel.* 30.3.

35 Malalas 12.30 (300 Bonn). On her sex being a factor in her treatment see SHA *Aurel.* 30.1–2; cf. below nn. 61ff.

36 Date of assumption see Estiot 1983: 15, esp. n. 41.

37 Zos. 1.59 (saying *all* the captives except Zenobia's son were drowned; an exaggeration, if not a total fabrication, since many turned up in Aurelian's triumph).

38 SHA *Aurel.* 30.4, cf. 31.3. For the settlement (Victor *Caes.* 39.43) see Chapter 9.

39 Zos. 1.60.1–2. Apsaeus may well be identical with the Septimius Apsaeus of *IGR* III 1049 (*CIG* 4487; cf. *RE* 2.276, 2A.1563).

40 Zos. 1.61.1.

41 *IGR* III 1029; *OGIS* 650: the wording, dedicated to Zenobia's health/safety, suggests that the Palmyrenes believed Zenobia was still alive in the spring of 273, or at least that they chose to regard her as such; cf. *OGIS* 651 and (more dubiously) *IGR* III 1049. Zenobia apparently claimed descent from (a Seleucid?) Antiochus: *Inv.* III 19 (*CIS* II 3946).

42 Zos. 1.60.2 (cf. 1.61.1); SHA *Aurel.* 31.1–2 ('Achilleus [*sic*]'). Polemius Silvius 49 (*Chron. Min.* I: 521) is confused between Vaballathus and Antiochus, perhaps supporting the latter's claim to be Zenobia's son. He may have been her nephew.

43 Zos. 1.61.1. Haddudan see M. Galikowski, 'Inscriptions de Palmyre', *Syria* 48, 1971: 420 (*Inv.* IX 40). The inscription mentions his priestly duties in 273 and 274, so the help he gave could have been in either 272 or 273; on his probable pedigree see Matthews 1984: 168, n. 38.

44 Zos. 1.61.1. On the exodus see below, n. 46.
45 SHA *Aurel.* 31.3, cf. 31.4–10, greatly exaggerating both the destruction and Aurelian's alleged cruelty, and suggesting (31.7–9) that the 3rd legion led the destruction of the 'Temple of the Sun' (presumably Bel is meant) which was subsequently reconstructed at Aurelian's command. The involvement of the 3rd legion is temptingly plausible (see Chapter 4, n. 15), but the letter in which all this information is contained is palpably fiction and the temple of Bel (who was not a sun god, see Chapter 11, n. 61) continued to function after the sack (above, n. 43); see Paschoud 1996: 156–7. See also E. Will, 'Le Sac de Palmyre', in R. Chevallier (ed.) *Mélanges d'archéologie et d'histoire offerts à André Piganiol*, Paris 1966: 1409–16.
46 Zos. 1.61.1; SHA *Aurel.* 31.3. Matthews 1984: 169; see also E. Will, 'Marchands et chefs de caravanes à Palmyre', *Syria* 34, 1959: 262–77. On the relocation of the trade route see Amm. 14.3.3. The city did continue to play a military role in the strategic defence of the eastern frontier, especially from the time of Diocletian.
47 The connection with Zenobia see SHA *Firm.* 3.1, 5.1; cf. Zos. 1.61.1; Blemmyes see SHA *Firm.* 3.3; cf. SHA *Aurel.* 32.2 (attempting something like Egyptian independence); *Firm.* 2.1–3 and 5.1 (seizing imperial power and issuing coins, directly contradicting *Aurel.* 32.2), neither is credible. Whether Amm. 22.16.15 (destruction of Bruchion etc.) refers to these events or to the fighting in 270 when Tenagino Probus and Zabdas struggled for Alexandria, is unclear (see J. Fontaine, *Ammien Marcelin Histoire, III, livres xx–xxii*, Paris 1996: 345, n. 1055; cf. Paschoud 1996: 158). Homo 1904: 115 and Mattingly 1939: 305, both linked this passage in Ammianus to Aurelian's subsequent campaign; but cf. Zos. 1.61.1, implying minimal fighting.
48 SHA *Firm.* 3.2–4.4 (esp. 4.3–4), 6.2.
49 Zos. 1.61.1; cf. SHA *Aurel.* 32.1–3 and *Firm.* 5.1 (both apparently alleging that Aurelian returned to Thrace between the destruction of Palmyra and the Egyptian campaign, see Fisher 1929: 143; Paschoud 1996: 158). He may have distributed a donative at this time to encourage the morale of his troops before the extended and probably unforeseen march to Egypt, see Estiot 1995a: 17.
50 SHA *Aurel.* 32.3 (stressing Aurelian's ferocity); Zos. 1.61.1. Firmus' end see SHA *Firm.* 5.2. Mattingly 1939: 305, believed in the full involvement of Blemmyes; on their supposed appearance in the triumph see SHA *Aurel.* 33.4; but see Chapter 10, n. 75.
51 Zos. 1.61.1 (cf. Chapter 10, n. 73). Estiot 1995a: 17, places the assumption of the consulship at Antioch and Aurelian returning to Rome in the spring; either chronology is possible.
52 Zos. 1.59; Zon. 12.27.
53 Before chariot see Eutrop. 9.13.2; Festus 24. The heavy chains and jewels see SHA *Tyr. trig.* 30.24–26; *Aurel.* 34.3. See also Jerome *Chron.* 222 (ed. Helm); Jordanes *Rom.* 291; and Chapter 10. The silence of

Syncellus and Zonaras on the triumph is odd, considering that was why she was brought to Rome.

54 Malalas 12.30 (300 Bonn).

55 SHA *Tyr. trig.* 30.27; cf. Stoneman 1992: 187–8. Retirement at Rome see Eutrop. 9.13.2; Jerome *Chron.* 223 (ed. Helm); Zon. 12.27; Sync. 721. The account in the *HA* may have been influenced by certain parallels with Mavia (*RE* XIV 2. 2330), a fourth-century Roman woman captured in the east and, because of her beauty, chosen by a Saracen sheikh to be his bride. After his death she declared war on the empire and in 378 made peace with the emperor Valens, travelled to Constantinople and lived there in retirement, her daughter marrying the Magister Militum Victor, see Wallinger 1990: 147–8.

56 Jerome *Chron.* 223 (ed. Helm); Eutrop. 9.13.2; SHA *Tyr. trig.* 27.2.

57 Sync. 721; Zon. 12.27. SHA *Tyr. trig.* 30.27 (living her retirement *matronae more Romanae*) neither supports nor contradicts this tradition.

58 Zos. 1.59 (linked to the erroneous account of Zenobia's premature death, and therefore untrustworthy).

59 SHA *Tyr. trig.* 27.2, cf. 30.27. On Vaballathus, Herennianus and Timolaus see Chapter 2, n. 32 and Chapter 4, n. 6.

60 Zon. 12.27 (allegedly contributing to Zenobia's decision to take her own life). Groag 1903: 1355, dismissed this story as fiction; but see Chapter 7, n. 57 in this book. (Note once again a possible parallel with Mavia, above, n. 55.)

61 Gibbon 1909: 325. Our view of Zenobia is very largely coloured by the extravagant fiction of the *HA*. See Wallinger 1990: 139–49.

62 Zos. 1.39.2; John of Ant. fr. 152.2 (*FHG* IV 599); SHA *Tyr. trig.* 27 1, 30.2–3.

63 SHA *Tyr. trig.* 15.8, 30.15.

64 SHA *Tyr. trig.* 30.12. Her attitude is presented as so extreme and unnatural that it suggests one who uses sex as an instrument of power, not unlike a seductress.

65 Cont. Dion. fr. 10.5 (*FHG* IV 197); SHA *Aurel.* 27, cf. 30.3.

66 SHA *Aurel.* 26.3, 26.5, 30.1–3; Zos. 1.56.2.

67 SHA *Aurel.* 26.3 (a woman, not a proper adversary); *Tyr. trig.* 30.5, cf. 30.10 (improper to lead a woman in triumph); *Aurel.* 30.2; cf. Zos. 1.56.2 (improper to put a woman to death).

68 SHA *Gal.* 13.2–3, 16.1; *Tyr. trig.* 12.11, in contrast to 15.8, 30.1, 30.10, 30.23; cf. (together with the spurious 'Victoria') SHA *Claud.* 1.1; *Tyr. trig.* 31.1, 31.7. See now Wallinger 1990: 141, 144–5, 147.

69 SHA *Tyr. trig.* 30.15–16. Wallinger 1990: 142–3, noting the parallels with Suetonius' description of Augustus (Suet. *Aug.* 79.2).

70 SHA *Tyr. trig.* 30.13–18, 15.8, 30.5–6.

71 SHA *Tyr. trig.* 30.18 (the textual emendation seems safe). Atalanta (like the much later Brunhild in the *Nibelungenlied*, who like Zenobia became 'tamed') feared the sexual act as it would result in a diminution in her

power. Chastity was also strongly associated with Christianity, of which the *HA* evidently disapproved.

72 SHA *Tyr. trig.* 27.1, 30.2, 30.19; *Aurel.* 27.3; cf. Zos. 1.59. See also Chapter 4, n. 29.

73 Dido see SHA *Tyr. trig.* 27.1, 30.2; cf. Gibbon 1909: 325.

74 For example, SHA *Tyr. trig.* 30.13–14, 30.19; *Aurel.* 30.1–3; Zos. 1.56.2; cf. SHA *Tyr. trig.* 16.1–2 (Herodes); *Aurel.* 31.1 (Palmyrenes/Syrians generally).

75 SHA *Tyr. trig.* 15.8, cf. 30.2 (Zenobia as 'foreign').

76 Gibbon 1909: 332.

77 Mattingly 1939: 302.

78 See Chapter 4, nn. 26–8. For the subsequent romanticization of Zenobia see Stoneman 1992: 197–200, cf. 111–18, 193–5.

79 Graf 1989: 160.

80 Zos. 1.57.4.

6 WAR IN THE WEST: THE REUNIFICATION OF THE EMPIRE

1 *CIL* II 5736; Eutrop. 9.9; Victor *Caes.* 33.12. (SHA *Tyr. trig.* 6.1; *Gal.* 7.1, that he was raised to be co-ruler by Postumus, is false.) See König 1981: 111, 140, 141–7.

2 König 1981: 140; Drinkwater 1987: 120.

3 P. Le Gentilhomme, 'Le désastre d'Autun en 269', *REA* 45, 1943: 233–40; König 1981: 148–55; Drinkwater 1987: 36–9.

4 *Pan. lat.* V (9) 4 (298); VIII (5) 4.2–3 (312). Date/duration see Drinkwater 1987: 178–9.

5 Bordeaux see Eutrop 9.10; cf. Victor *Caes.* 33.14. Victoria see SHA *Tyr. trig.* 5.3, 6.3, 7.1, 24.1, 25.1, 31.1–4 (cf. *Claud.* 4.4); Victor *Caes.* 33.14. See Drinkwater 1987: 39, 90, cf. 65–7 (accepting the Victoria story); cf. König 1981: 158–60. On the Victoria myth see Wallinger 1990: 149–53. Victorinus II (SHA *Tyr. trig.* 6.3, 7, 24.1, 31.2) is fictitious.

6 *CIL* II 2228 (König 1981: 208, no. 72; at Grenoble); König 1981: 148–50; on Alamanni see Chapter 2, n. 41 in this book.

7 Drinkwater 1987: 89f. (speculation based on a few oblique references in the literary sources), cf. 118–20 (admitting inscriptions offer no help to his hypothesis) 204 (admitting hoard evidence runs counter to it).

8 Drinkwater 1987: 242, cf. 120–1.

9 The debased 'silver' (billon radiates) was in steep decline from the final year of Postumus, through Victorinus: by the accession of Tetricus they averaged *c.* 2.5g in weight and as little as 1 per cent silver; by summer 273, *c.* 2.25g and less than 0.5 per cent silver: Besly and Bland 1983: 63; König 1981: 171; Drinkwater 1987: 155. The gold coinage also declined in weight: from 6g under Postumus, through 5g under Victorinus, to less than 4g in the early part of Tetricus' reign (but a

slight improvement in the winter of 272/3): Drinkwater 1987: 156–7; cf. Schulte 1983: 32f., nos. 30–42 (group 5).

10 Lafaurie 1975b: 943; Drinkwater 1987: 98f., 106f. (esp. n. 77), 124f., 184–7; cf. Schulte 1983: 66–9; König 1981: 166–7.

11 Victor *Caes.* 35.4 (Faustinus a '*praeses*' who won over some of Tetricus' soldiers with promises of money); Polemius Silvius 49 (*Chron. Min.* I 521–2, specifying Trier). Polemius' list only implies that Faustinus, and indeed Victorinus, were claiming imperial status at the same time as Aurelian was ruling the rest of the empire, not that either of them first assumed the purple in opposition to him. Tensions between Tetricus and the army at this time see Eutrop. 9.13.1; SHA *Tyr. trig.* 24.2; *Aurel.* 32.3; but cf. König 1981: 181; Drinkwater 1987: 76–8 (cf. 43, 82).

12 There is tenuous evidence that at least one of the British provinces switched its allegiance to Aurelian before he entered Gaul: König 1974; but see now Kettenhoffen 1986:140–1; Drinkwater 1987: 121–3.

13 Victor *Caes.* 35.4–5; Eutrop. 9.13.1. On the carnage see *Paneg. lat.* VIII (5) 4.3; Victor *Caes.* 35.3. These passages leave little doubt that the slaughter was fairly one-sided.

14 *Aeneid* VI 365: *Eripe me his, invicte, malis.*; Thus Eutrop. 9.13.1; Orosius 7.23.5; SHA *Tyr. trig.* 24.3; cf. *Aurel.* 32.3 and Victor *Caes.* 35.3–4 (without the quote). Victor alone supplies the details of how the surrender was effected.

15 Drinkwater 1987: 42–3.

16 Barbarian pressure on this frontier was almost constant under Probus and again under Maximian/Constantius. Note *Paneg. lat.* VIII (5) 4.3.

17 Drinkwater 1987: 42, 49–50 (esp. n. 15).

18 Note esp. SHA *Tyr. trig.* 24.4; the *caesae legiones* of Victor Caes. 35.3 leaves no room for remorse on Aurelian's part.

19 Victor *Caes.* 35.1–3 (but see Appendix A, n. 11 and Appendix B.2, n. 23). See Homo 1904: 121; Dufraigne 1975: 170, n. 3. But note Drinkwater 1987: 51–2, amending *Gallia* (35.3) to *Italia*, thereby providing a conclusion of the Alamannic invasion of Italy, absent from Victor's text as it stands, and the disappearance of the Germanic invasion of Gaul. Ingenious though the solution is, he is perhaps unduly influenced by a desire to prove Tetricus' standing as a defender of Gaul. On Alamanni, see further Chapter 7.

20 The archaeological evidence is inconclusive as to the precise dates of this refortification work; but on Dijon see Gregory of Tours, *Hist. Franc.* 3.19.

21 On the triumph see Chapter 10.

22 Eutrop. 9.13.2; Victor *Caes.* 35.5; *Epit.* 35.7; SHA *Aurel.* 39.1.

23 SHA *Tyr. trig.* 24.5. See *RE* 4: 1651f.; and Chapter 9, n. 36.

24 *CIL* VI 1641; *PLRE* I 'Anonymous 110'. On the possible implications of his career see König 1981: 70f., 181; Drinkwater 1987: 127–31; cf. H.-G. Pflaum, *Les carrières procuratoriennes équestres sous le Haut-Empire romain*, Paris 1960: 941–7 (esp. 946f.).

25 On this transfer and Aurelian's mints generally see Chapter 8, esp.
   p. 135 and n. 39.

26 Lyon not in Aurelian's control see Lo Cascio 1984: 178 (but see now
   Cubelli 1992: 81); political explanation of rejection of reformed coinage
   see H. Mattingly, 'The Clash of the Coinages circa 270–296', *Studies in
   Roman and Economic History in Honor of A.C. Johnson*, Princeton 1951:
   275–89, 285–8 (refuted by Crawford 1975: 577, n. 71).

27 Zon. 12.27 (11). See Groag 1903: 1400–1.

28 SHA *Firm.* 13.1: *qui* (sc. *Lugdunenses*) *et ab Aureliano graviter contusi
   videbantur*. Mattingly 1939: 309 (without citing either text); König
   1981: 181.

29 Eutrop. 9.17.1; *Epit.* 37.2; SHA *Prob.* 18.5.

30 SHA *Firm.* 13.4; *Prob.* 18.7. The entire book on Firmus, Proculus *et al.*
   is virtually worthless.

31 As König 1981: 181, admitting that Aurelian's relocation of the mint
   is a problem for this assertion.

32 On brigandage in Gaul in the late third century see J.F. Drinkwater,
   'Peasants and Bagaudae in Roman Gaul', *Classical Views* 3, 1984:
   349–71. For another explanation see Chapter 7 in this book.

33 Based on the phrase 'Galliarum imperium' in Eutrop. 9.9.3, rightly
   rejected by König 1981; see also R. Bland (review of Drinkwater 1987)
   in *JRS* 78, 1988: 258; cf. generally on the rejection of separatism,
   Watson 1991: 164–91.

7 THE END OF AURELIAN

1 SHA *Aurel.* 35.4: *ad Gallias profectus Vindelicos obsidione barbarica
   liberavit*, cf. 41.8. Groag 1903: 1401–2, and Mattingly 1939: 308–9,
   accept this account without hesitation; see now Paschoud 1996: 172–3.
   Zon. 12.27: again Γάλλους might be a loose term.

2 Alföldi 1939: 157, tried to combine Victor *Caes.* 35.1–3 (on which see
   Chapter 6, n. 19 in this book) and the *HA*; Mattingly 1939: 308–9,
   makes no reference to Victor at this point. On Probus' campaigns see
   Zos. 1.67–8; cf. SHA *Prob.* 13.5–8.

3 Near Perinthus (which acquired its new name in 286: see Magie
   1932: 265, n. 5; Paschoud 1996: 174). The earliest extant source
   to mention the place is Lactantius *de mort. pers.* 6.2; cf. *Chron.* 354
   (*Chron. Min.* I 148); Victor *Caes.* 35.8. Mentioning the two major
   cities: Eutrop. 9.15.2, Jerome *Chron.* 223 (Helm) and *Epit.* 35.8 (who
   copies Eutropius, but omits the name of the fort) all say Constantinople
   and Heraclea ; SHA *Aurel.* 35.5, Jordanes *Rom.* 291, John of Ant.
   fr. 156 (*FHG* IV 599), and Sync. 721 all say Byzantium and
   Heraclea.

4 Sync. 721; Zon. 12.27 (the wording is very similar in each case); SHA
   Aurel. 35.4–5.

5 Malalas 12.30 (301 Bonn).

6 For example, Groag 1903: 1360; Homo 1904: 322–3; Mattingly 1939: 309; Cizek 1994: 193–5; Paschoud 1996: 173, 174.

7 Explicitly: Eutrop. 9.15.2; Oros. 12.23.6 (without more); SHA *Aurel.* 36.6, cf. 35.5; John of Ant. fr. 156 (*FHG* IV 599); Zos. 1.62.3, cf. 62.1.

8 Paschoud 1996: 173, 174 (noting the *HA*'s use of 'Heraclea and Byzantium'), but he appears to have overlooked John of Antioch and Syncellus (see above, n. 3).

9 Zos. 1.62.1, 62.3 (who alone avoids the anachronism, 'Heraclea'). Zonaras (12.27) says merely that the deed was carried out at Thracian Heraclea.

10 Lactantius *de mort. pers.* 6.2; Euseb. *HE* 7.32.6; Jerome *Chron.* 223 (Helm); Oros. 7.23.6; Sync. 721, 722. On persecution see Chapter 11.

11 Victor *Caes.* 35.7–8, cf. 12; SHA *Aurel.* 36.3–4.

12 Malalas 12.30 (301 Bonn).

13 SHA *Aurel.* 6.2, 7.3–8.5. Aurelian had apparently suppressed a military coup at some previous point in his reign (see Chapter 11, n. 18), which might possibly have some bearing.

14 Zos. 1.62.1; Zon. 12.27; SHA *Aurel.* 36.4. Other sources do not name him, but some preserve his position: John of Ant. fr. 156 (*FHG* IV, 599); Victor *Caes.* 35.8; Eutrop. 9.15.2; *Epit.* 35.8. See Hohl 1911: 285–8. Paschoud 1996: 173–4, suggesting the mistake was already in the KG. This is not wholly convincing, and derives from the editor's thesis that the *HA* used no Greek source after Dexippus for the *vita Aureliani* (see Paschoud 1996: xxxix–xliii, 10–12, and his own works there cited; cf. Barnes 1978: 125; T.D. Barnes 'The Sources of the Historia Augusta (1967–1992)', *Historia Augusta Colloquia III, Colloquium Maceratense*, Bari 1995: 1–17).

15 These officers were probably *comites Augusti*. John of Ant. fr. 156 (*FHG* IV 599) calls them military tribunes and friends of the emperor; Eutrop. 9.15.2 and *Epit.* 35.8 say *viri militares amici ipsius*; Victor *Caes.* 35.8 says military tribunes (36.2: the ringleader was a *dux*); Zos. 1.62.2, members of the praetorian guard; Zon. 12.27, 'some powerful men'; Lactantius *de mort. pers.* 6.2, the emperor's friends (adding that they acted on false suspicion).

16 Zos. 1.62.2–3; Zon. 12.27; John of Ant. fr. 156; Victor *Caes.* 35.8, 36.2; Eutrop. 9.15.2; *Epit.* 35.8; SHA *Aurel.* 36.5–6 (cf. 35.5 on Mucapor).

17 Following Zosimus, Victor and the *HA*; rejecting Malalas.

18 SHA *Aurel.* 37.2 (claiming the execution was depicted on the emperor's tomb); cf. Paschoud 1996: 176, 177, pointing out that this form of punishment was appropriate to a slave (implying, perhaps, he was not a freedman).

19 Zos. 1.62.3; SHA *Aurel.* 37.1.

20 Contrast the events of 268: see Homo 1904: 325.

21 SHA *Aurel.* 37.3; Victor *Caes.* 35.12.

22 Good character see Eutrop. 9.16; *Epit.* 36.1; Victor *Caes.* 36.1. His rank see Victor *Caes.* 36.1 (consular); SHA *Tac.* 4.1; *Aurel.* 41.4 (including the right of first speech in the senate; cf. Paschoud 1996: 125–6, 194, 259).

23 Zon. 12.28; SHA *Tac.* 7.5–6; cf. Paschoud 1996: 192 (suggesting Zonaras meant Tacitus was elevated by the army in Thrace).

24 In that order, despite SHA *Tac.* 7.6–8.3 (a fiction on the theme of Tacitus' 'modesty').

25 His age see Zon. 12.28; supported by Malalas 12.31 (Bonn 301); cf. SHA *Tac.* 4.5ff. (note the possibility of exaggeration: Syme 1971: 245). An Illyrian general see Syme 1971: 217, 242, 245–7; Keinast 1990: 247–8; Paschoud 1996: 259–60. But cf. Christol 1986: 183–4 (no. 19); Callu 1996: 142, n. 39. See Chapter 10, n. 17 in this book.

26 Eutrop. 9.15.2; SHA *Aurel.* 37.4, 41.3–14 (a spurious and tendentious account, making out that Tacitus was still a *privatus*). The fact of the deification is borne out by inscriptions, see Chapter 11, n. 23.

27 SHA *Tac.* 3.4; *Prob.* 13.5.

28 Zos. 1.63.1; Zon. 12.28; SHA *Tac.* 13.2–3.

29 Victor *Caes.* 36.2; SHA *Tac.* 13.1; cf. *Prob.* 13.2. See Paschoud 1996: 176f.

30 Victory see Zos. 1.63.1; Zon. 12.28; SHA *Tac.* 13.2. Murder see Zos. 1.63.1–2 (mentioning the complicity of Aurelian's murderers); Zon. 12.28; SHA *Tac.* 13.5. The murder took place in Asia Minor, possibly in Pontus: Chron 354 (*Chron Min.* I 148); Jerome *Chron.* 223 (Helm); Jordanes *Rom.* 292; Sync. 722; Malalas 12.31 (Bonn 301); cf. Zos. 1.63.1. Victor *Caes.* 36.2, locates the murder at Tyana in Cappadocia; *Epit.* 36.1, at Tarsus (by error, see following note).

31 Thus *Epit.* 36.1, locating his death at Tarsus, where there was an outbreak of plague after Tacitus' death, and where his successor, Florian, met his end: Zos. 1.64.2–4; cf. Jerome *Chron.* 223 (Helm); Jordanes *Rom.* 292; Sync. 722; Malalas 12.32 (Bonn 302). These facts probably explain the error (see Syme 1971: 242). The same version of Tacitus' end is alluded to in SHA *Tac.* 13.5, and rather more ambiguously in *Prob.* 10.1 and *Car.* 3.7 (cf. Mattingly 1939: 312, n. 5: disease). For the date (*c.* June 276) see Appendix B.4.

32 Zos. 1.63.1, cf. 64.2. SHA *Tac.* 14.1 (full-brother) is certainly incorrect; SHA *Tac.* 17.4 (half-brother) is only marginally more credible: see Syme 1971: 246.

33 Zos 1.64.1; Zon. 12.29, showing the two elevations were more or less simultaneous; the idea of sequence in the Latin sources is due to the reign-by-reign arrangement.

34 Probus may already have been promoted to commander of the cavalry by Aurelian (as Claudius and Aurelian before him: see Paschoud 1996: 113), but at the time of Aurelian's assassination was probably absent from the Balkans, perhaps in the east. This would explain why he was not elevated immediately upon his mentor's death. Certainly he held the senior command in the east under Tacitus, though its precise nature is uncertain. The assertion that Tacitus promoted him to *dux totius orientis* (SHA *Prob.* 7.4) is as unreliable as all the other statements

concerning Probus' pre-imperial career in that biography (but cf. Mattingly 1939: 312–14, who accepts the testimony).

35 Zos. 1.64.2–4; Zon. 12.29; cf. SHA *Prob.* 10.8; *Epit.* 36.2. Florian was killed at Tarsus in Cilicia: see above, n. 33. For the chronology of this power struggle (summer 276) and the dates of Florian's reign see Appendix B.4.

36 Zos. 1.65; cf. Zon. 12.29.

37 SHA *Prob.* 13.2–3.

38 Gibbon 1909: 342.

39 Victor *Caes.* 35.9–36.1.

40 SHA *Aurel.* 40–1; *Tac.* 2.1–7.4. The *HA* also spins out the comparison with the interregnum after Romulus: *Tac.* 1. The two passages containing the decrees (SHA *Aurel.* 41.3; *Tac.* 3.2 [cf. 13.6]) were both introduced with very similar spurious formulas; note also the different names of the proposing consul 'Gordianus'. References to six months see *Aurel.* 40.4; *Tac.* 1.1, 2.1, 2.6. See Paschoud 1996: 194.

41 Gibbon 1909: 340, 343, accepted both at face value; a recent attempt to resurrect this view (Callu 1995 and 1996) must be rejected as misconceived: see Paschoud 1996: 190–2. Homo 1904: 335–9, rejected the early date for the death of Aurelian but accepted 25 September for the elevation of Tacitus; Cizek 1994: 205, took the latter as the date of Aurelian's death. Neither date carries any historical weight: see Appendix B.4.

42 Accepting the full six months see Mattingly 1939: 310; cf. also J. Schwartz, 'A propos des donées chronographiques de l'Histoire Auguste', BHAC 1964/1965, Bonn 1966: 197–210; recently revived by Callu 1995 and 1996 (see below). A more modest interregnum see Cizek 1994: 205–6 (almost 2½ months); Estiot 1995a: 18 (*c.* 2 months); Lafaurie 1975b: 990–2 (1–2 months); Chastagnol 1980: 76–8 (1 month, 24 days); Groag 1903: 1358–9, 1403–4 (*c.* 1½ months); Polverini 1975: 1020 (1 month); Homo 1904: 339 and Syme 1971: 237–9 (less than a month). See further Appendix B.4.

43 See Appendix B.4.

44 *Epit.* 35.10 (*Hoc tempore septem mensibus interregni species evenit*), 36.1 (*Tacitus post hunc suscepit imperium; vir egregie moratus*); cf. Eutrop. 9.16.1 (the same).

45 Victor *Caes.* 35.12 (*interregni species obvenit*); SHA *Tac.* 14.5 (*quasi quidam interreges inter Aurelianum et Probum*). The repeated reference to the other 'formal' interregnum at this point in the text is spurious and probably an interpolation; it is excised by most editors: see Paschoud 1996: 245 and 303.

46 *C.* six months see Eutrop. 9.16; SHA *Tac.* 13.5, 14.5; Oros. 7.24.1; Cassiod. *Chron.* (*Chron. Min.* II) p.148). Two hundred days see Victor *Caes.* 36.2; *Epit.* 36.1. Seven months see Malalas 12.31 (Bonn 301). Eight months, twelve days see Chron. 354 (*Chron. Min.* I 148). The interregnum is given as 6 months in Victor and *HA*, and as 7

months in *Epit.* 35.10. On the chronology of Tacitus' reign see Appendix B.4.

47 Eusebius *HE* 7.30.21; Jerome *Chron.* (ed. Helm) 222 (Aurelian), 223 (Tacitus). The figures here are very rounded: Aurelian's reign can only be said to have lasted 5½ years calculating from the summer of 270 to the winter of 275 (at the very beginning of which Tacitus acceded). Jerome's version is repeated elsewhere in the Latin literature: Eutrop. 9.15.2 (though this statement appears in only one manuscript tradition, π); *Epit.* 35.1; Oros. 7.23.3; Jordanes *Rom.* 290; Cassiod. *Chron.* 984 (*Chron. Min.* II 148); cf. Chron. 354 (*Chron. Min.* I 148), giving Aurelian, 5 years, 4 months and 20 days; Tacitus, 8 months and 12 days.

48 Malalas 12.30 (Bonn 299); John of Ant. fr. 156 (*FHG* IV 599); Sync. 721; Cedrenus (Bonn) 455; Zon. 12.27. The *HA* also grants Aurelian a reign of six years 'less a few days' (*Aurel.* 37.4), the 'few days' in question might reflect the fact that Probus' *dies imperii* fell rather earlier in the summer than Aurelian's. The attempt to amend this passage to fit in with the Latin tradition (by reading *annis < quinque mensibus > sex minus paucis diebus*) is unnecessary: the *HA* often fails to reconcile the information derived from different sources.

49 Florian is accorded 80 days in Eutrop. 9.16; 88 days in both Jerome *Chron.* (Helm) 223 and Chron. 354 (*Chron. Min.* I 148); 2 months in Malal. 12.32 (Bonn 301); scarcely 2 months in SHA *Tac.* 14.2, 14.5. Two months is about right, see Appendix B.4.

50 Thus Homo 1904: 339; Hohl 1911: 284. Also Syme 1971: 237–9, noting the tendency to exaggerate the gaps between emperors, as that in 264 after the death of Jovian (see Amm. 26.1.4, Zos. 3.36.3, where it is described as ἀναρχία).

51 Victor *Caes.* 36.1, 37.6; on both subjects, cf. Chapter 1. On the character of Victor's rhetorical prose see Appendix A. On the Tacitean echoes see Callu 1996.

52 In particular SHA *Tac.* 12, cf. 18–19. This is of course an elaboration of Victor (see preceding note).

53 See esp. SHA *Tac.* 10–11 (notably 10.3, 11.8). The allusion to Cornelius Tacitus was not only prompted by the coincidence of the *cognomen* but also by the textual references he found in Victor.

54 Syme 1971: 239–41; Syme 1983: 116, 119–20; Polverini 1975: 1020–3; Estiot 1995b: 53–4.

55 Doubts on the relationship between the mark, SC, and the exercise of genuine senatorial authority of the senate under the empire see R. Göbl, *Antike Numismatik*, Munich 1978: 79; Millar 1981: 70; lack of such a connection in the mid-third century is conclusively proved by its presence on the bronze coinage of Postumus: Watson 1991: 178–81, cf. 187–8.

56 Göbl 1953: 10–11, 16; and now conclusively D. Yonge, 'The so-called interregnum coinage', *NC* 1979: 47–60. Interregnum date see Webb

1927: 361. For the suggestion that these coins could be dated to 270/71 see H. Mattingly, *Roman Coins from the Earliest Times to the Fall of the Western Empire*, (3rd edn) London 1962: 134f.; Cubelli 1992: 13, remains undecided.

57 SHA *Aurel*. 45.5, 50.2; Zon. 12.27. The suggestion that Severina might herself have been the daughter of Zenobia (Callu 1996: 145, n. 47) is far-fetched; cf. above, Chapter 5, n. 60 in this book.

58 SHA *Aurel*. 10.2–15.2, cf. 38.2–3.

59 Thus Groag 1903: 1353; Homo 1904: 34–5, 141, n. 4; G. Barbieri, *L'albo senatorio da Settimio Severo a Carino (193–285)*, Rome 1952: no. 1766; Cizek 1994: 226. But see Syme 1971: 220 (cf. 4, n. 4, 100–1, 105, on the origin of 'Crinitus' lying in Eutrop. 7.2.1); Estiot 1995a: 9–10.

60 Without the title Augusta see *CIL* V 3330 [Italy]; *AE* 1894: 59 (*pia*) [Africa Procos]. With the title Augusta alone see *CIL* IX 2327, XI 2099 [Italy]; *CIL* III 472 [Asia]; *AE* 1900: 145 [Lydia]; *AE* 1934: 44; *Ins. Lat. Maroc.* p.25, no. 79 [Mauretania Tingit.] (cf. Sotgiu 1961: 92, nos 58–9). For other titulature of Severina see Chapters 10 and 11.

61 Estiot 1983: 16. On the date of the reform see Chapter 8 in this book.

62 *RIC* V.1 (p.313, Aurelian and Severina) 1–4; cf. Rohde 1881: 447–9; Gnecchi 1912: III, 65, nos 1–2.

63 The bulk of her coinage was issued at Ticinum and Rome; the relative output in her name was rather small at Cyzicus and Siscia (see Estiot 1983: 16; and Chapter 8 in this book on the mints). On her portrait style see Bastien 1992–4: 610–12, 645.

64 Some modern accounts are frankly fanciful: see e.g. Cizek 1994: 225–8. Göbl 1993: 246, n. 71, speculates that she may have been made genuine co-regent in 274 (enabling her the more easily to carry on after her husband's murder): the appearance of the plural AVGG on the reverse of the coinage *may* indicate more than usual participation by an empress, but this hardly amounts to proof.

65 Kellner 1978: 31, n. 1205 and 35, n. 1536; but cf. now Göbl 1993: 28, more convincingly dating these coins to the period following the victorious reintegration of Gaul in the second half of 274. See Plate 3, c–d.

66 Webb 1927: 253, and Mattingly 1939: 310, n. 2; Carson 1965: 233–5; Göbl 1993: 29–30; Cizek 1994: 206, 273, n. 14; Estiot 1995a: 10, 18, 31, 52, 54, 62, 88, 100–1; Callu 1996: 137–41. For iconography see Plate 2, c.

67 Estiot 1995a: 101; Callu 1996: 141. On Severina's symbolic relationship with the army, cf. Chapter 10 in this book.

68 The argument of Callu 1996: 142–5, that Victor deliberately suppressed information he received from the KG on Severina's interregnum is wholly unacceptable, not least because the author of the *HA*, who had access to the KG, would scarcely have done the same.

69 Estiot 1983: 20, 23, 25, could detect no identifiably separate series for Severina at the end of the reign at Siscia, nor at Lyon, which led her to

doubt the interregnum explanation. Göbl 1993: 41, 50, 56, 65, 68, detected such issues at Ticinum, Rome, Siscia (dated mysteriously to early 275!), Cyzicus and Antioch, respectively. Although Estiot has conceded the main point, see Estiot 1995b: 76–7, she still detects no such billon issue at either Siscia or Cyzicus, although she concedes the issue of gold (Estiot 1995b: 80–1, 87). Very recently, two coins have been put forward to prove the existence, after all, of such issues at Lyon and Serdica, see S. Estiot and F. Bonté, 'Aurélien et Séverine: trois raretés et un inédit', *BSFN* 1, 1997: 4–9, 7–9; but it should be noted that the Serdican type (reverse, CONCORDIA AVGG) somewhat undermines one of the strengths of the argument concerning the CONCORDIA AVG type from Antioch mentioned at n. 67. Other doubts were expressed by Lafaurie 1975b: 990.

70 Göbl 1993: 30 (cf. 245, n. 69), describes the interregnum issue for Severina as an 'indisputable fact', expressing incredulity at the doubts entertained by Estiot 1983 (above, n. 69); Göbl's view has now been accepted by Estiot 1995a (above, n. 66).

8 ECONOMIC REFORMS

1 On debasement generally see Burnett 1987: 48–50; M.H. Crawford, 'Money and Exchange in the Roman World', *JRS* 60, 1970: 40–8.

2 Jones 1953; Burnett 1987: 105–21; Drinkwater 1987: 206–11; see also R.A.G. Carson, 'The Inflation of the Third Century and its Monetary Influence in the Near East', in A. Kindler (ed.) *Proceedings of the International Numismatic Convention, Jerusalem 1963*, Jerusalem 1967: 231–50.

3 Nastor 1987: 137–42 (Aurelian), 142–3 (Perge under Tacitus); cf. K.W. Harl, *Civic Coins and Civic Policy in the Roman East, AD 180–275*, Berkeley 1987: 91–4; Burnett 1987: 51–65, esp. 63ff.; Homo 1904: 171–2.

4 For the revolt of the mint workers see Chapter 3. Another manifestation was the forgery of so-called 'barbarous radiates' in the west, see n. 58 below.

5 Göbl 1993: 79, cf. 80–2, on the various elements involved in these reforms.

6 *CIL* X 1214; V 6421 (respectively); *PLRE* I Sabinus (18); Cubelli 1992: 51, cf. 40–3; Crawford 1984: 251; Sotgiu 1961: 28, n. 55. The strong connection with north Italy might possibly suggest Sabinus was a native of the region. On the imperial mint at Ticinum and its connection with the coinage reform see n. 38 below. On Felicissimus and the riots see Chapter 3.

7 Homo 1904: 165f.; Webb 1927: 248f.; Carson 1965: 232; Crawford 1975: 575; Cubelli 1992: 17f., 51–4. The theory of Homo 1904: 163ff., later developed by Gatti 1961, that the revolt was a response rather than a cause of the mini-reform must be rejected.

8   Estiot 1995b: 54; cf. (February 274) Lafaurie 1974; Lafaurie 1975a: 99–107; (early summer 274) Carson 1965: 233–5 (but note first issue at Ticinum overlooked by Carson: Estiot 1983: 19); (autumn 274) Homo 1904: 166; Callu 1969: 323. The late date takes Zos. 1.61.3 to indicate precise relative chronology, which is unsound.

9   Zos. 1.61.3; for the significance of this passage see Cubelli 1992: 55, 67, 86–7; Estiot 1995b: 55.

10 V. Picozzi, *La monetazione imperiale romana*, Rome 1966: 19; Lafaurie 1975a: 88; Cubelli 1992: 56–7.

11 C.E. King and R.E.M. Hedges, 'An analysis of some third-century Roman coins for surface silvering and silver percentage and their alloy content', *Archaeometry* 1974: 195–8; Callu, Brenot and Barrandon 1979; Cubelli 1992: 57 (citing S. Bolin, *State and Currency in the Roman Empire to 300 AD*, Stockholm 1958: 292, n. 1, on the probable original silver content; but cf. Mattingly 1927: 221).

12 Lafaurie 1975a: 83; Cubelli 1992: 55–6.

13 Cubelli 1992: 67–89.

14 For example, Crawford 1975: 575–7; W. Weiser, 'Die Münzreform des Aurelian', *ZPE* 53, 1983: 279–95; full bibliography in Cubelli 1992: 68–70; cf. Callu 1969: 324–6.

15 For example, recently Lafaurie 1975a: 81–107; see Cubelli 1992: 70–2 for bibliography.

16 For example, Jones 1953: 299f.; Carson 1965; Callu 1969: 329; see further Cubelli 1992: 72–5.

17 Callu, Brenot and Barrandon 1979: esp. 246ff.; cf. also Keinast 1974: 553; Bastien 1976: 87; Cubelli 1992: 78–89; Estiot 1995b: 55. Note that the value-mark theory cannot adequately explain the relationship between the Aurelianic and Diocletianic coinage either: Cubelli 1992: 82–5.

18 Absence of reform marks see Cubelli 1993: 65, 81. Fineness see C.E. King, 'Denarii and Quinarii, AD 253–295', in R.A.G. Carson and C.M. Kraay (eds) *Scripta Nummaria Romana: Essays Presented to Humphrey Sutherland*, London 1978: 75–104: 104, Figures 17a and 17b, citing average weight at 3.55g but fineness at only 2.7 per cent. This differential cannot be quite as simply dismissed as Cubelli 1992: 81 suggests.

19 Bastien 1976: 36–8, confirming Rohde 1881: 285; Webb 1927: 251. See further Cubelli 1992: 60–1.

20 For example, Cubelli 1992: 51, 61; cf. Chapter 10 in this book.

21 The first group (Gnecchi 1912: II, 113, nos 1–3) average 18.73g; the smallest coins (Gnecchi 1912: III, 64, nos 5–18; 65, no. 2; 66, no. 1) average around 8g (Estiot 1988: 441, n. 6, gives 8.38g; Cubelli 1992: 61, n. 20, gives 7.93g); the double portrait group (Gnecchi 1912: III, 64, no. 4; 65, no.1) average 12.61g.

22 *RIC* 71–3; cf. Mattingly 1927; for arrangement, cf. P. Bastien and H.-G. Pflaum, 'La trouvaille de monnaies romaines de Thibouville (Eure) II', *Gallia* 20, 1962: 255–315, 277–81.

23 'Usualis': Mattingly 1927: 227; Callu 1969: 329. Quinquennalia: Manns 1939: 6; Estiot 1983: 38. Callu 1969: 328, dismisses the quinquennial explanation by saying that no such celebrations were held in the second and third centuries, but this is to overlook Postumus. See further Cubelli 1992: 77–8.

24 It used to be thought that Gallienus' Gallic mint was at Cologne and that Trier was a branch mint set up by Postumus' successors: Elmer 1941: 14, 30. For the reversal see now Besly and Bland 1983: 44–65, esp. 53–8; Drinkwater 1987: 143–6; Bland and Burnett 1988: 147–55; Watson 1991: 58–60. On Milan see Alföldi 1927: 201; Göbl 1953: 18–23; on Siscia see A. Alföldi, *Siscia. Vorarbeiten zu einem Corpus der in Siscia geprägten Römermünzen. I: Die Prägungen des Gallienus*, esp. 7–9; on the Asian mint see Alföldi 1938: 59–64; Göbl 1953: 30f. The location of the Asian mint at Cyzicus under Claudius is suggested by stylistic affinities with the local civic bronzes and by the presence of dots on the obverse as *officina* marks (Roger Bland, personal communication); cf. Göbl 1993: 62.

25 Rohde 1881: 297f.; Groag 1903: 1364; cf. (on the first Aurelianic issues) Manns 1939: 14–19; Estiot 1983: 17, 21, 30, 33; Bland and Burnett 1988: 132ff.

26 A coin from the Normanby hoard pertaining to the first issue at Cyzicus for Aurelian (obv. IMP C DOM AVRELIANVS AVG) which had been overstruck with the Divus Claudius dies is crucial in determining the date and sequence of these issues: Bland and Burnett 1988: 145. At Milan, these coins were only issued by the third *officina*.

27 Estiot 1983: 33–7 (suggesting the number of *officinae* rose from four to ten before finally settling back to six); Göbl 1993: 41–50; Estiot 1995b: 71–7. For the re-allocation of several solar types to this mint at this date see Kellner 1978: 20. On the closure of the mint at Rome being a motive rather than a result of the moneyers' revolt see Rohde 1881: 320; but cf. Estiot 1983: 16; Cubelli 1992: 14, 17 (Lo Cascio 1984: 170, is undecided); on the relocation of some of the workers see n. 34 below.

28 Estiot 1983: 17–19; Estiot 1991; Göbl 1993: 34–9; Estiot 1995b: 66–71; cf. Kellner 1978: 22–4. On output see n. 38 below.

29 Estiot 1983: 21–5 (cf. 16 for output); Göbl 1993: 50–6; Estiot 1995b: 77–81; cf. Kellner 1978: 25–31. On the early issues and their importance to Aurelian in his first few months see Estiot 1995a: 15.

30 Estiot 1983: 30–2; Göbl 1993: 62–5; Estiot 1995b: 84–7; cf. Kellner 1978: 36–40. The location of the mint under Aurelian is fixed by certain coins in the middle of the reign which bear a mint mark containing the letter C: Estiot 1983: 31; Göbl 1993: 62.

31 Göbl 1993: 65–8; Estiot 1995b: 87–90. On the arrangement of the post-Palmyrene issues for Aurelian see also Bastien and Huvelin 1969: 139–42, cf. 258–67 (the catalogue).

32 Estiot 1995b: 54; cf. Lafaurie 1975a: 99ff. For Alexandria in 270–2 see

Appendix B.3. The mint at Alexandria continued to mint down to his seventh regnal year (275/6); mysteriously there are some coins dated year VIII, although on any feasible arrangement of Aurelian's dates such a reckoning is impossible.

33 On the second Gallic mint and its amalgamation with Trier see Drinkwater 1987: 144, 146; Bland and Burnett 1988: 147–55 (esp. 153–5). See now Göbl 1993: 33; cf. Estiot 1995a: 40; Estiot 1995b: 66. For the Aurelianic coinage see below n. 39.

34 Manns 1939: 30, 44–7, 56–8; Kellner 1978: 33–5; Estiot 1983: 25–8 (noting that the workmen were brought with him from Rome); Göbl 1993: 56–60; Estiot 1995b: 81–2. The first coins issued here bear the mark SERD in the exergue: *RIC* 258, 265, 267, 272.

35 Manns 1939: 31, 33; Callu 1969: 233–4; Estiot 1983: 28; Göbl 1993: 60 (plausibly suggesting that it was originally a *moneta comitatensis* which was settled at Byzantium by the end of the year); cf. the caution expressed by Estiot 1995b: 83. Byzantium, a logical choice given the circumstances, would seem to be supported by *CJ* 5.72.2 (1 January of unspecified year, presumably 272) and by SHA *Aurel.* 22.3; but cf. Rohde 1881: 405; Webb 1927: 309 (both undecided); Kellner 1978: 31f., n. 1208 (Viminacium). Estiot 1983: 29–30, places the coins marked with a dolphin earlier than either Rohde 1881: 408–9, or Manns 1939: 42. The personnel were apparently withdrawn from Milan and later returned to Italy, where they reopened the mint at Rome.

36 Generally, see Göbl 1993: 60–2 (wrongly suggesting closure in 272); Estiot 1995b: 82–3; cf. Estiot 1983: 30 (last issue), 33 (transfer to Rome). On production level see Estiot 1983: 28; cf. (much lower estimates) Webb 1927: 309, n. 2; Kellner 1978: 31f., n. 1208.

37 The arrangement remains controversial: see Göbl 1993: 68; Bastien and Huvelin 1969: 143–4, cf. 168–70 (the catalogue); Callu 1969: 236; Webb 1927: 261. On the date and purpose of the mint's inauguration see Estiot 1995a: 106; Estiot 1995b: 89–90.

38 Göbl 1993: 40–1; Estiot 1983: 19–21, cf. 16 (output); Crawford 1984. The presence of Sabinus, and perhaps the centre of his operations, at Ticinum (see n. 6 above) and before that in northern Italy may partly account for the large output of the north Italian mints.

39 On Aurelian's Gallic coinage see Bastien 1976: 34–9; though Bastien's attribution of certain coins (p. 35 and pl. LXVIII, 1–3) to the second Gallic mint (at Cologne; here called Trier) is in error – on this, the transfer and mint at Lyon generally see Göbl 1993: 33–4; Estiot 1995b: 66; cf. also Elmer 1941: 93f.; Estiot 1983: 16; and for the circumstances, see Chapter 6 in this book; (on amalgamation with Trier see above, n. 33). Septimius Severus closed the mint at Lyon in 197, after his civil war victory over Clodius Albinus.

40 Callu 1969: 286–7, calculated an increase of as much as seven times; cf. Crawford 1975: 577. Such an increase would have fuel inflation.

41 See Estiot 1983; Kellner 1978; Göbl 1993. On the types mentioned here, see below, Chapters 10 and 11 in this book.

42 Homo 1904: 150–1; Palmer 1980: 220; cf. Paschoud 1996: 215–17 (more sceptical). SHA *Aurel.* 48.2; cf. *Prob.* 18.8; Victor *Caes.* 37.3; Eutrop. 9.17.2; and cf. *CJ* 11.58.1 (Constantine). The *HA* appears to have confused these measures with the subsidized sale of fiscal wine (see p. 128), and then greatly embroidered the story in the usual way.

43 See Chapter 9. This measure also was continued and extended by Probus.

44 Victor *Caes.* 35.7; SHA *Aurel.* 37.7–38.1, 39.3–4; cf Amm. 24.6.7–8. On the connection with customs and the walls see Palmer 1980: 218–20 (cf. Chapter 9 in this book).

45 SHA *Aurel.* 39.4; which for Palmer 1980: 219, is also interconnected with the above reforms to the supply of food and wine; cf. Paschoud 1996: 187f. A few other legislative measures of Aurelian's are preserved in the codes, the majority dealing with matters of private law: see Homo 1904: 149–50.

46 SHA *Aurel.* 45.1 (cf. 47.1); Paschoud 1996: 208–9, remains highly sceptical.

47 On the grain supply see *Epit.* 1.6; Joseph. *BI* 2.382–3, 2.385–6; Plin. *NH* 18.66–8; Suet. *Claud.* 18–19. On the organization see Wallace 1938: 31ff.; G. Rickman, *The Corn Supply of Ancient Rome*, Oxford 1980: esp. 97, 197, 253–6. On the reforms of the Severan period see F. Coarelli, 'La situazione edilizia di Roma sotto Severo Alessandro', in *L'Urbs. Espace urbain et histoire (Ier siècle av. J.-C.–IIIe siècle ap. J.-C.)*, Rome 1987: 448–56; Bell 1994: 84–7.

48 Wallace 1938: 45–6.

49 SHA *Aurel.* 35.1, 48.1; Chron. 354 (*Chron. Min.* I 148); Zos. 1.61.3.

50 SHA *Aurel.* 47.1.

51 Proc. *BG* 1.19; cf. Chapter 9.

52 Bell 1994. I am extremely grateful to Professor Bell for sharing much more information with me than appears here.

53 SHA *Aurel.* 48.1; Chron. 354 (*Chron. Min.* I 148); cf. Septimius, SHA *Sev.* 18.3. The Chronographer alone mentions the salt.

54 Victor *Caes.* 35.7; SHA *Aurel.* 35.2, 48.1; *CIL* VI 1156; Homo 1904: 181; Richardson 1992: 79, 174–5. See further Chapter 9, n. 29.

55 SHA *Aurel.* 48.1–4; *CIL* VI 1785. See Palmer 1980; cf. R.E.A. Palmer, 'Silvanus, Silvester and the Chair of St Peter', *Proc. Am. Philosoph. Soc.* 122, 1978: 222–47, 228–30; Richardson 1992: 81–2 (cf. 363–4); Homo 1904: 179–81. On the temple see Chapter 11 in this book.

56 SHA *Aurel.* 47.3; cf. Paschoud 1996: 213–15. These and other measures were quite properly relegated to a footnote by Homo 1904: 180f. (n. 3). Another like measure, a new forum at Ostia, may be more credible: see Chapter 9 in this book.

57 The local civic coinage includes coins depicting Annona with ears

of wheat bearing the legend, DONATIO COL CREMN: their interpretation is not certain, however. See Nastor 1987: 139–41.

58 Drinkwater 1987: 192–8, 212–13; see also C.E. King, 'The circulation of coin in the western provinces AD 260–295', in A. King and M. Henig (eds) *The Roman West in the 3rd Century AD* [BAR IS 109], Oxford 1981: 89–126; but cf. Crawford 1975: 577, stressing the comparative ease of transition across the empire, and explaining the make-up of western hoards in monetary terms: 'The dislocation of supply of money (never in any case more than an accidental consequence of supply of coinage to officials and troops) is hardly surprising in the circumstances.' For the Lyon output see above, nn. 19, 39. For the political explanations, see Chapter 6 in this book, at n. 26.

59 On the emperor's participation in such decisions see my lengthy discussion in Watson 1991: 37–44, and the works there cited; cf. Chapter 10 in this book, at n. 36.

9 PUBLIC WORKS AND ADMINISTRATION

1 The previous time was in 260/1: see Appendix B.3.

2 The date and circumstances of commencement are given explicitly in SHA *Aurel.* 21.9 and Zos. 1.49.2; and the date in Malalas 12.30 (Bonn 299) and in the *Consularia Constantinopolitana* (*Chron. Min.* I 229). This is compatible with most other accounts: SHA *Aurel.* 39.2; Victor *Caes.* 35.7; *Epit.* 35.6; Eutrop. 9.15.1; Chron. 354 (*Chron. Min.* I 148). The seventh-century *Chronicon Paschale* dates the beginning of the work to 273; Jerome *Chron.* 223 (Helm) and the *Chronicle* of Cassiodorus (*Chron. Min.* II 148) both suggest the last year of his reign. These dates are certainly too late for the initial stages, but might reflect significant stages in the construction of the walls. On the confirmation of an Aurelianic date from the archaeological evidence see Richmond 1930: 15–18.

3 SHA *Aurel.* 22.1; Malalas 12.30 (Bonn 299).

4 SHA *Aurel.* 21.9, 22.1 (consultation with the senate), is uncorroborated and thus suspect, but it would have been prudent for Aurelian to consult the senate and the policing of the walls was subsequently under the senatorial prefecture of the city.

5 Malalas 12.30 (Bonn 299–300). See Groag 1903: 1375; Richmond 1930: 28–9; Todd 1978: 43; cf. Homo 1904: 222, n. 2.

6 Zos. 1.49.2; Malalas 12.30 (Bonn 299–300).

7 *CIL* VI 1016 a–c, 31227; *CIL* VI 8594, though not a boundary stone, also sheds some light on the line.

8 The line of the walls see Richmond 1930: 7–9, 13–14, 17–18, cf. 205–17 (and Figure 11, p. 73); Todd 1978: 23–4; cf. Homo 1904: 222–39. On the strategic considerations on the west bank see Chapter 8, n. 51 in this book. For the thesis that Aurelian's walls followed the customs line in all but the eastern sectors see Palmer 1980: esp.

217–21, 223–4; he does, however, rather stretch the evidence (esp. his Appendix II.2, III.1–3, V.3, pp.231–3). See also below, n. 27.

9 The exclusion of the Pons Aelius would have been particularly odd if, as seems likely, the bridge of Nero no longer existed: see Richmond 1930: 20–6 (esp. 25f.); cf. Procop. *BG* 1.22, 3.36, 4.33; see also Homo 1904: 259, 270–1. On river walls see Richmond 1930: 18–20; cf. Procop. *BG* 1.19, 2.9; and on their appearance see below n. 24.

10 Richmond 1930: 10, 57–67; cf. Todd 1978: 24–31. The galleried sections were constructed either side of Porta Asinaria in the south, and east of Porta Pinciana in the north.

11 Richmond 1930: 62, 76–80; Todd 1978: 32–4.

12 For full descriptions see Richmond 1930: 191–200, 121–42, 109–21, 200–5 (respectively), cf. 245–6.

13 See Richmond 1930: 185–90, 93–100, 170–81, 100–9 (respectively), cf. 246.

14 Richmond 1930: 205–17; Todd 1978: 38–40; Richardson 1992: 306–7. The existence of the two flanking semicircular towers cannot now be proven, but the logic of the design demands it.

15 The exact location, the form and even the original name (Porta Aurelia?) of this gate is obscure. Strategically, it seems likely that Aurelian's original gate was in the river wall on the left bank; whether a postern was added later, on the right bank, is difficult to say. See Richmond 1930: 227–8.

16 It is not certain whether the original towers were semicircular, but it is difficult to believe this was a third-class gate: see Richmond 1930: 221–3. The gateway was distinguished from the foregoing by the name 'Pancratiana' in Procopius.

17 Richmond 1930: 142–59, cf. 254–5 (on Maxentius' restructuring) and 246–7 (on this class of gate generally); Todd 1978: 35–6, 53–7.

18 Richmond 1930: 159–69; Todd 1978: 59; Richardson 1992: 306. The original name is unknown: 'Pinciana' cannot antedate the fourth century. Further improved by Honorius, it was the scene of heavy fighting under Belisarius. For the offset, cf. the originally far more important Porta Tiburtina.

19 The original names of all three gates are uncertain. See Richmond 1930: 181–4, 217–19, 223–7; on Porta Chiusa cf. Todd 1978: 64; on Porta Septimiana, postulating that Aurelian incorporated a Severan monumental archway set up to demarcate the customs boundary near the important Cellae Nova et Arruntiana, cf. Palmer 1980: 223–4, 232.

20 Maxentius was apparently responsible for the blocking, at least at Ostiensis West. See Richmond 1930: 219–21 (P. Ostiensis W.), 229–35, 247 (other posterns and doorways, including one which served the Lateran Palace); Todd 1978: 47.

21 Their precise locations are uncertain: see Richmond 1930: 236–9. One probably served the road running in front of the mausoleum of Augustus; one served the quay known as 'the storks' (Ciconiae: on

which see Richardson 1992: 81–2), probably to be located just south of the modern Ponte Cavour; one probably served the ferry crossing to the Horti Domitiae; if the bridge of Nero still stood (see above, n. 9), then one must be assigned to it, if not then perhaps to a ferry which replaced it; one more further south.

22 Richmond 1930: 61–2, 243–8.

23 Homo 1904: 239–62 (overestimating the proportion), 265–70; Richmond 1930: 11–15, 63–4; Todd 1978: 26–8. On the mausoleum see above, n. 9.

24 Procop. *BG* 2.9; cf. Richmond 1930: 19. Procopius' suggestion that the walls were lower along the Tiber may simply reflect the fact that they were not heightened like the rest of the walls by Maxentius. On the possibility that Aurelian repaired the embankments as well see Chapter 8, n. 56 in this book.

25 Richmond 1930: 67, 242–5, 248.

26 Richmond 1930: 67 (whence quotation), 80, 242; Todd 1978: 34, 80–2; cf. I.A. Richmond, 'Five town walls in Hispania Citerior', *JRS* 21, 1931: 86–100. Of the contemporary Gallic and Spanish parallels, including Sanlis and Lugo, the closest is certainly Barcelona.

27 Thus Palmer 1980; the case is, however, somewhat over-argued, and his assertion (p. 219) that there were 37 gates in Aurelian's walls is wholly inaccurate. For evidence of fifth-century collection of customs at the Aurelianic Porta Nomentana see *Lib. Pont.* I 222 D.

28 This project is only mentioned in Chron. 354 (*Chron. Min.* I 148). On the possible correlation between some of the extant brickwork at the Baths and that found in the Aurelianic parts of the city walls see Richmond 1930: 61.

29 Chron. 354 (*Chron. Min.* I 148); cf. Symm. *Ep.* 9.57[54]; *CIL* VI 1156 (*ILS* 722); *Not. Sc.* 1909: 430–1. Water was supplied by the Aquae Virgo and Marcia. See Richardson 1992: 79 (castra urbana), 174–5 (forum suarium), both apparently east of the Corso and north of the via Condotti. On the probable connection with the distribution of pork see Chapter 8, n. 29 in this book.

30 SHA *Aurel.* 49.2 (portico), 45.2 (baths). On the Gardens of Sallust as an imperial residence in the fourth century, cf. *Pan. Lat.* 12 (IX) 14.4. The portico story (perhaps an imitation of the account of the porticoes of the Golden House in Suet. *Nero* 31.1: see Domaszewski, *Sitzungsb. der Heidelb. Akad.* 1916: 7.A, 13) is believed by some, e.g. Richardson 1992: 202.

31 *CIL* X 222, XI 556.

32 SHA *Aurel.* 45.2.

33 Dijon and Orleans see Homo 1904: 212–13 (cf. Chapter 6, n. 20 in this book); Richborough see Todd 1978: 79–80; cf. J.S. Johnson, *The Roman Forts of the Saxon Shore*, London 1976: 34–62. Milestones: note especially *CIL* VIII 10374; cf. others in Sotgiu 1961: 81ff.; Homo 1904: 350ff.

34 Victor *Caes.* 35.7–8; SHA *Aurel.* 39.5.

35 *AE* 1991: 1736 note (p. 481); cf. *CIL* VIII 20836. The most decisive evidence is provided by the procurator of Sardinia, Septimius Necrinus: *Eph. Ep.* VIII 775 (*v.e.*), 796 (*v.p.*).

36 On Tetricus see Chapter 6, nn. 22–3. At least two other regions (Venetia and Campania) attest such governors in the reign of Carinus. Correctors of both Italy as a whole and separate regions are still attested under Diocletian. See Homo 1904: 144–5 (esp. 144ff., n. 1).

37 Victor *Caes.* 33.3; Eutrop. 9.8.2; Festus *Brev.* 8; Oros. 7.22.7; Jordanes *Rom.* 217; Alföldi 1939: 151–2; Mócsy 1974: 209. Dacian legions at Poetovio see V. Hoffiler and B. Saria, *Antike Inschriften aus Juguslavien. Heft I, Noricum und Pannonia Superior*, Zagreb 1938: 144ff. The implication of a partial withdrawal under Gallienus was rejected by Cizek 1994: 139–40; but for the suggestion the withdrawal began even under Philip see Potter 1990: 233–4.

38 See Appendix B.1.

39 SHA *Aurel.* 39.7; Jordanes *Rom.* 217. See Alföldi 1939: 152–3; Mócsy 1974: 211–12.

40 Cizek 1994: 123–52, esp. 125–7, suggesting a date no earlier than summer 273 for the withdrawal based largely on the evidence of one hoard. The hoard may well have been buried due to the invasion of the Carpi in the autumn of 272. On the reinforcement of bridgeheads on the left bank of the Danube at this time see Cizek 1994: 151 (cf. 145).

41 Thus Homo 1904: 314; R. Vulpe, 'Considérations historiques autour de l'évacuation de la Dacie par Aurélien', *Dacorum. Jb. Ost. Lat.* I, 1973: 41–51, 49. On the internal arrangement of the sources see Appendix A.

42 *RIC* 108 (*Normanby* 1258; Manns 1939: 13. Homo 1904: 314, n. 2, expressly denied the relationship between the coin and the withdrawal; but see Mattingly 1939: 301; cf. Cizek 1994: 125.

43 Eutrop. 9.15.1; Festus *Breu.* 8; SHA *Aurel.* 39.7; Jordanes *Rom.* 217; Sync. 722; Malalas 12.30 (301 Bonn). Homo 1904: 314–21; Mócsy 1974: 211–12; cf. generally H. Vetters, *Dacia Ripensis*, Vienna 1950. On the continuation of a considerable Daco-Roman presence north of the Danube after this time see Cizek 1994: 142–5 (though he goes too far in denying a civilian evacuation altogether).

44 The literary sources, except Festus *Brev.* 8, suggest a single province: either Festus is anachronistic, or the rest are oversimplifying. *AE* 1912: 200, implies the existence of two Dacian provinces by 283 at the latest; see Syme 1971: 223; cf. Mócsy 1974: 211–12 (also p. 273, on the later expansion westward of the new Aurelianic province of Dacia under the Tetrarchy); Cizek 1994: 150 (*CIL* III 12333 and 13715, which he cites here, are probably not Aurelianic: see now Kettenhofen 1986: 140f.).

45 Victor *Caes.* 39.43. That the desertion of farmland was a real concern to Aurelian and to the imperial government in general during the later third century, see Chapter 8.

10 THE EMPEROR, THE SENATE AND THE ARMIES

1 Nephew see Eutrop. 9.14; *Epit.* 35.9; cf. SHA *Aurel.* 39.9, 36.3. Son-in-law see John of Ant. fr. 155 (*FHG* IV 599); cf. SHA *Aurel.* 42.1–2 (mentioning a married daughter; but see Appendix A). More generally see John of Ant. fr. 156 (*FHG* IV 599); Eutrop. 9.13.1, 9.14; *Epit.* 35.9; SHA *Aurel.* 21.5–8, 36.3, 38.2, 39.5, 39.8–9, cf. 6.1 ('severitas inmensa'), 40.2 ('severissimus princeps'), 44.1–2 ('ei clementia defuerit', 'nimia ferocitas'). For a detailed analysis of the *HA*'s portrait of Aurelian with regard to cruelty see Mouchová 1972.

2 Lactantius *de mort. persec.* 6.1; Oros. 7.23.3–12; Zon. 12.27; cf. Julian *Symp.* 313–14 A (ed. Hertlein). On the pervasive influence of the Christian tradition see Mouchová 1972: 191–4.

3 Malalas 12.30 (299 Bonn); cf. Chapters. 5 and 6 in this book. The charges of cruelty in the *HA* are often encased in fiction.

4 On Gallienus and on the rhetorical framework generally see Chapter 1; on Claudius see Syme 1971: 204–6 (cf. 237–47); Syme 1983: 68–70; on the 'interregnum' and Tacitus see Chapter 7 in this book (esp. nn. 51–3). On the sources themselves see Appendix A.

5 Zos. 1.49.2; SHA *Aurel.* 18.4, 21.6, 38.2, 39.8; Eutrop. 9.14. See Cubelli 1992: 46. For all these events, see Chapter 3 in this book. The use of the plural in SHA *Aurel.* 18.4 (*seditiones*), and 21.5 (*seditionum*) may suggest that the senators who supported the provincial revolts were not the same as those who joined and perhaps orchestrated the revolt at Rome (which may have centred on one Urbanus: see Zos. 1.49.2).

6 Cont. Dion. fr. 10.1 (*FHG* IV 197); Zon. 12.27 (not specifying Ravenna).

7 Amm. 30.8.8 (cf. 31.5.17); Jerome *Chron.* 244 (Helm), apparently one of Jerome's own annotations. Mentioning cruelty only see SHA *Aurel.* 21.5–6, 39.8. See Gilliam 1972: 143–4: 'Aurelian's harshness was a commonplace and doubtless a fact, but his exactions from the rich I do not find specifically mentioned in the *vita.*'

8 Groag 1903: 1406–7 (cf. 1374–5); Cubelli 1992: 46–9; cf. the more balanced view in Lippold 1995.

9 Cubelli 1992: 51, 61, suggesting that Aurelian formally removed the right of minting bronze from the senate and linking this to the rebellion of 271; cf. Homo 1904: 79, 163; Gatti 1961; Lo Cascio 1984: 170. See Chapter 7, n. 55 in this book.

10 The link between the mint workers' revolt of 271 and the idea of a hostile senate coining behind Aurelian's back was first mooted by A. Sorlin-Dorigny, 'Aurélien et la guerre des monnayeurs', *RN* 1891: 105–34, the idea has been picked up and elaborated upon in various ways by numerous scholars since. Linked to the GENIVS PR coinage see Turcan 1969; cf. above Chapter 7, n. 56 in this book. Linked to DIVO CLAVDIO coinage see Groag 1903: 1372–4; Bernareggi 1974; cf. Estiot 1988: 441, quite rightly rejecting the link. Cubelli 1992:

5–25, 30–49, appears prepared to believe either; but see now Estiot 1995b: 53–4.

11 According to *Epit.* 34.4, he was *princeps senatus* under Claudius, which clearly demonstrates his eminence in the senate around the time of Aurelian's accession. See Christol 1986: 100–1, 221–4 (no. 49); Syme 1971: 203, n. 1; *PLRE* I Bassus (17); *CIL* VI 3836 (31747; *IGR* 1137); *ILS* 5056; *AE* 1906: 128. For his pedigree see *PIR*[1] P.525–6.

12 *PLRE* I, Antiochianus; Christol 1986: 110, 131–2.

13 Christol 1986: 110, 132, 270–1 (nos. 63–4); *PLRE* I, Orfitus (2).

14 *CIL* VI 31775 and XIV 2078 (= *ILS* 1209–10). The exact chronology of his eastern provincial governorships is not certain, but they must both have fallen between 272 and 277: *PLRE* I, Lupus (5); Christol 1986: 263–70 (no. 62). On the new pontifical college see Chapter 11 in this book.

15 *CIL* VI 1417; Christol 1986: 193–5 (no. 27). Disgrace is a doubly dangerous deduction, since he may well have served a complete year as successor to rather than predecessor of Bassus.

16 Christol 1986: 111, 238–9 (no. 51), 207 (no. 39). Although Veldumianus' *nomen* has been supplied, it is a fairly safe supposition; he may have become urban prefect at some unknown date (*CIL* VI 319). For Suagrus see Christol 1986: 132.

17 For the traditional view see *PLRE* I, Tacitus (2–3); but see now Christol 1986: 111–13, 153–8 (no. 12); cf. Paschoud 1996: 259f. Christol takes *PLRE* I, Tacitus (1) to be the son of this Caecina; but Caecina was *praeses* of Baetica prior to his consulship, and it is generally accepted that the governors of Baetica were only thus styled after 276, making the consulship in 273 an impossibility (but cf. Chapter 7, n. 25 in this book). The question remains open.

18 The epithet, used in SHA *Aurel.* 37.3, is not found elsewhere, and is probably the author's own invention.

19 As *vp praefectus vigilum* on *CIL* XII 2228 (*ILS* 569; Grenoble 269); as *vc praefectus praetorio* on *CIL* XII 1551 (Vaison, date uncertain). See Homo 1904: 66, n. 3, 142–3; Howe 1942: 82; Christol 1986: 199–200 (no. 32).

20 *PLRE* I, Marcellinus (1), (2) and (17); Groag 1903: 1400; Homo 1904: 143; Christol 1986: 113–14. On Marcellinus at Verona see *CIL* V 3329 (*ILS* 544, *c*. 265).

21 Sotgiu 1961: 82f, nos. 7–10; cf. (erased) *CIL* III 7586; see also A. Stein, *Die Legaten von Moesien*, Budapest 1940: 106; *PLRE* I, Sebastianus (4), though the date is here in error and *PLRE* I, Anon. (113); cf. also *CIL* III 14460; *PLRE* I, Anon. (114).

22 *CIL* III 15156; Sotgiu 1975: 1059; cf. *PLRE* I, Aper (3) and (2).

23 See Chapter 7, n. 34.

24 Jerome *Chron.* 222 (Helm); Alföldi 1939: 162; but cf. Barnes 1994: 18.

25 *PLRE* I, Mucapor.

26 SHA *Firm.* 3.1; *PLRE* I, Firmus (2); Barnes 1978: 70–1 (governor of Crete and Cyrene).

27 Tenagino Probus had been governor of Numidia (*AE* 1941: 33; *CIL* VIII 2571; *AE* 1936: 58) before becoming prefect of Egypt (*AE* 1934: 257; SHA *Claud.* 11.2; Zos. 1.44.2; see Barnes 1978: 70f.). He is not to be confused with M. Aurelius Probus, the future emperor (as unquestionably has happened in SHA *Prob.* 9.1 and possibly 9.5).

28 *PSI* X 1101; see *PLRE* I, Marcellinus (20), cf. (19) and (21). It should be noted that his rulings were still cited some time later, in the sole reign of Aurelian, implying he did not suffer official condemnation for his actions under the Palmyrene regime.

29 See Rea 1969 and his analysis of *PSI* X 1102, *PSI* X 1101 and *P. Wisc.* 2 (on dating see Appendix B.3). On the identity of Ammianus see also *P. Oxy.* 2711; cf. *PLRE* I, Ammianus (1) and (5).

30 *P. Mert.* 26; *OGIS* 71; SHA *Firm.* 3.1.

31 Alföldi 1939: 217–18; cf. Eadie 1967: 169–72; Luttwak 1976: 186–7.

32 Alföldi 1939: 218–19.

33 *CIL* III 327 (*ILS* 2775); *PLRE* I, Claudius Dionysius (10) and Claudius Herculanus (2).

34 SHA *Aurel.* 6.2, 7.3–8.5 (note the gory details supplied in 7.4); on the title *restitutor exerciti*, see n. 48 below.

35 *FHG* IV 188, fr. 12. On the significance of this passage regarding Aurelian's attitude to divine right see Chapter 11 at n. 18.

36 Campbell 1984: 19–156; Nock 1972: II, 736–90; R.W. Davies, 'A Note on Lorictitis', *BJ* 168, 1968: 161–5. On the controversial question of the relationship between symbolism (especially on the coinage) and imperial authority see in particular A.H.M. Jones, 'Numismatics and History', in R.A.G. Carson and C.H.V. Sutherland (eds) *Essays in Roman Coinage Presented to H. Mattingly*, Oxford 1956: 13–33; C.H.V. Sutherland, *The Emperor and the Coinage*, Oxford 1976; M.H. Crawford, 'Roman Imperial Coin Types and the Formation of Public Opinion', in C.N.L. Brooke *et al.* (eds) *Studies in Numismatic Method Presented to Phil Grierson*, Cannes 1983: 47–64; Watson 1991: 18–22, 36–44.

37 Such vows were taken in anticipation of these special anniversary years (*vota suscepta*) as well as once they had been achieved (*vota soluta*). On the interpretation of VSV (on *RIC* 71–3) as a reference to Aurelian's quinquennalian celebrations see Chapter 8, n. 23.

38 Bastien 1992–94: 640 (pl. 116.6 = Bastien 1976: 134, no. 2b).

39 *CIL* V 29 [Italy]; as *mater castrorum et senatus et patriae* see *AE* 1930: 150 (Sotgiu 1961: 91f, no. 56) [Tarraconensis]. The latter also accords her the titles *domina sanctissima* and *piissima*.

40 *RIC* [Severina] 2, 4, 8, 13, 18, 20 (see Plate 2, c; on the possibility of some of these being minted after Aurelian's death see Chapter 7); cf. *RIC* [Severina] 1 (CONCORD MILIT, Concordia seated = Bastien 1976: nos. 4, 6, 8, 10).

41 For example, *RIC* 87, 101–3, 166–8, 192–5, 199–202, 216–19 (cf.

Watson 1991: 269, Table A:5). Types referring to *Concordia Augusti*, which reflects the support of the general public as well as that of the army, were also produced for both emperor and empress.

42 FIDES MILITVM (or abbr.), see, for example, *RIC* 28 (*Normanby* 1242); *RIC* 109 (*Normanby* 1257); *RIC* 328; and the gold types see *RIC* 93, 90 and 94 (but cf. Manns 1938: 15, 17), 91 (but cf. Estiot 1991: nos 2–3). With rev. iconography, 'Emperor between two standards' see *RIC* 46 (*Maraveille* 26).

43 VIRTVS MILITVM, *RIC* 408 (*Maraveille* 598ff.); for gold, cf. Manns 1939: 41; VIRT MILITVM see *RIC* 407 (*Maraveille* 601f., 631); *RIC* 56 (*Maraveille* 23–5).

44 VIRTVS EQUIT, *RIC* 115; [aureus] *RIC* 100 (Estiot 1991: no. 10). VIRTVS ILLVRICI, *RIC* 388; [aureus] *RIC* 378–80; cf. Manns 1939: 33, 43. GENIVS ILLVR, *RIC* 204, 223 (*Maraveille* 398ff.); [aureus] *RIC* 172–3; – ILLV, *RIC* 110 (*Normanby* 1255f.). GENIVS EXERCITI, *RIC* 345 (*Maraveille* 632).

45 At Milan: VIRTVS or VIRT MILITVM, *RIC* 147–8 (*Maraveille* 137 etc., 282 etc.); VIRTVS AVG, *RIC* 149 (*Maraveille* 132ff.). At Siscia: VIRTVS MILITVM, *RIC* 242 (*Sirmium* 492ff.) (see Plate 2, f–g); VIRTVS AVG, *RIC* 241 (*Sirmium* 495ff.); also note [aureus] *RIC* 184.

46 At Siscia: VIRTVS MILITVM, *RIC* 212; VIRTVS AVG, *RIC* 211. Note also, at Milan: VIRTVS AVG, *RIC* 116; cf. VIRTVS EQVIT, *RIC* 115.

47 *Cohors Pimasensis Aureliana*, AE 1908: 136 (*Sotgiu* 1961: 93, no. 65); *Legio III Augusta Aureliana*, CIL VIII 2665 (*ILS* 584; set up by the commander M. Aurelius Fortunatus). On Commodus see Dio 72.15.2 (cf. SHA *Comm.* 17.8). See Campbell 1984: 88–93 and J. Fitz, *Honorific Titles of Roman Military Units in the Third Century* AD, Budapest/Bonn 1983. See also above at n. 33.

48 *RIC* 366 (*Maraveille* 673) see plate 2 d.

49 *CIL* III 12456. Coins see VICTORIA GERN [*sic*] *RIC* 355; VICTORIA GOTHIC *RIC* 339; VICTORIA PARTICA [*sic*] *RIC* 240; on the concept *victoria aeterna* see below n. 51.

50 The complexities are made worse by apparently impossible combinations of consular and tribunician numberings in the evidence for Aurelian: see Peachin 1990: 87–91 (cf. 75–84, on Gallienus).

51 Peachin 1990: 383–405, nos 40–1, 66, 77–9, 110–12, 121, 128; and see now Daguet 1992: esp. 176–7 (cf. 186 and add *AE* 1992: 1847). Note also references to the concept *victoria aeterna*: Estiot 1983: 31 (*RIC* -); *CIL* XI 6309.

52 *RIC* 300–3. For inscriptions and papyri see Peachin 1990: 383–405. On the history of the title and its wider applications see Berlinger 1935: 20–2; Imhof 1957; and S. Weinstock, 'Victor and Invictus', *H. Th. R.* 50, 1957: 211–47. On Invictus as a divine epithet, in particular in relation to Sol, see Chapter 11.

NOTES (CHAPTER 10)

53 *CIL* VI 1114 [Rome]; *CIL* XIII 8997 [Lugdunensis]. On interpretation
see D. Romano, 'La *Historia Alexandri* di Giulio Valerio e l'Ideologia
Politica di Aureliano', *Ann. del Liceo Classico* 3–4, 1966/67: 218–28; cf.
J. Scarborough, 'Aurelian: Questions and Problems', *CJ* 68, 1972/73:
334–45, 344; cf. *'magno perpetuo imperator'*: *AE* 1983: 696 [Lugdunum].

54 *Invictissimus* see Peachin 1990: 397–9, nos 113, 116, 127. *Super omn[es
pr]incipes Vic[toriosis]simo Imp(eratori)*: *CIL* XI 3878. [Italy]. Perpetuo
Victoriosissimo Indulgentissimo Imp(eratori): *CIL* VIII 20537 (Sotgiu
1961: 89, no. 48) [Mauretania Sitifensis]; *CIL* VIII 10205 (restored);
10217 (*ILS* 578); *AE* 1981: 917; *AE* 1992: 1847; Sotgiu 1961: 87f.,
nos 38, 41, 43; *Victorissimo* [*sic*]: *CIL* VIII 10177; Victrisissimo [*sic*]:
Sotgiu 1961: 87, no. 37 [Numidia]. *[Fortis]simo et Victoriosissimo Principi*:
CIL VI 1112. [Rome]; cf. *Victorioso Augusto*: *CIL* XI 1214. [Italy].

55 The early issues see *Sirmium* 1566, 1568 (*RIC* 351); *Sirmium* 479
(*Maraveille* 405/*RIC* 234); *Sirmium* 157 (*Maraveille* 118/*RIC* 140).
In general see Peachin 1990: 383–405, nos 10, 27, 53. Note also his
titles *pacator orientis* (below, n. 64) and *imperator horientis* [*sic*]: *AE* 1936:
129.

56 Peachin 1990: 383–405, nos 9, 11, 13, 26, 29–30, 32, 37, 51–2, 55,
57–9, 63–4, 78–9, 101, 111–12, 117, 124, 129, 132. That he took the
title in 272 directly after the initial victory over Palmyra, see Estiot
1983: 15. For an example of the coin types see Plate 2, e.

57 *Restitutor patriae*: *CIL* III 7586 [Moesia Inf.]. *Conservator orbis*: *CIL* V
4319; cf. ὁ γῆς σωτήρ, *CIG* II 2349n (cf. Homo 1904: 358). On
Peachin 1990: 396, no. 102 (*conservator patriae*), cf. Kettenhofen 1986:
140–1.

58 *RIC* 400–2; *RIC* 235; *RIC* 366, respectively.

59 Peachin 1990: 398–9, nos 127 and 116 respectively; the restorations are
conjectural.

60 *CIL* V 4320; VIII 15450; both dating to the first few months of
Aurelian's reign.

61 Peachin 1990: 395–400, nos 101, 132; *RIC* 4, 6–7. The title *pacator
orbis* was first applied to Commodus.

62 PACATOR ORIENTIS *RIC* 231 (Manns 1939: 39, for date).
Pacatissimus see Peachin 1990: 385–8, nos 15, 33, 39.

63 Although fragmentation does not permit of precision, the following
breakdown gives an approximate idea of the relative frequency of
each title on the corpus of Aurelianic inscriptions: Germanicus, 22;
Gothicus, 28; Parthicus/Persicus, 12–14 (7 Parthicus; 5–7 Persicus);
Carpicus, 14. On the *cognomina victoriarum* in general see now Ketten-
hofen 1986; also Sotgiu 1961: 17–27; Peachin 1990: 91f. On dates, cf.
Estiot 1983: 14–16. To these lists should be added *AE* 1991, 944
[Lucitania]. On the victory titles in the papyri see Bureth 1964: 123.
Orfitus' inscription: *CIL* VI 1112.

64 Thus Homo 1904: 141; Groag 1903: 1356f.; Kettenhofen 1986: 146;
Peachin 1990: 91f.; although Sotgiu 1961: 26, dissents.

65 Arabicus see *CIL* II 4506 (*ILS* 576); *AE* 1936: 129; Palmyrenicus see *CIL* V 4319 (*ILS* 579); see Kettenhoffen 1986: 138–9, 143–4; cf. Sotgiu 1961: 24.

66 The only certain attestation of Dacicus Maximus for Aurelian is *CIL* XIII 8973 (*ILS* 581), on which inscription Carpicus Maximus is also mentioned. *AE* 1925: 57 was accepted by Sotgiu 1961: 82, no. 6, but rejected by Kettenhofen 1986: 142, 144–5.

67 Kettenhofen 1986: 139–40, 140–1, 144–5; cf. Sotgiu 1961: 21f.; Peachin 1990: 396, no. 102. Kettenhofen's rigour is to be accepted, given the present state of the evidence; on Britannicus cf. König 1974; on Sarmaticus, cf. Saunders 1992: 312–15.

68 Dexippus (*FGH* 100) fr. 6, esp. 6.2–3. For the context of this passage see Chapter 3 and also Appendix B.2. *Adlocutio* was occasionally advertised on the coinage of the period, though no such coin types are known for Aurelian.

69 On the historical worth of Dexippus see Appendix A, n. 13; on this passage, cf. Millar 1981: 40.

70 Estiot 1991: nos 9, 25–9 (cf. *RIC* 9, wrongly placed at Rome. See Plate 3, b. Note also the magnificent reception which awaited Aurelian at Rome on his return from the east at the end of 273: Zos. 1.61.1 (this is usually, but probably wrongly, taken to refer to the triumph, of which Zosimus makes no specific mention). The importance of *adventus* at a date only slightly posterior to Aurelian's time is reflected in the *panegyrici latini*. See Alföldi 1934: 88ff.

71 The Persians as among the 'vanquished' though it is doubtful Aurelian had any serious military confrontations with them: see Chapter 5, nn. 25, 32.

72 On the coincidence of imperial consulships and quinquennalian and decennalian celebrations see R. Burgess, 'Quinquennial Vota and Imperial Consulship, 337–511', *NC* 148, 1988: 77–96, 77–81.

73 Eutrop. 9.13.2. This corresponds more or less exactly to SHA *Aurel.* 32.4: 'Thus Aurelian . . . directed his journey toward Rome, in order to parade before the eyes of the Romans his triumph over Zenobia and Tetricus, that is over east and west.' Other notices supplied in Jerome *Chron.* (ed. Helm) 222; Oros. 23.5; Zon. 12.27; cf. SHA *Tyr. trig.* 24.4. Zosimus 1.61.1 has conventionally been taken to refer to the triumph, erroneously placed before the defeat of Tetricus (but cf. Kienast 1990: 231, postulating on the basis of this passage that Aurelian held two triumphs, one before the defeat of Tetricus and one after): it may rather be that Zosimus is here referring to Aurelian's reception (*adventus*) at Rome in 273, in which case he makes no reference to the triumph at all.

74 SHA *Aurel.* 33–4; *Tyr. trig.* 30.24–6. The account is more or less accepted at face value by Homo 1904: 122–30 (esp. 123: 'naturellement nombre de détails sont sujets à caution, mais . . . l'ensemble est authentique'); see also Groag 1903: 1392–4; and, more discerningly, Merten 1968; Paschoud 1996: 160–9.

75 On captives see Merten 1968: 120–2; J. Straub, 'Aurelian und die Axumiten', *BHAC 1972/74*, 1976: 269–89; G.W. Bowersock, 'Arabs and Saracens in the Historia Augusta', *BHAC 1984/85*, Bonn 1987: 71–80, 78–9; Barnes 1994: 13. On the stag-chariot (cf. Zon. 12.27: elephants) see Homo 1904: 123; Merten 1968: 111–16 (noting that Pompey triumphed in an elephant-drawn chariot: Plut. *Pomp.* 14.4); E. Alföldi-Rosenbaum, 'Heliogaballus' and Aurelian's Stag Chariots and the Caesar Contorniates', *Historiae Augustae Colloquia, II Colloquium Genovese*, Bari 1994: 5–10.

76 On the gradual development of the imperial title *dominus* see K.J. Neumann 'Dominus', *RE* 5.1, 1903: 1305–9, 1307–9; Alföldi 1935: 91–4. On Aurelian's coins see Chapter 11, n. 25 in this book.

77 Severina see *AE* 1930: 150 (Sotgiu 1961: 91f, no. 56) [Tarraconensis]; cf. *CIG* II 2349° (p.1069) [Andros, Achaea]. Aurelian see *IGR* I 591 (Peachin 1990: no. 150), an imperial title first attested in the Severan era.

78 B.M. Feletti-Maj, *Iconografia romana imperiale da Severo Alessandro a M. Aurelio Carino* (222–285 d.c.), Rome 1958: 95, no. 22 (pl. V.12); Alföldi 1935: 148. On the diadem in imperial iconography generally see Bastien 1992–4: 143–66, esp. 143–6.

79 Gnecchi 1912: I, pl. 26.7; J.M.C. Toynbee, *Roman Medallions*, New York 1944: pl. xlvi. 4; Alföldi 1935: 148f.; Bastien 1992–4: 145, pl. 102.11, cf. pl. 102.5 (Iconium); and cf. SHA *Gal.* 16.4. N. Hannestad, *Roman Art and Imperial Policy*, Aarhus 1986: 295, argued the lack of clarity is deliberate, but this would have been self-defeating. On Constantine's types see Bastien 1992–4: 156–8.

80 *Epit.* 35.5; Malalas 12.30 (299 Bonn); accepted as an Aurelianic innovation by Groag 1903: 1405, among others; but cf. Victor *Caes.* 39.2, making the same claim for Carus.

81 On Severina and the stephane (often incorrectly termed a diadem) see Bastien 1992–4: 610–12. For examples, see Plate 2, c and Plate 3, c.

11 THE EMPEROR AND THE DIVINE

1 Inscriptions see Homo 1904: 350ff; Sotgiu 1961: 81ff. Interpretation see Berlinger 1935: 1–20.

2 PIETAS AVG, *RIC* 138 (*Maraveille* 127, 166, 248); Pontifex Maximus is mentioned on both coins and inscriptions. Severina see *AE* 1930: 150 (Sotgiu 1961: 91f, no. 56) [Tarraconensis].

3 See Nock 1972: II, 653–75.

4 RESTITVTOR ORBIS, *RIC* 369 (*Sirmium* 1802), minted towards the end of the reign at Cyzicus. Σευηρεῖναν θεὰν νείκην: *AE* 1927: 81 (Sotgiu 1961: 92, no. 57). On Victoria as an important goddess in her own right see S. Weinstock, 'Victoria', *RE* 8.A2, 1958, 2501–42.

5 Zanker 1988: 192–215.

6 MARTI PACIFERO (etc.), Estiot 1991: 469–80, nos 1, 5, 12; *RIC* 33,

112, 270–1. MARS INVICTVS, *RIC* 357–8 (Mars and Sol); cf. the parallel contemporary RESTITVTOR EXERCITI in Chapter 10, n. 48. The titular reverses see e.g. PM TBP VI COS II PP and PM TBP VII COS II PP, *RIC* 186, 16; cf. Manns 1939: 54; see Plate 2, j.

7   VIRTVS AVG, *RIC* 41, 97–8, 179–83, 341; Bastien 1976: no. 36 (cf. *RIC* 1); Elmer 1941: no. 887 (cf. *RIC* 5). VIRTVS AVG (emp. and Mars), *RIC* 149, 241. VIRTVS ILLVRICI, *RIC* 378–80, 388. FIDES EXERCITI, *RIC* 393. Obverse types see *RIC* 219 (Manns 1939: 39, cf. 31, 42); cf. Bastien 1992–4: 206, 441. See Plate 2, g, h, i and cf. Plate 2, f; and on this symbolic nexus generally see Watson 1991: 127–32.

8   VIRTVS AVG, *RIC* 57–8, 316–18; Manns 1939: 56 (RIC -). *Herculi Aug(usto) consorti d(omini) n(ostri)*, *CIL* XI 6308, cf. 6309.

9   PROVIDENT(ia) AVG, *RIC* 335 (cf. Manns 1939: 18, suggesting Minerva). VENVS VICTRIX, *RIC* – (S. Estiot, 'Un antoninien inédit d'Ulpia Severina', *BSFN* 1994: 918–21); VENVS FELIX (Venus with Cupid), [Sev] *RIC* 6. On the temple and its associations see R. Mellor, 'The Goddess Roma', *ANRW* II.17.2, Berlin 1981: 950–1030, 1020–24. The cult form of Venus most closely associated with the imperial line was Venus Genetrix, which commonly appears on the coinage of empresses in third century, though no such types are known for Severina.

10   AETERNITAS AVG, *RIC* 326 (AD 271: Manns 1939: 18). ROMAE AETERNAE (etc.), *RIC* 142 (minted over a number of issues at Milan: *Maraveille* 138ff., 181ff., 209, 311ff.) Plate 3, b; *RIC* 337; *RIC* 405; cf. *RIC* 84–5 (Gnecchi 1912: III 65, nos 15–16; cf. Manns 1939: 52, bronze, AD 275).

11   Chron. 354 (*Chron. Min.* I 148).

12   MINERVA AVG, *RIC* 334 (*Sirmium* 1538); PM TRP PP COS (Neptune with dolphin and trident), *RIC* 324 (Manns 1939: 20); both dated to the first six months of his reign.

13   PROVIDENT(ia) AVG, *RIC* 336. The statue see *Bull. Arch. Com.* 1882: 151, no. 545 (Homo 1904: 361). Obv. types see *RIC* 221, 228 (Rohde 1881: nos 147, 190); *RIC* 394, 408 (Rohde 1881: nos 186, 401) see Plate 2, m. Manns 1939: 29, interpreting these types as relating both the emperor and Mercury to the Germanic god Wodan, is certainly to be rejected. See Groag 1903: 1393, 1406; P. Bastien and C. Arnold-Biucchi, 'Busto Monetale come Mercurio (Gallieno, Aureliano)', *RINSA* 84, 1983: 73–85, 75–6, 84–5, and now Bastien 1992–4: 391–400. FORTVNA REDVX, *RIC* 128, 220–1, 331–2 (note: no. 221 has a Mercury obv.).

14   APOLLINI CONS(ervatori), *RIC* 22 (*Normanby* 1245); *RIC* 160–2; cf. PM TRP COS (Apollo seated with branch), *RIC* 157 (Manns 1939: 19, both double aureii, doubtless intended as donatives, minted at Siscia in celebration of Aurelian's first consulship). CONSERVATOR AVG (Aesculapius), *RIC* 258 (AD 271, perhaps implying an illness that summer).

15 IOVI STATORI, *RIC* 333 (Manns 1939: 18, AD 271); *RIC* 267–8 (Manns 1939: 30; Estiot 1983: 27, AD 271). IOVI VICTORI, *RIC* 49 (Manns 1939: 42f., AD 273). *CIL* III 12456 (restored); *CIL* VIII 2626.

16 *RIC* 48 (Rome); *RIC* 129, cf. 131 (Milan); *RIC* 174, 225, 227 (Siscia); *RIC* 259–66 (Serdica); *RIC* 346 (Cyzicus); *RIC* 394, cf. 395 (Byzantium). At Milan and Siscia especially these types were minted over a considerable period: *Maraveille* 214ff., 217f., 219ff., 224, 226, 227 (= *RIC* 129); *Maraveille* 420ff., 426, 428f., 431, 432ff., 439ff., 452f., 456, 457ff., 461f., 463ff., 467ff. (= *RIC* 225). See Plate 2, l. On the globe and divine investiture see Bastien 1992–4: 502–3.

17 CONCORD MILITVM, *RIC* 342 (*Maraveille* 636ff.); FIDES MILITVM, *RIC* 344 (*Maraveille* 634f.); IOVI CONSER, *RIC* 346 (*Maraveille* 639ff.). See Plate 2, k; cf. Plate 2, l.

18 Petr. Patr. fr. 6 (*FHG* IV 197). On the importance of the purple as an element of imperial insignia see W.T. Avery, 'The *Adoratio Purpuriae* and the Importance of the Imperial Purple in the Fourth Century of the Christian Era', *MAAR* 17, 1940: 66ff.; cf. Alföldi 1935: 49f. On the theme of divine pre-ordination see Nock 1972: II, 252–70; Fears 1977. On the obv. type declaring Aurelian born to his destiny to become the divine master of the Roman world, see below n. 25.

19 P. Bastien, 'Egide, Gorgoneion et buste impérial dans le monnayage romain', *NAC* 9, 1980: 247–83; Bastien 1992–4: 341–65, esp. 354, cf. 270.

20 JVNO REGINA (Juno with peacock) [Severina], *RIC* 7 (Gnecchi 1912: III, 66, no. 1); *RIC* 14 (cf. 15, rejected by Rohde).

21 On the imperial cult and its political, social, cultural and religious significance see Price 1984. On the DIVO CLAVDIO coinage see Chapter 3, n. 37.

22 As ὁ μέγιστος καὶ θειότατος see Peachin 1990: 402, no. 141, cf. 144 (μέγιστος alone); note also the formula ὁ ἐν θεοῖς: *P. Oxy.* LI 3613.5 (Peachin 1990: 401, no. 135). *Sanctissimus*, *CIL* XI 3878; *sanctissima*, *AE* 1930: 150 (Sotgiu 1961: 91f, no. 56).

23 *CIL* VIII 11318 [Africa Procos.] (originally reading *L. Domiti Aureliani*, later amended to *divi Aureliani*). *Divo Aureliano*, *CIL* VIII 25820 [Africa Procos.]; *CIL* VIII 10961, Sotgiu 1961: 86–88, nos. 28, 39, 44 [Numidia]; *CIL* III 9758 [Dalmatia]. SHA *Tac.* 9.2 (not reliable).

24 *Deo Aureliano*, *CIL* XI 556 (*ILS* 5687) [Italy]. *CIL* II 3832; *AE* 1938: 24 (Sotgiu 1961: 81, no. 1; cf. *AE* 1972: 284) [Tarraconensis]. *CIL* VIII 4877 (*ILS* 585) [Numidia]. Sotgiu 1961: 84, no. 15 [Africa Procos.]. Greek see *CIG* II 2349n (p. 1069); for Severina see above, n. 4.

25 Radiate obverses: IMP DEO ET DOMINO AVRELIANO AVG, *RIC* 305; DEO ET DOMINO NATO AVRELIANO AVG, *RIC* 306. (In both cases the reverse is the standard RETITVT(or) ORBIS type.) On interpretation see Groag 1903: 1406; Homo 1904: 191–3; Sotgiu 1975: 1043f.

26 Suet. *Dom.* 13; Dio 67.4.7; Victor *Caes.* 11.2. On *dominus*, cf. Chapter 10.

27 Zanker 1988: 50–1, 144, 183–92. (To commemorate the triumph over the orient, Augustus dedicated two obelisks, at the Circus Maximus and his new horologium: *CIL* VI 701, 702.)

28 On light and solar imagery in the representation of imperial authority see Alföldi 1934: 111–18; Alföldi 1935: 107f., 139–44; Kantorowicz 1963: esp. 131ff.; Fears 1977: 326ff.; Bastien 1992–4: 103ff.; cf. SHA *Gall.* 16.4, 18.2–4 (probably apocryphal).

29 AETENIT AVG (Sol), *RIC* 20 (AD 270). PM TRP/COS, *RIC* 325; PM TRP COS PP [aureii], *RIC* 158–9 (Manns 1939: 19, January 271); cf. above, n. 14.

30 ORIENS AVG (Sol with globe), *RIC* 397 (for date, Estiot 1983: 29); (Sol with whip), *RIC* 230 (for date, Estiot 1983: 24). (An early Solar type from Cyzicus, RESTITVTOR ORIENTIS, cited by Manns 1939: 37, lacks confirmation.)

31 The dates are drawn from the catalogues in Estiot 1983 and Göbl 1993.

32 The subtle variations have made classification very difficult, especially among the numerous billon radiate types. For the arrangements see Kellner 1978; Estiot 1983; Göbl 1993; and cf. Watson 1991: 282–6 (Tables A15–16), 354, n. 123. For examples of the standard iconography see Plate 3, h and i. Unusual types include: ORIENS AVG (Sol with the attributes of Apollo, laurel branch and bow), *RIC* 64 (see Plate 3, g); SOLI INVICTO (Sol driving quadriga), Gnecchi 1912: II, 113, nos 2–3 (Manns 1939: 44).

33 *Soli Invicto Sacr(um) pro salute et incoluminate Perpetui Imp(eratori)*, *CIL* VIII 5143 (*ILS* 580) [Numidia]; cf. *CIL* VIII 23924 (restored) [Africa Procos.].

34 CONSERVAT AVG, *RIC* 383–5; and aureii, *RIC* 371–3; cf. PM TRP VI COS II PP (Sol) [aureus], *RIC* 185. Solar investiture types: SOLI CONSERVATORI, *RIC* 353 (Rohde 1881: 349–50); ORIENS AVG, *RIC* 282–3; SOLI INVICTO, *RIC* 312–15; RESTITVTOR ORBIS, *RIC* 367; cf. RESTITVTOR ORIENTIS [aureii], Manns 1939: 54; VIRTVS AVG, *RIC* 316–17; cf. also APOL CONS AVG, with same iconography, Rohde 1881: 67 (Estiot 1995a: 83, and note f.)

35 VIRTVS AVG (Hercules and Sol), *RIC* 318; MARS INVICTVS (Mars and Sol), *RIC* 357–8; MARTI INVICTO, *RIC* 359. See Plate 3, j, k. The solar type, IOVI CONSER(VATORI) (Emperor receiving globe from Sol holding whip) [Serdica], *RIC* 274–5 (Rohde 1881: 189), lacks recent confirmation: it may have been a die cutter's error or an error of Rohde's decipherment (i.e. that 'SOLI CONSERVATORI' was the intended or actual legend).

36 *RIC* 152–3, 189, 256, 284–5; *RIC* [Severina] 9, 10; see Plate 3, c and d. This continues the theme of the earlier Jovian coins see above, n. 17.

37 PACATOR ORBIS (Sol with whip), *RIC* 6 (minted at Lyon, see Bastien 1976: nos 1, 3, 5, 7, 9; cf. earlier type for Postumus, Elmer 1941: no. 599, itself based on a Severan prototype).

38 Manns 1939: 52 (cf. *RIC* 75–6, 79–81); Plate 3, e.

39 Sol and Luna on breastplate see *Sirmium* 1431 (*RIC* 260: rev. IOVI CONSER, *c.* end 272). On the lunar affiliation in Severina's portraits see Bastien 1992–4: 645 (pl. 116.1; [Severina], *RIC* 16). Raised hand see Plate 3, f (the reverse of which is as Plate 3, e); Bastien 1992–4: 562, 568, in general 559–72; cf. Alföldi 1935: 107–8.

40 *RIC* 319–22 (Rohde 1881: 444–6; Manns 1939: 45); Plate 3, l, m. These coins are usually attributed to Serdica: thus Rohde 1881; Webb 1927; Manns 1939; and also Homo 1904: 372; Bastien 1992–4: 568; Estiot 1995a: 78, 83 (classified as double radiates on the basis of the analysis in Callu, Brenot and Barrandon 1979); but Göbl 1993: 49–50, re-allocates them to Rome and classifies them as sesterces (but cf. Estiot 1995b: 75–6, 82). For the restoration 'consul' see Homo 1904: 184, 372; Halsberghe 1972: 139–40.

41 For an over-interpretaion of the coins, relating them to a mythical imperial edict, see Homo 1904: 184–5; Halsberghe 1972: 139.

42 The text of Zos. 1.61 implies that the temple was begun at this date, before Aurelian left to reclaim the western provinces in 274.

43 Philocalus *Fast. 354* (*CIL* I² p. 278; cf. 338f.); Julian *Or.* 4.156B, C. On the significance of the winter solstice as the date of the consecration see J. Noiville, 'Les origines du Natalis Invicti', *REA* 38, 1936: 144–76; cf. H. Kähler, 'Zum Sonnentempel des Aurelians', *RM* 52, 1937: 94–105. Jerome *Chron.* 223 (Helm), reflects the belief that 274 was the date of consecration.

44 Chron. 354 (*Chron. Min.* I 148); *Notitia reg.* VII (referring to it as a temple of Sol and Luna). Richardson 1992: 363–4, cf. (81–2); Halsberghe 1972: 142–3; Palmer 1980: 220; on the fiscal wine see SHA *Aurel.* 48.4; cf. *CIL* VI 1785; and on Ciconiae and S. Silvestro, cf. Chapter 8, n. 42.

45 Eutrop. 9.15.1; Victor *Caes.* 35.7; SHA *Aurel.* 28.5, 35.3, 39.6; Zos. 1.61.2; Sync. 721 (Bonn); cf. Jerome *Chron.* 223 (Helm). SHA *Aurel.* 10.2, adds the spurious detail that there was a painting depicting the glorious martial exploits of Aurelian and his 'father', Ulpius Crinitus, displayed in the temple.

46 Codin. *De Antiq. Const.* I 4 (66, ed. Banduri), following Belisarius' recapture of Rome from the Goths.

47 Chron. 354 (*Chron. Min.* I 148); Jerome *Chron.* 223b (Helm); Julian *Or.* 4.155 B (201, ed. Hertlein); Philocalus (loc. cit., n. 43 above), writing on the festivals of 354, eighty years or exactly twenty cycles after 274, notes games in honour of Sol on this day.

48 SHA *Aurel.* 35.3: the reading *pontifices* is not certain, but see Paschoud 1996: 172.

49 Cf. Halsberghe 1972: 145–6, avoiding the obvious inference.

50 Homo 1904: 184–8; cf. for example Halsberghe 1972: 138–48; Cizek 1994: 178–82.

51 *CIL* VI 31775 [Rome].

52 It was this Sol to whom Augustus dedicated his obelisks (above, n. 27): see generally, Richardson 1992: 364–5.

53 The conclusion, or rather the premise, of Halsberghe 1972: esp. 140, 149, 156, 158; reiterated in G.H. Halsberghe, 'Le culte de Deus Sol Invictus à Rome au 3e siècle après J.C.', *ANRW* II.17.4, Berlin 1984: 2181–201.

54 Halsberghe 1972: 120, rightly points out the danger of such an assumption with regard to Mithras, but fails to apply the same logic to Elahgabal. This renders the argument of his book, in large measure, invalid. On the widespread use of Invictus see Imhof 1957: 199–215; Richter 1909–15: 1141–50. The deities who sported the epithet Invictus included Jupiter, Hercules and Mars, all of whom became associated with deities of eastern origin.

55 The most famous example is the black stone in the Kaaba in Mecca, an ancient Semitic cult which later became the central focus of Islam. The black stone was represented on the coinage of Elagabalus. The Baal and Baalat (equated with Helios/Sol and Selene/Luna, respectively) at Hierapolis were also aniconic, the point being emphasized by the presence of empty thrones in the temple: Lucian *De Dea Syria* 34 (cf. Halsberghe 1972: 128–9; the *sigillum* he notes at 126, n. 10, means a 'sign' or 'mark', i.e. something aniconic, not a 'little image'). On association with Jupiter see below, n. 61.

56 SHA *Aurel.* 25.3–6; on which Paschoud 1996: 143–5; and on the mischief, Richter 1909–15: 1147. By the late fourth century, when syncretism had progressed far further down the road to a pagan solar monotheism, such a link would seem only natural.

57 Halsberghe 1972: 157–8, citing *CIL* VI 2151. On Mithras and other Dei Invicti see Richter 1909–15: 1143ff.; Imhof 1957: 213ff.

58 See above, nn. 32 and 34.

59 Zos. 1.61.2. In such a context the term ἀγάλματα can only mean cult statues: see Price 1984: 176–9. For Halsberghe 1972: 141–2, this showed that 'images of other gods' were set up in the temple as an expression of the syncretic lengths to which the emperor was willing to go to accommodate Roman views. On two cults sharing the same cultic space see Nock 1972: I, 202–51.

60 Teixidor 1979: 1–46. On Yarhibol see also the entry by P. Linant de Bellefonds in *LIMC* V.1, 1990: 624–6; and on Aglibol see that by M. Le Glay in *LIMC* I.1, 1981: 298–302.

61 SHA *Firm.* 3.4 (*Iuppiter consul vel consulens*). See K. Winkler, 'Iuppiter Consul vel Consulens (zu Hist. Aug. *quad. tyr.* III 4–6)', *Philologus* 102, 1958: 117–26; E. Will, 'Une figure du culte solaire d'Aurélien – *Iuppiter consul vel consulens*', *Syria* 36, 1959: 193–201; but cf. the scepticism expressed by J. Straub, 'Iuppiter Consul', *Chiron* 2, 1972: 545–62. Note also SHA *Aurel.* 31.7–9 (Halsberghe 1972: 133, 141, 157, strains this evidence unduly; see Chapter 5, n. 45 in this book). Various forms of Baal were identified with Jupiter (e.g. Heliopolitanus,

Damascensus, Dolichenus) and at Rome there was confusion as to whether these cults (including Elahgabal) were to be seen as Jovian or Solar (Teixidor 1979: 50). In general see H. Seyrig, 'Le culte du soleil en Syrie à l'époque romaine', *Syria* 48, 1971: 337–73.

62 Rome, e.g., *CIL* VI 2185 (= 31034), 710, 712, 31036; for inscriptions in Numidia and the Danube (e.g. *CIL* III Suppl. 7956, [Dacia]) see Richter 1909–15: 1150; H. Seyrig, 'Antiquités Syriennes, 22: Iconographies de Malakbêl', *Syria* 18, 1937: 198–209, 200–206; cf. above, n. 22, for Aurelian and Severina. More generally, see Teixidor 1979: 13, 47–52.

63 *Notitia regio.* VII; cf. also, on the prevalence of such twin cults in the Near East, Teixidor 1979: 42ff.

64 See above, nn. 32 and 34, for Sol types with Apollonian associations.

65 Groag 1903: 1398–1400, postulating that the new religion drew upon and incorporated elements from a number of different solar cults, particularly those of oriental origin, transcending them in a way which allowed their original, largely Semitic, identities to be left behind. See also G. Wissowa, *Religion und Kultus der Römer* (2nd edn), 1912: 366–8.

66 SHA *Aurel.* 4.2, 5.5, 35.3; cf. Sextus Pompeius Festus, *De verborum signif.* 18 (Teubner, p.22). Believed by Homo 1904: 28; Halsberghe 1972: 130–1, cf. 138, 140, 148; Cizek 1994: 12–14; but cf. Paschoud 1996: 73. On solar cults, including Mithras and Malakbêl, in the Balkans and among the troops stationed there, see above, nn. 57 and 62.

67 Bastien 1992–4: 465, citing *Consularia Constantinopolitana* (*Chron. Min.* I 228) which applies the term *levatus* to designate an accession first to Aurelian. For the ritual in its developed form see Corippus *de laud Iust.* II 137–58; for its origin and development see Alföldi 1935: 54; Kantorowicz 1963; Bastien 1992–4: 464–5.

68 Julian *Caes.* 313–14 A (ed. Hertlein); see Homo 1904: 188f., rightly dismissing the idea of fanaticism but overplaying the political motivation.

69 The general thesis can be seen in Groag 1903: 1404–5; Homo 1904: 184–95; Halsberghe 1972: 134–55, esp 134–6, 149–50, 152–3; Cizek 1994: 16 ('absolutisme théocratique'). For a contrary (and in my opinion more sustainable) view see Wardman 1982: 121–3.

70 N.H. Baynes, *JRS* 25, 1935: 83–4; cf. Nock 1972: II, 252–70; Fears 1977. For the idea of Sol on earth see Homo 1904: 191–3; Halsberghe 1972: 153–5.

71 *Contra* Homo 1904: 192–3; Halsberghe 1972: 152–5. On the exaggeration of the 'slide into despotism' see Chapter 10 of this book, and Watson 1991.

72 Particularly guilty here is Halsberghe, whose work on this subject (1972, and that cited in n. 53 above) is still, regrettably, regarded by many as seminal. On the Judeo-Christian outlook as a serious impediment to our understanding of paganism see Price 1984: esp. 11–15; and in this specific context, Wardman 1982: 122.

73 Halsberghe 1972: 137, 154; also Homo 1904: 195; but cf. Wardman 1982: 122–3. On the persecutions see Chapter 1 of this book and on Aurelian's persecution see pp. 200–1.

74 Election see Jerome *Chron.* 220 (Helm). First synod see Euseb. *HE* 7.27.2, 28.3, cf. 30.3. Second synod/excommunication see Euseb. *HE* 7.28.4–29.1; Jerome *Chron.* 221 (Helm); Zon. 12.25. Activities see Euseb. *HE* 7.30.7–12. Overall, see Millar 1971: 11–12.

75 On his defiance see Euseb. *HE* 7.30.19. On the widespread appeal of Paul's theology see Friend 1965: 443–4 (with reference to the near contemporary *Acts of Archelaus*); and for the Palmyrene connection see Chapter 4.

76 Euseb. *HE* 7.30.19; see Baldini 1975.

77 Euseb. *HE* 7.32.6; Lactantius *de mort. persec.* 6. See Friend 1965: 444. His principal motivation, as with Decius, Valerian and Diocletian, was almost certainly his extreme conservatism in all matters.

78 Homo 1904: 375–7; Friend 1965: 444–5.

79 Kantorowicz 1963: esp. 120ff.

APPENDIX A: EXCURSION ON SOURCES

1 For a full discussion of the literary sources, still of value today, see Homo 1904: 3–20.

2 Of numerous articles and books, the work of Sir Ronald Syme has been particularly trenchant (Syme 1968, 1971, 1983); in addition there have been a number of colloquia devoted to this source.

3 The hoax was first exposed by H. Dessau, 'Über Zeit und Persönlichkeit der *Scriptores Historiae Augustae*', *Hermes* 24, 1889: 337–92; and Dessau, 'Über die *Scriptores Historiae Augustae*', *Hermes* 27, 1892: 561–605. The single authorship is now fairly widely accepted, as is a date of composition around 395–7. See now Paschoud 1996: esp. x–xxxvii, and bibliography there cited.

4 Syme 1968: 138–9; Syme 1983: 125–6.

5 See now Paschoud 1996: xii–xviii; cf. Fisher 1929: 142, 147; Syme 1968: 197f., 207f. (on the possibility that the author was a *grammaticus* in the circle of the Symmachi-Nichomachi). Also see generally Mouchová 1972; Lippold 1972; Lippold 1995.

6 On early life/career see Paschoud 1996: 70–106; cf. (somewhat generously) Homo 1904: 27–35. Among the inventions are both 'Ulpius Crinitus' and a great-grandson named 'Aurelianus', said to have served as 'proconsul' of Cilicia (Aurel. 42.1–2) whose existence must be deemed as improbable as his title: see Magie 1932: 278f., n.1; Syme 1968: 164, n.1. On the *vita Aureliani* and its fictions in general see Fisher 1929; Paschoud 1996.

7 On the lost books of Ammianus and the references to this period in the extant portion of the work see Gilliam 1972.

8 A. Enmann, 'Eine verlorene Geschichte der römischen Kaiser und das

Buch *de viris illustribus urbis Romae*. Quellenstudien', *Philologus* Suppl. 4, 1984: 335–501. On the *Annales* and the KG being the only sources used by the author of the HA for the *vita Aureliani*, see Paschoud 1996: 10–12.

9 Examples include the revolt of the mint workers and the evacuation of Dacia (see Chapters 3 and 9 respectively).

10 Notoriously in his account of the aftermath of Aurelian's assassination (see Syme 1983: 160; and Chapter 7 in this book).

11 The lacuna see Dufraigne 1975: 168f., n. 6, 169, n. 1; cf. Callu 1996. See Chapter 6, n. 19 and Appendix B.2.

12 See Millar 1969; for a more sceptical view, cf. Potter 1990: 73–90.

13 Zosimus' fairly full, if somewhat confused, account of the Gothic Wars must derive from Dexippus; his lengthy description of Aurelian's Palmyrene Wars from Eunapius. Whether Eunapius was also a source for the account of these and other events in the *HA* is a matter of some debate: see Barnes 1978: 112–23; but cf. Paschoud 1996 (above, n. 8); see also G. Zecchini, 'La storiografia Greca dopo Dexippo e l'Historia Augusta', *Historia Augusta Colloquia, III Colloquium Maceratense*, Bari 1995: 297–309 (note esp. bibliography cited in n. 8, p. 298).

14 The identity of the 'Continuator', his relationship to Peter and the attribution of the extant fragments between them remain doubtful: see Potter 1990: 70–94, 356–69, 395–7.

15 On the Sibylline Oracle see A.T. Olmstead, 'The Mid-Third Century of the Christian Era', *CP* 37, 1942: 241–62, 398–420; and now esp. Potter 1990.

16 See esp. Graf 1989; de Blois 1975.

17 For example Lafaurie 1975a; Estiot 1991; Cubelli 1992; Göbl 1993; cf. Estiot 1995b (a review of these last two). Works on individual hoards see Kellner 1978; Estiot 1983; Estiot 1995a; and more generally Besly and Bland 1983; Bland and Burnett 1988. Of the older works, Rohde 1881, Webb 1927 and Manns 1939, are still useful, though much has been superseded by subsequent research.

18 A. Blanchet, *Les trésors de monnaies romaines et les invasions germaniques en Gaule*, Paris 1900; more recently, Cubelli 1992: 33ff. But note the caveat in S. Estiot, 'Le troisième siècle et la monnaie: crise et mutations', in J.-L. Fiches (ed.) *Le IIIe siècle en Gaule Narbonnaise. Données régionales sur la crise de l'Empire*, Sophia Antipolis 1996: 33–70, 56–63.

19 Note especially: (coin analysis) Callu, Brenot and Barrandon 1979 (and see also Chapter 8 in this book); (typology) Bastien 1992–4.

20 On Aurelian see Sotgiu 1961; Kettenhofen 1986; Daguet 1992. On the period as a whole see Peachin 1990.

21 In addition to *PIR* and *PLRE*, see in particular Christol 1986 and the numerous contributions in this field of H.-G. Pflaum.

22 On the imperial mint at Alexandria see Vogt 1924; Milne 1933.

23 Thus especially: (on chronology) Rea 1972; Rathbone 1986; (on titulature) Bureth 1964; Peachin 1990.

APPENDIX B: PROBLEMS OF CHRONOLOGY

1 Alföldi 1939: 721–3 (= Alföldi 1967: 436–9).

2 Potter 1990: 57f., prefers Claudius, both because of Claudius' reputation and because Aureolus would have been unlikely to rise in revolt after such a great victory. The earlier date of Aureolus' revolt (see Bastien 1984) removes the second objection; the first only implies that Claudius *did* win a significant victory over the Goths, not that Gallienus did *not* do so.

3 SHA *Gal.* 13.6, 13.7; cf. Sync. 717 (general route/sack of Byzantium).

4 Zon. 12.26.

5 Zon. 12.26; Petr. Patr. fr. 169 (= *FHG* IV 196 '*Cont. Dion.*' 9.1); cf. Cedrenus, I 454, 12ff. But note Sync. 717; SHA *Gal.* 13.8; Zos. 1.39.1 (placed rather too early in the narrative of Gallienus' reign); Victor *Caes.* 33.3; Eutrop. 9.8.2.

6 SHA *Gal.* 5.6–6.1 (possibly confused with the Claudian invasion).

7 Sync. 717; cf. SHA *Gal.* 13.9; Zos. 1.39.1 (both without place name).

8 Zos. 1.43.2 (note that the battle is not described as a triumphant victory), 1.45.1 (mentioning Naissus); cf. (without place name) SHA *Claud.* 9.9; Victor *Caes.* 34.5; Sync. 720 passes over Claudius' campaign very briefly.

9 Amm. 31.5.15–17 (cf. Zos. 1.44.1).

10 *FGH* 100, fr. 6–7 (*FHG* III 682–6, fr. 24).

11 *FHG* IV 188, fr. 12.

12 *FHG* IV 197, fr. 10.3; *Epit.*, 35.2 (on his mistaken belief that Placentia was a victory see Chapter 3, n. 45).

13 Zos. 1.49.2; *Epit.*, 35.3–4; SHA *Aurel.* 18.4, 21.5–6.

14 Thus, e.g., Groag 1903: 1368; Homo 1904: 60ff.; Magie 1932: 226f, nn. 3–6; Mattingly 1939: 298–9.

15 Alföldi 1967: 427–30 (= A. Alföldi 'Über die Juthungeneinfälle unter Aurelian', *BIAB* 16, 1950: 21–4); the thesis was partially prefigured in Alföldi 1939: 156–7.

16 Saunders 1992 (accepted by Paschoud 1996). Another eminent scholar not to follow Alföldi is Demougeot 1969: 510–15.

17 Saunders 1992: 320–1: surely correct on the former point, though rather too sceptical on the latter.

18 Zos. 1.48.1: see, e.g., Magie 1932: 227, n. 5; Mattingly 1939: 298–9. Zosimus may possibly have misunderstood his source and thereby unwittingly confused Rome and Ravenna, which in the fifth century was the capital of the western empire and which Aurelian did visit at the outset of his reign (see Chapter 3). On Zosimus in this context see Saunders 1992: 316–17.

19 Saunders 1992: 321–4, though I do not entirely agree with his reasoning (see below at n. 22).

20 Saunders 1992: 319.

21 Cubelli 1992: 36–7.

22 Dexippus *FGH* 100, fr. 6.1 (introduction), 6.4 (the Juthungi boast of having captured cities on the Danube). The principal problem left unsolved by the proposed solution is how to explain Zos. 1.49.1. Part of the explanation may lie in Zosimus' conflation of two invasions: see Appendix B, pp. 200–1.

23 Zos. 1.49.1. Groag 1903: 1370; Homo 1904: 73; Alföldi 1939: 156f.; also Cubelli 1992: 33ff. (using the evidence of coin hoards to trace two simultaneous invasion paths; but this is not wholly convincing; cf. Appendix A, n. 18). Victor *Caes*. 35.2 (an invasion of Italy by the Alamanni, apparently in 273–4) is often cited as referring to the events of 270/1 (Homo 1904: 73ff.; Mattingly 1939: 299; Dufraigne 1975: 169f., n. 2), but this is plainly wrong, since the earlier invasion would have been described by Victor in a section of the work that is now lost (on the textual lacuna see Appendix A, n. 11).

24 Saunders 1992: 317–18, suggests that Zosimus confused the campaign against the Vandals with the Gothic campaign of the following year (which Zosimus otherwise fails to mention). Although not impossible, such an explanation is unnecessary and on the whole unlikely.

25 *AE* 1993: 1231 (not available to Saunders).

26 L. Bakker, 'Raetien unter Postumus – Das Seigesdenkmal einer Juthungenschlact im Jahre 260 n. Chr. aus Augsburg', *Germania* 71, 1993: 369–86, 378. It is not clear when (prior to 11 September 261) Raetia went over to Postumus, nor when it reverted to central imperial control (though Bakker, pp. 381–2, rightly observes it was certainly before the final defeat of Tetricus in 274). In all probability it was before Gallienus' campaign in Gaul (see Chapter 2, nn. 41, 43).

27 Syme 1983: 147–8, 154–5. The Augsburg inscription specifically refers to the Juthungi as 'Semnones'; cf. Saunders 1992: 315f. (esp. n. 20).

28 SHA *Aurel*. 18.1 refers explicitly to Aurelian's achievements under Claudius and 18.2 is introduced with the phrase *iisdem temporibus*, 'at this same time'.

29 Alföldi 1967: 428, postulated that the Quadi (a Suebian people living east of the Marcomanni) assisted the Vandals (here wrongly called Sarmatians); cf. Saunders 1993: 315–16. On the evidence for Sarmaticus Maximus (including SHA *Aurel*. 30.5) and on the triumph see Chapter 10 in this book.

30 On the significance of the Egyptian material see Appendix A.

31 Last for Claudius from the Arsinoite, *P. Stras*. I.7.21 (20 September 270); last from Oxyrhynchus, *P. Oxy*. XIV 1646.32–4 (Phaophi, year III: 28 September–27 October 270; cf. J. Rea, 'The date clause of *P. Oxy*. XIV 1632–34', *ZPE* 26, 1977: 227–9). On date of Claudius' death see also Rea 1972: 12–26; Rathbone 1986: 120–4.

32 Rea 1972: 23–4; Price 1973: 81–5. The coinage for Quintillus at this mint was slight, Milne 1933: nos. 4296–8; cf. Vogt 1924: I, 212.

33 Seventy-seven days see Chron. 354 (*Chron. Min.* 1 148). 'A few months' see Zos. 1.47. Twenty days see SHA *Aurel*. 37.6. seventeen days:

Eutrop. 9.12; Zon. 12.26; SHA *Claud.* 12.5; Jerome *Chron.* 222 (Helm); Oros. 7.23.2; cf. Jordanes *Rom.* 289. 'A few days' see *Epit.* 34.5. The Egyptian dating makes 77 days impossible.

34 Quintillus was proclaimed between two and six weeks before Aurelian and probably lasted for about three weeks after, allowing for the quantity of his coinage. See H. Huvelin and P. Bastien, 'Emissions de l'atelier de Rome et chronologie des règnes de Claude II, Quintille et Aurélien', *BSFN* 1974: 534–9.

35 Mattingly 1936: 111–12.

36 Earliest known consular-dated papyrus is *P. Stras.* gr. 255c (12 October); the earliest joint naming for Aurelian and Vaballathus is *P. Oxy.* XL 2921.6–11 (second week in December): see Rathbone 1986: 123; and the other works mentioned in n. 31 above.

37 Peachin 1990: 43. On the travel times involved see Rathbone 1986: 102; Peachin 1990: 26 (esp. n. 5; cf. his caveat: 20, n. 48). Rathbone 1986: 122, doubts the Palmyrene invasion had anything to do with the consular dating.

38 Aurelian year I see Milne 1933: 103, nos. 4299–4302; only one *officina* was apparently working at this time.

39 Earliest joint issues from the mint see Milne 1933: 103, nos. 4303–7. For the subtle variations and the change in regnal years at about this time and for the papyri see Chapter 4.

40 Alföldi 1939: 176–7, set Odenathus' murder (in Cappadocia) in April 267. In spite of the re-dating (for which see below, n. 43), others still continue to follow the old dating: e.g. Isaac 1990: 222 (266/7 in Emesa).

41 See Chapter 4.

42 Last joint see *P. Oxy.* XL 2904.15–23. First for Aurelian alone see *P. Oxy.* XL 2902.16–18.

43 Rea 1972: 20–5; Price 1973; Rathbone 1986: 122–4; Peachin 1990: 43–4.

44 Aurelian year II see Milne 1933: 105, nos 4354–7 (the error being due to ignorance coupled with inertia).

45 Among the most useful recent studies may be cited: Polverini 1975: 1018–23; Chastagnol 1980: 76–7; Rathbone 1986: 125; Keinast 1990: 231; Peachin 1990: 44, 46–7. See also Paschoud 1996: 190–4 (cf. 252–3).

46 Milne 1933: nos 4466–87; *P. Oxy.* XII 1455.20–6; cf. Peachin 1990: 44.

47 Consul see *P. Cair. Isid.* 108.17–19 (= *SB* V 7677); Peachin 1990: 44, 92. The existence of an aureus type referring to 'consul designatus II' (*RIC* V.1 [Tacitus] no. 1) also suggests he reigned for a period of more than just a few days before the end of the year. For a different, but in my opinion erroneous, view of Tacitus' tribunician renewal see I.F. Kramer and T.B. Jones, '"Tribunicia Potestate" AD 270–275', *AJP* 64, 1943: 80–6, 83. Tacitus' tribunician years and consulships remain controversial.

48 *C.* six months see Eutrop. 9.16; SHA *Tac.* 13.5, 14.5; Oros. 7.24.1;
    Cassiod. *Chron.* (ed. Mommsen) p.148. Two hundred days see Victor
    36.2; *Epit.* 36.1. Seven months see Malalas 12.31 (Bonn 301). One
    source, Chron. 354 (*Chron. Min.* 148), even grants him as much as 8
    months and 12 days. See Rathbone 1986: 125; Peachin 1990: 46.

49 The output of the Alexandrian mint for Probus in his year I (275/6) was
    sufficiently large to occupy some time, though the estimate of over
    three months in Milne 1933: xxiv, is surely an exaggeration. Note also
    O. Mich. I 157.1 (year I). See Rathbone 1986: 125; Peachin 1990: 46–7:
    'Tacitus must have survived into (roughly) June 276.'

50 *CIL* XIII 8973 (cf. XVII 498; *ILS* 581), which gives Aurelian a seventh
    tribunician year, may indicate that news of his death had still not
    reached as far as Orleans by 10 December. Furthermore, the length of
    Aurelian's reign in the literary sources suggests a later date for his death
    (though this length might well include the interval between his death
    and Tacitus' proclamation).

51 *Consularia Constantinopolitana* (ed. Mommsen, *Chron. Min.* I 229).

BIBLIOGRAPHY

[This bibliography only includes modern works cited more than once.]

Alföldi, A. 1934 'Die Ausgestaltung des monarchischen Zeremoniels am römischen Kaiserhofe', *RM* 49: 1–118.

—— 1935 'Insignien und Tracht der römischen Kaiser', *RM* 50: 1–117.

—— 1939 'The Invasions of Peoples from the Rhine to the Black Sea'; 'The Crisis of the Empire (AD 249–270)'; 'The Sources for the Gothic Invasions of the Years 260–270', *CAH* XII: 138–64; 165–231; 721–3.

—— 1967 *Studien zur Geschichte der Weltkrise des 3. Jahrhunderts nach Christus*, Darmstadt.

Alföldy, G. 1966 'Barbareinfälle und religiöse Krisen in Italien', *BHAC* 1964/5, Bonn: 1–19.

Baldini, A. 1975 'Il ruolo di Paolo di Samosata nella politica culturale di Zenobia e la decisione di Aureliano ad Antiochia', *Riv. Stor. Ant.* 5: 59–78.

Barnes, T.D. 1978 *The Sources for the* Historia Augusta, Brussels.

—— 1994 'The Franci before Diocletian', *Historiae Augustae Colloquia II, Colloquium Genevese*, Bari: 11–18.

Bastien, P. 1976 *Le monnayage de l'atelier de Lyon: de la réouverture de l'atelier par Aurélien à la mort de Carin (Fin de 274–mi 285)*, Wetteren.

—— 1984 'L'Atelier de Milan en 268', *La Zecca di Milano, Atti Conv. Int. di Stud. Milano 1983*, Milan: 133–45.

—— 1992–4 *Le Buste Monétaire des Empereurs Romain*, Wetteren.

Bastien, P. and Huvelin, H. 1969 'Trésor d'antoniniani en Syrie', *RN*: 231–70.

Bell, M. 1994 'An Imperial Flour Mill on the Janiculum', *La ravitaillement en blé de Rome et des centres urbains des débuts de la République jusqu'au Haut Empire [Actes du Colloque International de Naples 1991]*, Naples/ Rome: 73–89.

Berlinger, L. 1935 *Beiträge zur inoffiziellen Titulatur der römischen Kaiser*, Breslau.

Bernareggi, E. 1974 'Familia Monetalis', *NAC* 3: 177–91.

Besly, E.M. and Bland, R.F. 1983 *The Cunetio Treasure. Roman Coinage of the Third Century AD*, London.

Bivona, L. 1966 'Per la chronologia di Aureliano', *Epigraphica* 28: 101–21.

Bland, R.F. and Burnett, A. 1988 *The Normanby Hoard and other Roman Coin Hoards*, London.

de Blois, L. 1975 'Odaenathus and the Roman–Persian War of 252–264 AD', *TAΛANTA* 6: 7–23.

Bowersock, G.W. 1983 *Roman Arabia*, Cambridge.

—— 1986 'Hellenism and Zenobia', in J.T.A. Koumoulides (ed.) *Greek Connections: Essays on Cultural Diplomacy*, Notre Dame: 19–27.

Brandt, H. 1995 'Die "Heidnische Vision" Aurelians (HA A. 24, 2–8) und die "Christlische Vision" Konstantins des Grossen', *Historiae Augustae Colloquia III, Colloquium Marceratense*, Bari: 107–17.

Bureth, P. 1964 *Les titulature impériales dans les papyrus, les orstraca et les inscriptions d'Egypte, 30 a.c.–284 p.c.*, Brussels.

Burnett, A. 1987 *Coinage in the Roman World*, London.

Callu, J.-P. 1969 *La politique monétaire des empereurs romains de 238 à 311*, Paris.

—— 1996 'Aurélius Victor et l'interrègne de 275: Problèmes historiques et textuels', *Historiae Augustae Colloquia IV, Colloquium Barcinonense*, Bari: 133–45.

Callu, J.-P., Brenot, C. and Barrandon J.-N.1979 'Analyses de séries atypiques (Aurélien, Tacite, Carus, Licinius)', *NAC* 8: 241–54.

Campbell, J.B. 1984 *The Emperor and the Roman Army 31 BC–AD 235*, Oxford.

Carson, R.A.G. 1965 'The Reform of Aurelian', *RN*: 225–35.

Chastagnol, A. 1980 'Sur la chronologie des années 275–285', in P. Bastien *et al.* (eds) *Mélanges de numismatiques, d'archéologie et d'histoire offerts à Jean Lafaurie*, Paris: 75–82.

Christol, M. 1986 *Essai sur l'évolution des carrières sénatoriales dans le 2e moitié du IIIe s. ap. J.C.*, Paris.

Cizek, E. 1994 *L'Empereur Aurélien et son Temps*, Paris.

Crawford, M.H. 1975 'Finance, Coinage and Money from the Severans to Constantine', *ANRW* II.2, Berlin: 560–93.

—— 1984 'La zecca di Ticinum', in E. Gabba (ed.) *Storia di Pavia I (L'Età Antica)*, Como: 249–54.

Cubelli, V. 1992 *Aureliano Imperatore: la rivolta dei moneteriere e la cosidetta riforma monetaria*, Florence.

Daguet, A. 1992 'L. Domitianus Aurelianus *perpetuus imperator*', *Antiquités Africaines* 28: 173–86.

Demougeot, E. 1969 *La Formation de l'Europe et les Invasions Barbares, I , Des Origines Germaniques à l'Avènement de Dioclétien*, Paris.

Downey, G. 1950 'Aurelian's Victory over Zenobia at Immae, AD 272', *TAPA* 81: 57–68.

Drinkwater, J.F. 1987 *The Gallic Empire. Separation and Continuity in the North-Western Provinces of the Roman Empire, AD 260–274*, Stuttgart.

Dufraigne, P. 1975 (ed. and trans.) *Aurelius Victor Livres des Césars*, Paris.

Eadie, J.W. 1967 'The Development of Roman Mailed Cavalry', *JRS* 57: 161–73.

Elmer, G. 1941 'Die Münzprägung der gallischen Kaiser in Köln, Trier und Mailand', *BJ* 146: 1–106.

Estiot, S. 1983 'Le trésor de Maraveille', *Trésors Monétaires* 5: 9–115.

—— 1988 'Un "as" d'Aurélien appartenant à la collection H.-G. Pflaum', *BSFN* 43: 439–41.

—— 1991 'Or et billon: l'atelier de Milan sous Aurélien (270–274)', in *Ermanno A. Arslan Studia Dicata, II: Monetazione Romana Republicana ed Imperiale*, Milan: 449–93.

—— 1995a *Ripostiglio della Venèra. Nuovo Catalogo Illustrato, II/1 Aureliano*, Rome.

—— 1995b 'Aureliana', *RN*: 50–94.

Fears, J.R. 1977 *Princeps a diis electus. The Divine Election of the Emperor as a Political Concept at Rome*, Rome.

Fisher, W.H. 1929 'The Augustan Vita Aureliani', *JRS* 19: 125–49

Freeman, P. and Kenedy, D. (eds) 1986 *The Defence of the Roman and Byzantine East* (BAR IS.297), Oxford.

Friend, W.H.C. 1965 *Matyrdom and Persecution in the Early Church*, Oxford.

Gatti, C. 1961 'La politica monetaria di Aureliano', *PP* 16: 93–261.

Gibbon, E. 1909 *Decline and Fall of the Roman Empire*, (ed. J.B. Bury) I, London.

Gilliam, J.F. 1972 'Amminus and the Historia Augusta: the lost books and the period 117–285', *BHAC 1970*, Bonn: 125–47.

Gnecchi, F. 1912 *I Medaglioni Romani*, I–III, Milan.

Göbl, R. 1953 'Der Aufbau der römischen Münzprägung in der Kaiserzeit. V.2, Gallienus als Alleinherrscher', *NZ* 75: 5–35.

—— 1993 *Die Münzprägung des Kaisers Aurelianus* (270–275), Vienna.

Graf, D.F. 1989 'Zenobia and the Arabs', in D.H. French and C.S. Lightfoot (eds), *The Eastern Frontier of the Roman Empire*, I, Oxford: 143–67.

Groag, E. 1903 'Domitius (36) Aurelianus', *RE* V.1, Stuttgart: 1347–419.

Halsberghe, G.H. 1972 *The Cult of Sol Invictus*, Leiden.

Hanslik, R. 1972 'Zenobia', *RE* (2nd edn) 10A, Munich: 1–7.

Harl, K.W. 1987 *Civic Coins and Civic Politics in the Roman East*, Berkeley.

Hohl, E. 1911 'Vopiscus und die Biographie des Kaisers Tacitus', *Klio* 11: 178–229, 284–324.

Homo, L. 1904 *Essai sur le Règne de l'Empereur Aurélien (270–275)*, Paris.

Hopkins, K. 1983 *Death and Renewal*, Cambridge.

Howe, L.L. 1942 *The Praetorian Prefect from Commodus to Diocletian*, Chicago.

Imhof, M. 1957 'Invictus (Beiträge aus der Thesaurusarbeit, X)', *Mus. Helv.* 14: 197–215.

Isaac, B. 1990 *The Limits of Empire: The Roman Army in the East*, Oxford.

Jones, A.H.M. 1953 'Inflation under the Roman Empire', *Economic History Review* II, 52: 293–318.

Kantorowicz, E. 1963 '*Oriens Augusti – Lever du Roi*', *DOP* 17: 117–77.

Kellner, W. 1978 *Ein Römischer Münzfund aus Sirmium*, Vienna.

Kettenhofen, E. 1986 'Zur Siegestitulatur Kaiser Aurelians', *Tyche* 1: 138–46.

Keinast, D. 1974 'Die Münzreform Aurelians', *Chiron* 4: 547–65.

—— 1990 *Römische Kaisertabelle*, Darmstadt.

König, I. 1974 'Eine Beobachtung zum Zerfal des gallischen Sonderreiches und der Titel *Britannicus Maximus* Kaiser Aurelians', *Latomus* 33: 51–6.

—— 1981 *Die gallischen Usurpatoren von Postumus bis Tetricus*, Munich.

Lafaurie, J. 1975a 'Réformes monétaires d'Aurélien et de Dioclétien', *RN*: 73–138.

—— 1975b 'L'empire Gaulois. Apport de la numismatique', *ANRW* II.2, Berlin: 853–1012.

Lippold, A. 1972 'Der Einfall des Radagais im Jahre 405–6 und die Vita Aureliani der Historia Augusta', *BHAC 1970*, Bonn: 149–65.

—— 1995 'Kaiser Aurelian (270–275). Seine Beziehungen zur Stadt Rom und zum Senat in Spiegel der *Historia Augusta*', *Historiae Augustae Colloquia III, Colloquium Marceratense*, Bari: 193–207.

Lo Cascio, E. 1984 'Dall 'antoninianus' al 'laureato grande': l'evoluzione monetaria del III secolo alla luce della nuova documentazione di età dioclezianea', *OPUS* 3: 133–201.

Luttwak, E.N. 1976 *The Grand Strategy of the Roman Empire from the First Century AD to the Third*, Baltimore.

Magie, D. 1932 'Scriptores historiae Augustae', III, London.

Manns, F. 1939 *Münzkündliche und Historische Untersuchungen über die Zeit der Illyrerkaiser: Aurelianus*, Wurzburg.

Matthews, J. 1984 'The tax law of Palmyra: Evidence for economic history in a city of the Roman East', *JRS* 74: 157–80.

Mattingly, H. 1927 'Sestertius and denarius under Aurelian,' *NC*: 219–32.

—— 1936 'The Palmyrene Princes and the mints of Antioch and Alexandria,' *NC*: 89–114.

—— 1939 'Imperial Recovery,' *CAH* XII: 297–351.

Merten, E.W. 1968 'Zwei Herrscherfeste in der Historia Augusta', *BHAC 1966*, Bonn: 101–40.

Millar, F.G.B. 1969 'P. Herennius Dexippus: The Greek World and the Third-Century Invasions', *JRS* 59: 12–29.

—— 1971 'Paul of Samosata, Zenobia and Aurelian', *JRS* 61: 1–17.

—— 1977 *The Emperor in the Roman World*, London.

—— 1981 *The Roman Empire and its Neighbours*, (2nd edn) London.

Milne, J.G. 1933 *Catalogue of the Alexandrian Coins in the Ashmolean Museum*, Oxford.

Mócsy, A. 1974 *Pannonia and Upper Moesia*, (trans. S. Frere) London.

Mouchová, B. 1972 'Crudelitas Principis Optimi', *BHAC 1970*, Bonn: 167–94.

Nastor, P. 1987 'Monaies impériales de Pamphylie et de Pisidie sous Claude II le Gothique et Aurélien', in H. Huvelin, M. Christol and G. Gautier (eds), *Mélanges de Numismatiques Offerts à Pierre Bastien*, Wetteren: 131–43.

Nock, A.D. 1972 *Essays on Religion and the Ancient World*, I–II, Oxford.

Palmer, R.E.A. 1980 'Customs on market goods imported into the city of Rome', *MAAR* 36: 217–33.

Paschoud, F. 1996 (ed., trans., commentary), *Histoire Auguste*, V.1: *Vies d'Aurélien et Tacite*, Paris.

Peachin, M. 1990 *Roman Imperial Titulature and Chronology, AD 235–284*, Amsterdam.

Polverini, L. 1975 'Da Aureliano a Diocleziano', *ANRW* II.2, Berlin: 1013–35.

Potter, D.S. 1990 *Prophecy and History in the Crisis of the Roman Empire: A Historical Comentary on the Thirteenth Book of the Sibylline Oracle*, Oxford.

Price, M.J. 1973 'The Lost Year: Greek Light on a Problem of Roman Chronology', *NC*: 75–86.

Price, S.R.F. 1984 *Rituals and Power*, Cambridge.

Rathbone, D. 1986 'The dates of the recognition in Egypt of the Emperors from Caracalla to Diocletian', *ZPE* 62: 101–31.

Rea, J.R. 1969 'The Date of the Prefecture of Statilius Ammianus', *Chron. d'Egypte* 44 [84] 1969: 134–8.

—— 1972 *The Oxyrhynchus Papyri*, XL, Oxford.

Richardson, L. 1992 *A New Topographical Dictionary of Ancient Rome*, Baltimore.

Richmond, I.A. 1930 *The City Walls of Imperial Rome. An Account of its Architectural Development from Aurelian to Narses*, Oxford.

Richter, F. 1909–15 'Sol' in W.H. Rocher (ed.), *Ausführliches Lexicon der griechischen und römischen Mythologie*, IV: 1137–52.

Rohde, T. 1881 *Die Münzen des Kaiser Aurelianus, seine Frau Severina und der Fürsten von Palmyra*, Miskolc.

Saunders, R.T. 1992 'Aurelian's *Two* Iuthungiann Wars', *Historia* 41: 311–27.

Schulte, B. 1983 *Die Goldprägung der gallischen Kaiser von Postumus bis Tetricus*, Frankfurt.

Seyrig, H. 1971 'Le culte du soleil en Syrie à l'époque Romaine', *Syria* 48: 337–73.

Sotgiu, G. 1961 *Studi sull'epigraphia di Aureliano*, Cagliari.

—— 1975 'Aureliano', *ANRW* II.2: 1039–61.

Stoneman, R. 1992 *Palmyra and its Empire: Zenobia's Revolt against Rome*, Ann Arbor.

Syme, R. 1968 *Ammianus and the* Historia Augusta, Oxford.

—— 1971 *Emperors and Biography*, Oxford.

—— 1983 Historia Augusta *Papers*, Oxford.

Teixidor, J. 1979 *The Pantheon of Palmyra*, Leiden.

Todd, M. 1978 *The Walls of Rome*, London.

Turcan, R. 1969 'Le dédit des monétaires rebellés contre Aurélien', *Latomus* 28: 948–59.

Vogt, J. 1924 *Die Alexandrianischen Münzen*, Stuttgart.

Wallace, S.L. 1938 *Taxation in Egypt, Augustus to Diocletian*, Princeton.

Wallinger, E. 1990 *Die Frauen in der* Historia Augusta, Vienna.

Wardman, A. 1982 *Religion and Statecraft Among the Romans*, London.

Watson, A. 1991 'The Representation of Imperial Authority: Problems of Continuity in the Mid-Third Century AD', unpublished Ph.D. thesis, London.

Webb, P.H. 1927 *Roman Imperial Coinage*, V.1, London.

Zanker, P. 1988 *The Power of Images in the Age of Augustus*, Ann Arbor.

INDEX

Abrittus, battle of 24–5, 28, 39,
 55
Aegean 8, 40, 43, 46, 205, 215
Aemilianus 25
Aesculapius 185
Aglibol 195–6
agri decumates 33, 35
Alamanni 9, 25, 39;
 agri decumates overrun by 33–5;
 Gaul, threat to 94, 102, 108;
 infantry units of, employed by
  Aurelian 170;
 Italy invaded by 34–5, 43, 94,
  158, 217–18, 220;
 wedge between Rhine and
  Danube armies 35, 90–1
Alaric, Rome sacked (410) by 152
Alexander the Great 72, 103, 208
 imperial imagery and 173–4,
  180–1, 188
Alexandria (Egypt):
 mint of 132, 134–5, 214,
  221–4;
 coinage produced at, for:
  Aurelian 129, 134, 222, 224;
  Aurelian and Vaballathus
   jointly 67–8, 134, 223;
  Claudius 221;
  Quintillus 222;
  Severina 114, 128–9, 134;
  Vaballathus 69, 134, 223;
  Zenobia 69, 223;

recaptured by Tenagino Probus
 (270) 62;
retaken by Palmyrenes 62;
retaken in Roman
 counter-invasion (272) 71,
 223;
revolt in (273) 82–3
Alexandria ad Issum (Iskenderun)
 72
Alps 25, 34, 49–50, 95, 137, 218;
 Alpine passes 50, 91, 93.
Amandus and Aelian, revolt of 98
Ammianus Marcellinus 162, 210,
 216
Ammianus, Statilius (prefect of
 Egypt) 168–9
Anatolia: *see* Asia Minor
Antioch 26, 32, 70, 168;
 mint of 63, 74, 132, 134;
  coinage produced at, for:
   Aurelian 129, 134, 222–4;
   Aurelian and Vaballathus
    jointly 64, 68, 134, 223;
   Claudius 63, 223;
   Severina 115, 134;
   Vaballathus 69, 134, 223;
   Zenobia 69, 223;
 Palmyra and 63–4, 70, 72–5;
 Paul of Samosata, bishop of
  63–4, 199;
 recaptured by Aurelian (272)
  74–5;

287